THUNDER
IN THE SKIES

THUNDER
IN THE SKIES

A CANADIAN GUNNER IN THE GREAT WAR

DEREK GROUT

FOREWORD BY ERNEST B. BENO, BRIG-GEN. RET'D

DUNDURN
TORONTO

Editor: Britanie Wilson
Design: Janette Thompson (Jansom)
Cover design: Sarah Beaudin
Cover image: composite — Canadian Artillery loading limbers, May 1918, courtesy of Library and Archives Canada, PA-002587; barrage map, courtesy of Madeleine Claudi
Printer: Webcom

Library and Archives Canada Cataloguing in Publication
Grout, Derek, author
        Thunder in the skies : a Canadian gunner in the Great
War / Derek Grout ; foreword by Brigadier-General Ernest B. Beno.

Includes bibliographical references.
Issued in print and electronic formats.
ISBN 978-1-4597-3093-9 (paperback).—ISBN 978-1-4597-3094-6 (pdf).—
ISBN 978-1-4597-3095-3 (epub)

        1. Sargent, Bert. 2. World War, 1914-1918—Artillery operations, Canadian.
3. Canada. Canadian Army. Canadian Field Artillery—Biography. 4. World War,
1914–1918—Personal narratives, Canadian. 5. Artillerymen—Canada—Biography.
6. Soldiers—Canada—Biography.I. Title.

D547.C2G79 2015   940.4'1271   C2015-901031-4
                                                 C2015-901032-2

1 2 3 4 5   19 18 17 16 15

We acknowledge the support of the **Canada Council for the Arts** and the **Ontario Arts Council** for our publishing program. We also acknowledge the financial support of the **Government of Canada** through the **Canada Book Fund** and **Livres Canada Books**, and the **Government of Ontario** through the **Ontario Book Publishing Tax Credit** and the **Ontario Media Development Corporation**.

Care has been taken to trace the ownership of copyright material used in this book. The author and the publisher welcome any information enabling them to rectify any references or credits in subsequent editions.

— *J. Kirk Howard, President*

The publisher is not responsible for websites or their content unless they are owned by the publisher.

Printed and bound in Canada.

VISIT US AT

Dundurn.com | @dundurnpress | Facebook.com/dundurnpress | Pinterest.com/dundurnpress

Dundurn
3 Church Street, Suite 500
Toronto, Ontario, Canada
M5E 1M2

In memory of
Bert, Jim, Walter, Hal, "Biff," Bob, and the other
43,908 members of the Canadian artillery who served
their country so well during the Great War, among
them Acting Sergeant 303659 Ernest Victor Grout,
Third Brigade CFA, who died of wounds
October 3, 1918.

Have I not heard great ordnance in the field
And heaven's artillery thunder in the skies?

The Taming of the Shrew
Act 1, Scene 2

Contents

Foreword

Early June 2014 — After having spent the past 10 days in Normandy attending the seventieth anniversary of D-Day, I arrived in the Belgian town of Ypres. Under an overcast sky, a friend and I were enjoying an early-morning 10-kilometre walk. The fields along our track were ploughed recently, and muddy with sparse clumps of plants, including poppies swaying in tufts of grass. It was quiet and peaceful.

About a kilometre off the track we spotted a small, isolated Commonwealth War Graves Commission cemetery with a prominent white cross bearing an inverted bronze sword. A brown stone wall shielded the perimeter of this sanctuary and the encased register at its entrance.

As we crossed the field to pay our respects, mud sucked at the soles of my shoes. Bits of rusted steel were evident in the ground — remnants of artillery shells fired 100 years ago. I tried to avoid the mud by taking a shortcut along a narrow ditch (most likely a trench so many years ago), but lost my footing and slid down into the putrid cold water, soaked to my knees. I pulled on the grass to get up the steep bank where prickly nettles stung my hands, arms, and legs, leaving a welt and burning rash. Determined to visit these lads in their final resting place, I followed another line of approach, with boots sloshing and stinking.

The neatly groomed cemetery revealed rows of white tombstones lined up like silent sentinels to mark the graves of young soldiers from Britain, Canada, Australia, and Newfoundland. They were shockingly young, cut down in the prime of life in battle conditions that are impossible to imagine. Their ages ranged from 15 to 29, with the majority in their early twenties. Some could not be identified and are *"Known only unto God."* Here and there graves were adorned with colourful flowers or a small Canadian flag fluttering gracefully in the breeze. My eye caught the marker of a young German soldier, off to one side. His presence with our fallen sons is an acknowledgement of the cost on both sides to achieve the peace in our time for which these men and so many others fought and died.

As a retired Canadian Army officer, I am proud of the accomplishments of the Canadians who fought in the Great War. However, these graves before me serve as a grim reminder of the painful cost of victory.

Later that rainy and thunderous day I visited Vimy Ridge. The white twin-pillared monument is the centrepiece of a 100-hectare preserved battlefield park that encompasses a portion of the ground over which the Canadian Corps made their assault. Vimy was the first occasion on which all four divisions of the Canadian Expeditionary Force participated in a battle as a cohesive and victorious formation, and thus it has become a national symbol of historic achievement and sacrifice.

In the next days we passed through Passchendaele, Cambrai, Loos, Arras, Beaumont Hamel, and many other towns and villages whose names are battle honours emblazoned on the colours of our Canadian regiments. All the while, I asked myself, *How can I learn more about this era? And what can we do to ensure future generations remember the heroes of that era?*

When I got off the plane in Canada, I received an e-mail from Derek Grout, a writer I had never met. He asked me to read his manuscript and consider writing a foreword to his book, *Thunder in the Skies: A Canadian Gunner in the Great War.*

This wonderful book brought life and meaning to my experiences during my visit to Flanders. It presents accurately the Canadian battlefield experience of the First World War by the soldiers who witnessed it. As a Canadian soldier and gunner, it was easy for me to identify with Bert Sargent, who joined the Army in Montreal in late 1914 to be part of the "Great Adventure." He trained in England, met the love of his life, and departed with his friends to fight a brutal war. As I turned the pages, I empathized with Bert as he endured the harsh realities of combat so vividly described in this book, and I understood that he was fighting for what he believed in, and for his friends.

Derek Grout brings new light and context to the challenging world that faced hundreds of thousands of young Canadians a century ago. His outstanding research brings Canada's contribution into focus and allows us to appreciate the dauntless soldiers of that era, especially their feelings, motivation, love of life, and basic humanity. We learn how, individually and collectively, regardless of rank or position, they all played a meaningful role in creating the foundation of our great nation and in making Canada the land of the free.

Bert Sargent's story struck a chord with me as an ex-gunner and a gun end officer, and I felt a bond of service along with a feeling of deep respect and awe for what they endured and what they achieved. Bert and the gunners in this book are not unlike the Canadian gunners I have seen in Afghanistan — skilled, talented, professional, highly motivated, and thoroughly dedicated to supporting our infantry and combat teams, no matter what. Our regiment hasn't changed that much over the past century. The ethos of giving our all for the supported arm still motivates us and life on the gun position hasn't really changed. Then and now we have great soldiers, great Canadians.

Finally, I would like to thank Derek for telling the story of the guns and gunners of Canada and the Canadian Corps in the First World War. In my many visits to gunner units at home and abroad, as colonel commandant of the Royal Regiment of Canadian Artillery, I reminded our soldiers of the importance of maintaining the skills, standards, dedication, and bravery of the Canadian gunners who paved the way to victory at Vimy, Hill 70, Passchendaele, and the Hundred Days. What a magnificent soldier Bert Sargent was, and again, thanks to Derek for bringing his story to life. This book has been a wonderful learning experience for me, as it will be for all Canadians.

Ernest B. Beno, Brigadier-General (Retired)
Kingston, Ontario

Acknowledgements

Many people contributed to making this book a reality. I owe them all a great debt for generously sharing stories, letters, and photographs. They have made the past come alive and have helped to ensure that the wartime exploits of an extraordinary generation of men are not forgotten.

Special thanks are due to Madeleine (Sargent) Claudi and Ronald Claudi for sharing Bert's story with me, for making their family papers freely available, and for great patience in answering my numerous and frequent questions. I also owe a special debt to Ernest Beno, former colonel commandant of the Royal Regiment of Canadian Artillery, for his generous foreword.

To the following institutions and people: the Royal Archives (Pamela Clark); the McCord Museum (Nora Hague); the Rare Books and Special Collections Division of McGill University Libraries (Dr. Richard Virr and David McKnight); McLennan Library of McGill University; McGill Archives (Mary Houde and Tina Witham); Stewart Museum (Bruce Bolton and Normand Trudel); Floyd Low; Royal Montreal Regiment Museum (Ron Zemancik and Nino Lambertucci); Maritime History Archive of Memorial University of Newfoundland (Paula Marshall); Douglas Sinnis; Colonel James Dodd (retired); Gordon McWhaw; Bibliothèque Nationale du Québec; Commonwealth War Graves Commission; the staff of Montreal's Mount Royal Cemetery; Lakeview Memorial Gardens (Rainer Schmalhaus); Library and Archives Canada; Lennox and Addington County Museum and Archives (Jennifer Bunting); Vincent Scully and William Scully Ltd.; Deseronto Public Library (Ken Brown); Newcastle Public Library (Catherine Reid); Frances Itani; Statistics Canada (for 1911 census data); Canadian Centre for Architecture (Renata Guttman and Anne-Marie Séguin); Reverend Patrick Wheeler; Peter Gordon; Donna Lockwood; Concordia University Archives (Nancy Morelli); George Metcalf Archival Collection of the Canadian War Museum; Société de transport de Montréal (André Vigneau); Jay Underwood; Stewart Sargent; Master Gunner Donald Greene (retired); Reverend James A. Ramsay (St. Barnabas Church); Cathy Clubb.

I am grateful to the following for permission to quote material: Her Majesty Queen Elizabeth II for the correspondence of the Duke of Connaught; Madeleine (Sargent) Claudi for the letters and diaries of her father, Albert Elbridge Sargent; Laura Norris for making available additional correspondence and photos, as did Ken Darling, another member of the extended Sargent family; my former high school classmate, Gary Whittaker, for various written items belonging to his grandfather, James D. McKeown, including the only surviving copy of Bert Sargent's *Official History*; John Fetherstonhaugh for the transcribed letters of his father, Harold Fetherstonhaugh, and the transcribed letters and diary of his uncle, Edward Fetherstonhaugh; Cathy (Notman) Fetherstonhaugh for the letters of Wilfred Notman; Elisabeth Sunerton for the letter of Dr. Alvah Gordon; Eric Hyde for the letters of Walter Hyde; Library and Archives Canada for the War Diaries of various units and formations of the Canadian Expeditionary Force; Ronald and Elaine Hale for the letters of their grandfather, Robert Hale; Grace Keenan Prince, for extracts from the diaries of her uncle, John Patrick Teahan, published as *Diary Kid*; Janet Bishop and the New Brunswick Museum, for the letters of William Harrison and Douglas Murdoch; Nancy Kuehn for the unpublished memoirs of Hew Cochrane; Acacia House Publishing Services Ltd. and Arthur Bishop for extracts from *Winged Warfare* by William A. Bishop; Atherton Wallace, for extracts from *Transfusion*, detailing his father's experiences in the CAMC; Geoffrey Kelley for excerpts from Canon Frederick Scott's *The Great War as I Saw It*; and Ken MacPherson for excerpts from his father's *A Soldier's Diary*.

Special thanks are also due to Jean MacLean for permission to reproduce a number of photographs taken by her father, Simon Campbell; and to Joni Crosby-Boyd of the Pointe Claire Public Library, who ferreted out obscure books and numerous microfilms that provided essential background for this work. My eagle-eyed editor at Dundurn, Britanie Wilson, offered numerous insightful suggestions and improvements to my manuscript, for which I am very grateful.

To all, my heartfelt thanks.

Derek Grout
Pointe Claire, Quebec
April 2015

Introduction

On the morning of March 26, 2004, I was helping at a church book sale, sorting hundreds of periodicals into piles.

"Where do you want these?" a voice demanded.

I looked up as a tall, silver-haired man heaved an old canvas-and-leather bag onto the table. Clearly, it had seen better days; the brass fittings were tarnished and the sides had been split so it could be used as a carrier. When he removed a stack of *National Geographics*, I noticed a name in faded block capitals and, on closer inspection, the letters CFA.

"That's a military antique you've got," I observed.

The man paused to wipe his forehead. "It belonged to my father-in-law," he said. "Served in the artillery in World War I. Joined the ranks in 1914 and finished up as a lieutenant with a Military Cross."

I was impressed. "He survived?"

"Yes. One of the lucky ones." He chuckled. "Never got a scratch."

Lucky indeed!

We introduced ourselves and started chatting, the magazines forgotten momentarily.

"We've got his letters, diary, and photographs," my acquaintance added, almost as an afterthought, as he picked up the bag and turned to go.

Letters? Diary? Photos? The amateur historian in me was piqued. I knew little of a gunner's daily life and how it might have differed from a frontline soldier's. We exchanged telephone numbers.

A few days later I was ushered into a cozy sitting room where a card table held a variety of items together by elastics. Even if Bert Sargent, like many veterans of the Great War, never spoke about his wartime experiences to his children, it was evident he was determined

Memories. *Author's photo.*

not to forget. My fingers trembled as I flicked through stacks of sepia postcards from a long-vanished world, unfolded barrage maps, and skimmed through letters at random. A quick glance was enough to show that Bert was a gifted writer and a keen observer. There were letters from training camp in England, and others written under shellfire by the light of a guttering candle. They were wonderful, describing artillery life in an intimate, easy fashion, and in a way — 90-plus years after — that deserved to be heard. These letters would lead me on a three-year odyssey, though that was still far in the future.

From what I could see, Bert participated in almost every major Canadian engagement from early 1916 onward. Even better, his experiences were wholly typical of any gunner in the Canadian Field Artillery (CFA). Thus his story is the story of many; he epitomized the citizen soldiers of Canada who served their country so ably in time of need and, the war over, returned to pick up their lives in a nation radically changed in their absence. Fortunately, he'd never been wounded, so there was a continuous record with no long break as he convalesced in an English hospital.

From out of the blue, an idea struck me. *Perhaps I could "follow" him around for four and a half years, "seeing" the Great War through his eyes....*

1

A City Goes to War

In the autumn of 1914, Canada's largest city was caught up in the fever of war.

Already, the First Contingent, comprising 30,617 men and 7,697 horses, had sailed in an armada of 30 chartered vessels from Gaspé Basin. Thereafter, Montreal's English and French newspapers featured stories from the sprawling training camp — a tent city — set up for the Canadians on Salisbury Plain.

For Canada, with a population of seven and a half million, equipping and training the First Contingent represented a remarkable achievement. At the outbreak of war on August 4, when Britain declared war on Germany to defend Belgian neutrality, Canada had just 3,100 regular soldiers and 57,500 partially trained and partly equipped militia. The government's appeal for recruits to the Canadian Expeditionary Force (CEF) had been highly successful; large numbers of men flocked in naïve enthusiasm to the colours, hoping the war would not end before they reached France. Although two-thirds of the early enlistees were British-born, among the First Contingent were members of some of the oldest and most socially prominent families in Montreal.

Though no Canadians had yet seen action, Montrealers were stunned by the enormous number of casualties in the first months of fighting. In August and September alone, France lost some 350,000 men — killed, wounded, prisoners, or missing. What began as a war of mobility degenerated that autumn into a static conflict when the German Army, checked on the Aisne and too tired to move, dug itself into well-sited defensive lines. British and French troops opposite them dug in, as well, and soon a continuous line of trenches extended 450 miles from the North Sea to the Swiss frontier. It was a stalemate; for the first time in the long history of warfare, there were no flanks to be turned. The only possible attack was a frontal assault.

These lines of trenches, separated by what was termed "No Man's Land," would scarcely change over the next three and a half years. Entrenched troops, equipped with breech-loading magazine rifles, defended by machine guns and accordions of barbed wire, and supported by deadly artillery, could be dislodged only at great cost to the attacker. And, when changes *did* occur, the "butcher's bill" was staggering, far out of proportion to what was gained. Jingoistic newspapers painted a lurid and misleading impression of trench life. Carefully filtered stories made it all seem somehow romantic and exciting, a larger-than-life adventure lifted from the *Boy's Own Paper*, where plucky British soldiers overcame all odds and won out in the end.

By autumn, the sight of marching soldiers was no longer a novelty in Montreal, though with khaki uniforms in short supply, citizens could see new recruits clad in a hodgepodge of costumes, including postal uniforms. Banks and other major companies formed Home Guard units, and paid for the new Ross Mark III rifles the men would carry. Periodic spy scares kept citizens on edge, with various foreigners arrested on suspicion of being enemy agents. Armed soldiers patrolled the harbour and the Lachine Canal, while sentries guarded both ends of the Victoria Bridge, which spanned the St. Lawrence River and provided an essential rail link to Atlantic Canada and the United States.

Like every other Montreal organization, McGill University, the country's finest institution of higher learning, was enmeshed in the war. Early on, McGill pledged a field hospital, and McGill's Canadian Officers' Training Corps (COTC) offered a four-month training program to all men of military age who were "desirous of fitting themselves as soldiers." The response was overwhelming. As the *McGill Daily War Contingent Supplement* put it, "It was difficult to train properly the large number of recruits who offered themselves immediately after the commencement of the war."

Even before the First Contingent reached England, it was apparent more men would be needed from Canada. The war, at first widely expected to be over by Christmas, showed no sign of ending. On October 6, the cabinet in Ottawa pledged a Second Contingent of 22,000 to the War Office in London, thus presenting an opportunity for men who had been too slow to join the August volunteers. It was a popular move; ALL CANADA ENDORSES SECOND CONTINGENT was a typical headline. As with the First Contingent, the Second would comprise not only infantry but also all the supporting branches, including a complement of artillery and its related formations, and engineer, cyclist, signal, and administrative units. And, as in the First, every man was a volunteer. Conditions of enlistment were similar, too: a minimum height of five foot three inches, a minimum chest measurement of thirty-three and a half inches, age between eighteen and forty-five. Married men were accepted only with the written consent of their wives.

Orders went out from Ottawa on October 21 to begin recruiting infantry for the Second Contingent. In Montreal, posters blossomed around the city, urging citizens to enlist in one of the newly authorized battalions, both English- and French-speaking, and militia regiments in their respective armouries geared up for an influx of men. By the twenty-seventh, the *Gazette* reported that recruiting was as brisk as for the First Contingent. In the second week of November, recruiting for overseas infantry battalions ended, their ranks filled. In all, in 15 working days, 1,500 men had been recruited in Montreal. It was a very satisfactory showing for Canada's commercial, transportation, and industrial capital, though Toronto had contributed more men. Battalion medical officers had been particularly diligent in rejecting prospective recruits for minor problems, which in later years, when recruiting fell off dramatically, would be cheerfully overlooked.

Men of the Second Contingent had a slightly better understanding of what they were getting into. As Bert Sargent later observed:

The men who were now to be enlisted were men who realized to the full that they were embarking on "The Great Adventure" and that they would not see the Europe as described in the guide books and featured in the posters of Thos. Cook & Son, but rather a Europe full of mysterious horrors vaguely discernible between the lines written by various war correspondents.

On November 5, the *Daily Star*'s front page headlined: FIELD ARTILLERY AND AMBULANCE ARE TO BE RECRUITED IN MONTREAL. "Montreal men who have been holding back from enlisting because they prefer any other branch of the service than infantry now have their chance. Orders were received this morning from militia headquarters at Ottawa to recruit for one battery of field artillery and one field ambulance." All over the city, men whose jobs were lost in the two-year recession began to think of military service. The artillery was more than gun-laying and, as the *Field Service Manual* makes clear, it offered jobs in a variety of trades. Drivers, especially, were in demand; harnessing and driving a team of six horses hitched to a field gun was no easy task and, under combat conditions, it required great skill.

The Second Contingent would have three field artillery brigades, the 4th, 5th, and 6th. Each brigade was composed of three batteries of six 18-pounder guns, for a total of 54 guns. In December, even as units were recruiting, this organizational scheme was modified. Thereafter, brigades consisted of four batteries of four 18-pounders, a total of 48 guns. As well, each brigade contained a Headquarters Section and an Ammunition Column.* This latter was responsible for transporting artillery and small arms ammunition from a central depot to the guns. It was an important unit. Timely arrival of shells of the right calibre at the right place was critical on the battlefield. There was, after all, nothing more useless than a fieldpiece that could not be fired for a lack of ammunition.

More than two inches of snow blanketed the city on November 11, the first significant accumulation of the season. Hundreds of men loaded snow into horse-drawn carts, and only the main streets and streetcar routes were cleared. Three days later, as the city returned to normal, further details were published on the sole artillery unit Montreal would contribute to the Second Contingent.

---

*After the reorganization, the breakdown was as follows: 4th Brigade (13th, 14th, 15th, and 16th Batteries); 5th Brigade (17th, 18th, 19th, and 20th Batteries); and 6th Brigade (21st, 22nd, 23rd, and 24th Batteries).

Artillery to Recruit

Recruiting will start this evening at the Craig Street Drill Hall for a battery of field artillery, offices for that purpose being opened at the Drill Hall. For this battery 131 men of all ranks will be required to go with the next contingent. The recruiting will be under Capt. W.G. Scully of the 3rd Battery, CFA, while the medical examinations will be made by Capt. H. Pavey, of the 3rd Victoria Rifles, who will be at the Drill Hall each afternoon and evening. Thirty-two men have already volunteered for this work, and it is expected that the battery will be enlisted within a few days.

The city's young (and not so young) men began to trickle down to the cavernous Drill Hall on the north side of Craig Street, four blocks east of St. Lawrence Boulevard, opposite the small greensward of Champ de Mars. Built to house four regiments of the Montreal garrison, the Drill Hall, with its soaring sloped roof, had been a landmark since the mid-1880s. The sombre facade of grey stone was done in Romanesque Revival style, with large, round-headed windows.

Montreal's Craig Street Drill Hall, where the 21st Battery began recruiting in November 1914. *Author's photo.*

In apartment 35 of the fashionable Grosvenor Apartments at the south-west corner of Sherbrooke and Guy Streets, a 26-year-old mechanical engineer named Albert Elbridge Sargent — "Bert" to his family and friends — read of each day's developments in Europe with rising concern. The war, it seemed, would go on longer than expected. Though the Sargent family had no tradition of military service, Bert, a native Montrealer, was anxious to do his bit.

Bert Sargent had the lean, well-proportioned build of an athlete, and an air of calm self-possession. He stood five foot ten inches, taller than most of his generation, and his dark brown hair was cropped short. And, though in 1914 most men were clean-shaven, he had a small, neatly trimmed moustache. He had been named after his father, who died two months before Bert's arrival into the world in 1887. Since his mother's death in 1909, he'd lived with his sister, Flora, and her husband, George Darling, while attending McGill. The Sargent family was a large one: Bert was the youngest of nine surviving children — six sisters and two brothers, spread across Canada and the United States.* The family traced its roots to Loyalists who had settled north of the Vermont border.

Bert's schooling had been conventional. He attended the prestigious Montreal High School, which served the city's Protestant community, and received his degree from McGill in May 1913. After an extended trip that summer to New York and New England, he began work in the engineering and design office of Darling Brothers Limited in Montreal. The company was a well-known manufacturer of industrial products such as pumps, heat exchangers, and elevators, and enjoyed a reputation for financial probity and sound engineering. It was a family firm founded in 1888 by George Darling — Bert's brother-in-law — and his two brothers.

As with the firm's other junior engineers, Bert divided his time between the head office at 112 Prince Street and the foundry around the corner. The work was interesting but, after August 4, he found himself wondering whether he couldn't do something more useful

---

*These were, in birth order, Flora, Stella, Lotta, Lena, Charles, Alice, Edyth, Grover. Their names appear frequently in Bert's letters.

for the war effort. Not the infantry, for medical officers at this time were rejecting any applicant who wore glasses — Bert, who suffered from myopia in both eyes, had worn them since childhood. Not that it had affected him in the least, for he was a gifted athlete. He'd been captain of the McGill hockey team, playing left wing on the squad that defeated teams in Boston and New York in January 1911 to win what the New York press termed the "Amateur Hockey Championship of North America." In the latter game, Bert scored the winning goal in the last seconds of play, breaking a 3–3 tie. In baseball he played second base, and he was an experienced canoeist and member of the Hudson Heights Boat Club. Recognizing his talents and exemplary character, Bert's 37 classmates in science and engineering bestowed on him a high honour, electing him class president.

Over breakfast Bert scanned the *Gazette*, as he did every day. In mid-November an article caught his eye. *If not the infantry ... well then, perhaps some other branch ... a technical arm, where his degree might prove useful....* Disconcerted to find the nearest unit of the Canadian Engineers was recruiting in Ottawa, he looked for another opportunity. In the next days he began putting his affairs in order and wondered how to break the news to his family.

Elsewhere in Canada's metropolis, hundreds of other men were making similar decisions that would affect themselves, their families, and their country. Though they came from a wide range of backgrounds, a considerable number were from Montreal's close-knit, middle-class, English-speaking community. They knew, or knew of, each other from their days at the High School or from McGill. Two hundred yards from the distinctive copper dome of the Grosvenor Apartments, in a three-storey townhouse of red sandstone, Wilfred ("Biff") Notman, the fourth grandson of William Notman, the noted Montreal studio photographer, was thinking along the same lines. The 22-year-old, born and raised in Montreal, lived with his newly widowed mother at No. 22 Summerhill Avenue; he looked for more excitement than he was finding as a clerk, and military service offered an opportunity to see something of the world. Men whom he'd known since high school were joining the artillery....

On tree-lined Mance Street, in a residential neighbourhood near McGill, a 27-year-old newspaperman, Walter Gordon, felt much the same way. A native of New Brunswick, Walter was a 1909 arts graduate of McGill who had played halfback for the university's second team. Shortly after graduation he joined the *Gazette* as a reporter, later becoming sports editor and city editor in 1912. He was an easygoing, gregarious man who made friends easily and, thanks to his newspaper activities, was well known in Montreal's sporting and social circles. At the outbreak of war, he joined the McGill COTC, convinced the war would last longer than the pundits predicted. With the course about to end, he was having a difficult time deciding which unit to join. At this stage of the war there was no assurance he would qualify for a commission, despite his COTC training. He gave notice to the paper and prepared to vacate his top-floor flat in the greystone York Apartments.

Architect Harold ("Hal") Fetherstonhaugh (McGill 1909) dissolved his business partnership and volunteered for officers' training at the Royal School of Artillery, located in Kingston. Born in Montreal in 1887, Hal was a tall man — five foot ten inches — with fair hair and penetrating blue eyes. With officers' positions for the Second Contingent largely filled by early November, Hal hoped for a lieutenant's billet in the Third Contingent.

Twenty-two-year-old Walter Hyde, another Montreal architect, put his professional plans on hold. While service in the infantry might be a waste of his talents, he knew there were other branches where his skills could be used to greater effect. He soon found himself in artillery school at Kingston, seeking to qualify for the rank of lieutenant.

John Archibald ("Archie") Gordon, a 20-year-old clerk who lived on Sherbrooke Street not far from Bert and Hal, stayed in touch with former classmates from Montreal High School, hoping to get himself into the Second Contingent....

2

Into the 21st Battery

On November 14, the first day of formal recruiting for the 21st Battery, 24 men were accepted, with a number of others having been turned away, mostly for medical reasons. The following Monday, 15 more were enlisted. On Wednesday, November 18 — 106 days into the war — the *Gazette* announced that recruiting for the Second Contingent was now practically complete, "as far as the infantry is concerned," adding that "volunteers will continue to be accepted to provide for reinforcements." Almost as an afterthought, the lead paragraph of the Ottawa-datelined column continued, "The artillery for the second contingent are not yet all enlisted."

It was on this afternoon after work that Bert Sargent picked his way through the mounds of snow on Craig Street. It had warmed considerably from the morning low of -16° C and the earlier gusts had abated. It was, the papers claimed, the coldest snap for 13 years, and Montrealers knew winter had truly arrived. Bert left Darling Brothers earlier than usual and, in the fast-approaching darkness, he passed many figures, huddled deep into their overcoats, heading for home. Crowded trams clanged along Craig Street, heading toward the Canadian Pacific Railway's Viger station, while shopkeepers contemplated the lack of business and awaited the end of the day. On the corner of St. Lawrence Boulevard, the newspaper rack at Robert's Pharmacy displayed the *Daily Star*'s headline: BRITISH LINES AROUND YPRES STILL OBJECT OF VIOLENT GERMAN ATTACK.

A beige streetcar stopped opposite the Drill Hall, disgorging a half-dozen soldiers.

Bert stepped past a sentry and entered the Drill Hall, its interior lit by the last rays of sunlight flooding through the skylights. Once his glasses unfogged, he looked around. Inside, all was bustle and purposeful activity. Voices echoed from the high, trussed roof, while men hurried to second-floor offices clutching stacks of paper. In the middle of the floor, an immense open space measuring some 125 by 300 feet, panting men in civilian garb were going through a routine of physical training, jumping jacks and push-ups. Elsewhere a squad of six similarly clothed men was getting a first lesson in close-order drill from a leather-lunged sergeant of the 85th Regiment, whose voice betrayed frustration at their inability to keep in step. From a basement range came the sharp crackle of pistol fire.

Over the past weeks the Drill Hall had acquired a rich aroma, an amalgam of cigarette smoke, sweat, cooking, disinfectant, wet serge, and toilet facilities threatening to back up from overuse. There was something else about the place, as well: a sense of imminent adventure and grand purpose, a sense of belonging to some small part of a greater, unknown whole, and devotion to a cause. Since there were no permanent facilities in Canada where the Second Contingent could muster in winter, the minister of militia had authorized local training for all recruits. For the 21st Battery, a corner at the north end of the Drill Hall had been transformed into a barracks area. Blankets, hung on wires suspended from the roof trusses, provided some degree of privacy for the men who lounged on two-tier bunks. Above them, a few spectators looked down from the second-floor viewing balcony at the north end of the Hall.

In another corner, roped off and guarded by one unarmed soldier, were four field guns of Boer War vintage, complete with two-wheeled limbers, filled with dummy shells. They were not 18-pounders; almost every gun of this calibre in Canada — 96 in all — had gone to England with the First Contingent. But the four 12-pounders were breech-loaders and sufficient for training purposes. They lacked the hydraulic recoil system of the 18-pounders, which meant they had to be pushed back into position and re-aimed after each shot — but this hardly mattered, as the 21st Battery would not be shooting live ammunition for many months. Had Bert been able to get close enough, he would have smelled machine oil, brass polish, and freshly applied dubbing on leather, for the Field Artillery made a religion of equipment maintenance and cleanliness, and these obsolete fieldpieces had been lovingly tended to by the new recruits.

Along one wall, lines of men snaked backward from folding tables, at each of which sat a soldier in uniform. Hand-printed signs on the wall behind each table indicated the branch of service being recruited: AMMUNITION COLUMN, FIELD AMBULANCE and — *ah, there!* — 21ST BATTERY. Bert joined the half-dozen men queuing for the 21st. The table was manned by an officer engaged in earnest conversation with a potential recruit. Bert was surprised to find he knew the officer: Fred Baker had also attended Montreal High School.

Finally, it was Bert's turn.

The two men greeted each other warmly. Baker, a civil engineer, explained he'd been granted a commission just six days earlier, and attached to the 21st since the previous Friday. A short discussion ensued on the 21st Battery's need for men with a technical bent. Finally, Baker reached for a pale blue attestation paper, the form volunteers were required to fill out and sign, signifying their willingness to serve in the Canadian Overseas Expeditionary Force. Baker's finger traced the personal details Bert would have to furnish, including previous military experience, profession, marital status, and details of next of kin.

After Bert indicated he was willing to be attested, he signed the top portion of the form, and Baker signed as a witness. Bert signed and dated the declaration, agreeing to serve for one year, or the duration of the war plus six months. Again, Baker witnessed his signature, pleased. Another engineer would be a useful addition to the battery. Consulting a list of serial numbers, Baker assigned Bert a number — 85150 — and the rank of bombardier (Bdr). It was the most junior non-commissioned officer (NCO) rank in the artillery and entitled Bert to wear a single chevron on each sleeve. Bert supposed he would find out in due time what *exactly* a bombardier was supposed to do.

As Baker turned to the next in line, Bert took his attestation paper upstairs to Captain Robert Allen's office on the west side. A staircase at each corner of the north end gave access to the upper floor. From open doors came the discordant jangle of telephones and the babble of voices.

Allen, from the 1st Heavy Battery and Ammunition Column, was one of many officers appointed by Order-in-Council in early November as temporary Justices of the Peace for the purpose of administering the oath of allegiance to new recruits. He'd been busy in the past few days, with dozens of men passing through his office. After Bert had sworn to be faithful and bear true allegiance to His Majesty George V, he signed the appropriate space, and Captain Allen witnessed the signature with an elaborate flourish.

A few doors down, Medical Officer Captain Harry Pavey occupied a small office. Pavey, born in 1878, was another McGill man who had received his MD in 1902 and was on secondment from the Victoria Rifles. Like Robert Allen, Pavey was a busy man. Each recruit was examined individually, a process taking 10 minutes at most. In the past few days there had been enough men in the Drill Hall to fill Pavey's days. The doctor did not waste much time on the obviously fit man in front of him. The McGill community was a small one, and Pavey knew of Bert Sargent and his hockey exploits. Still, Pavey had a job to do. Describing the duties of a medical officer, Pavey later wrote: "He must examine all recruits to ascertain they are free from contagious or infectious disease, and to see they are physically and mentally fit to train for overseas service. Every man when he reaches the front line should be able to fight: he must be physically fit and trained accordingly." Pavey filled in the basic medical information on the reverse of Bert's attestation paper, then, affirming he considered Bert fit for duty, signed the form. He extended his hand and wished Bert good luck.

Bert was one of just eight men accepted on the eighteenth of November.

To his surprise, Bert was instructed to return home for the next few nights. Until the 85th Regiment moved out, there wasn't enough space in the Drill Hall. He was, though, instructed to return the following afternoon.

Over dinner that night he broke the news to Flora and George Darling. Then it was time to tell his brother, Grover, and his sister,

Lena. No one was particularly shocked by the news and, if pressed, they might have admitted they were surprised it had taken him so long to enlist. At Darling Brothers the next day Bert arranged to pass his files to another junior engineer. There were good-natured back slappings and congratulations mixed with scarce-hidden envy, and probably a secret wonder whether they'd ever see him again.

The next evening, Bert was back at the Drill Hall. Even before he received a uniform, he was assigned to the recruiting desk, taking over from the battery's newly commissioned adjutant, Lieutenant Matthew ("Hew") Cochrane, guiding men through the same process he'd gone through a day earlier. During his shift, he witnessed the signature of 29-year-old William Meunier, who signed on as a gunner (Gnr), one of five men accepted that day.

In addition to a medical examination, each recruit underwent a rigorous dental examination. Those with problems "were told to get their ivories attended to so they might be able to properly masticate the food they are liable to get at the front. It was pointed out that in all probability it would be anywhere from six months to a year before the men in the active service regiments would be able to secure the services of a dentist again, so that they had better get any latent defects fixed up before they left." As a result, city dentists were swamped. Determined not to be refused on account of his teeth, Bert scheduled an appointment with his dentist, Ernest Hutchison, whose office was located on St. Catherine Street.

As a bombardier, Bert received $1.05 a day, and was eligible for a field allowance of 10 cents per day. While the $1.05 a day represented good money to some of the recruits, a labourer removing snow for the city of Montreal was paid $2.25 per day, itself less than half the $5.00 a day Henry Ford paid his workers in Detroit.* Adjusting for inflation, Bert's daily pay was equivalent to $19.00 in 2004 dollars. Compared to a British "Tommy," who received a shilling a day, the men of the CEF were well paid — a Canadian private making $1.00 per day earned four times what his British counterpart received.

---

*Pay rates for Canadian soldiers remained unchanged throughout the war. By 1918, soldiers and their families were feeling the pinch of wartime inflation.

A day or two later Bert moved into the Drill Hall, bringing a few things from the Grosvenor. While officers could decide whether to live in barracks or take rooms elsewhere, NCOs and other ranks (ORs) had no choice. Having done well on his first shift at the recruiting desk, Bert found himself back on the same duty on the twenty-third, relieving Captain Allen and Lieutenants Baker and Cochrane, this time witnessing the signature of Driver Albert Lawton.

On the twenty-sixth, Bert presented himself at the adjutant's office. Hew Cochrane, acting officer commanding (OC) while Captain William Scully was in Kingston qualifying for promotion, was a 1908 graduate of the Royal Military College and worked as a civil engineer. The two men reviewed a number of topics, including the need for engineers in the Field Artillery. They also discussed Captain Scully, whom Bert had not yet met, and he was pleased to learn that everyone held the OC in high regard. Scully, Bert learned, went to great lengths to protect his men and tolerated no outside interference. "Efficiency is his aim and he demands that every man give his best and that orders and tasks be carried out as delivered." Then Cochrane took Bert's attestation paper from a folder on his desk and signed that he was satisfied with its correctness.

The last hurdle had been cleared.

3

Training and the "Mysteries of Barrack Life"

In the following days, men of varied backgrounds slowly filled the ranks of the 21st Battery. Some gave up successful professional positions in order to enlist, and there were others whose age and education might normally have led them to seek commissions. But the CEF already had a surplus of officers, and so they enlisted in the ranks. They cared less for rank than for an opportunity to serve their King and Empire, accepting low ranks merely to get in on "the show." In the coming years, their abundant talents would win them promotions and honour.

Biff Notman enlisted in the 21st Battery on the sixteenth; Archie Gordon, a day later, was assigned to the Headquarters Section. On the twenty-third, Walter Gordon joined the battery as a gunner. His abilities were quickly recognized and he was promoted first to bombardier, then to corporal. Biff, Walter, and Archie were soon joined by other familiar faces, and the Drill Hall began to resemble a class reunion. Recruiting progressed well enough that by November 25 a total of 82 men had been accepted, just over half of the battery's nominal strength.* Three days later, under a column headlined FIELD ARTILLERY NEARLY RECRUITED, the *Gazette* reported:

---

*The nominal strength of the 21st Battery was four officers and 151 ORs, as it was for each of the 22nd, 23rd, and 24th Batteries, the other batteries comprising the 6th Brigade. The nominal strength of the Brigade's Ammunition Column was four officers and 152 ORs. With a Headquarters Section of five officers and 36 ORs, the 6th Brigade's nominal strength amounted to 817 all ranks.

Good progress is being made with the enlistment of the men for the Field Battery which is to go to the front with the second contingent and which is being recruited at the Craig Street Drill Hall. The recruits are being examined by Capt. H. Pavey and the men are put through a very strict examination so as to reduce the likelihood of any further thinning out under actual work.

It is expected that the Field Battery will be recruited up to strength in a few days. So far the men are drilling with garrison supplies, and it is not yet known whether they will have guns to take with them, or finish their training and secure their guns in England.

All NCOs and private soldiers drew their first issue of kit from Quartermaster-Sergeant Arthur Henry, himself only recently enlisted. If they were lucky, and of the right size, they also got a uniform. Reflecting the Canadian winter, the kit included a greatcoat, woolen undershirt and drawers, balaclava cap, and woolen gloves. Along with this came a variety of toilet articles, sewing kit, and eating utensils. These items would be added to over the next months, first in England and, later, at the front. In England, as the tight-fitting Canadian tunics wore out, they were replaced by the looser and more comfortable five-button British version. Along with all this, the men received brown leather boots. NCOs and ORs were also issued a five-pouch 1908-pattern bandolier of tanned pigskin to hold 50 rounds of .303 ammunition. Each man also received two identity discs, with his name, initials, number, unit, and religious affiliation.

Kit inspection was a regular feature of barracks life and took place generally once a week. On these occasions, every man's kit items were laid out for inspection. If any items were missing, his pay was docked and he could expect to be assigned extra fatigues as punishment.

The standard khaki service dress, adopted in 1902, consisted of a high-collar, single-breasted serge tunic with seven metal buttons, large patch pockets, and shoulder straps; a shirt; serge trousers; and puttees. These latter, woollen strips some six feet in length and four inches wide, were intended to make a neat seal between the boot and trouser leg. Sergeants patiently showed their men how to roll the puttees.

Unlike the infantry, artillery and mounted units rolled them from the knee down. Along with their uniforms the men received brass collar badges and CANADA shoulder badges. NCOs, depending on their rank, also received one or more *V*-shaped chevrons to be sewn on the sleeves. Once their uniforms were squared away, the next stop for most recruits was the studio of a local photographer for a portrait, either alone or with a group of comrades. The result was usually made into a postcard and mailed to the folks back home.

In barracks, great attention was paid to personal grooming. Short, severe haircuts were the order of the day. Each man was issued a cut-throat razor and shaving soap as part of his kit, and he was expected to use both every day, in quarters and in the field. Moderate moustaches, like those worn by Bert and Walter (and about a quarter of the 21st's men), were acceptable; full beards, which adorned a previous generation of Canadian soldiers, were not. Those who could afford it purchased a Gillette safety razor with replaceable blades, though at $5.00 apiece, they were an expensive luxury. To the military, personal hygiene was paramount. In crowded barracks and the Drill Hall, contagious diseases could spread easily. Thus, a Shower Bath Parade was generally held once a week, usually on Tuesdays.

Recruits to the battery ate their meals at the Drill Hall, with various messes allocated to officers, sergeants, and privates. Typically, it cost the government about 75 cents to feed a man for a day and most men had no complaints about the food. Across town, at the Grenadier Guards, the diarist of the 2nd Divisional Ammunition Column recorded: "As an example of the excellence of the food, men received two eggs each day and chicken once a week."

In an age of widespread belief, Sunday morning Church Parade was an important aspect of barracks life. Officers inspected the men to make sure buttons were polished and uniforms neatly brushed, reflecting credit on the battery. Church Parades were announced in the newspapers, and often hundreds of citizens lined the streets as various regiments marched to local churches.

Training in the 21st Battery began immediately on enlistment.

First, the men were instructed in what the *Gazette* called "the mysteries of barrack life." Then, as the paper related, "they were taught how to handle their kits and look after their quarters." After this, basic training could begin in earnest. At the outset, as men and officers were still being taken on strength, training consisted mainly of physical drill and squad drill, intended to build up a recruit's fitness. Drills were usually conducted five and a half days a week, with Saturday afternoons and Sundays off.

Route marches were important, for the armies of 1914 moved largely on foot. NCOs set a brisk cadence: 120 paces per minute, with a 10-minute rest every 50 minutes. With practice, units could cover 15 miles or more in a day with gear, though it was a gruelling routine. For young recruits, like 18-year-old Gunner Frederick Peverley, and the fit, like Bert Sargent, route marches presented no difficulties. For others in the battery, like 44-year-old Gunner John Entwhistle and 44-year-old Sergeant George Ginsberg, a Boer War veteran, weeks passed before they could keep up with their comrades. "It is the plan," the *Gazette* explained, "to gradually increase the length of these marches, in order to harden the men for the work ahead."

In time, the regimen of regular meals with good food and physical training began to pay off. By late December the *Gazette* noted, "The men are getting hardened in their work, so that a ten-mile route march is easy for them." Route marches and drill sometimes had to yield to Montreal's winter. In late December, the paper advised: "During the present cold weather, there will be little platoon or company drill on the Champ de Mars, as this is too trying on the men."

In parallel, training in the basics of gunnery, and courses in specialized skills like map reading and signalling, began. Recruits learned of the two types of guns in use by the Field Artillery: the 18-pounder field gun (similar to their obsolete 12-pounders), which fired a projectile of 18.5 pounds over a fairly flat trajectory to a distance of about 6,500 yards. And the 4.5-inch howitzer, of which there were just a handful in all of Canada. It fired a 35-pound projectile up to 7,000 yards in a high trajectory, which meant the shell plunged onto its target. It was intended to collapse trenches and emplacements, something the 18-pounder could not do.

The men also learned that, unlike previous wars, they would rarely see the enemy they were shooting at. Instead, their fire would be indirect, supported by a forward observer in contact with his guns by telephone or other means. In this new type of artillery warfare, signalling was of particular importance. Signal personnel were required "to send and receive Morse code at 12 words per minute by buzzer, flag and lamp, semaphore at the same rate and to thoroughly understand telephones, communication systems, director and range finder."

Four-gun batteries like the 21st were divided into two "sections," each of about 70 men, and commanded by a lieutenant. Sections were broken down further into two "sub-sections," the four sub-sections being designated A through D. Each sub-section, headed by a sergeant, was equipped with one 18-pounder.

It took six men to fire the 18-pounder. Under their sergeant, every gunner and bombardier learned the specific tasks to do his job as a member of the crew, so the gun could deliver accurate, sustained fire on an enemy position. Each man learned the functions of every other member in the sub-section, so he could take over in case of injury. Once the men of each sub-section learned to work together, the four sub-sections had to be moulded into a battery.

It was not for many months that the men would actually fire their weapons. "Gun drill" consisted of bringing the gun and its limber from a travelling mode to the point where it was loaded with a dummy round and ready to fire on a target. To accomplish this, the gun crew performed a series of precise moves, carefully choreographed so the men did not get in each other's way. It was tedious, repetitive work but essential if a crew was to bring its gun into action with the minimum of delay under actual battle conditions. For drivers, it was the same. Men needed to control a six-horse team pulling a gun and its limber; thereafter, the teams had to manoeuvre and come into action as a whole. Drivers of the 21st Battery faced one major problem: there were no horses at the Drill Hall.

Much of the training the gunners received was a waste of time; a good deal was useless. Some of it was just plain wrong, though this would not become apparent in many cases until they had reached the front. Artillerymen of the Second Contingent were being prepared for a war still imperfectly understood, unlike any other fought to date. Training was based on the concept of mobile warfare, something not seen again on the Western Front until the last months of 1918. In reality, the lines were so static by mid-1915 that field guns remained in position for months at a time.

Training also included classroom time on a variety of subjects, 90-minute lectures given by officers reflecting the latest thinking from the War Office, and condensed into various softcover manuals. All of this was intended to reinforce the idea that the basic mission of the field artillery was to support the infantry's advance by destroying, neutralizing, and suppressing the enemy by superiority of fire. Among the first lecture topics were "Discipline and Interior Economy"; other topics included "Military Law," "Ammunition," "Signalling," and "Gunnery." Lectures were repeated so the lessons would sink in.

In a 12-week training program, physical drill was held daily, and beginning in the second or third week, so were foot drill (for gunners) and battery drill (for NCOs and drivers). Those assigned as signallers received instruction in various signal techniques. By week four, ceremonial drill was added, so the men would know the proper procedures for a variety of military functions. Week five saw a route march added to the program. At week seven, by which time the men had route marches four days out of six, all-day marches were introduced. By week eight, working with their 12-pounders, gunners practised loading, and received further lectures on "Equitation," "Driving," and "Ammunition — 18-Pounder," along with a lectures on "Employment of Artillery in the Field," "Battery Drill and Movement," "Gunnery," "Gun Laying," "Battery Tactics," "Map Reading," "Bivouacs," "Emplacements and Concealment," and "18-Pounder Equipment."

They also learned to use the various tools of their new craft: clinometer (to measure angles of elevation), rangefinder, telescopic gunsight (for the few occasions when they would shoot at targets they could actually see), dial sight, fuse indicator, and how to remove, clean, and stow the above for transport.

Had horses been available, by week nine gunners would have received instruction in "Harnessing and Saddling," while drivers practised "Section Gun Drill." These two programs would have been conducted on an almost daily basis until they were second nature. In the event, these aspects of training would have to wait until the

21st Battery arrived in England. And, with horses, came lectures on "Stable Duties and Management," "Animal Management" (the latter two given by an officer from the Veterinary Corps), and some basic information on the treatment of minor ailments to horses. The unit's medical officer would also have provided instruction on sanitation, hygiene, and basic first aid.

By week 10, were there a full outdoor rifle range at the disposal of the 21st, recruits would have received appropriate musketry instruction and practice. Instead, the battery made do with the basement range of the Drill Hall, using pistols and .22-calibre rifles. Training with .303 service rifles would have to wait until they arrived in England. As the lectures and practical aspects of the training curriculum increased, route marches decreased to one a week. With training coming to an end, and anticipating a departure from Canada, lectures came on "Ship Discipline"; and, if the battery was taking horses, "Care of Horses on Board Ship."

As if the pattern of lectures, physical training, and route marches was not enough, officers faced an extra burden. Notices appeared in barracks in the second week of December that classes would be held "to instruct the officers in the language of the enemy." By the time the Second Contingent sailed for England, officers were expected to have a working knowledge of German. "Between drills and lectures, [officers] are already working more than union hours," the *Gazette* noted. "Any special linguistic training will have to be subtracted from sleeping time."

Newspaper articles provided useful information for the battery's fledgling gunners, and first-hand accounts of artillery action were dissected for possible lessons. The *Illustrated London News* began a series in November entitled *A Dominant Factor in Modern War: Artillery*, and contained a wealth of detail. An official report from London on January 5, 1915, dealing with the effect of British heavy guns, was summarized in the *Gazette* a few days later. "Experiences in this war have caused many profound modifications of theories commonly held before it broke out. But no factor was so underestimated as the effect of high-explosive projectiles fired by guns and howitzers.

"The gunner has come into his own, for this arm of the service has assumed importance greater probably than it has ever before possessed, and certainly greater than it has known since the time of Napoleon, an artillery officer himself."

Officers and men of the 21st read with equally great interest an article appearing in the Montreal *Daily Star* a few weeks later. Headlined BRITISH HOWITZER IS PROVING SUPERIOR TO GERMAN'S HEAVY GUNS, the Canadian Press story cited the official "Eye Witness," who wrote: "A great feature of the recent fighting has been the accuracy of our artillery fire. On one occasion our guns accomplished the feat of blowing the Germans out of trenches they were occupying on an embankment, although it was only forty yards from that which we were holding."

On occasion, lectures were given in Montreal by officers of other units, to which men of the 21st Battery might be invited. When Lieutenant Shirley Templeton Layton of the 2nd Montreal Brigade of Heavy Artillery addressed the Canadian Society of Civil Engineers on December 3, officers and non-coms of the 21st Battery with a background in science were probably in attendance. They would also have attended the Society's next session on January 14. Lieutenant James Brunton, a McGill lecturer on military engineering, reviewed the use of field artillery since the Franco-Prussian War of 1870, the development of quick-firing breech-loaded guns, and the great increases in power, range, and effectiveness that had been achieved since then.

Brunton went on to discuss the howitzer, and many of the military men in the audience craned forward, for this was a topic of considerable interest. The war, the lieutenant pointed out, had seen the reintroduction of an obsolete weapon, the howitzer, firing projectiles at a very high angle, "so that they would drop into covered positions and cause much trouble to the men concealed in them."

4

"A Great Credit to Your Country"

As training progressed, the men of the 21st developed a growing confidence in their abilities and a sense of pride in their unit. New friendships were forged in the Drill Hall, many of which would outlast the war. At the end of November, a total of 102 men had been accepted for the battery, and the ranks of the ammunition column were similarly being filled.

On December 7 the Montreal garrison turned out to welcome the prime minister, Sir Robert Borden. Long before the review, a steady stream of citizens began to converge on Fletcher's Field, a park on the east side of Mount Royal. The afternoon parade, the *Gazette* promised, would be an impressive one, made more so by the "knowledge that the greater number of the men will be making history at the front within a few months, and that in all human probability a proportion of them will not return, but remain in obscure graves on Belgian and German battlefields, martyrs to British defence of the world's liberties."

In all there were 3,133 officers and men, of whom 133 came from the 21st Battery — virtually its entire strength. The gunners left their 12-pounders at the Drill Hall. Led by the McGill COTC's band, the prime minister passed slowly down the khaki-clad lines, stopping here and there to exchange a few words with several officers. Afterward, Borden addressed the officers and NCOs of the units he had reviewed. Gathered in the assembly hall of the Peel Street Barracks, the leader of the Conservative Party spoke for about 10 minutes, summing up his impressions and offering encouragement for what lay ahead.

"It has been," he said, "a great privilege to see the troops which have been mobilized and are being trained, and also the training corps of McGill University. I congratulate Canada on the spirit of the country, which, in response to our call, has brought us officers and men more quickly than we can arm or equip them. This is not a great military country, and we were not prepared to meet all the demands of the occasion on the instant, but you may rest assured all that can be done is being done with the greatest expedition possible."

Knowing many of the soldiers felt they were ready to meet the Germans right away, Borden urged caution and patience:

It would be highly foolish to send to the front men not fully trained and not properly equipped. And if the training of the men is important, that of the non-commissioned officers and officers is even more so, wherefore it is to be expected that when the time comes that you can be accommodated across the sea, there may be further training for you. But no one who recognizes the spirit, the resourcefulness and the courage of the Canadian people will entertain the slightest doubt as to the showing you will make.

Borden was right. In time, the Canadian Corps would be among the finest troops on the Western Front.

"This war," Borden concluded, "is not of the Empire's seeking, but it has come, and it involves all that our fathers established, and that we have sought to extend. We are face to face with the greatest military power in the world, but when I see training and discipline such as I have seen this afternoon, combined with a courage and a loyalty of which I need not speak, I feel we have all that we can desire." Then he gestured around the assembly hall. "I hope the arrangements for your comfort are satisfactory, and can assure you it will not be our fault in Ottawa if they are not."

Amid good-natured laughter and sustained applause, Colonel Erastus Wilson, General Officer Commanding (GOC) of Military District No. 4, of which Montreal was a part, rose to thank the prime minister for his remarks. Wilson commended the officers under his command, terming them "the most conscientious and hard-working men in Canada." He ended by saying he was absolutely certain Canada would have good cause to be proud of the expeditionary force she was sending.

On December 9 the 21st Battery learned that Ottawa had appointed a commander for their 6th Brigade, Lieutenant-Colonel Edward Rathbun, a native of Deseronto. Rathbun was to report for duty at once in Montreal and "proceed with the organization of the artillery from this district for the Second Contingent." Rathbun arrived the next day. A man of medium height whose fair hair was turning to grey, he was a Victorian renaissance man with a wide range of interests. In his younger days he had worked in the manufacturing company founded by his grandfather. From gristmills, lumbering, and cartage, the business expanded into railways, steamships, cement, chemicals, and terracotta tiles. Taking over the firm on his father's death in 1903, Rathbun also served three years in the Ontario Legislature. He joined the militia in 1900 as a lieutenant and, within six years, rose to the rank of lieutenant-colonel (Lieut.-Col.), commanding the 9th Field Artillery Brigade whose headquarters were in Deseronto. And, in 1912, he had served as president of the Artillery Association.

One of Rathbun's first acts on arriving at the Drill Hall was an inspection, witnessed by a *Gazette* reporter. "After the regular drill, he inspected the 21st Canadian Field Artillery. The unit turned out with four guns and 43 men, with the ammunition column also up to strength, and after the parade, Lieutenant-Colonel Rathbun briefly complimented the officers and men on their appearance and work."

The four batteries comprising Rathbun's new command were spread across eastern Canada. The 21st Battery mobilized in Montreal under Captain William Scully. The 22nd was being raised in Kingston and Belleville (Military District 3), while the 23rd and 24th were forming in Fredericton (MD 6) and drew on New Brunswick and Nova Scotia for manpower.

Canada's governor general, HRH Prince Arthur, Duke of Connaught and Strathern, arrived in Montreal on December 17 to inspect various military units then undergoing training. The 64-year-old Duke, third son and seventh child of Queen Victoria, was a lifelong military officer, appropriate for a prince whose godfather was the Duke of Wellington. The Duke's first stop was the snow-covered Champ de Mars. Here, in the early afternoon, as the Royal Standard fluttered in a light breeze, the khaki-clad Duke reviewed the 24th Battalion Victoria Rifles. He passed up and down the ranks of soldiers, each with rifle and fixed bayonet, stopping before almost every other man, asking about their nationality, previous military service, and sometimes offering a few words of kindly advice.

Then it was the battery's turn. The Duke and his entourage descended the steps to Craig Street. As onlookers and streetcars were held back, the vice-regal party entered the Drill Hall, where "over seven hundred men of various branches of the service were drawn up for inspection. These included the 6th Brigade Canadian Field Artillery under Lieut.-Col. Rathbun, an ammunition column under Lieut. Cochrane....

"His Royal Highness made the same keen inspection of these units as he had done with the 24th. He passed slowly up and down each line, talking to a number of the men.... 'Are you an old country man or Canadian?' he asked many of the recruits. And to others, perhaps noting a military bearing, 'Have you seen service before?'"

At the close of the inspection the men formed into close order as the Duke ascended to the second-floor reviewing stand, where he could be seen and heard by every man. He first complimented the troops on their fine appearance, especially the artillery. Then, warming to his subject, he continued, "I am sure that you are going to be a great credit to your country and Empire and the Service in the hard work that lies ahead of you. In that work I must impress upon you that discipline and sobriety are of first importance to the work of a soldier. I trust that you will set a good example in both respects, and keep up the good name of the Royal Field Artillery, which is one of the finest services in the army." From the balcony, he led the troops in cheers for his nephew, the King. The men returned it with hearty cheers for the Duke.

In a letter to George V dated December 17, the Duke provided details of his hectic inspection tour.

... I returned yesterday from 5 days of inspection of the new units of the 2nd Canadian Division which are being trained in different towns in Canada. I visited St. Johns, Province of Quebec, 1 hr. by train from Montreal, Montreal, Kingston & Toronto. At Montreal I saw the 24th Battn, an exceptionally fine Regt. & very smart. I also inspected there a smart Field Battery, of which the men were nearly all English-[speaking]. 7 Companies of Army Service Corps and 2 Field Ambulances, the material of all was good. I also inspected in the University grounds the newly formed McGill University Regt: over 1000 strong, several of the companies have not got their uniforms yet but the material was excellent & Officers & men are showing the greatest keenness.

After describing his impressions of other units in Kingston and Toronto, the Duke concluded:

Everywhere I went over, the barracks, or improvised Quarters & found everything clean & tidy. At each place I addressed the Officers urging the importance of discipline & sobriety & the necessity for their setting a good example. From what I saw I have every confidence that this new Division will be an efficient one in every sense of the word; they are working very hard & are all being trained by the Officers Commanding the Districts from where they come & they are quartered in their Districts.

In the last 10 days of December, two events of note occurred that involved the men of the 21st Battery. On December 20, military headquarters in Ottawa announced that each soldier would be allowed 25 cents for extra rations for Christmas. The money "would be used to add a number of extras which the soldiers' tables are ordinarily strangers to. For the men in barracks the special allowance will be used in buying oranges, apples, nuts, raisins, sauces, pickles, ginger ale and other delicacies." Twenty-five cents per man might not sound like much but, with purchases in wholesale lots by shrewd Army Service Corps buyers, it would "go quite a long way."

A day later the 21st Battery and the ammunition column received orders to vacate the Drill Hall. With their kit transported in wagons, more than 200 men in greatcoats marched four abreast with Captain Scully through the snowy streets to take up residence in the old High School Barracks on Peel Street, just north of St. Catherine Street. With them went the unit's mascot, a young terrier.

The men would return to the Drill Hall for training, as they'd left the 12-pounders behind. Two half-hour marches in the winter months would toughen them for the rigours of war.

5

New Homes

Sold to a real-estate speculator in 1912, the former Protestant High School occupied almost the entire block between Peel and Metcalfe Streets, extending to Burnside on the north. Disused since its sale, it was offered as a barracks to the government — rent-free, as a patriotic gesture — when recruiting for the Second Contingent began. Military authorities were quick to appreciate the building's potential. Modifications were hurriedly effected, transforming the school into a regulation barracks capable of holding more than a thousand men, with cooking facilities, dining rooms, and showers. Nonetheless, it was somewhat on the small side and soon became crowded as the 23rd and 24th infantry battalions continued to recruit.

The Peel Street Barracks (to use its new name) was thoroughly inspected by Major-General Sam Hughes, Minister of Militia and Defence, in late November. At Hughes's insistence, lighting in various rooms was improved and more space set aside where men could read in their leisure hours. "You must," Hughes admonished the commanding officers gathered in the assembly hall, "look after these men so that they have reasonable comfort. The Dominion can afford it, and owes it to them and I intend to see that they are properly looked after." The bombastic Hughes was as good as his word. By the time the 21st Battery, the ammunition column and 6th Brigade headquarters arrived, taking over the south wing, the building was in good shape from a soldier's perspective. In the barracks area, a partition was erected between the 21st Battery and the infantrymen. Newly installed pay phones meant the men could call their families.

Though crowded, the new quarters were an improvement over the Drill Hall. Given the large number of men in barracks, arrangements were made for artillery privates and NCOs to take their meals at the nearby YMCA. For Bert, Walter, and Biff, all of whom had attended school in the building more than a decade earlier, the transformations came as a shock. It was a curious sensation to walk down corridors that had once echoed with the laughter of schoolboys and girls and the chant of Latin verbs. Now they were filled with uniformed men, and the halls echoed to shouts of command.

Within a few days, so no one could doubt the identity of the south wing's occupants, a three-line, printed sign appeared over the former girls' entrance:

HEADQUARTERS 6TH BRIGADE ARTILLERY C.E.F.

Shortly afterward, Major Scully had the battery assemble outside for a formal photograph, a customary act for almost every military unit prior to going overseas on active service. Underneath their new sign, the 114 officers and men recruited to date for the battery and the column, along with their terrier mascot, gathered around their commander. The ground was snow-covered and the weather seasonably cold; the men struck a jaunty pose in their fur hats and greatcoats.

The Peel Street Barracks occupied a choice parcel of land in the heart of Montreal's new commercial district, a stone's throw from the busiest intersection in the city. Nearby was James Ogilvie's new department store, where officers desiring something other than barracks fare could enjoy a four-course lunch for 40 cents. Two blocks south was the elegant Windsor Hotel, the city's hotel of choice. A 15-minute walk eastward on St. Catherine Street brought the men to Montreal's entertainment area, where escape artist Harry Houdini was a favourite headliner at the Orpheum, and burlesque and vaudeville shows promised to distract soldiers with time on their hands.

And, for Bert and Biff, the barracks had one further attraction: it was but a short walk to their homes.

As Christmas neared, there was a general easing of drill among the various units. Men from the Montreal area, unless their services were required on Christmas Day, received leave to spend the holiday with their families. Those from nearby towns lined up for reduced-rate rail tickets, a patriotic gesture by the railways to men in uniform. Recruits from more distant locations would enjoy a fine Christmas meal in their respective barracks.

The elaborate Christmas dinner at the barracks received good coverage in the local newspapers. MEN HAD REAL CHRISTMAS headed one column in the *Gazette* of December 26, but no amount of gaiety could hide the fact that the 500 men at the long tables were soldiers who would soon be called to duty. "There is a general feeling that both officers and men are engaged in a venture which may mean many casualties, and they are determined to enjoy what will in all probability

Major William Scully, officers, and men of the 21st Battery, 6th Brigade, taken in December 1915 outside their headquarters in the former Montreal High School. Bert Sargent is circled on the right; Walter Gordon, centre. Note the unit's mascot, to the right behind Bert. *Courtesy of Vincent Scully.*

be the last Christmas for some of them. It is a sobering thought, that before another Christmas comes along, these men will have had their turn at the front, whence a good many of them will never return."

With most of the 21st Battery coming from Montreal, the south wing was virtually deserted. Bert, with a two-day respite from duty, spent the time at the Grosvenor, enjoying a traditional dinner with the extended family, and visiting friends. Battery personnel trickled back to barracks on Sunday, December 27, as the mercury plunged to -26° C. Normal activity resumed the following morning, and the weather moderated somewhat. Recruiting continued through the holiday period; seven more men were added to the battery's roll between December 22 and 31.

Though Bert managed to get off duty for New Year's Eve, he was back in barracks on the first, participating in a time-honoured tradition. All units in the Montreal garrison held a New Year's reception and open house at their various barracks, with senior officers paying courtesy calls to each other's messes. The *Gazette* explained the protocol:

According to custom the officer commanding, Col. Wilson, will hold a reception at Divisional Headquarters early in the morning, after which, accompanied by his staff, Col. Wilson will call on the officers of the different regiments. Receptions will be held at all the armories on New Year's morning, as usual, with the addition of the active service men. Lt.-Col. Gunn and the officers of the 24th Victoria Rifles will be "At Home" during the morning, as also will the artillery officers who are headquartered in the Peel Street Barracks.

Drill and classes resumed the next morning when reveille sounded in the barracks, rousing the men of the 21st Battery.

Early in the new year the Montreal Riding Academy offered an equestrian course to officers of Montreal's active service units. Artillery officers, especially, needed to ride, as horses were the sole means of moving the guns in the field, and officers needed to keep up with their units. The course, given by Captain Théophile Reeb, a former French cavalryman, was not for the fainthearted. "The officers have a hard time of it, working first on practically barebacked horses, then with saddles stripped of stirrups, after which they learn how to handle the reins with either one or two hands, and then take their jumps or fall off, as the case may be." Once the lessons were over, officers of the 21st were expected to continue riding, though this presented a problem since the horses were stabled a couple of miles away in the suburb of Verdun.

Architect Walter Hyde, having completed artillery training at Kingston and in the process of receiving his lieutenant's commission, returned to Montreal just before the Christmas holiday. Posted to the 6th Brigade's ammunition column, his attestation paper was dated January 10. Five weeks later he transferred to Lieutenant-Colonel Rathbun's Headquarters Section.

On the thirteenth, Bert returned to the Grosvenor with a surprise for Flora and George. The sleeves of his uniform tunic bore a second chevron: he'd been promoted to corporal. It meant a pay increase of five cents per day. Within a couple of weeks, having had an opportunity to demonstrate his talents, Bert won a further promotion, this time to sergeant. Along with his third stripe came a welcome increase in pay; a sergeant received $1.35 a day plus a daily field allowance of 15 cents. By common consent, "Sergeant Sargent" would have been too comical; everyone in the battery, including the officers, called him "Sergeant Bert," a typical Canadian informality.

In early January it became apparent that the old High School would soon be dangerously overcrowded and the authorities decided the 21st Battery, along with the ammunition column and brigade headquarters, would have to move. A return to the Drill Hall was not possible because other units had since moved in. However, a nearby building formerly occupied by the R.J. Tooke company, a manufacturer and retailer of men's shirts and accessories, happened to be vacant. Rathbun made a quick inspection of the five-storey stone building at the southwest corner of Craig Street West and St. Francis Xavier and decided it could be the battery's new home, provided some modifications were made; these were agreed to by Colonel Wilson, who then secured a lease on January 19.

On January 29, the 6th Brigade held a Vaccination Parade, with Captain Harold Muckleston administering the first of two anti-typhoid inoculations (the second dose was given on February 8). Regulations allowed each recruit so vaccinated to be put on the sick list for 48 hours. While most men did not become physically ill, the dose was sufficiently strong that arms became very sore and the men were unable to drill properly. No one much liked the vaccinations: men were required to refrain from alcohol for 24 hours prior to the injection and 48 hours afterward. As January ended, only 10 names had been added to the roll of the 21st Battery; its strength (excluding officers) stood at 122, still 30 short of the nominal strength.

In Kingston, newly commissioned Hal Fetherstonhaugh, originally expecting to join the Third Contingent artillery, agreed to a last-minute switch with a McGill classmate who'd been assigned to the Second Contingent. His training complete, Hal was assigned to the 6th Brigade's ammunition column. On February 1 he presented himself at the Peel Street Barracks and was taken on strength. Like others, he was surprised by the transformation of his former school. Gunner Herbert Edwards, a Kentish-born 35-year-old steamfitter who had joined the column on January 25, was assigned as Hal's batman, or servant. Like other batmen, Edwards trained as a member of a regular gun crew and was expected to take his place in the gun pits when the battery went into action.

A cold snap in the first week of February caused outdoor drill to be cancelled, replaced by complete kit inspections and typhoid inoculations for the latest recruits.

A new man, Gunner Robert Hale, joined the brigade's headquarters section on February 8. Born in London in 1893, Hale emigrated to Canada at the age of 18, having served a year and a half in the 7th London Field Artillery Brigade. A moulder in a steel works in civilian life, Hale was a signals specialist. Unmarried, his sweetheart was 22-year-old Alice Heath in the suburb of Verdun. Bob Hale had his own reasons for enlisting — "I shall always have the satisfaction of knowing I did not stay at home when there was some work for men to do." He offered another reason, as well: "I was told on more than one occasion I was afraid to go to the war. Now I am going to prove to those people I am not afraid."

It took two weeks to transform the Tooke Building into a completely equipped barracks, for Rathbun had paid careful attention to the building's sanitary facilities. On February 9, the 6th Field Artillery, some 309 men, marched down Peel Street. With the temperature a reasonable -7° C it made for a pleasant enough day. Police halted traffic as the 21st Battery, ammunition column, and Headquarters Section returned to the older section of town. "Within a few hours the men were comfortably fixed up in their new quarters." Lice, no stranger to Montreal's crowded tenements, would not be given an opportunity to infest the men of the 21st Battery. "All men going into barracks were either plainly clear of undesirable population, or else were fumigated at the Meurling Institute," explained the *Gazette*. "Any man who subsequently showed any insectiverous infection was at once separated from the rest and given the necessary treatment, so that the men at the barracks were clear of the usual troubles of soldiers on active service."

For nearby eateries like the New World Lunch Room and the Power Buffet, and watering holes like Krausmann's (surprisingly, still advertising a wide selection of German draft beers), the arrival of 300-odd artillerymen was a windfall. Hungry, well-behaved young men with money in their pockets were always welcome.

Inspections by senior officers were a way of life in the army. In the afternoon of Friday, February 12, it was the turn of Major-General François Lessard, inspector-general for eastern Canada, to conduct a thorough review. The 21st mustered at the Drill Hall, a short distance from the Tooke Building. Lessard seemed pleased with what he saw. "In general efficiency and physique," he told an audience of reporters, "the men whom I had the pleasure of inspecting today are fully the equals, if not the superiors, of the soldiers who left Canada with the First Contingent. Moreover, I found them remarkably well up in their drill."

The battery being recruited by Major Scully was representative of the male population of Canada's largest and most cosmopolitan city — with one glaring exception. Despite being raised in a city whose residents were about 50 percent French Canadian, there were virtually no francophones in the 21st. Though many of the Quebec-born men, Bert and Hal Fetherstonhaugh among them, had some knowledge of French, few francophones joined the artillery, where passable English skills were a virtual requirement. Unlike the infantry, the artillery never attempted to recruit French Canadians and all training was in English. In almost all other respects, the battery reflected the English-speaking society from which it was largely drawn. Like other early CEF formations, the majority of volunteers were British-born; native-born Canadians represented only 38 percent of the 21st Battery.

Edward Rathbun, eldest son and grandson of Victorian captains of industry, was not a patient man, and he itched to take his brigade to England, feeling his men were ready — or as ready as they could be made in barracks in Montreal, Fredericton, and Kingston. In mid-February Rathbun chanced to be in Ottawa when, as Nicholson relates, "an urgent call was received asking for the immediate dispatch overseas of the '6th CFA.'" Elated, Rathbun insisted this meant *his* brigade, and Ottawa ultimately acquiesced: the 21st would depart Montreal on February 17. It was a signal honour. Rathbun's gunners were the first of the Second Contingent to sail for England, ahead even of the infantry they were supposed to support in battle.

Compared to other artillery brigades training in Canada, the 6th was *not* yet ready, despite Rathbun's vigorous assertions. The brigade had limited experience with horses, and had not yet learned to work as a disciplined team with drivers and gunners. By comparison, the 16th Battery, then in Guelph, would spend twenty-four and a half weeks in training before being shipped to England; the 21st and its three sister batteries received just 13 weeks training before going overseas. As well, they — like many others — were ignorant of the new realities of modern warfare; it would have been folly to send them into the meatgrinder of the Western Front.

The men of the 21st, badly short-changed in Canada, would spend months in England making up for the haste with which they were sent overseas.

6

"Berlin or Bust"

The artillery had always been popular in Montreal, and citizens greeted the news of the 21st's departure with a sense of pride though, for others, the event was tinged with sadness. These men were brothers, husbands, and fathers heading off to war, and no one knew what fate awaited them overseas. For their part, the men were elated. Most occupied themselves with last-minute paperwork. Bert, for example, filled out a form specifying that $10.00 a month from his pay be assigned to his sister Lena, beginning on March 1. The money would be paid into her account in Montreal, to be used in any manner Bert specified.

ORs and NCOs with family in Montreal, with the approval of their superiors, managed to spend a last night at home, saying tearful farewells. It was a time for parting gifts and souvenirs, photos and locks of hair from wives and sweethearts. Long before sunrise these men returned to barracks, often bleary-eyed from lack of sleep. They found the Tooke Building humming with activity. Batmen scurried on last-minute errands for officers, procuring necessities for the train ride to Halifax. Extra luggage was sent ahead by motor transport to the Grand Trunk's ornate Bonaventure Station, a half-mile away. Kit bags were inspected and packed, belts and bandoliers received a final polish, buttons and insignia gleamed. Bert, an amateur photographer, packed his Kodak with care, as did Hal Fetherstonhaugh. Uncertain whether the men would be fed on the train, Alice Heath packed a small lunch for her soldier, Gunner Bob Hale.

Few occasions were capable of bringing together the three levels of Montreal society, but the departure of the 21st Battery was surely one of them. Bound by concern for the men going off to God knew what, elegant ladies from the Square Mile mingled with day labourers in threadbare jackets, both contrasting with the fine coats and hombergs of middle-class businessmen and office clerks. On the sidewalks, people jostled for positions and waved miniature Union Jacks as the gunners emerged from the Tooke Building, formed ranks, then swung west onto Craig Street, four abreast, at the regulation pace.

At the station, a family friend approached Hal Fetherstonhaugh's mother. "Don't worry about our boys," the friend advised. "I have reliable word from England that the war will be over very shortly and they will never see any fighting." It was, according to Hal's father, an idea embraced by many.

The emotion-charged send-off was front-page news:

Officers and men of the 6th Brigade, Canadian Field Artillery, about four hundred in all, left Montreal this morning. The men lined up behind their headquarters on Craig and St. Francis-Xavier Streets and then marched to the Bonaventure station where they embarked. The train pulled out shortly before 11 o'clock.

The 6th Brigade, consisting of the 21st Battery, under the command of Major Scully, and the Ammunition Column, under Capt. [Philip] Cook, is commanded by Lieut.-Col. Rathbun, and is the first unit of the Second Contingent to leave Montreal.

The men marched down to the station in two detachments, the first leaving early this morning, the other shortly before the train left. Hundreds of friends and relatives were outside the headquarters at an early hour. Visitors were allowed inside the building and there were many touching scenes.

At the station thousands had assembled to bid the troops "God Speed." The soldiers, ever cheerful, as it behooves the British Tommy, were received with rousing cheers as they marched onto the platform. They replied with enthusiastic hurrahs and the singing of *It's a Long Way to Tipperary*.

Each man carried his own kit, consisting of blanket, knapsack and cartridge belt. After these had been deposited in the cars, they found that they still had a few minutes left for leavetaking.

There were those who bid mother and father and sister and brother and a big ring of friends goodbye. Others took leave quietly with wife and mother, hugging the baby who looked on, open-eyed with astonishment. Some, apparently, did not know anybody in particular, but they must say goodbye. So they shook hands with utter strangers and cheered for the Entente and the flag and the officers and the Brigade until they were hoarse and red in the face.

An elderly, well-dressed lady blessed her son with smiles. When he turned away and left, she suddenly lost control and fainted in the arms of her husband.

One woman became hysterical and had to be escorted out. But most of the adieus were cheerful, the soldiers themselves looked to that, although it was harder in most cases than they had expected.

The railway carriages were decorated with chalk inscriptions. One read: BERLIN OR BUST, another FREE RIDE AT LAST.

When the train at last pulled out there were salvos of cheers, ending in the soldiers singing *Tipperary*.

Three hundred and eighteen miles to the south, while clocks in Manhattan chimed noon, tugs hauled the White Star's RMS *Megantic* away from Pier 60. While her stern swung slowly into the Hudson, her engines rumbled to life. Soon the steamship passed through the Verrazano Narrows and the office towers fell astern. *Megantic* steamed slowly northeast, bound for Halifax, some 650 nautical miles away, the first leg of her passage to England. She had been contracted to transport the men of the 6th Brigade, a fact known only to her master, George Metcalfe, and a few of Lieutenant-Colonel Rathbun's staff. With the United States still neutral, there was no secrecy surrounding *Megantic*'s departure from New York, nor her intermediate port of call.

White Star Line's RMS *Megantic*, aboard which Bert and the 6th Brigade sailed to England, February 1915. *Author's photo.*

The 4-6-2 locomotive of the Intercolonial Railway looped through industrial areas along the Lachine Canal. Gathering speed, it cleared the Point St. Charles yards and started across Victoria Bridge. As Montreal faded from view across the frozen river, the men settled down for the overnight 841-mile journey to Halifax. Some would sleep, lulled by swaying coaches; others would pass the time chatting, playing cards, or wiping fogged windows to peer at the snow-covered farms of rural Quebec. With a consist of 13 cars,* the Pacific-class locomotive would stop about every 130 miles, roughly every two hours, to take on water. There were also stops at three divisional points — Levis, Campbellton, and Moncton — where new train crews took over. For those so inclined, these brief halts were an opportunity to alight and stretch their muscles.

---

*The train, in the Intercolonial's Pullman Red livery, was made up of one baggage car, one commissary car, one table car, eight colonist cars, one first-class dining car for officers, and one first-class sleeper for officers. The men were accommodated in colonist cars. Normally holding up to 72 per car, troop trains typically had 54 per car.

Bob Hale, in a carriage with the Headquarters Section, began a letter to Alice:

There are 14 of the HQS together ... all very nice, the pick of the staff.

The food on the train was excellent but we were very glad of that lunch. We did not have dinner until 3 o'clock. For dinner we had boiled mutton, caper sauce, potatoes, rice pudding and coffee. Supper — stew, preserves and tea. Breakfast this morning — porridge, sausages, bacon, and coffee.

After we left yesterday some of the bunch got drunk, but not any of our crowd. We were all in bed last night at 9 o'clock and up at 6 o'clock this morning.

Others, like Lieutenant Hal Fetherstonhaugh, sent telegrams:

FEBRUARY 18.   JUST A LINE. GETTING OUT AT NEWCASTLE FOR 20 MINUTES' EXERCISE. WILL WRITE FROM HALIFAX. NOTHING NEW. WONDERFUL WEATHER. WE DO NOT ARRIVE UNTIL LATE TONIGHT. WE GOT A GREAT SEND-OFF.

At Newcastle, to honour the 21st Battery, schools let out for the morning and flag-waving children lined the streets as the men were paraded. A few days later, the *North Shore Leader* reported: "The school children gave flags to the soldiers as they were passing through Newcastle. Names were written on some of them and already a number of them have received letters and cards from the soldiers."

The train arrived at the Intercolonial's North Street Station late on Thursday night. Officers were put up at the King Edward, a modest hotel immediately adjacent. NCOs and ORs would spend a second night in the coaches. With dawn came a good breakfast on the train, following which the men were paraded and the roll called. Then they shouldered their gear and marched smartly to the nearby docks where *Megantic* awaited her military passengers. A salt tang hung in the air and a light mist lingered over the harbour as the men neared the giant ship. At the foot of the gangway, each man's name was checked off as he stepped up to the transport officer. Once on deck, crewmen directed officers, NCOs, and ORs to their respective quarters. Officers were billeted in first-class cabins, with NCOs and ORs in second- and third-class cabins. Quickly stowing their gear, the men began to explore the ship that would be their home for the next fortnight.

Megantic was a familiar sight to many. She had been a regular on the summer St. Lawrence route between Montreal and England since her maiden voyage in the summer of 1909 when she was much admired "for her elegant and luxurious furnishing, as well as the bright and airy manner in which her staterooms are fitted up, not a detail that could add to the comfort of her patrons being neglected." Her sea-going qualities also came in for favourable comment: "... some of her passengers, who have crossed the Atlantic on many occasions, stated they had never travelled on a steadier or more comfortable vessel."

In this early stage of the war, significant numbers of civilians still crossed the Atlantic. As there were not sufficient men in the 6th Brigade to fill *Megantic* (she could carry almost 1,700 passengers), White Star sold off the remaining berths. Despite shortages of food and rising prices, steamship companies tried hard to maintain pre-war standards. For soldiers who had eaten government-provided meals for the past three months, *Megantic* was a welcome change, and the printed menus for each meal were a nice touch.

The brigade's remaining batteries arrived by special trains. The 23rd and 24th showed up on February 19 from Fredericton, after an impressive send-off by civic authorities. They were soon joined aboard *Megantic* by the 22nd from Kingston. A surviving *Megantic* menu from February 19 reveals how well the officers were treated. Dinner began with giblet soup, followed by fish, then a choice of meats with vegetables, a choice of desserts, along with assorted fruits and nuts, ending with a cheese plate and coffee.

German naval policy with respect to submarine blockade of the British coast became a matter of public record while *Megantic* waited at Halifax. On February 18, Germany proclaimed the waters around the British Isles a "War Zone," in which all ships, regardless of their flag, would be sunk on sight. U-boat commanders were instructed "... to regard all merchantmen found within the blockaded area for the purpose of convoying anything to Britain as enemy ships engaged in illegal operations. The submarines are to approach the merchantmen, if possible, without being seen and torpedo them immediately without the slightest examination regarding their nationality or in any way concerning themselves as to the fate of the crew."

To those with cameras (and there were not many, for Kodaks were expensive novelties), *Megantic* offered a variety of new subjects and backgrounds. Batmen or cabin stewards were pressed into service as photographers. They were handed a camera and given quick instructions on how to take a photograph. Groups of officers or men then assembled for souvenir snapshots, officers striking jaunty poses with their walking sticks.

Bob Hale began another letter to Alice:

Did you get the other letter I sent from Halifax? I did not post it myself, but we went on parade and, as we were not allowed to leave the ranks, I had to give it to a civilian and trust him to mail it for me.

It is a nice bright day but very cold. There are two warships lying out in the harbor and they look fine too. There is not a bit of snow here in Halifax. You must excuse this bad writing; I am in my bunk. All the boys are in the reading room, singing songs, and I came here to be alone with you and to kiss that little piece of hair you gave me. I have only been away from you for two days and it seems so long to me.

There are four of us in this cabin. We have just had supper. We had fish, cheese, butter, jam, and tea and as much as we wanted. It is reported we are going to sail on Sunday but nobody knows anything.

Nobody is allowed on shore. We have had two deserters up to now, so they are getting very strict.

In the army, few things went quite as planned. *Megantic*'s departure was delayed while *Missanabie* and *Vaderland*, the other liners making up the small convoy, were loaded. George Metcalfe, completing his third voyage as *Megantic*'s master, paced his bridge impatiently, though there was nothing he could do; his sailing orders came from the Admiralty and he was a lieutenant in the RNR.

The following day, *Megantic* slipped her lines and anchored in the harbour. "We are to wait here," Bob Hale recorded, "until the remainder of the contingent have embarked and then proceed to sea with our escort. The weather here is very cold but bright and pleasant.

"The food on board is good. This morning for breakfast we had porridge, fish, eggs and bacon and marmalade. Dinner — soup, roast beef, potatoes, peas, fruit pudding, ice cream, one orange and one apple. Supper — stew, jam, peaches and rice.

"Our accommodation is excellent. We are berthed in the second-class cabins amidship, and we have a porthole in our cabin."

Up in first class, Hal Fetherstonhaugh was frustrated:

We are still here with not any news as to when we are to move off. All the men are on board; no passes except to officers, and all are anxious to move. We are living in the lap of luxury — splendid meals, orchestra, etc.

We had a muster parade this morning, checking off every man in the Brigade. It took quite a long time, from nine until eleven-thirty. We had a chance to see how the [Ammunition] Column compared with the other Units. It was not disappointing. They are pretty solid-looking and the sun is beginning to tell on their faces.

I hope we move out soon.

As I write, some officers of the 23rd have just arrived. They say we will get out into the stream tomorrow morning.

Bob Hale evidently had a dry sense of humour:

Monday, February 22

This morning we got up at 6 and had a good breakfast at 7 o'clock. At 9:30 we went on parade and were presented with tobacco and pipes. After that we did physical drill for an hour and then dinner at 11:30. After eating an excellent dinner we rested until 2 o'clock and then we paraded for boat drill.

Our lifeboat is number six, but it is right on the top boat deck about a mile away from our cabin. I don't think if anything does happen that I will bother about getting into my boat. I shall just make a dive for the one nearest.

The weather here today was beautiful, not too cold. We are laying here now with steam up. I expect we will be moving tomorrow.

7

At Sea

Hale's prediction was accurate. On Tuesday, an hour and 11 minutes before low water, *Megantic*, *Missanabie*, and *Vaderland*, with two Royal Navy escorts, departed Halifax. For security reasons the event was not mentioned in the local papers, though almost every Haligonian knew of the three liners that carried 4,000 men, the lead elements of the Second Contingent, drawn from every corner of the Dominion. The convoy was shepherded by the 16-gun *Canopus*-class battleship HMS *Glory* and HMS *Essex*, an obsolete three-stack frigate. Capable of 23 and 18 knots respectively, their speed would be restricted to that of the slowest vessel, *Vaderland*. For *Megantic*, it meant a normal six-day Atlantic crossing could well be doubled.

Bob Hale described their departure:

At 8:15 this morning we weighed our anchor and steamed slowly out of Halifax harbor. The band of HMS *Essex* played us out with *It's a Long Way to Tipperary* and other war songs. The tugs and other ships in harbor bid us farewell with their whistles. *Essex* is leading the line and, as *Megantic* is the fastest of the three transports, we bring up the rear.

We had not been out of port an hour before I was seasick, accompanied by several others. For breakfast I had fish and I guess when it smelt the sea it was impatient to get back again, so I let it go and was very glad when it was over. I missed dinner and supper but the boys were good and brought me up several little snacks. The Brigade had boat drill again today.

Wednesday, February 24

I got up at 6 AM and went for a walk on deck before breakfast. I ventured down to the dining room, but I had to beat a hasty retreat after eating a little porridge and taking a cup of coffee. There was liver and bacon for breakfast, but I could not wait for that.

Essex is now out of sight but I don't doubt that she is knocking around somewhere ahead.

I could not go down to supper again tonight but I hope I shall soon be better.

Our escort has come back to us again and *Glory* is about 10 miles in our rear.

That afternoon Captain Walter MacLean, brigade medical officer ("Pills," to the men), administered the second typhoid shot to those who had missed it earlier. "My arm is very sore, so that between seasickness and a sore arm I am [not] feeling very good," Bob Hale lamented.

Recruiting for the 21st Battery continued even aboard *Megantic*, to make up for the pair who had deserted before arriving in Halifax. The last man taken on strength was one of the ship's passengers, English-born Charles Player, aged 31, a groom by trade, who enlisted as a gunner. He received his physical examination aboard *Megantic* by the medical officer (MO); the attestation paper records his place of enlistment as "High Seas." In the absence of a magistrate, the oath was administered by the ship's master, George Metcalfe.

Free time was spent in a variety of ways. In first class, officers entertained themselves as passengers would have done in peacetime. They played shuffleboard and quoits; where a table could be found, there were card games, chess, and checkers. Also, *Megantic* boasted a small library from which officers could borrow books. In second and third class, card games could be found at any time of the day or night; dominos and checkers were also popular. The third-class dining saloon had a piano, and it was not hard to find men in the group who could play well.

Hal began chronicling the 2,445-nautical-mile passage across the Atlantic. It was an easy crossing, a relatively rare occurrence on the North Atlantic in winter.

Now that I am really settled on board, I shall start a letter which I hope to keep up if anything of interest happens.

Our duty program has been rigidly adhered to. It consists of about 5 hours work a day for the men and 6 1/2 for us, besides the "Interior Economy" or office work. We have physical drill in the morning, signalling and foot drill in the afternoon, also lectures.

The passengers have given prizes and Wednesday, Thursday and Friday are to see all the events run off. There is great competition amongst the various units, and the ammunition column has entries for every event. I hope we will come out well. It is extraordinary what talent you come across in 150 men.

The sea trip has done most of them good, and they are all very contented. There are about 1500 troops on board — a wet canteen — and up to the present there has not been the slightest row of any kind.

We are hoping we are to be kept together as a Brigade, but at present we know nothing.

We receive wireless messages, but none are sent.

Essex keeps in the lead and *Missanabie*, *Vaderland* and *Megantic* follow. *Vaderland* is a tub and a great nuisance. Several times she has swung in ahead of us in a most alarming manner, and the language from our decks was illuminating.

I was Officer of the Guard last Tuesday. It was quite the most strenuous duty I have had. We started at 2 PM and had 24 hours straight without sleep. Each hour I had to report to the bridge that our guards were at their posts, and each hour a complete round of the ship, in and out, had to be made. It kept me busy and it does seem unnecessarily long when there are so many subalterns on board, but we all have our turn.

The watches are doubled for tonight and we are told the electric lights will be switched off. All the shutters are closed at 5 PM, and it is a serious offense to allow any light to show. There is lots of talk about submarines, but I have not lost any sleep on that account.

The colonel [Rathbun] has insisted on a great many boat drills, and it has been very interesting. The ship's crew are responsible for getting the boats out, and every man knows his place. I don't look forward to a rowing picnic. But my crew is very husky. All the lowering of boats is left to the crew; we just have to be there, ready to lend a hand.

Bob Hale described events from the perspective of an OR.

Thursday, February 25

We ran into a fog today early and we were very nearly in a collision with one of the other transports, but just managed to avoid it. Our whistle is blowing constantly. The ship is rolling heavily today and there are a lot of men sick on board. I am one of the sick ones. I shall be very glad when this voyage is finished because I must admit I am a very poor sailor.

All our portholes have to be covered at night in case we meet any hostile ships, but I don't think there is much danger just yet, but we might have to be still more careful about next Tuesday. Still I believe with luck we will get through.

Friday, February 26

Vaderland has been in trouble yesterday and today, and we have had to go much slower — worse luck. I am very glad I did not go on the *Vaderland*, for she pitches terrible.

There has been nothing out of the ordinary today, I am feeling a little better and eating a little more now.

Essex was signalling for about an hour. I tried to read the signal but when it was finished I could not make head or tail of it. It was probably a code message.

Saturday, February 27

It was very dull this morning and later turned to rain. We have made 1100 miles up to noon today.

Sunday, February 28

Sunday night, and I have just come down from the deck. It is very stormy now, much worse than this afternoon. There are a lot of the boys on deck and they are nearly all looking the same way, towards *Vaderland*. She is rolling very heavily and she steers very badly. I cannot understand how they dared to leave port under such conditions. The waves as you stood on deck were as high as the rails and you would think they were going to bury the ship.

We went to church this morning and the skipper took the service and it was very nice indeed. It brought back old memories.

We are getting toward the danger zone now. There is a big cargo of copper on board this boat and from the way some of the boys talk you would think they had cold feet, for some of them are continually talking submarines.

Monday, March 1

We had a very pleasant day today. It was a little foggy this morning but it cleared up later. About 9:30 AM we sighted a ship but she turned out to be going towards Canada and home. When we first saw her all hands were excited.

Our sports were a great success and we had lots of fun. The weather cleared up very fine and the sea got quiet; it is quite calm now. *Megantic* and *Missanabie* have now left *Essex* and *Vaderland* behind and we are going at full speed ahead, the first time since we started. *Vaderland* was dangerous at night. Last night we were all woke up by the ship's whistle and this morning we were told that *Vaderland* had come within twenty yards of hitting us. They are taking all precautions on board now in case of accidents. All the lifeboats have been uncovered and prepared to be instantly launched, and they have all been restocked with water and fresh biscuits.

Tuesday, March 2

We have had a nice day today but it was foggy this morning again. We finished our sports today, except the boxing and that will be finished tomorrow. We were just in the middle of a good match when the bugle went for boat drill and that finished it for today.

Hal Fetherstonhaugh related what happened after the bugle call. "Everybody had to rush down to get on lifebelts, then back up on deck again. It only took about ten minutes."

At last, orders came down to the brigade to get their kit ready. Bob Hale finished washing some clothes, while Gunner Herbert Edwards packed Hal Fetherstonhaugh's kit.

Wednesday, March 3

It was a grand day today, sun shone fine and warm. We were all busy getting ready to launch. This afternoon *Essex* ordered us to Queenstown [now Cobh] at full steam. The other ships got out of our way and we went ahead, followed by *Missanabie*. The warship is still standing by *Vaderland*. It is now night and

Boxing match aboard ship. *Author's photo.*

no moon and we are moving some. The ship is shaking all over from end to end from the strain of the engines.

I have just come down from deck and it is quite exciting the way we are going full speed and without a single light. I think there must be something wrong or we would not be going at this speed without an escort.

Thursday, March 4

We arrived here safe and *Missanabie* a little later. *Vaderland* and *Essex* arrived about four hours later OK. We were all ready to disembark when we received orders to stay on the ship. This is not our destination so I suppose we just ran in here for shelter. We are lined up here by the wharf — all three ships. *Essex* has gone into the naval yard.

Everybody in town is on the wharf and the boys are going crazy. Nobody is allowed on shore.

With the men confined to their ships, Hal wrote, "We do not know whether we go on or not. I don't think we were expected and we may go on to Liverpool." Posting his letter in Ireland, he started another: "We arrived at Queenstown and prepared to disembark, but no orders arrived. The authorities were delighted to see us, but had no idea we were coming. They gave the ship a great reception, showering oranges, cigarettes, etc. on the men. The vendors made a great day of it selling Irish handkerchiefs."

Finally new orders arrived: only officers were permitted ashore. Some ladies from town came down and invited some junior officers to afternoon tea. Hal and two other lieutenants from the 21st were taken to a fine home on the hill overlooking the harbour. It took the authorities a while to decide what to do with the Canadians. At noon the next day a cable from the Admiralty arrived. Two destroyers, HMS *Lion* and HMS *Loyal*, steamed into Queenstown at 5:30 p.m. and escorted *Megantic* out to sea at 7:00 that night, leaving *Missanabie* and *Vaderland* behind.

Bob Hale described the final 280-mile leg of their passage:

We went very slow until we got out of the harbor because it is all mined. We then dropped the pilot and steamed full speed. It was very exciting. It was just dark and suddenly searchlights flashed on us from out at sea somewhere. One of our guards answered and we were in darkness again.

We have not the slightest idea where we are bound, for it is now 9 AM, but we can see no land yet.

Three hours later *Megantic* arrived at Liverpool, at the mouth of the River Mersey, and tied up at the Landing Stage. Kits were packed and the men trooped unsteadily down the gangplank. The 6th Brigade formed up in the large square beside the Landing Stage; after roll call, they marched to the adjacent railway station for their special train.

As the men boarded, Bob Hale and several others were detailed to look after the officers' luggage. "We were nearly finished," he related, "when the train started. We just threw the rest of the stuff on and then had to run for it. If you had seen us going, you would have laughed."

All things considered, it was a fine passage. No deaths or accidents occurred on any of the three liners, and 4,000 more Canadians had been added to the British Army.

Before they could do their bit, additional training would be required. Too green to know just how unprepared they were for trench warfare, months would pass before any were ready for the front. But, when they'd learned their lessons in England, France, and Belgium, these men would form the backbone of the Canadian Corps.

8

Shorncliffe

As the train departed, the men cheered wildly. "At each station we went through they raised a tremendous row," wrote Hal. The train bearing the 6th Brigade did not stop in London, leaving the men with a vague impression of endless row houses, red-tile roofs, smoking chimneys, and bridges. "We passed through London and it gave me a funny sensation to see stations I had been at before. It was just a long shriek through the city, with the men spelling out "C-A-N-A-D-A."

As for accommodations in England, the Second Contingent was far luckier than the First. Recognizing the inadequacies of the sprawling camp on Salisbury Plain where the First Contingent had been dumped, the War Office allocated the permanent base at Shorncliffe to the arriving Canadians. It was situated on high ground overlooking the English Channel, two miles west of the port of Folkestone, whose pre-war population of 20,000 was swollen by war refugees. In 1915 it was one of the best military posts in Britain, with brick barracks, adequate stables for horses, along with hospitals, workshops, and other amenties.

The brigade arrived at its destination about 2:00 a.m. on Monday, March 8. Clambering down from the train at Shorncliffe Camp Station,* burdened with luggage, the *Daily Star* related, "They met a very hearty reception from the garrison staff. They marched in darkness to the camp. On arrival they were delighted to find a hot meal

---

*Since renamed Folkestone West.

provided, while fires were burning in the barrack rooms. Needless to say, this hospitable reception was much appreciated, as were also the comfortable camp beds."

The first day in camp was marked by a blustering snowstorm. Highly unusual for England, it made the Canadians "feel quite at home." Officers had their own mess and quarters in Moore Barracks. "All the officers," wrote Hal, "are in one large building with a fine, large dining room, billiard room, lounge and large bedrooms with a fireplace in each. From my window we can see the Channel and the destroyers are patrolling up and down. I hope we stay here; it seems almost too good to be true."

NCOs like Bert and Walter were housed and messed together, though in less style than the officers. ORs, four to a room, occupied "small brick houses which hold about twenty." The men liked what they found. "We are situated on top of a hill overlooking the sea and the country is very pretty," recorded Bob Hale. "Folkestone is a nice town but at night it is in total darkness. You cannot see a light so we don't go far in case we lose our way."

Most men found a few minutes to write to their families. Nova Scotian John Hamm, who would become a good friend of Bert's over the

Moore Barracks, Shorncliffe. ORs, four to a room, occupied these brick barracks, which each housed about twenty men. *Author's photo.*

next years, sent a postcard noting that "We arrived safe" and "We had a lovely trip across," promising a letter "after we get all settled down."

It was soon apparent a grave mistake had been made. When the War Office had asked Ottawa for the 6th CFA, it had really wanted the 6th Field Ambulance. Indeed, even as Hal disembarked at Liverpool, puzzled observers asked, "Where are your stretchers?" As Lieutenant-Colonel Rathbun and the 6th Brigade settled into daily life and the routine of training, they wondered about their future and their continued existence as a unit.

"We have six guns for training now, and horses are arriving," Hal informed his brother on March 23, and also told him he'd been named to command the ammunition column. "So far there are only sixty horses for the whole Brigade. Each Battery has a whack at them." And, as 18-pounders were needed in France, the 6th Brigade was training with old 12-pounders — just what they'd had in Montreal, with a slight difference. As Bob Hale related, "Our guns are painted all kinds of colors: green, yellow, brown, red, black, grey and everything else. They look very funny — just like a circus. That is to disguise them when they are in the open country. You cannot tell what they are from a distance."

For city men with little riding experience, working with horses took some getting used to. "We were at riding drill yesterday for two hours and I feel so sore now I can hardly sit down," Hale confessed. "Some of the boys are worse than me. You would laugh if you could see them."

The welfare of the Montreal units was a concern, and newspapers sought to reassure the folks at home their boys were well looked after. The *Daily Star* had its own correspondent at Shorncliffe, who filed a story headed 1ST DETACHMENT OF NEW ARRIVALS WELL CARED FOR. The *Gazette*, relying on the Canadian Associated Press, carried a column captioned CANADIANS ARE DELIGHTED WITH SHORNCLIFFE CAMP. Shortly after, the *Daily Star* ran another story: MEMBERS OF CANADIAN SECOND CONTINGENT HAVE ALL BARRACKS COMFORTS. The articles were devoured with great interest in Montreal. No letters from the brigade had yet arrived in Canada, so newspapers offered the only clues as to how the men of the Second Contingent were faring. The stories, filed by cable from England and subject to censorship, sought to reassure Canadians that their men were being well treated, in fact, far better than the First Contingent. "The first detachment of the Second Contingent is now established in barracks instead of huts and tents. The men have splendid quarters which are well heated. When the men first heard they were going into huts, they complained, thinking they would have the same type as those erected for the First Contingent. Instead they found brick buildings, admirably suited for barracks, paved streets and almost all the comforts of home. All are in good health and spirits...." the *Daily Star* told readers.

The *Gazette* painted Shorncliffe in resort-like terms: "An English fashionable watering place, the south coast camp has a magnificent situation overlooking the English Channel. Special instructions have been issued by the War Office that everything should be done to render the quarters as comfortable as possible for the new contingent. Expansive parade grounds afford ample scope for military work and means of recreation are not lacking." The papers knew what was expected of them and what their readers wanted to see. The new arrivals "... have already created a favorable impression by their smart appearance and keenness for work. Although they have been only two days in the camp, they are already seriously engaged in their military duties." And, "The men appreciate the excellence of their military environment and are naturally keen to prove themselves fit for the front."

The first inspection took place on Friday, March 12. Bob Hale reported to Alice that the garrison commander, Major-General P.S. Wilkinson, "was well pleased with the show. The Canadians are a much smarter-looking crowd than the regular troops round here, but that is because the best of the British troops have gone to the front, and they have had to take smaller men to make up the regiments." Hal similarly recounted, "It came out in orders that the General was much pleased with the steadiness shown in the ranks."

Despite the glowing comments in the Montreal papers, the newly arrived Canadians were initially regarded with near hostility by the people of Folkestone. Word of mouth had convinced the locals that most men from the Dominion, apparently, could not handle their alcohol. "I think the First Contingent got the Canadians a rather bad name," observed Bob Hale, on March 9. Writing to Alice about attending Evensong in Folkestone, he said, "I was the only Canadian and from the way folks looked, you would have thought I had committed a crime." Three months later, the Canadians hadn't made much headway in impressing the locals. Visting the 24th Battalion, Hale confided, "They are a disgrace to the uniform. They are always drunk in town here and in my opinion there is nothing that looks worse than to see a man in uniform drunk." Writing in mid-March, Hal noted sourly, "The Canadian reputation here is made. "Drunken Canadian" is the general description given to a man with CANADA on his shoulder straps, quite irrespective of his condition."

Some, though, found an immediate warm welcome in Folkestone. Albert Bates, a 29-year-old former plumber and now a bombardier in Hal's ammunition column, was born in Folkestone and his mother still resided in the east end of town. Albert's friends soon became frequent visitors at 4 Thanet Gardens. Local merchants, whatever their private feelings, also welcomed the well-paid Canadians. Former law student Corporal William O'Brien observed sourly, "The shopkeepers found the boys from Canada very fine pickings indeed and the highest prices were charged for everything."

Ross Barracks, Shorncliffe, into which Bert and other members of the Reserve Brigade moved after vacating Moore Barracks. *Author's photo.*

The Canadians discovered the town was populated by more than English citizens. "There are a great number of Belgian refugees here, mostly women and children, and you would feel so sorry for them if you could see them," Bob Hale wrote. "We see them often when we are out on a march. Every night we are visited by little boys who come and ask us for bread and meat, or anything we can spare. We are glad to get rid of it because we get more than we can manage. They sing songs and clean our boots sometimes, but that is an extra and we each give them a few coppers for their services."

Shortly after his arrival, Hale described conditions at Moore Barracks:

All the boys are writing letters and waiting for dinner. Cookhouse has just blown now. The food here is not as good as it was in Montreal. What I mean is, it is good but it is served up very rough and some of the boys are much surprised. They have got much to learn about the army yet.

The weather here is a little better today but it is very muddy. We had a good stroke of luck this morning. We managed to buy some milk so tonight at supper we are going to do things in great style.

Less than a week later, he could report: "We are getting fine food now, roast beef, potatoes, jam, marmalade, bread, butter, cheese, condensed milk, and kippers or haddock, soup and tea. This is served out to us every day and we get lots of it."

The daily routine, Bob Hale found, was scarcely different than in Montreal.

We get up at 6 AM. Physical drill from 6:30 to 7:30 AM. Breakfast at 7:30 AM. Drill parade at 9 AM to 11:30. Dinner at 12 noon. Drill parade at 2 PM to 4:30. Supper at 5 o'clock, then we are allowed out till 10 o'clock. Lights out at 10:15. Today is Saturday and we were dismissed at 10 o'clock.

On Sundays there was Church Parade at 8:45 a.m. Attendance was not compulsory and it was sparsely attended. As the 43rd Battery's diarist noted sarcastically, "A church parade entailed more shining of buttons and general polishing than any other parade; it was a succession of inspections and re-inspections, forming fours, and abrupt springings to attention. For, in order to appreciate the chaplain's message, the men must be drawn up just so, and every bit of their accoutrements agleam."

In addition to training, ORs were assigned various duties, or "fatigues." "I am Room Orderly today," Hale wrote on March 18. "That is, clean up quarters and scrub floors. Imagine me on my hands and knees." Later he recorded, "I was on cookhouse fatigue today. I learned quite a few points on washing dishes and greasy pots." Batteries were also assigned stable duties, feeding, watering, and grooming the horses, and mucking stables. On April 11, Hale noted, "It is a grand day today — Sunday — but our battery is Duty Battery for the week, so we have to go to stables three times today. We have been twice so far and we have to go again at 3:45. After that we can go out, except the men who are told off for guard." Taking care of horses was not without danger, as he discovered. "One of the boys in our house got bitten. It was funny. The horse caught him by the shoulder and threw him out of the stall. The lad was hurt but he is getting better now."

The highlight of any soldier's day was the bugle announcing mail call, with the prospect of letters and packages from home. Photographs of wives and sweethearts were passed around, while hometown newspapers, gifts, and small treats were shared with comrades. "I just had some maple sugar that Archie Gordon had sent him this morning from Canada," Hale recorded after one such call. "It was fine, believe me." On another occasion, he related, "Archie Gordon had a gramophone sent him today. We have got Columbia Records and one of the songs is *Just a Little Love, Just a Little Kiss*."

Recognizing that packages from home were a valuable morale booster, the British government decreed the previous November that goods sent as presents to individual soldiers or to bodies of men in the CEF would be admitted to the United Kingdom duty-free. For the next five years Canadians would send a cornucopia of supplies to their men in the field to remind them of home. By November 1916, 20,000 parcels a week passed through the post office in Montreal, destined for the troops overseas — a number that increased further with the Christmas rush. Postal rates were reasonable: packages to soldiers in England cost 12 cents per pound, with a weight limit of 11 pounds. Packages to soldiers in France had two tariffs. Up to three pounds, the cost was a flat 24 cents; from three to seven pounds, the cost was 32 cents. With such rates, Canadians could afford to send plenty to Europe — and they did.

Canadian and American newspapers were prized items, for they gave a better impression of the war than their British counterparts. "We have seen a few casualties in the papers and have heard many rumors, but the truth is harder to get here than at home," Hal wrote. Home news was always welcome, as Bob Hale noted. "We have a lot of Montreal [Daily] Stars here one of the boys had sent over, so the rest of the bunch are all reading us the news." Once at the front, though, the papers from home seemed somehow ludicrous. "Whenever I see a Montreal or Canadian paper," Hal later commented, "I am always struck by the fearful amount of exaggeration that goes on. They speak of things happening to us which are absolutely without foundation. It annoys me intensely, for I know it must make people anxious."

Pay Parade was held once a week, usually on Monday so the men could not go on a weekend binge. "We drew £2 18s 9d and they owe us to today for 18 days. We will have lots of money. I am going to put some in the bank," exulted Bob Hale. A week later he wrote, "The boys have just been paid so they are all feeling in good spirits."

Some officers purchased motor vehicles so they could tour the countryside. Hal Fetherstonhaugh, along with two fellow lieutenants, purchased Royal Enfield motorcycles. When a unit was suddenly posted to France, often with little warning, men scrambled to dispose of their vehicles. "There will be a bargain sale of motors round our lines when we move off — no less than 13 cars and three motorcycles," wrote Royal Ewing of Montreal's 42nd Battalion.

Biplanes of the Royal Flying Corps made an impression on most men. Observed Bob Hale, "We see aeroplanes over here every day and they are quite a sight." Hal was similarly struck. "Nearly all the time there was a humming in the air and, at one time, three aeroplanes were over our heads. There is a station near here which I hope to visit soon."

On March 15, the artillery officers moved to separate quarters in the nearby village of Sandgate, though the men stayed on at Shorncliffe. At month's end the officers moved again and were billeted in private homes in Folkestone, taking their meals in shifts at Chichester Memorial Hall. For junior officers like Hal, the daily activities by late March consisted of the following:

6:15–7:15 a.m.	Route march
8:30 a.m.	Fall-in. Parade for drill
12:00 noon	Dismiss; orderly office and inspection of quarters
2:00 p.m.	Fall-in
5:00 p.m.	Dismiss
6:00–7:00 p.m.	Lectures
7:15 p.m.	Dinner

One of the busiest men at Shorncliffe was Major Arthur Jarvis, Jr., 52, assistant provost marshal (APM) of the 2nd Canadian Division. At the time of his enlistment in 1914, Jarvis was a rancher in Alberta; previously he served 31 years with the Royal Northwest Mounted Police. He was a level-headed, no-nonsense officer, responsible for a variety of matters, from arresting drunks, providing security, watching for suspected German spies, investigating civilian complaints, and apprehending men who had deserted or overstayed their leave. Early in April the APM laid out routes for patrols ("picquets"), and established guardrooms at the various sub-camps where Canadian units were based. As more Canadian soldiers poured into the Folkestone area, Jarvis and his MPs were kept busy.

That spring, southeastern England enjoyed a stretch of fine weather. "The roads have all dried up," Hal reported. Extended route marches began, intended to keep the men in condition and build endurance. Bob Hale described one march in early April. "Yesterday afternoon and this afternoon we had long marches. I feel very tired but very well." Conversation was one way to make marches seem less tiring.

"All the boys were just talking of the reception we will get when we come home again, but I am afraid there will be a great many of us who will not come back."

Some days seemed long indeed. On April 12, after a tiring march in the morning, Hale and his group "went over to the gun park and started trench digging. We had lots of fun, but it was hard. We got home from that and Archie Gordon, myself and six more were told off for Town Picquet from 6:30 till 10:00 PM. The duty of the Town Picquet is to arrest all drunks or any disorderlies. We did not have any trouble so we did not mind. If it had been payday I guess we would have had some work to do."

Evenings often ended on a pleasant note for tired soldiers. "We are just going to make some cocoa and toast, and then to bed."

The long Easter weekend of April 3–5 provided a welcome break for the weary Canadians. Though it rained steadily for three days, the men took it in stride. Those desiring diversion from Moore Barracks obtained a pass and wandered into Folkestone, or boarded a train to nearby Canterbury. Bob Hale and a buddy went to a show in town and, while waiting to be admitted, witnessed "a terrible fight between some Imperial troops. There were some women with them and they were all drunk. You never saw anything like it. It was awful."

Practice trenches, Shorncliffe, summer 1915. *Courtesy of Madeleine Claudi.*

For Sergeant Bert, still nursing a sore arm from the vaccination "Pills" MacLean had administered a few days before, the Easter week-end proved to be memorable. He'd received an invitation to dinner at the Folkestone home of a young woman named Hilda Austin. For the occasion Bert cleaned and pressed his uniform, polished his boots, and rolled his puttees with extra care.

Also present that Saturday evening at 15 Cheriton Place were two of Miss Austin's oldest friends, Emily and Rosalie James. The sisters, who lived with their parents in London's East End, had come down for the weekend, an early celebration of Emily's twenty-fourth birth-day. Glasgow-born Rosalie — who had turned 21 in January — was an accomplished pianist and, as was common at the time, the guests pre-vailed upon her to play for the small gathering. Bert was quickly taken with the petite, fair-haired Rosalie. Her nickname, he soon learned, was "Cud," shortened from "Cuddles," a pet name from childhood when she liked to snuggle in her mother's lap.

As the evening drew to a close, he asked whether he might see her again. Suitably impressed by the quiet, well-spoken sergeant six years her senior, Rosalie assented readily. The engineer-gunner seemed so unlike the Canadians she and Emily had been warned against.

9

"We Are a Depot Brigade"

By late March rumours concerning the fate of the 6th Brigade were rampant. Hal was one of the first to learn their destiny: "It is settled now that we shall not go out as a brigade," he lamented on March 23. "Drafts will be taken from us as they are needed."

On Easter Monday Rathbun convened a meeting with his officers to review the organization changes. Henceforth, he said, they would no longer be a brigade at all, but simply a depot,* from which officers and men would be drawn to replace losses in other active units. The four original batteries and the ammunition column were folded into three batteries. Hal's column ceased to exist. Rathbun, "much to his disgust, instead of leading his brigade into action, was placed in command of this pool."

Major William Scully was given command of No. 1 Battery, composed mostly of the former 21st Battery and the ammunition column. Among his officers were Lieutenants Hal Fetherstonhaugh, Walter Hyde, and Fred Baker; among the NCOs, Sergeant Bert and Corporal Walter Gordon. As well, the Headquarters Section was disbanded. The men, including signal specialist Bob Hale, were distributed among the three new batteries, with most going to Scully's 1st Battery. As signalling with flags had been rendered obsolete by field telephones, Hale was soon learning gun drill.

---

*Officially this was designated the Reserve Brigade CFA and later changed to the Canadian Reserve Artillery.

"This is now an instructional school," wrote Hal after the meeting, "and as the men are brought up to a certain standard of efficiency, they will be sent to France as required. We are to have 60 trained gunners and 60 trained drivers ready at any time for a draft." Understandably, officers and men who had trained together for five months were bitter. Their units were being disbanded and they would be separated from men whose friendship they had come to value. "I honestly felt quite badly over it," admitted Hal. "You see, I had been with [the Column] since its birth, so to speak, and I had a feeling that we were quite attached to one another." Of the men formerly under his command, he was generous in his praise. "They were all great enthusiasts and I am sorry they are not to be together any more." Gone was a sense of belonging. "The Column *liked* being the Column."

Determined their original unit should not be forgotten, officers and men of the former 23rd Battery posed for a series of photos in front

Gun drill, Shorncliffe, April 1915, with the camouflaged 12-pounders. In this classic firing position, the No. 1 (the sergeant), with his hand on the spade, instructs the rest of the gun crew. No. 2 is to the right of the breech; No. 3 is ready to fire the gun, while No. 4 has the dummy shell in the correct position, ready to place in the bore. No. 5 (not seen) is at the limber, to the left of the gun, setting the fuse and handing the next shell to No. 4. No. 6, standing in front of the limber, prepares the ammunition and hands it to No. 5. *Courtesy of Madeleine Claudi.*

Sergeant Bert, directing his 12-pounder crew. Shorncliffe, probably April 1915. Note the dummy shell on the ground; the limber appears almost empty. *Courtesy of Madeleine Claudi.*

of the barracks. These, along with a nominal roll, were included in a 30-page souvenir booklet, printed in London the following month.

By mid-April, NCOs and ORs of the reserve brigade were putting in a full day:

5:30 a.m.	Reveille
6:00 a.m.	Stables
7:30 a.m.	Breakfast
8:30 a.m.	Parade
9:00–12:00 noon	Rifle practice
12:30 p.m.	Dinner
1:45 p.m.	Parade
2:00–4:00 p.m.	Lectures
4:15 p.m.	Stables
5:30 p.m.	Retreat

Sergeant Arthur Montgomery of the 21st Battery, ready for kit inspection. Shorncliffe, Spring 1915. *Courtesy of Madeleine Claudi.*

Batteries of the Reserve Brigade rotated as "Duty Battery," and on April 16, it was the turn of Battery No. 1. Hal described what this entailed: "We furnish all the guards, picquets, etc. for the week. We also look after the stables, so the week has been a busy one, with early morning parades, which get me out of bed at 5 AM. No, I do not like it, and I won't pretend I do, but it just must be done."

Continuing losses in France and Belgium meant more men were urgently required; the Reserve Brigade was electrified when it was learned a hundred men from the former 22nd Battery, raised in Kingston, would go to the front in the second week of April. A touch of jealousy surged through the Montreal men, all anxious to see action. This emotion was misplaced: the Kingston men went to reinforce the Horse Artillery.

Leave for the Reserve Brigade was allocated in small doses. "The men are getting six days' leave, 5% per week," Hal wrote on March 23, "but

I'm afraid at that rate some will not get off. We are not allowed leave until the saluting improves. So far we have not heard whether the general in command of the division [Major-General Samuel Steele] thinks it better or not. Of course we do not believe we are the offenders."

London, the largest city in the world with 7.5 million people, was a magnet for the Second Contingent. The YMCA at Shorncliffe distributed free copies of *Seeing the Old Country Through the Red Triangle*, and frequent rail service meant the capital was just over two hours from Folkestone. To Bob Hale, it was a familiar city: he was a Londoner by birth and his parents were still there. Only a few Canadians, Hal among them, had seen it before. To most, including Bert and Walter, it was a place to be explored, steeped in history and tradition, and somehow larger than life. As the diarists of the 43rd Battery recorded, "Most of us found London a great revelation and will never forget it. It was the largest, the best, the wickedest, the most beautiful and the ugliest city that many of us had ever seen or ever will see."

Sergeant Bert, having just met Rosalie James, now had an additional reason for seeing the metropolis. A week after Easter he took the train to London and visited the two sisters at their home in East London. The comfortable, middle-class Victorian brick row house at 237 Browning Road was identical to those stretching up and down both sides of the street. One may conclude that the visit was a success: as he was leaving, Emily asked him to sign her autograph book. He was the first of many Canadians to do so over the next four years, made welcome by the sisters and their parents.

Canadian soldiers with a couple of days' leave took in the main sights ... Trafalgar Square, the Houses of Parliament, Westminster Abbey, St. Paul's, the Tower. With sufficient time and money they took in a theatre or music hall performance and enjoyed a meal in one of the city's landmarks. Above all, it was a place to meet old friends and catch up on news of other Canadian soldiers and transplanted Montrealers. It was also the place for officers to purchase "extras" for the front. "I got a certain amount of kit in London, a good map case, a kit bag, and a watch with illuminated numbers," wrote Hal Fetherstonhaugh. "I am getting a prismatic compass in a few days, also field glasses."

Noon stables. The horses were lined up for inspection before being groomed and watered. *Courtesy of Madeleine Claudi.*

With time, attitudes in Folkestone toward the Canadians changed. Attending a reception at a hotel in honour of Canadian officers on April 20, Hal commented, "Our name and reputation is not quite as bad as it used to be." A week later, after the Canadians had held the Ypres Salient against the first gas attack on the Western Front, attitudes improved even further. "The Canadians are now quite popular in Shorncliffe, and the people are awfully decent."

Success at Ypres — "Wipers" to the soldiers — came at a high price. "On Monday the officers' casualty list came out," Hal wrote, "and you may imagine there were a great many on it who will be a big loss to the force." In the lists were many familiar names. "Of course we must expect casualties, but it seems doubly sad when our own friends are taken."

On April 27, No. 1 Battery moved into Ross Barracks from Moore Barracks, so the latter could be used for a hospital* to accommodate the growing number of Canadians wounded in Flanders. Ross Barracks, traditionally used for artillery, was well located. "The stables

---

*This later became the No. 11 Canadian General Hospital and remained at Shorncliffe for the duration of the war.

Watering the horses, Shorncliffe. *Author's photo.*

are right behind, and it will make things quite a lot easier to manage."
ORs were four to a room, with a fireplace in each. "We have all got
our girls' pictures on the mantelpiece," Bob Hale told Alice. "Quite a
picture gallery. I often lie in bed and look at your picture."

Infantry units of the Second Contingent slowly made their way
to England. First was the 18th Battalion, arriving at Shorncliffe on
April 29 with 36 officers and 1,081 ORs. Next was the 21st Battalion,
with 42 officers and 1,059 ORs. "This district is very full of troops,
and a good many fields, formerly green, are now tramped hard and
brown, or dug up for practice entrenchments," wrote Hal on May
10. Soon it became even more crowded. The 24th Battalion, raised
from the Victoria Rifles in Montreal, arrived on May 21. "The McGill
Hospital and the 24th have both arrived," Biff Notman noted, "and
it is mighty good to see someone from home." By the end of May,
more than 10,000 Canadians crowded into a small corner of Kent.
A base like Shorncliffe could not hope to accommodate such a large
number, even for a short time, and satellite camps sprang up in the
surrounding area. "This whole district is Canadian now, and every
large field and hilltop seems to have its encampment," wrote Hal.
"Quite a lot of the Second Division are here already, and there are
dozens of friends arriving all the time." The newly arrived units were

put through training programs to supplement the instruction they'd received in Canada. Artillery batteries arriving from Canada carried out their training independent of the Reserve Brigade, adding further to the isolation felt by Rathbun's men.

As April turned to May, the weather warmed and the Canadians at Shorncliffe got sunburned from working ever-longer hours outdoors. "We have to keep on drilling until 5:30 PM now," Bob Hale recorded. "The instructors who are with us say we are further advanced than the First Contingent batteries were when they went to the front. They are just making us go the whole way now from 5:30 AM to 5:30 PM. I don't mind because we are training with an end in view and for a good purpose."

On May 1, a call went out for volunteers from the Reserve Brigade's 1st Battery. "Every man on parade volunteered," Hale wrote with evident pride. "They only wanted 50 men so they gave the NCO[s] the first chance. So we will have to wait a while longer. I guess it won't be long now; the sooner the better. Yes, dear, you can count on my killing a few for you and some for myself." Bert and Walter (now promoted to sergeant), not among the NCOs selected to go, would have to wait.

Reserve Brigade gunners at Shorncliffe reading Montreal's *Daily Star* of Sunday, May 9, 1915, whose headline describes the sinking of the *Lusitania*. *Courtesy of Madeleine Claudi.*

After the gas attack at Second Ypres and *Lusitania*'s sinking, the mood at Shorncliffe turned more bellicose. "What do you think of the war now?" demanded Bob Hale. "When I go to the front, I will not take any prisoners. I don't think any of the boys here will. All these stunts they are pulling off now. We will remember when we get there."

More artillery drafts for the front took place. While the men selected on May 12 were pleased, those left behind grew ever more restless and resentful. "I came over to fight, not for a holiday in England," Hale griped. Typically, men picked to go to the front were given a few days' notice, then confined to barracks until departure in case anyone should have a change of heart. No one knew where they were headed, and a week or so later the men at Shorncliffe would get a letter from "Somewhere in France."

Proficiency with a rifle was an essential skill for every soldier in the British Army — even artillerymen, who might one day be called upon to defend their guns from an advancing enemy or who could, in an emergency, be pressed into service as infantrymen. "Musketry" the British called it, a term harking back 200 years to the era of flint-locks and smoothbore muzzle-loaders, a far cry from the high-velocity

"The Sgt.-Major, QMS and four Nos. 1 of the old 21st Battery taken the morning Hack left for the Front. This is the only photo we have of the old crowd." Bert is in the front row at left. *Courtesy of Madeleine Claudi.*

bullets and clip-loaded rifles of the Great War. The Universal Musketry Course, in three parts, was welcomed by the gunners — a sign they might soon be leaving England and going up the line. Instruction was given at the Hythe School of Musketry, a short distance from Shorncliffe. To their delight, the Canadians were given British .303-inch No. 1 Mark III Lee-Enfields. Utterly reliable, and one of the finest military bolt-action rifles ever produced, the Lee-Enfield was far superior to the Canadian-made Ross Mark III rifle, then being used (and cursed) by the Canadians in Flanders. The bolt of the straight-pull Ross had a disconcerting tendency to jam when the breech was fouled with mud, or when the weapon was hot.

Biff Notman described his experience at Hythe in mid-May:

We spent the first three days of last week down at the ranges qualifying in musketry. Although I am no crack shot, I guess I am good enough for an artilleryman. We had to shoot five rounds at 100 yards, prone position, taking your own time; five rounds same way at 200; five at 200 snap-shooting, when the target stays up for four seconds; five rounds in 30 seconds, and

Hythe School of Musketry. *Author's photo.*

five more at 300 from the kneeling position — so you see we had plenty of variety.

Bob Hale did well on the range:

This rain makes it hard shooting but I did not do so bad. The first course at 100 yards, I got two bulls and three inners. The second course at 200 yards I got three bulls and two inners. The third course was what they call "snapshooting." The range is 300 yards and the target is supposed to be a man's head, as it would appear at that range. The target comes up for four seconds, then disappears. You have to aim and fire in that time. I hit it twice in the center and three times just outside the circle. That is considered good shooting.

With the encouragement of senior officers, a program of sports began at Shorncliffe on the theory that men who played sports while off-duty were less likely to create problems in surrounding towns. Baseball was a favourite; most men of the Second Contingent grew

Bert Sargent (left), player-manager of the Reserve Brigade's baseball team. Shorncliffe, spring 1915. *Courtesy of Madeleine Claudi.*

up with the game and its nuances. Teams were formed and competition was fierce. Gloves, catchers' masks, bats, and balls were provided free by the Canadian YMCA, reprising its role in the Boer War. Locals gaped at the games in amusement. Bert Sargent served as player/manager for the reserve artillery team, filling in where needed at second base, shortstop, and even pitcher. Writing on May 24, a half-holiday to mark Empire Day, Biff commented, "Regarding that game of baseball when we played the 21st Battalion, we were very badly beaten, but it was a lot of fun. They took moving pictures of the game, which were shown in London, and I suppose they will have them in Canada later. They took one of me at bat, and I was lucky enough to get a two-bagger." Empire Day also featured a match between the artillery and the McGill Hospital, and Hal and another Canadian officer escorted two Englishwomen to the game. "They have never seen baseball before, so I shall have to brush up on my knowledge of the subject," Hal confessed.

With many Canadians being drunk in Folkestone and creating a disturbance, the authorities adopted stern measures in early June. The artillery, the only group with access to significant numbers of horses, was handed a special responsibility. "Our three batteries are each confined to barracks one night in three," Bob Hale stated. "In case of any more trouble they can send a full battery downtown to stop it."

In late May, Fortune smiled on Walter Hyde. Posted to the 10th Battery, the lieutenant was soon at the Front, among the first of the former 21st men to see action. By early June he was able to write "... I am in a forward observing station about 200 feet from Mr. Fritz's front line and you may be sure it is interesting and a trifle warm." He went on to describe his routine: "We put in 2 days FOO,* 2 days at the Battery and two days with the Horse Lines in our back billets. It's all very interesting but, believe me, I'd willingly can the interest in exchange for a bath, a decent night's sleep or a square meal." He had one other complaint: "The trouble now is not that there is little to write about, but that there is very little we *may* write about."

---

*Forward Observation Officer.

"The sort of drill and stuff we pored over at Kingston and Shorncliffe is useless here as everything is different, and we have to forget all we learned and do things chiefly by common sense." A day later, he added, "I wish I could send you photos of things here, but as only one camera per battery is allowed, and as I am not the possessor of it, I can't manage it."*

Hal was similarly fortunate a week later. Detailed with two other officers to take a draft of 332 men to France, it was an opportunity to gain some useful experience and "to pick up some tips." Though the assignment lasted only a few days, it offered the young subaltern a welcome change from Shorncliffe. On his return, he secured permission to keep the horses in their stables on June 7. "We had them all disinfected, blankets, harness, stables, and everything. They are so much in use that the drivers don't get enough time to get them in good condition, but a day like today gives them all a new start."

As the summer progressed, frustration in the Reserve Brigade mounted. "I wish we were going over to France," lamented Bob Hale. "We are tired of being here now." The uncertainty of their future began to weigh on the men. "There is a rumor that the whole bunch of us here are going shortly. We have heard so many rumors we don't know when to believe them or not. I hope it is true anyway." Just one in a draft of thirty men, Biff Notman left for France in mid-June, joining the 2nd Artillery Brigade.

On inspections, the men of No. 1 Battery did well. "I must tell you how successful we were in getting our harness into shape, harness which had not been cleaned since Salisbury," Hal recounted with pride. "Our Battery was complimented on Saturday morning on its condition."

Casualties from France continued to arrive at the Moore Barracks hospital. Even without a big push at the front, the daily wastage of troops was staggering. "We have a lot of men with us now who have been to the front and come back wounded," wrote Bob Hale. "Some of the tales they tell are funny and some are terrible." As casualties

---

*That would soon change; all private cameras were forbidden at the front, though a few dedicated shutterbugs continued to take pictures.

mounted, the gunners counted themselves lucky. Telling Alice she worried too much about him, Hale tried to reassure her, though his words probably had the opposite effect. "You know the artillery don't have half the danger that the infantry have sometimes, although when we do get it, it generally comes all at once."

Dominion Day, July 1, found the members of Rathbun's command engaged in drill, making up for two previous days of rain. Infantry of

Field exercises, Shorncliffe, summer 1915. At the head of the Reserve Brigade is Bert Sargent, closest to the camera; beside him is the OC, Lieutenant-Colonel Rathbun. *Courtesy of Madeleine Claudi.*

Field exercises with the 12-pounders, Shorncliffe, summer 1915. *Courtesy of Madeleine Claudi.*

the Second Canadian Division, by contrast, were granted a half-holiday for the purpose of sports, in recognition of their good work over the previous month. In the evening, to celebrate the nation's forty-eighth birthday, Canadian regimental bands played in a Folkestone park. Bob Hale and others with free time made plans to attend.

Longing for a touch of domesticity and seeing no end to their stay in England, some 1st Battery gunners adopted a pet. "We have the cutest little cat here in our room," Hale told Alice. "It is sitting on my knee as I am writing this letter. We feed it milk and other things. It is just full of fun."

With little advance notice, Hal was posted to Belgium, to the 1st Battery of the 1st Artillery Brigade. Soon he was writing to a rapt audience about conditions at the front:

I am on duty till 5 PM tomorrow evening, my job being to stay where the opposing trenches can be seen, and watch developments, and if artillery assistance is needed, to check our fire and make corrections. There are three of us here, two telephonists and myself. The dugout is in preparation and will be very comfortable when completed. We cannot do any cooking here, so a loaf of bread, some cheese, butter, fresh water and marmalade will do me till I get back to my billet.

A day later another letter provided more details:

Nothing very much happened yesterday, but for a new arrival there is always lots that is interesting to see, such as aeroplanes being shelled, captive balloons, batteries firing and all that sort of thing. Then the things coming the other way have to be watched. I am beginning to learn what the various sounds mean. It is a very important study. They send over some very noisy ones that can be heard a long way off.

At night, things were very different. "Every few moments the Germans send up star shells, and let go if they see anything, or think they do. Between flares sometimes it is absolutely quiet. At other times there is the rattle of musketry, the pumping of the machine guns, and sometimes the artillery joins in." The work was certainly interesting:

> Up at the forward observing station, we keep a watchful eye on the front. We are in constant touch with the battery, and report any noticeable feature of the day's operations and any new work [the Germans] are doing. We get the guns registered on any points we consider it advantageous to be able to turn on, at a moment's notice. All calculations of angles are kept, also barometer readings, temperatures, and the direction of the wind. It may sound complicated but it is not, though experience is a great factor in turning out a good gunner. The maps

Pen-and-ink sketch by Lieutenant Hal Fetherstonhaugh of his billet at Ploegsteert, autumn 1915. *Courtesy of John Fetherstonhaugh.*

are excellent and, being so long in one position, we get a good chance to get used to the country opposite.

Hal left his Kodak in England. Determined to record life behind the lines, the young architect took out his sketchpad and got to work. By mid-September he had completed six five-by-eight-inch pen-and-ink drawings of scenes around his position in Belgium.

Pen-and-ink sketch by Lieutenant Hal Fetherstonhaugh of the Sergeants' Mess, near Ploegsteert, September 1915. *Courtesy of John Fetherstonhaugh.*

10

"Dear Folks ..."

Bert Sargent's surviving correspondence begins with a lengthy letter from the third week of July. Throughout the spring and summer he had kept a detailed diary and sent letters home on a regular basis. In Montreal, these were typed at Darling Brothers, with multiple carbon copies, and distributed by Flora and George to members of the Sargent clan.

By this time Bert and Walter had become fast friends and, as sergeants, shared the same quarters in Ross Barracks. Bert's friendship with Rosalie had blossomed and the two were corresponding on a regular basis. Accompanied probably by Walter, Bert had at least one leave in London, where he stayed at the Cecil on the Embankment. With double rooms at $2.25 per day, and three decent meals for under $3.00, it made a nice change from Shorncliffe.

Though the first page of his letter, in which he described an outing on horseback, is missing, it was evident Bert was enjoying himself:

> Coming home we cut off over the hills to the coast and came through Dymchurch, New Romney and Hythe. It was really a beautiful trip and to my mind horseback is the ideal way to make a trip like this, as you are able to see everything.
>
> Thursday night, July 22: — A miserable cold, rainy night and only a candle to write by. Sounds cheerless, does it not, particularly as we have no coal to make a fire with. Will not be surprised if I beat it to bed very shortly as I am tired and anyway it's much more comfortable there.

Grover's cigarettes (200) arrived safely on July 10th. He could not have chosen a better brand. They smoke so well, in fact, that they are more than half gone already. Not, of course, that I wish to hint at a repeat order, but they *are* good. I have discovered a very practical use for the "quid" that George sent. We have had a great deal of rain so far this month, and I am beginning to feel the need of a raincoat so I am going to purchase one on Saturday at 22*s* 9*d*.

We had a couple of big inspections here last week. The first one on Friday by [Brigadier-] General [James C.] MacDougall in command of the Canadians here at Shorncliffe, and then one on Saturday [July 17] by the premier [Robert Borden] and Sam Hughes. There were between 20,000 and 25,000 troops on parade; made quite a showing.* I have it on good authority that both these inspections are only preliminary to an inspection by His Majesty, but we have heard nothing further.

I have some more snapshots to send to you and will hold this letter over until tomorrow to enclose them. They are not very good as the photographers hereabouts are so busy they try to rush the work through and consequently spoiled a great deal of it. I am hoping to go up to London again a week from Saturday. Walter will probably go with me this time and if our finances will permit, will stay four days.

The other day I was over at stables when one of the men came in to say a couple of officers were waiting for me in the

---

*Private Noel Chipman, a friend of Hal Fetherstonhaugh's, described the impressive event: "They finally came and the whole parade came to attention, while big massed bands, stationed at intervals along the line, played popular airs. After a long time they got through inspecting us and went to the saluting base. All the bands then massed together and, as their regiments passed, each took its turn in playing."

Afterward, GOC Second Division, Major-General Samuel Steele, issued a Divisional Order placing on record "his appreciation of the appearance and behaviour of the troops of the 2nd Canadian Division," and noted that "the review reflected very creditably on all concerned." APM Arthur Jarvis noted in his War Diary that "the troops presented a splendid appearance and carried out various movements with smartness and precision."

Hotel Cecil, a favourite haunt of Canadian soldiers on leave in London. *Author's photo.*

square. Imagine my surprise at walking over and meeting Capt. Ernest Hutchison and a friend, both with the Dental Corps.

You probably know by this time that the first McGill Company reinforcing the Princess Pats left last Friday for France and the second company arrived on St. Martin's Plain a week ago Saturday. I have not been over to see them as yet, but believe there are some old classmates of mine amongst them.

Good night all, with love and lots of it.

This looks more like an essay than a letter but it was the only paper I had handy; you see, I have run out of Hotel Cecil paper, so it is time I went after some more.

Tuesday night, July 27th

Another sample of how time flies, but this is going to be mailed tonight without fail.

A little scheme I have which requires Grover's or Ken's careful attention. It is a clever little scheme, too, only wish I had thought of it sooner, but here goes. I want that grey-checked suit of mine sent over to me, just the coat and one pair of pants, and two shirts. Do them up in a parcel and mail them to me c/o R.B. James, 237 Browning Road, Manor Park, E. London. I have a hunch I may want to use them and wish you would mail them just as soon as possible.

Everything has gone along very much as usual this week: have been in the saddle most of the time and enjoy every minute of it. We have had a rather novel experience the last two mornings in having to be out at the Hythe Rifle Ranges at 5 AM to act as instructors. Our men have the Range from 5 to 6:30 AM, so Walter and I have been turning out at 3:30 and ready to leave barracks at 4. Tomorrow morning is the last of it for a week at least. It means an eight-mile walk with an hour and a half on the range before breakfast. Not too bad at all but these beautiful days it is so fine early in the morning that we try to kid ourselves into thinking we enjoy it.

Had a splendid ride last Saturday afternoon with Major Scully and Capt. Cochrane. I go out with the Captain quite often but this is the first time the Major has joined us. They are both corkers and when on parade are *on parade*, but when off parade it is a different matter. The Major showed us one of the prettiest rides I have had yet, right through the fields and woods, through gates and over stiles. I don't suppose we were on the main road one-quarter of the time we were out. We had some splendid canters and a couple of good races.

As I have a beautiful little black horse now that can travel where he wants to, I was right up there all the time. The Major thinks this horse of mine the best-looking in the Brigade and he is not far off. He formerly belonged to the Adjutant [Capt. Arthur Irwin] but he threw him one day and so the Adj. discarded him. Two or three of the other officers tried him out and could not manage him.

He matches my gun team, which is made up of black and dark chestnuts; it is the best team in the Brigade, both as to looks and as to the way they work. However, that is probably the reason for my getting the black saddle horse. I expected he was going to give me a bad time but have had no trouble with him at all. I have made a great pet of him and he *does* like to be petted. When I first took him over he had a bad habit of side-passing and would not take the right rein at all, but I have him in fine shape now and can do nearly anything I like with him.

I took a picture of him the other day and will send it along as soon as possible. I have quite a few other snaps to enclose in this letter. Hope they are arriving safely as I only remember your having mentioned one batch, and I think I have sent three at least.

Another matter: this time for Lena's attention. About two weeks ago Walter and I ordered two pairs of Strathcona boots* from Mort Packard** in Montreal. They are very expensive here (about £4 10s) so we thought we could get them more reasonably there. I am going to have him send my bill to Lena for settlement. Kindly ask her to attend to this for me; and by the way, is my assigned pay coming through regularly? I ought to have sixty dollars there by the end of this month. If it isn't coming through, let me know at once and I will attend to it.

Those cigarettes Grover sent me were great, but did not last long. I opened the first box on the 10th and finished the last of the 200 on the 24th. I gave some away but no more than I usually do, less, if anything, as I liked them too well.

As summer progressed, frustration and discouragement plagued the Reserve Brigade. Those left behind when drafts were taken had no immediate prospects beyond stable duties, gun drill, route marches, and endless equipment and harness cleaning.

One of Bert's few pleasures in this period was the opportunity to ride at frequent intervals. That he, a sergeant, could ride with senior officers illustrates the informality and egalitarian spirit of the CEF.

---

*A high brown leather riding boot, first issued to Canadian officers and men of Lord Strathcona's Horse in the Boer War (1899–1902). English-made boots were available at Shorncliffe, but they weighed considerably more than their Canadian counterparts.

**Vice-president of L.H. Packard Co. Ltd. at 15 St. Antoine Street.

A rest stop during field exercise. Bert Sargent, right, drinks from his canteen. *Courtesy of Madeleine Claudi.*

Bert drinking from his canteen, field exercises, July 6, 1915. *Courtesy of Madeleine Claudi.*

Aug. 3/15

Very little of import has occurred in the last fortnight.

Forty-some new recruits from Vancouver have been added to our Brigade, bringing its strength up over the thousand mark, and we are more cramped for space than ever. Also, we have a

Bert Sargent, Shorncliffe, July 30, 1915, probably riding "Billy." *Courtesy of Laura Norris.*

great many more men to look after. I now have 49 men in my sub-section and it is being added to at the rate of about 4 a week, men returning from hospitals. Very nearly every morning I go through my room and find some new face I have never seen before. You can imagine how hard it is to keep track of them all and see none of them loaf. These boys that have been to the front take every opportunity, of course, to avoid work; [I] can hardly blame them, but still they have to do their work the same as the others and it is up to me to see that they do.

At times I get very much fed up on the work and if it wasn't for the horses and the riding, [I] would be very sore at being kept here so long, but I am more fond of horses now than I ever was and am perfectly happy as long as I am in the saddle, so I can stick it a while longer until something turns up.

Our weekends are as enjoyable as ever. We can always get a bunch together to go out through the country somewhere Sunday afternoon for tea and usually we manage to have a good time on these rambles. The last three of four Saturday afternoons I have been riding with the Captain [Hew Cochrane] and the Major [William Scully]. We always go across country through the fields and lanes where the footing is soft and we can let the horses out. It is simply beautiful country and I enjoy these trips more than anything else.

We had another big inspection today in preparation for the review tomorrow by [Andrew] Bonar Law.* It rained, as it always does on these occasions. The 1st Contingent men say they have not had a review yet but what it rained and neither have we. The inspection tomorrow is evidently to be on a fairly large scale. Of course, Sam Hughes is to be in it too and I believe Bonar Law is to speak in Folkestone at night. Tomorrow will be the anniversary of the declaration of war, so I presume that is the excuse for all the fuss. These affairs are very tiresome though and we will all be glad when it is over.

From what we hear, things have been very quiet at the front the last six weeks. Seems a great shame we weren't prepared to do something at this time for, from what we can see, this would have been the time to strike while the Germans were so busy on the Russian frontier. From letters we have had, the men have been just killing time and waiting for something to happen. I suppose, however, in another week or so, they will be having all they want of it.

How is my assigned pay coming, Lena? Does it come regularly and how much have you received so far? A good many of the men have had trouble with theirs, so let me know if it is not right.

It is just 9:30 now and "Last Post" is being sounded in all the camps. Some of them use six to eight trumpeters on it and it sounds great.

---

*Secretary of state for the colonies.

I met young Willie Birks* down in Folkestone the other night;
he has a commission in the 42nd Highlanders and was with
another friend of mine, [James] Art[hur] Mathewson (Arts '12,
Law '15 McGill). Birks has a Ford 5-passenger and they are having
a big time travelling round the country.

I have another bunch of snaps to send. I don't know what
you have been doing with the others I have sent; only hope you
are keeping them together for me.

Will close this now, as I want to write another before retiring
and 5:20 AM comes around very quickly.

In Montreal, knowing his brother-in-law was certainly worthy
of a commission and concerned the war might end before Bert was
promoted, George Darling began lobbying on Bert's behalf. George,
named president of Darling Brothers in March on his brother's death,
was well connected in Montreal business circles. One of the first men
he approached was Erastus Wilson, commandant of the Montreal
Military District. Outside of his militia job, Wilson served on the
boards of several Montreal firms and was the local representative
of a major insurance company. Besieged with many such requests,
Wilson did not commit himself on Bert's behalf. Another person
George approached was Brigadier William Dodds, then at Shorncliffe
commanding the 5th CFA Brigade. Prior to the war, Dodds was an
insurance executive and a keen supporter of local sports. Meanwhile,
at Shorncliffe, Major William Scully, who also believed in the bright
young engineer, encouraged Bert to try for a commission. At this time,
the CEF had more officers than the First and Second Divisions could
use. Only later, with four divisions in the field and after horrific casualties, would men like Bert and Walter receive commissions. Ironically,
had the two been five years younger and straight out of university,
they would probably have been offered commissions on enlisting. For
the moment, though, they would have to be patient. Had they transferred to the Royal Field Artillery (RFA), both men would have received
immediate commissions. So strong, however, was the Canadian esprit

---

*A scion of the noted Montreal jewellery firm and another Montreal High
School man.

de corps that they (and many others) preferred to remain as NCOs in the CFA, waiting their turn.

Bob Hale finally got lucky; in early August he was posted to the 2nd Brigade's 6th Battery. "There is one thing we have lots of here," he wrote. "That is mud. My word! I never saw so much mud before." He made light of conditions at the front, hoping Alice wouldn't worry. "The guns are going some tonight. The star shells make it look very pretty at night. From a distance it looks just like a big firework show. It is quite a sight to watch them."

Aug. 10/15

Dear Folks,

Nothing of any consequence has happened since I wrote last week. I had a nice letter from Charles [Sargent] and one from Flo of July 22nd. For some reason or other we didn't receive any Canada mail last weekend but no doubt it will be along today or tomorrow.

The Strathcona boots which Walter and I ordered have arrived and are most satisfactory. They are not nearly as heavy as the ankle boots we are being issued now and so soft and comfortable that they will be a treat. I have written to Mort to send the bill to Lena and trust she will attend to it promptly for me.

Flo's last letter was very interesting; was so pleased to hear of the work at the [Engineering] Shop and how well they are carrying on with it. I am so glad to see they [Darling Brothers] have gone in for munitions work so extensively, as it is just as important that all available men should work at this as it is for them to enlist. I would like to see Grover get into some work of this kind, as I don't see how he could get by in the kind of work we are doing on account of his eyes, unless he were to take up a commission, and even then he would have to wear glasses. This may sound strange from me, as my eyes are not what you would call good, but then I am used to wearing glasses and with them I am just as good as the next man. I grant that the men who are on the combatant end have the most interesting work to do, but then this other work is just as important.

Over here, thousands of girls are taking over work which was formerly carried out by men, such as ticket collectors at the railway stations, driving taxis and delivery vans, etc. and men are being recruited for the munitions work much as they are in the army; and any man who is not in khaki and cannot show a good reason for not being in it, is made to feel very uncomfortable and often is given a rough time of it.

We had to go through another big inspection the other day (Wed.), this time by Bonar Law and it rained, as usual. We formed up on the Plain about 15,000 strong. At about 2:30 PM it tried to rain intermittently until about 3:30 when it finally succeeded and came down in actual torrents. The men took it as a joke at first but after it had continued for about twenty minutes and everyone was well soaked-through and standing up to their ankles in water, they began to grouse a bit at the delay. Bonar Law appeared about 4:00 PM and the "march past" began about 4:15. The men marched splendidly in spite of their condition but Bonar's popularity was not increased perceptibly by the review.

We were lucky, as we only had about 10 minutes' walk back to [Ross] Barrack[s], but most of them had from 3–5 miles to make before reaching camp, and I can imagine how pleased the men must have been by the time they got there. These reviews are useless procedures at best and fail to accomplish any good that I can see.

By the time this reaches you, you will no doubt have sent on my grey suit I asked for. I am now going to ask you to mail me my raincoat. It is such a light one that it will roll up into a small parcel and come through OK. I figure I might just as well have the benefit of it here as not. I have intended buying a service raincoat but have not done so as yet; will probably do so when I am in London next time.

More cigarettes will certainly be appreciated. Those Melachrinos beat anything I have had in a long time. Fruit cake and candy come through the mail very well!

The Colonel [Rathbun] and the Adjutant [Captain Arthur Irwin] are over in France just now, to be gone two weeks. There

Sergeant Bert, summer of 1915, probably taken at Browning Road on a visit to Rosalie's home. *Courtesy of Madeleine Claudi.*

are rumors of a move of some sort but, if anything, it will simply be moving this Depot [Brigade] to France, which I doubt very much.

From Emily's autograph book, it is apparent that Bert did not visit 237 Browning Road alone. On most of his leaves, he was accompanied by at least one member of the Reserve Brigade. Thus, during the summer of 1915, Walter Gordon signed her book, as did Quartermaster Sergeant Frank ("Chubbie") Jennings. Over the next years, as Bert visited London on leave, his travelling companions would add their names, units, and dates to her book.

From London Bert wrote the following on Hotel Cecil letterhead.

18/8/15

Just nearing the end of a short holiday and a very pleasant one it has been.

There have been rumors lately of a move in the very near future to France. Of course, these rumors have been with us before so we don't attach much credit to them but in this case they look slightly more reliable. The Colonel and the Adjutant have been in France the past two weeks and rumor has it they are over there making arrangements to move our whole outfit over and establish the Depot there, where it will be more handy than it is at present. What strengthens this theory is the fact that the medical authorities require our barracks for their work, so we will probably have to move somewhere, and why not direct to France?

During the last two or three weeks we have been thoroughly inspected at different times by the Premier, Sam Hughes, Bonar Law and Maj.-Gen. Steele. Everything points to a move and here's hoping it comes off this time.

By the time this letter reaches you, George [Darling] no doubt will have told you of the chance there is of my getting a commission. I would never have thought of applying for it had not Major Scully suggested it and offered to push it through for me, and even then I doubt if I would have done anything about it if we were going over as a battery. However, the way things have gone lately, the Major is experiencing a little more difficulty than he had expected, I think, and if I do get it, it will be a long time coming. It was about two months ago when he first suggested this but I have not said anything about it before, as I know how indefinite these things are and also I knew the amount of influence required to put them through.

I think I told Ken [Darling] in a postcard last week of my meeting two old classmates of mine here in London last Friday night. It certainly is wonderful how I run across people I know over here, but then I suppose it is not so strange after all, as I am sure all my friends are over here somewhere and one does get accustomed to meeting them when you least expect it. The McGill men have certainly turned out splendidly. It does not matter what corps you meet, you are sure to find some McGill men in it.

Wonder if you have received that photo I had mailed to you some days ago and what do you think of it? It took about an hour to have that taken as my horse is very lively and would not stand still long enough.

He gave me quite a doing about two weeks ago when I took him out for about an hour to run over to St. Martin's Plain to see Ern Hutch[ison]. Was coming down a very narrow road with loose wire fences on either side when about halfway down we met one of these large military motor trucks. I expected trouble as he was feeling very frisky and had shied at everything we had passed and it is just as well I was prepared. He wheeled around just as the truck met us and jumped clean over the wire fence, and how it was he did not get tangled up in the loose wire and go down beats me. The only mark he got was a scratch on the haunch where the truck struck him when he wheeled and that only took the hair off and didn't even cut the skin, so I considered we were very lucky.

Will have to close now, as it is time I was away. Expect to spend the afternoon in a music hall, that is, until 4:30 when I have some friends to meet and will be with them until my train leaves for Shorncliffe at 9:15 tonight.

Had breakfast at 11:10 this morning, for the last time for some weeks probably; it will be great to get up at 5:30 again tomorrow! Have forgotten the sound of a trumpet now but I imagine I will recognize that old "reveille" in the morning just the same.

Haven't had any mail for about two weeks but imagine it is waiting for me at camp.

George V, accompanied by Lord Kitchener and other dignitaries, arrived at Shorncliffe on Thursday, September 2. A royal inspection was usually a sign that a unit would shortly be leaving England and, for the Second Division, this proved to be true. For once the weather co-operated and the sun shone during the King's inspection, heavy rains setting in only after the three-hour ceremonies at Beachborough Park concluded at 12:30 p.m. APM Jarvis noted, "the Division looked splendid and the King and Kitchener were obviously impressed." The visit was choreographed in detail; four pages of instructions were distributed to all unit commanders, indicating the proper protocol to be followed ("There will be no cheering") and indicating the space allocated to each unit on the parade ground.

Private Noel Chipman had a perfect vantage point. "All of a sudden a single bugle note was sounded. Immediately the whole body came to attention. Then two bugle notes were blown and the parade sloped arms. The King and Staff galloped up to the saluting base. Then Gen. [Richard] Turner rose on his stirrups and gave the 'Present Arms!' and the band played *God Save the King*. The *click, click, click* of 'Present arms!' sounded awfully well, and when they came back to the slope it looked like a forest of bayonets."

The King directed Major-General Turner, GOC 2nd Canadian Division,* to inform all commanding officers that he considered the Division one of the best he had inspected since the beginning of the war. Later, the following message from the King was received and published:

Officers, Non-Commissioned Officers and men of the 2nd Canadian Division: —

Six month ago I inspected the 1st Canadian Division before their departure for the Front. The heroism they have since shown upon the field of battle has won for them undying fame. You are now leaving to join them, and I am glad to have had an opportunity of seeing you today, for it has convinced me that the same spirit which animated them, inspires you also.

The past weeks at Shorncliffe have been for you a period of severe and rigorous training, and your appearance at this inspection testifies to the thoroughness and devotion to duty with which your work has been performed.

You are going to meet hardships and dangers, but the steadiness and discipline which have marked your bearing on parade today, will carry you through all difficulties.

---

*Turner had succeeded Samuel Steele as divisional commander on August 17, 1915.

History will never forget the loyalty and readiness with which you rallied to the aid of your Mother Country in the hour of danger. My thoughts will always be with you. May God bless and bring you victory.

Camps surrounding Shorncliffe began to empty. First to go, on September 5, was the Divisional Supply Column; in the next days, infantry and ancillary units departed, leaving behind the frustrated men of the seemingly forgotten Reserve Brigade CFA. Apart from one brigade, the Second Division's artillery did not accompany it to France, due to a shortage of guns. As Second Division battalions took their places in the line, they were mainly supported by guns of the Royal Field Artillery.

11

"Soldiering More Than We Have Done Since We Arrived in England"

As Shorncliffe emptied, two events of note touched Bert Sargent.

On September 10, William Scully was named to command the 2nd Canadian Divisional Heavy Battery. Though no one begrudged him the appointment, it was a heavy blow to the men who had been with him since the 21st Battery was recruited ten months earlier. They had come to know and respect him as a firm disciplinarian, whose primary concern was the men under his command.

Then, on the thirteenth, a new unit — the 8th (Howitzer) Brigade CFA — was formed at Shorncliffe by the transfer of officers and men from the Reserve CFA Brigade. Given the nature of trench warfare, the Canadians in the field had an urgent need for 4.5-inch quick-firing howitzers, whose plunging fire could destroy German trenches. The 8th was the first howitzer brigade in the CEF and came under the command of Lieutenant-Colonel William King, who had seen service in France as a major with the First Contingent and was wounded while in command of the 10th Battery CFA. A widower of 38, with 22 years in the militia, King was the right man for the job, and his period at the front left him with no illusions as to what his gunners would face "over there." The new brigade consisted of three four-gun batteries, the 29th, 30th, 31st (each commanded by a major, with one captain, and three lieutenants); a Headquarters Section;

and one brigade ammunition column (commanded by a major, with two lieutenants).

Bert's next letter was written on letterhead embossed with the crest of the Royal Field Artillery.

Tues. Sept. 14/15

Have had letters this week from Flo (2), Lena (2), Stella, Grover, Charles, Lotta and Ede, and they were all very nice too!

The cigarettes which Grover sent were as usual very much appreciated and are now a joy of the past. Mamie McRae also sent me 50 of the same blend last week and I am trying to make them last by careful handling until payday.

I am so glad you all like that photo I had taken. I have some more copies waiting for me at the photographers but I hope to be able to rescue them this payday.

That reminds me. In Lena's last she enclosed a small cheque for me to endorse and return. It was indeed kind and thoughtful of her to send it but surely she didn't expect to see it back again. It came in very handy downtown last night when I was caught with very little but bus fare home in my jeans. I managed to raise 4s 6d on it at my tobacconist and this saved a very painful situation.

If there is one thing army life teaches you, it is resourcefulness in raising money at a moment's notice. I have seen the time when the five of us here in this house have planned a little outing somewhere but, when we have come to reckon up, we have found our combined funds about equal to the bus fares; so we scatter among our friends, be they gunners, drivers, NCOs or officers, and if we are not able to raise a couple of pounds between us, the raising is considered very poor. We travel together most of the time and the one that has the most money usually foots the bills, then when payday comes around again, there are a few rapid transactions and we are all squared away for another fortnight.

Talking about losses, we did sustain a real one last night, one we have all felt very keenly. Major Scully has been given command of the heavy battery at Otterpool (about 7 miles from here). He took over his new duties last night, and leaves with his battery for France tonight.

It was all done so suddenly we are just now beginning to realize what it is going to mean to us. Up to Saturday, all arrangements had been made for the Major to take command of the ammunition column of the new Howitzer Brigade which was in the process of formation here. Everything looked very nice, as we had picked out all the best of the men who had come over with us from Montreal and although we weren't very keen on being in the Ammunition Column, still we were happy at the thought of going out as a unit and having the Major with us. Then came this sudden change of plan and everything is now chaos. Maj. [Ernest] McColl is taking command of the Column and we don't know where we will end up. However we have quit worrying now and don't care where they put us, so long as they get us out of here with a fair chance of getting across the water in a couple or three months.

It seems ridiculous that the Second Division men are going to the front before we do. It is not generally known, I suppose, but the Second Division began moving over to France last Friday and will probably all be over by the end of the week. If we are taken out of here by the end of the week, as we expect, it will require at least two months hard work to get the brigade in shape and fit for the front. That will mean about Xmas before we can expect another move.

I am really becoming ashamed to write to my friends and tell them I am still in England. We have had a couple [of] week[s] of beautiful weather but I am told to expect the unsettled winter weather to set in any time now.

Formal orders confirming the posting of Sergeants Walter Gordon and Bert Sargent to the new brigade's ammunition column appeared on October 1:

The following men, late of the Reserve Brigade CFA are taken on the strength of the 8th Howitzer Brigade, for pay, rations and discipline from this date....

Kit inspection at Shorncliffe of the men selected for the 8th (Howitzer) Brigade, September 18, 1915. *Courtesy of Jean MacLean and P.E.I. Public Archives and Records Office.*

Posted to the Headquarters Section were 25 men; to the 29th Battery, 129; 30th Battery, 135; the 31st Battery, 131; and the Ammunition Column, 113. More would be assigned in the coming days to bring the units up to strength.

The 8th Howitzer Brigade was formally a part of the 2nd Canadian Division, a positive development for the "orphaned" men of the Reserve Brigade. At last they belonged to a division that was actually *at* the front. And, though the brigade might not be going anytime soon, there was no doubt they *would* go.

Among the junior officers of the Howitzer Brigade was James ("Jim") McKeown, a fresh-faced lieutenant from Montreal, another of the old High School group. Just 22 and newly graduated from Artillery School in Kingston, McKeown had been in England only six weeks when he was posted to the 31st Battery. The paths of Bert and Jim McKeown would cross many times in the following half-century. Also posted to the brigade was Simon Alexander Campbell, a 25-year-old native of Prince Edward Island, a clerk who had enlisted in Calgary the previous November. A camera enthusiast, he had been photographing almost every aspect of his military service, a practice he continued as a howitzer gunner.

On September 17, the 8th Howitzer Brigade was ordered under canvas at Otterpool, a satellite camp located in the middle of a racecourse outside the hamlet of Westenhanger. Other 2nd Division artillery units were already at Otterpool. The 5th Brigade, 844 strong, had arrived a month earlier, only to find the camp's sanitation and water facilities inadequate, and spent the next two weeks getting the camp into shape. By the time Bert and the rest of the Howitzer Brigade arrived, Otterpool, though crowded, was up to Canadian standards.

An advance party from the 8th Brigade went out on the seventeenth and, just before noon two days later, 12 officers and 433 men fell in on the barrack square at Shorncliffe. Carrying 24-hour rations, and with good march discipline — "no stragglers," as the War Diary put it — the unit arrived at Otterpool where the men drew equipment and began pitching 12-foot-diameter bell tents, each capable of holding 10 men.

There was much they needed. Indents for horses were sent off at once and the unit requested a veterinary officer. Three 4.5-inch howitzers arrived early on the twentieth. Gun drill and lectures began the same day, part of what Jim McKeown called "the intensive training so necessary to turn a batch of men into a well-organized unit, each department equally efficient in the performance of its special duties." Few in the brigade had even seen 4.5-inch howitzers before, and they were examined with great interest. Along with the guns came the cloth-covered *Handbook of the 4.5-in. Q.F. Howitzer*. Officers, gunners, and artificers spent the next days poring over the manual, learning every detail of their formidable weapon. For the next three years, the well-thumbed *Handbook* and its periodic amendments were always close at hand.

Corporal William O'Brien, a member of the 31st Battery, described Otterpool as "an ideal camp in fine weather but a rotten dump in rainy weather — and we had lots of the latter." More men arrived almost every day for the new unit, including Medical Officer Captain William Kenney and veterinary sergeants. Equipment flooded in: dummy shells for practice, telephones and cable, water carts, transport and ammunition wagons, horse blankets, nose bags, mess carts, saddlery and harnesses, tarpaulins, shovels — in short, all the equipment needed by a field artillery brigade on active service. On the twenty-fifth, 340 more draft horses arrived; these were followed by 136 saddle horses the next day. Musketry, for those not yet qualified, took place at Hythe. As the weather cooled, groundsheets and woollen blankets, four per man, arrived at Otterpool.

Summing up this period, McKeown wrote: "Work was the order of the day. Horses, howitzers, signalling and other equipment soon arrived, and grooming, breaking-in of horses, driving drill, riding, gun-laying, signalling and other forms of training kept all ranks busy from dawn till dark."

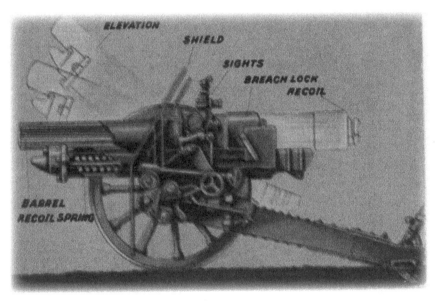

The 4.5-inch QF howitzer. *Author's photo.*

"Panorama of Otterpool Camp taken soon after we arrived there about the end of September. This green turf did not last long." *Courtesy of Madeleine Claudi.*

Bert's first letter from Otterpool was upbeat and enthusiastic.

Sept. 27/15

Here we are at last in a real live unit and soldiering more than we have done since we arrived in England.

We received word last Friday night to leave Ross Barracks at 8:30 AM Saturday and no one knew where we were going to. By the time kits were examined and everything squared away it was 11:00 o'clock and the new brigade moved off about 11:15, arriving here at 2:30 PM.

Some march! Saturday was particularly hot and our men do not do a great deal of marching anyway, so they weren't sorry when it was over, especially as they had no dinner. In fact they did not get any supper either, and very little breakfast the next day — but not a grumble out of any of them.

The camp we have taken over was vacated a couple of weeks ago by the [2nd] DAC and they certainly did not care how dirty they left it. The majority of the tents were old and poor, so we have spent most of our time this week cleaning up and putting the camp in shape. It has been a very interesting week as I have not had much experience under canvas and I have enjoyed it fully. We have been very fortunate in having wonderful weather, clear, cool days and bright moonlight nights, but tonight it has turned to rain and we are experiencing our first wet night under canvas. Walter and I have a tent to ourselves and we are gradually fitting it out as comfortably as possible.

The Reserve Park who were in camp just below us moved out to France last night, so today I took a wagon down there with a fatigue party and helped myself to several new tents, tables, chairs, etc. etc. The best table I secured came into our tent and I am writing on it now. It is a much better table than the colonel [Lieut.-Col. King] has and our OC sent a man down for it this afternoon, but he did not get it.

I am writing this by the flickering light of a candle with occasional outbursts of conversation between Walter and Don Peppler (a Toronto boy, Sergeant in the 29th Bty) so it is no wonder I make a few slips here and there and have trouble in keeping my mind on what I am writing.

Walter and I had another big disappointment last week but now that we are settled in this brigade, we don't think so much of it as we did at the time. Last Thursday night we received orders for a draft of 28 men from our battery for France, the first draft we have been asked for in three months. As Major Scully had just left a few days previous, [Lieutenant-] Col. Rathbun took it upon himself to pick out the men who should go. When the list came down, it included ten of my men, the best I had in my sub-section and almost all the old crowd I brought over from Montreal. Walter lost some of his good men too, but I was the greatest loser.

However, that wasn't our greatest disappointment. We were both absolutely fed up on this kind of soldiering around Ross Barracks and it didn't take us long to find our new major [Ernest McColl] and tell him our troubles. We just told him we had to get over to France and would gladly go as gunners if he would see the colonel and have our names on the list. He gave us some encouragement and beat it to the colonel, so we thought our chances were rather good. However, a couple of hours later he sent word that the old colonel would not change a single name on the list.

That was just a little too much for both of us. It was the second time we have volunteered to drop our stripes to go, but it was no use, we didn't care what happened that night. If it hadn't been for this brigade moving out so soon, I don't know what we would have done.

Sunday afternoon: — Had to put this aside the other night and this is the first opportunity I have had to continue. I said previously that we were soldiering now; I am more convinced every minute such is the case. Such a busy day we have had of it!

Saturdays and Sundays are just like any other days now and we certainly have to be on the job all the time. We were on duty from 5:30 AM Saturday to 1:30 AM Sunday, then up again at 5:30, and what with stables, Church Parade, exercise ride, etc., have been at it all day, and now I have just been detailed to take a party of 15 men to Westenhanger station at 11:30 tonight to get some saddle horses that are expected in about 1:00 AM. I can see that I will be in bed about 3:00 AM and, as I am Brigade Orderly Sergeant, tomorrow I will have to be up at 5:30 and will be on duty until 10:30 anyway.

Tuesday night I am in charge of the Town Picquet at Lympne (about 2 miles from here); the Picquet mounts at 4:00 PM and comes off duty at Lympne at 9:30 PM. So that means bed again at about 11:00 PM.

Wonder what they can find for me to do Wed. night!!

This brigade is certainly coming along in great shape. We have just been here a week Sat. and have the majority of our equipment already. Lieut.-Col. King DSO, our new OC, looks like a real man. He is a young man who has made a big name for himself at the front and he is certainly hustling things along in fine shape. He is such a treat compared to the old woman [*i.e.* Lieut.-Col. Rathbun] we had at Ross Barracks. Major McColl is in charge of the Ammunition Column. He is now at Larkhill with the majors of the three batteries taking a course in howitzer work.

The 4.5 QF [Quick Firing]* howitzers which we are using are beautiful guns, even better, I think, than the 18-pounders. They are certainly a more interesting gun, more accurate I believe, and one which requires more skill to handle.

We are in the Ammunition Column, a part of the unit I have never had any use for, but which on further acquaintance I find very interesting. We have managed to keep the remnants of the old 21st Battery together here and that is worth a big sacrifice. Both Walter and I had several offers to go with each one of the batteries in the Brigade but we chose to go with the Column so as to be with our old crowd and we are not a bit sorry now, as

---

*"Quick firing" meant that, thanks to its recoil system of hydraulic buffers and springs, the gun did not need to be "re-laid" (aimed) by the gunners after each shot. Maximum rate of fire was four rounds per minute.

we have a better bunch of men than any of the other units. The work is very interesting and, when we get to the front, is very exciting as, from what I hear, it is more dangerous than on the guns. Then if we get fed up on this work we will be able to go with one of the batteries practically whenever we want to.

It does seem so good, though, to be with a real live unit once more and I don't care how much work I get now, as with the prospect of going over soon I will do it willingly.

Happened to be in the office the other day and overheard the colonel dictating a letter in which he said: "The way things are going now we will without doubt be ready by the end of November and I am confident we will be across before Xmas." Sounds good, doesn't it? He looks like a man that means what he says, too!

We have our full complement of horses in now, 151, and they are a very likely looking lot. We paired them off today and separated them according to color: blacks and dark browns, greys, roans and light bays, and chestnuts.

There are only three sub-sections in the Column and we tossed for choice. I won, and took the black and dark browns. I have about 40 blacks and 10 dark browns; they do look fine too and when they are cleaned up will make a fine showing.

I have picked out a couple of saddle horses that show some promise; am anxious to give them a trial tomorrow, as it is hard to tell what a horse is like until you have ridden it. From the looks of them, though, I don't think either of them will come up to Billy, whom I was very sorry to have to leave behind me at Ross Barracks.

Monday night: — We are both very grateful to George for what he has done for us through Col. Wilson. Although we are quite content to carry on as we are now, still we have not given up the idea of getting commissions eventually.

Had a nice heavy box of fudge sent to me from Montreal and maybe the boys didn't enjoy it. There must have been about 3 lbs. of it but it didn't last long.

Wonder if anyone is sending me any underwear. I had five suits when I came over but am reduced to the suit I am wearing now. I find the riding plays h— with it.

Bert's blacks at Otterpool Camp, early October 1915. *Courtesy of Madeleine Claudi.*

Sergeant Bert on a Sunday morning, outside the bell tent he shared with Walter Gordon. Taken at Otterpool shortly after their arrival on September 19, 1915. *Courtesy of Madeleine Claudi.*

Sergeant Walter Gordon, who shared Bert's bell tent at Otterpool. Note the Strathcona boots, which both Walter and Bert ordered from Montreal. *Courtesy of Madeleine Claudi.*

It turns very cold at night here; now my hands are so cold I can hardly write, so [I] think the best thing to do is to roll up in my blankets and get warm. We have certainly been fortunate as far as the weather is concerned for, with the exception of the one rainy night mentioned previously, we have had beautiful weather.

This camp life agrees with me and I am taking on weight. Just tipped the beam at 175 lbs. the other day, the best I have ever done. Will climb in now and say good night to all.

12

Zeppelin Attack

By early October, the Howitzer Brigade's ammunition column and three batteries were nearly up to strength. Musketry instruction at Hythe ended, with all the new men qualifying. "Stores coming in freely," recorded Colonel King on October 4, among which were three No. 7 dial sights, directors* and stands. With their arrival, gun-laying classes could commence at last.

On October 11, the brigade held its first mounted parade. The sight of so many horses, guns, and wagons was certainly something to behold — and to hear. Observed the First Contingent's Private John Teahan:

> Nothing has so impressed me in this war as the sight of Artillery in full marching order on the move. There is jingle and rhythm to an artillery brigade that is lacking in any other fighting unit on the move. The guns, limbers and wagons make a dull rumbling sound and the harness chains on the lead horses jingle as they pass.
>
> They resemble a circus parade except that they move in a close formation so that when the leading horses halt, there is

---

*Like a theodolite, mounted on a tripod, used to measure angles from a gun position relative to two aiming posts. Gunners used this to aim their weapons for indirect fire (e.g. when their target was not visible and the fall of shot could be corrected by an observer).

a great pulling up of horses all along the line. The guns are not bunched but are followed by limbers or wagons loaded down with all sorts of truck.

On the night of October 13/14, London suffered its largest Zeppelin raid to date, with five of the giant airships striking the capital, killing 71 civilians. The same night, Otterpool Camp came under air attack, probably one of the London raiders attracted (as Jim McKeown put it) "by neat rows of well-lighted bell-tents." Powerless to resist, the Canadian gunners could merely watch in shock as the 600-foot-long Zeppelin dropped a stick of bombs and cruised off into the darkness at 60 knots, leaving behind the first casualties in the 2nd Divisional artillery. Next morning the men gaped at bomb craters 12 feet across and five feet deep.

Corporal William O'Brien, in Jim McKeown's battery, confided to his diary:

The most exciting feature of our stay at Otterpool was the visit of the Zeppelin to our quarters. I had just finished mailing a letter home from my tent when the order "Lights Out" came down the line. We had learned to do things on the jump and this prompt action probably saved our lives. As it was, the tent where I lived was punctured by some of the shrapnel. Six bombs were dropped in the heart of our camp and our unwelcome visitor faded away as fast as he came.

In his report the next day to headquarters at Westenhanger, Lieutenant-Colonel King described the attack:

Shortly after nine o'clock last night, it was reported to me that a Zeppelin was approaching. I ordered "Lights Out" and after seeing the Zeppelin for myself, as well as hearing it, I ordered Captain [George C.] Riley* to report to Westenhanger and any other places he could get in communication with, that a

---

*Riley, a Montrealer, had crossed in *Megantic* with the 21st Battery.

Zeppelin was approaching our lines from the southwest. As previously arranged, the brigade Trumpeter sounded "Lights Out."

Lights were quickly extinguished and probably a minute afterwards I heard the bombs dropping and ordered all ranks to lay down. Four bombs were dropped in quick succession, the nearest being just across the road from the 29th Battery.

Two men were killed and three wounded from the 29th Battery and one man of the Sub-Staff Brigade Headquarters was wounded by flying fragments.

Accompanying King's report was a fragment from one of the bombs.

Nearby, the 5th Brigade had 13 killed and six wounded, along with 16 horses killed and three wounded.

The night after the raid, "Lights Out" was ordered at 7:00 p.m. With October's early darkness this soon proved impractical and the men were permitted to use candles in their tents until 9:00 p.m., though as Bert noted, "a candle is not much good for reading or writing." On the assumption German spies were guiding the Zeppelins to targets in England, picquets from Otterpool, consisting of one officer, one NCO, and nine men, were ordered to watch for motor cars on the coast road and suspicious lights.

Some of the horses killed by bombs from the Zeppelin attack at Otterpool Camp on the night of October 13/14, 1915. *Courtesy of Jean MacLean and Donald Campbell.*

Training was suspended in late afternoon on the fifteenth for the funerals of the men killed in the air raid.

On Sunday, October 17, the weather was fine and warm; there was Church Parade for the Howitzer Brigade in the morning, and the men enjoyed a quiet afternoon. On Monday, as good weather continued, the brigade held its first mounted march, followed a day later by the first brigade route march. "Horses beginning to get into shape," Lieutenant-Colonel King recorded with satisfaction. In the evening, Bert began an extended letter.

Seems to me as though I am continually grousing about the lack of sufficient time in which to write letters. Well, I can't help repeating it again here, only now I have just cause and reason for it, where formerly it was possibly partly imagination.

Ever since we moved to this Camp we have been absolutely on one mad rush from 5:30 AM to 6:30 PM, Saturdays and Sundays included, with scarcely time to wash and eat between parades. That is no exaggeration whatever. In fact, there have been days when we have not had time to wash or shave even. Everything has been rush! And what work we have done since coming to this country has been but child's play to what we have been through the last four weeks.

The only consolation now is that we are beginning to obtain results, but even with that one feels very much like laying back and refusing to go any more until you can catch your breath for a fresh start. We have certainly been up against it for fair in this Column for, even when up to full strength, we haven't enough men to carry on the work as it should be carried on, but when you have men in hospital, on command, or absent without leave, you can imagine the amount of work it throws upon those who are left.

As an example, take my sub-section. To begin with, I had 32 men on my roll and 41 horses. Of these 32, five men were taken for signallers; three went on permanent duty on the sick-horse lines; one went on command to take a course in telegraphy, two were transferred to headquarters, three went to hospital the first week (two of them are still there) and after the first payday, seven of them went absent without leave, one of whom is still away; the others returned or were brought back five or seven days later.

Altogether that made 21 men away, leaving 11 men to carry on with. Out of these, I had to appoint a tent orderly, a mess orderly, and one sanitary fatigue every day, leaving me as a rule seven or eight men to look after 41 horses, and that means not only grooming but exercising, and, believe me, it is a different matter looking after and feeding horses on picket lines out in the open to what it is in a stable. And then, the first couple of weeks when the horses were strange to one another, they kicked one another so badly we had to peg every one of them down with heel ropes. It sure was some work and I won't forget it in a hurry.

Down in Ross Barracks we thought we were working when we turned out one six-horse team per sub-section every morning. Here we leave stables about seven o'clock in the morning and by 8:20 we have to get breakfast, clean up (which includes shaving) and have five six-horse teams hooked in to the wagons ready to move off by 8:30. And as soon as we receive the remainder of our harness, this will be increased to seven teams per sub-section. It is quite a sight to see one brigade move off every morning at 8:30 with anywhere from 48 to 56 teams in line. We made our first route march this AM and made a very creditable showing.

I was over at Lympne last night in charge of the Town Picquet, and as I did not have time to finish the letter, I dropped Flo a postcard just to let you know this letter was on the way. Was very glad to get Flo's letter today and to hear that all are well and the [artillery] shell business is going on apace. Also received a further consignment of 300 cigarettes from Grover. They arrived on the 9th but as I had the remains of a half-pound box which I had bought to finish up, they are lasting better than formerly.

Cigarettes are devilish expensive here now since a war tax of 50% has been put on them. My tobacconist here put me wise to it the night before the tax was put into effect, so I purchased a pound (about 425) but they have disappeared. Tell Grover the Melachrinos are certainly a beautiful cigarette and I like them better than anything I can get here, but they do seem expensive. If Benson & Hedges (plain), Murad or some other good Turkish cigarettes are less expensive, they would probably satisfy me just as well.

You really can't understand how good it is to get things like this from home. It doesn't matter what it is, a piece of chocolate or a 15¢ box of cigarettes — as long as they come from across the water they bring a little bit of home with them and consequently appear far bigger than they are.

Thursday, 21st

Another interruption; as I only have a few minutes in which to write now, I don't expect to get very far. I am on picquet at Lympne again tonight and as it has been raining most of the day and does not seem to have finished yet, I anticipate an uncomfortable night. However, as I have my big boots and a good cavalry raincoat, I will be as nearly dry as possible.

If Grover is considering going into the game, tell him by all means to pick out the branch he wants, then take a course somewhere and secure his commission. There is plenty of time for him to do it all and yet see some of the fun. Of course, if he wants to come over here he can secure a commission in the Imperial Army without any trouble.

By all means, Grover, keep out of the Infantry.

Panorama of Otterpool Camp. "Tent marked 'X' was occupied by Sergts Gordon & Bert. Our horse lines were originally between the two lines of tents but had to be moved to the end of the lines on account of the mud." The photo was taken about the first week of November 1915 before the Howitzer Brigade moved to huts at St. Martin's Plain. *Courtesy of Madeleine Claudi.*

The 8th Howitzer Brigade had a short life. On October 25 it was renumbered, becoming the 6th Howitzer Brigade CFA. The (new) 6th Brigade consisted of the same three batteries as its predecessor, though these were now renumbered respectively as the 21st, 22nd, and 23rd. The three batteries also received new commanders. Appointed to the 21st was Major Andrew McNaughton, well known to the Montrealers, who had just recovered from a shell wound at Ypres. The 22nd was given to Major John Mackay; the 23rd to Major Hamilton Geary. The Column, with Bert and Walter, remained under Ernest McColl.

Bert's letter resumed a few days later.

Tuesday, October 26

I went up to London again last week-end for a change; went up Sat. noon and back Sunday night, and believe me, that change came just in time as I was absolutely fed up on the work here and something would surely have happened if I hadn't been able to get away from it for a few days.

Had a real quiet and *delightful* time up town. Stayed with my friends the James' and it sure was a bit of "home" and how I did hate to leave it Sunday night. Say, can you imagine me climbing out of a real feather bed (with sheets, etc.) about 10:15 AM and, after a nice bath, getting into a comfortable grey-checked suit and sauntering down to a breakfast beside a blasting coal fire and a couple of nice young ladies to wait on me. It was about the biggest treat I have had since I have been over here.

That suit, though, was about the best ever! You honestly can't begin to imagine how good it felt to get into it again after being in the uniform for over eight months. If I never get a further opportunity to get into it, I will feel it was well worth the bother of having it sent over. I just lay around in it all day and, as it was cold and raining, we just stayed around the fire and enjoyed life. Came back on the 9:17 that night and made a record run by arriving in Westenhanger at 10:50 (60 miles or more), had a walk of two miles to camp and was in bed at 11:35.

Thursday

"Lights out" at nine o'clock interrupted this message Tuesday night.

We have had one of those real nasty English winter days: cold, rainy and wind all day, and it certainly has been far from comfortable under canvas. Gives one a slight idea of what those poor devils must have put up with on the [Salisbury] Plain last winter. I invested in a pair of rubber boots the other day and they sure have been useful.

The Zeppelins have been very active of late; this foggy weather we are having evidently just suits their method of operation. About two weeks ago they made a determined raid on London and, from what I have heard from some of my friends up there, it must have been a grand sight, though most terrifying. They did quite a bit of damage, though not sufficient to cause any great worry.

The same night they located two of the Canadian camps and caused *some* excitement as well as a few casualties. I am not at liberty to give any details but may get something through next time. These Zeppelins are truly most terrifying, as you feel so helpless and have no way of defending yourself. The bombs they drop are evidently of large size and very high explosive; they make a terrific row and shake everything for miles. When four of them are dropped in a row about 50 feet apart, and at about a 3-sec. interval, the din is terrible and the havoc wrought *considerable*. Pieces of these bombs have been picked up 500 yards from where it struck.

We have just finished night stables. The poor horses are out in the open and have been rained on steadily since midnight last night. We have just had one of the heaviest showers I have been in for a long while; simply came down in sheets for about 20 minutes. The old horses don't seem to mind it a great deal, but it can't be very pleasant.

Rumors have been rife of a move into huts somewhere in the neighborhood where shelter could be found for the horses, but we never know more than a day ahead what the authorities are pulling off.

Drilling and training is going on apace, and Colonel King still maintains we will be ready for the front by the end of next month. Things are going a bit smoother now that Major McColl has taken over and we are introducing a little system. Walter and I are still in the Amm. Column. Major [Andrew] McNaughton (McGill Science '10) who came over here with the 1st Contingent in command of the 5th Battery from Montreal and who is back from the front, is now in command of the 21st Battery.

Am still hoping a set or two of underwear will be forthcoming. Will write George at first opportunity of what we have done in connection with our commission[s]. It will be some time before anything is done.

Received Grover's cigarettes, also cigs and sox from Mamie McRae. Great!

As October came to an end, men and horses continued to suffer from the abysmal weather. To help the animals endure the cold and constant wet and muddy conditions, veterinary officers ordered that each animal was to receive an extra ration of three pounds of bran per day.

The following entry from the War Diary is wholly typical:

Oct. 28. High wind. Heavy rain all day. Lectures in place of [gun] drills owing to weather. Condition of horses not improving.

13

"I Have Seen No Better Brigade This Year"

The weather did not improve with the change of month. An all-day route march planned for November 2 was cancelled due to very heavy rain and high winds. The following day was cold and dry, enabling the route march and various manoeuvres to take place. That evening, instead of the usual lecture, Lieutenant-Colonel King convened his NCOs and officers and critiqued the day's activities.

Some good news came through on November 4: Lieutenant-Colonel King learned that huts at St. Martin's Plain, a satellite camp just a 15-minute walk from Ross Barracks, would be available for his brigade the following week. Just in time, too, for the temperature was dropping and, on the sixth, the walkways at Otterpool iced over. And, though the chilled men in bell tents at Otterpool were not complaining about their lot, huts would be a decided improvement over canvas.

If anything, the pace picked up in November. Apart from Sunday morning Church Parade, the training did not let up. Gun layers were qualifying rapidly, and King reported on the sixth, "Good progress being made by all ranks." Most days saw the ammunition column and batteries in the field on manoeuvres and exercises, with officers having further lectures in the evening while the men looked after their gear or, if possible, relaxed.

High winds and exceedingly heavy rain cancelled a planned all-day route march on the ninth, to be replaced by lectures on Gun Laying.

With over an inch of ice on the ponds, the brigade conducted another route march with manoeuvres on the fifteenth, with the evening devoted to reviewing the day's performance. "Distinct improvement shown by all ranks," was Lieutenant-Colonel King's terse assessment in the War Diary.

On the seventeenth, under clear and cold conditions, the brigade conducted a short and uneventful route march to St. Martin's Plain. Jim McKeown, with a fine sense of humour, recalled, "Great was the joy of all ranks when the Brigade marched, or rather slid, along ice-covered roads to St. Martin's Plain, where the men lived in huts and the horses had stables."

The men spent the next day drawing supplies and getting settled.

16/11/15

We are still in Otterpool and up to our knees in mud, but we have orders to move Wed. and Thursday, and will probably be settled by the time you receive this. We have been very busy ever since we have been here, on the go all the time. We have got things down to a system now though, and are getting results in spite of all the handicaps and inconveniences.

We are having the same experiences as they went through on [Salisbury] Plain last winter, as we have several men who came over with the first contingent and admit that this camp is every bit as bad as the Plains were last winter at their worst. The men are coming through wonderfully well and it's surprising what little "grousing" they do.

We have had practically steady rain and cold weather for three weeks and the camp is nothing but mud. There is not a place where you don't at least go up to your ankles in it, and most of the time you are halfway up to your knees. Of course, the horses are the chief sufferers but the men (except those few who have been able to buy rubber boots) go around with wet feet from morning to night, and every day the same. Even with the rubber boots, they get damp inside and you have no way of drying them. We have had a few days of sunshine scattered here and there but it never lasts long enough to dry things up very much.

In spite of it all, though, we are doing very good work and accomplish a great deal. We have had two very successful field days when the brigade has been out for the day on maneuvers and, as a unit, we have done very well at drill and had some splendid route marches through this part of the country.

We underwent a rather critical inspection last Thursday by [Brigadier-]General [James C.] MacDougall and the Column was rather highly complimented on its good work. In fact, as far as horse and harness were concerned, we were told we were in a class by ourselves. The boys have certainly worked hard and deserve it all. Can you imagine the job it is to keep harness clean with continual rain and mud?

It is rather nice to have [Captain] Ern Hutchison with us now; Rus has been with us for some time and now Ern is attached to us as Dental Officer. He was down to see me yesterday afternoon (Sat.) but I was busy and didn't see much of him.

Was more than glad to get that suit of underwear you sent, Grover. It is great stuff and just the right weight and size. It is larger than what I would wear ordinarily, but with all the riding I am doing, I find it lasts longer when large.

Have another great horse, a stocky little chestnut cob with silver mane and tail. He's, if anything, too full of life and I have a devil of a time holding him and making him go and do what I want. He is very excitable, too, and at first I got so disgusted with him I very nearly gave him up; but he is coming around fine now and I think with a little more training will make good.

Had an awful time getting him in the first place, as one of our officers, [Lieutenant Angus] Meikle (used to play hockey for Queen's) took a fancy for him and decided to take him over. However, Meikle isn't a very strong rider and "Billy II" used to take him wherever he wanted to go, and the second or third day he threw Meikle off, and Meikle has never ridden him since. He asked me to ride him for a few days until his leg (which he had hurt) was better, but would not give him up. Meikle was transferred to the 22nd Battery the other day and I have the horse. I took a snap of him the other day and if it turns out well, will send it along.

Tuesday night

Just a word as I have to mail this tonight. Cigarettes arrived and disappeared almost immediately. Come again.

Will write again at first opportunity. Moving to St. Martin's Plain tomorrow.

On the twentieth, six brand-new 4.5-inch howitzers arrived at St. Martin's Plain and were unloaded eagerly. Other tools of the gunner's craft followed: clinometers, sights, and fuse indicators. These latter, in brass, were similar to a large slide rule and showed a gunner the proper time setting to be applied to a shell fuse so that a shrapnel shell would burst in the air at the proper point for a given range.

Despite the change of locale, the men's activities varied little. Gunnery drill and tactics, route marches, battery tactics, exercise rides, inspections of men, kit and horses, Church Parades — all served to keep the unit hard at work from before the first traces of dawn to "Lights Out." Lieutenant-Colonel King, it seemed, was a firm believer in the old theory of "Train hard, fight easy; train easy, fight hard — and die."

26/11/15

Have just finished a parcel of news which came in by the noon mail. Letters from Madge and Mamie McRae, Auntie Stearns, and one from one of my former drivers, now in France. Am feeling so happy and amiable I simply have to write to someone.

Auntie's letter made me feel quite ashamed of myself, for she enclosed £2 which she said was waiting for me at the house when I left Montreal, and she had expected I would call to say good-bye. It was indeed a surprise to me and a very happy one, too, for at the moment I had exactly 5d in my pocket and pay-day five days off. Think it is much more welcome now than it would have been 10 months ago.

I had letters from Grover, Flo and Lena last week. The apples and underwear have not come to hand as yet. Hope to G— they turn up, though, as I have my mouth already set for the apples.

We are back in Shorncliffe and we are all sincerely happy again. The last three or four weeks at Otterpool were terrible and I don't think any of us will ever forget them. To get into huts where everything is dry and comfortable, and to be able to wear leather boots again and keep your feet dry is absolutely the height of contentment. The men are all happy again and the horses are showing improvement every day.

We expect another move very soon as the Brigade expects to go to Larkhill (on Salisbury Plain) on the 3rd of December for firing practice. However, I don't expect the Column will go along but will remain here and hold down the camp.

I haven't yet grasped the idea of being in the Artillery and not having charge of a gun. Even so, none of us yet regret having gone to the Column instead of a battery, as the experience gained here will be invaluable to us when we do go to a battery.

We moved in from Otterpool last Wednesday, the 17th. It was also Walter's birthday. I was left out there that night in charge of the base detail to strike the camp, so the little celebration we had planned had to be postponed. The celebration will be all the more joyful when it does come off.

Three or four days before leaving Camp, we woke up one morning to find the tent quite dark although it was fairly light outside. On opening the tent flaps a great bunch of snow fell in. It had been snowing all night and the ground was covered almost six inches deep. It sure did seem like home again. That night the moon was quite bright and Walter and I walked over to Lympne (about 2 miles). It was for all the world like walking around the mountain [Mount Royal] at home on a winter night; we *did* enjoy it!

Today has been cold and stormy with several heavy snow flurries but the sun has come out in between times, so it disappears as fast as it comes down. I have become quite accustomed to the climate here and don't mind the cold at all now, although it is bitter and damp at times. I have taken some snaps of the Otterpool Camp which I will enclose; some were taken when we first went out there and some just before we left, but the latter are on such a small scale it is hard to distinguish the mud.

Otterpool Camp, after the overnight snowfall of November 15/16, 1915.
Courtesy of Jean MacLean and Donald Campbell.

December slipped by, almost unnoticed by men whose transformation into a fighting unit was nearly complete. The weather was cheerless; in the first three weeks of the month, entries in the brigade's War

6TH CANADIAN HOW BDE
CAN. EX. FORCE

2ND DIVISIONAL ARTILLERY
1ST CANADIAN CORPS

Christmas card from the 6th Howitzer Brigade, December 1915. Each battery arranged for its own distinctive cards. The card was printed by Gale & Holden Ltd. of Aldershot. *Author's photo.*

Diary are depressing, to say the least. "Cold and cloudy" is repeated like a mantra day after day.

14/12/15

I intended to have this letter mailed tonight so it would catch the midnight mail for Canada, but unless I can find someone going downtown later on, I'm afraid it will have to wait for Thursday's mail, and that won't reach you until after Xmas.

To begin with, I want to acknowledge with thanks the receipt of several very nice parcels, the contents of some of which were appreciated by all in the hut. Ede's box with the fruit cake, fudge, nuts and raisins, etc. was simply great. If she could have seen the way the boys went for that fudge, she would indeed have been flattered. I consider myself a rather good judge of fudge and that was better than any I have tasted yet. The fruit cake was "top hole" but I have been more conservative with that and have dealt it out in smaller doses; the flavor of the frosting particularly appeals to them.

St. Martin's Plain, Christmas Day, 1915. This is the hut occupied by Bert's men. The soldier walking alongside the hut is Corporal Albert Bates, who would be the first man in Bert's section to die in Belgium. *Courtesy of Madeleine Claudi.*

The 500 Fatimas which Grover ordered from New York came through OK and are being consumed, along with 250 Melachrinos and 250 Virginias from the firm, who also sent a fine big box of Baker's Chocolates in cakes, which is great stuff to carry when we are out for the day.

Lena sent me a very nice diary and Pokette a two-lb. box of Huylers.

The two sets of underwear arrived just when they were required and are giving great satisfaction. They are just the right weight and size. Have three good suits now, which ought to last for some time.

Tuesday December 21/15

Well, a fat chance there is for this to reach you for Xmas. Lucky if it gets to you by New Year's.

Though Bert originally expected the brigade to proceed to Larkhill for shooting trials on December 3, the date was pushed back and it was not until December 23 that arrangements were finalized. Plans called for the brigade to entrain on the night of December 26/27 for the town of Amesbury and then march to Camp 22 at Larkhill. In the

Larkhill, on Salisbury Plain. *Author's photo.*

event, the entrainment went very smoothly, and all units were on board their respective trains, four in total, before the departure time. There were no incidents, and the brigade arrived at its destination in the afternoon of the twenty-seventh.

Larkhill, consisting of more than 800 buildings on a hilltop on Salisbury Plain, was a new creation, built in the autumn of 1914 by a small army of workmen on the site of a firing range established in 1899. According to Private John Teahan, "Larkhill now looks like a city: huts of wood, tin and canvas cover the Plains, laid out in 'streets,' numbered one way and lettered the other, with canteens, a moving picture show, laundry, etc. The railway, its siding filled with freight cars, gives the camp a real metropolitan appearance."

On the twenty-eighth, the brigade drew ammunition from ordnance stores and passed the rest of the day going through final gun drills for the trial shoot. In two days of tests (December 30 and 31) on the rolling West Down ranges — the first time most of the men had actually fired their guns with live ammunition and heard the distinctive bark of the 4.5-inch howitzer — the brigade vindicated their commander's faith in them. "All batteries did exceedingly well," Lieutenant-Colonel King recorded in the War Diary on the thirtieth. The next day, despite

Sergeant Bert, Larkhill, December 31, 1915. "There was some mud here."
Courtesy of Madeleine Claudi.

rain and poor weather for observation on the range, King wrote: "Very good shooting done by batteries. General Drake complimented [the] Brigade." And for good reason, as McKeown related: "On the last target engaged — a house — six direct hits were obtained in succession, all guns of the [23rd] Battery being given the necessary corrections, and firing, after one gun only had been ranged on the target."

Having last seen the 2nd Divisional Artillery at Otterpool in late September, Brigadier Bernard Drake was impressed with the progress made in three months. "All ranks know their work, the drill at the guns is good and quiet, and good effect was obtained," he wrote. "I consider them the best Divisional Artillery I have seen this year on Salisbury Plain." Of the 6th Howitzer Brigade, Drake observed, "This brigade is ably commanded by Lieut.-Col. King, and the training has been very thorough. It is well horsed, the turnout is good, and I have seen no better brigade this year. The three battery commanders know their work well."

In all, it was a fine way to end 1915.

Drake's comments were passed on to the men. As the Howitzer Brigade entrained for Shorncliffe at 9:25 on New Year's Eve, all could take pride in their achievements, feeling they were now closer than ever to getting to the Front.

Bert found a few minutes in which to write a postcard to George Darling.

> Larkhill
>
> Pulling out of here at midnight and will be back in Shorncliffe about 10:30 AM New Year's Day. Can't realize at all that this is New Year's Eve. Remember where we were this time last year?
>
> The Brigade did wonderfully well in its shooting and has been very highly praised by General Drake of the Imperial Army, who said we were the best Howitzer Brigade he has yet seen on Salisbury Plain, not excepting the Imperial Brigades.

On New Year's Day, fine and cold, the brigade detrained at Shorncliffe station without casualties to men or horses. Normal activity resumed at St. Martin's Plain the next day with an exercise ride and gun drills, to ensure the men did not lose their fine edge.

Tuesday, Jan. 4

A few more acknowledgments: letter from Flo, socks and cigarettes from the McRaes, a book and a box of chocolates from the Am[erican] Pres[byterian] Church.* Parcel from Alice and Edythe with handkerchiefs, writing tablet, etc. (the handkerchiefs were very welcome as well as the tablet).

Letter from Mildred with a cheque enclosed. A box of candies and fruit from Lotta from California and a fruit cake from Virginia. The box of apples arrived and are simply great, they are perfectly sound and a great treat.

Altogether we have had a splendid Xmas and if it hadn't been broken up by having to leave the next day for Salisbury Plain and not getting back until New Year's Day, it might have been a whole lot better.

We had quite an experience at Larkhill and altogether the Brigade did wonderful work and was highly complimented by the Generals who witnessed the firing. The weather while we were away was just as bad as we have had all along, but apart from that the work was very interesting. I was acting QMS for the trip and enjoyed the work very much as it gave me the chance to get around the country a bit and witness the firing as well. I was in the saddle practically all the time I was away.

Larkhill itself is a wonderful camp; it will accommodate about 68,000 troops; huts all laid out like a big city, with metal roads and electric lights. As soon as you get off the roads you are halfway up to your knees in mud, but that seems only natural to us now and we will miss the mud if we ever do get away from it.

The horses are having a hard time of it, due to their having wet feet all the time and I suppose 15% at least are down with cracked heels and unfit for service until they get better.

It is hard to say just when we will be moving across, but the condition of the horses will without a doubt keep us back. We

---

*Located in Montreal on Dorchester Street, at the corner of Drummond. It was to this church that the former 21st Battery had paraded on Sundays; George and Flora were probably members of the congregation.

are supposed to be under orders from the 11th of January, but I doubt if we will get away before the middle of February. There is a rumor around we may be sent to Egypt, but I hardly think it probable. However if at all possible, I will cable you the day we leave and if we are leaving for France, the cable will read "Arrived Safely" and if for Egypt or some other place, it will read "All well."

Of course a letter addressed to me with my number and unit on it will be forwarded to me wherever we go.

We are getting our final leave and Walter and I hope to get up to London together for four days at the end of this week. If we do get those four days, they will be *real ones*!

There are two or three things I would like to know, and hope those concerned will answer the questions. 1st Did Flo ever receive that colored photo of myself and my horse, which I had mailed registered some time ago?

2nd Does Lena receive my assigned pay regularly, and what is my balance in the bank at present?

3rd Did Mildred ever receive that hockey ring of mine?

4th Did my Xmas cable go through and when was it received?

Alice and Ede's cable reached me Xmas Day and, as you may imagine, I was *delighted*. I also received Charles' Xmas letter and will look up those boys he mentions as soon as I have the opportunity. A draft of 750 came into Ross Barracks the other day and they are probably part of it.

I sent you all cards from Larkhill; trust they arrived. I have a few more snaps to enclose and also a package of postcards which I want you to keep for me. They are of some of the places I have visited and I would like to keep them and think the safest way is to send them home.

The same day he mailed a second letter, this time to George Darling at the firm.

I have just finished a letter to the folks tonight which I think contains all the news of any consequence for the last fortnight. I am writing you however to thank you and the firm for the very acceptable Xmas box which was sent me. You really could not have sent anything I would have appreciated more.

Cigarettes are a luxury over here now, particularly a real good Turkish, as the prices have gone up so, and that cake chocolate is "jake" stuff to carry with you when going out anywhere for the day and a lunch has to be carried. The other boys are rather fond of it too, so it is not the only use it is put to. Please tell the other members of the firm how much I appreciated it and thank them for remembering me.

Walter Gordon and I expect to get up to London for a few days the end of this week and, as this is the last leave we will get before going across, I may need a little money. If I do, George, I am going to cable you for it and have you collect from Lena who has charge of my bank account.

I trust business is as good as ever and that your next order for shells* will be for 35-pounders as, when we get these howitzers of ours over there, we would like to throw a few homemade articles over into the German trenches. Believe me, if the boys keep up the wonderful shooting they did at Salisbury Plain last week, we will soon get back at them for the little visit they paid us at Otterpool some time ago, when we had no way of retaliating.

We can certainly handle these howitzers, even if we are the first and only Canadian Howitzer Brigade, and General Drake of the Imperial Army said on Salisbury Plain that if the New Army (Kitchener's Army) were half as good as the Brigade, he would be satisfied.

Enough for now. Good night, George. Remember me to all the boys in the office and shop.

On January 6, veterinary officers inspected every horse in the brigade to ensure they were fit for service at the Front. Four days later, another inspection took place, this time for mange, with a few cases being found among the horses of the 6th. As mange was highly

---

*In late 1915, Darling Bros. received its first munitions contract; the company expanded its machine shop facilities to handle the order.

contagious, those afflicted were immediately separated from the others for treatment.

On the twelfth, Brigadier-General Edward Morrison, commander of the Second Division artillery, inspected the brigade in marching order, the first time he'd inspected the unit. Morrison was relatively new to his command, having taken over on October 2 from Brigadier-General Herbert Thacker, who had gone to the 1st Division. The next days passed with drawing clothing from stores, exercise rides, gun drill, and kit and barrack inspections, with final preparations being made for overseas transportation. In response to a War Office directive, all horses were clipped before embarkation. The 5th and 7th Brigades of the 2nd Divisional Artillery, equipped with 18-pounders and having completed similar training programs over the past months, were likewise preparing to depart England.

For a number of officers and men of the Howitzer Brigade, this was a time of bitter disappointment. To get his brigade down to its war establishment strength, Lieutenant-Colonel King was obliged to return 76 men to the reserve brigade at Shorncliffe, where they would form a nucleus of gunners trained on the 4.5-inch howitzer. When the list was posted, Bert and Walter heaved a sigh of relief — their names were not among those to be returned.

At long last they were going to war.

14

To the Front

January 17 was wet and cloudy, but no one in the 6th Brigade's ammunition column minded.

In all, according to Lieutenant-Colonel King's Operation Order No. 1, the 6th Brigade required nine trains: two for the column, two each for the three batteries, and one for the Headquarters Section. It was all spelled out with great precision, so each unit knew where and when it was supposed to entrain.

Embarking strengths were as follows:

	Officers	ORs	Horses	Guns	Wagons
Brigade Headquarters	6	48	38	—	—
21st Bty	4	134	126	4	8 4-wheel 2 2-wheel
22nd Bty				as above	
23rd Bry				as above	
Amm. Col.	3	106	132	—	17 4-wheel 1 2-wheel
Totals	21	556	548	12	48 (all types)

At 8:00 a.m., after loading nine four-wheeled wagons, one-half of the ammunition column — consisting of two officers, 53 ORs, and

66 horses — boarded train No. X1088 at Shorncliffe station; it was the first howitzer unit to entrain for Southampton docks. An hour later the second half departed. The column's horses, wagons, and men arrived at the docks without mishap, no small feat. Though just under 100 miles, the journey took almost six hours. The men brought with them the "unconsumed portion of the day's ration and one day's extra rations, cooked." Horses, as always, were well looked after: nosebags were filled at Shorncliffe and one day's feed was carried. Immediately on arrival at the docks, they were detrained, fed, and watered.

Waiting for the 5th, 6th, and 7th artillery brigades were three transports, *Maidan*, *Anglo Canadian*, and *Novian*. It was to the first and largest of these vessels that Bert's ammunition column was directed. Launched in 1912, the 500-foot *Maidan* had spent two years in the India trade until requisitioned by the Admiralty for cross-Channel troop-carrying duties.*

Under cloudy skies the following day, while Bert, Walter, and the rest of the column settled aboard *Maidan*, the three batteries of the Howitzer Brigade boarded trains to join their comrades. "We were a day and a half aboard the boat," Bert recounted, "and that was the most comfortable part of the whole trip, as we were the first unit to go aboard and consequently were able to 'get next' to the head steward. Four of us arranged for a cabin and had our meals in the saloon with the officers. As some of the officers were not able to secure cabins, we considered ourselves rather fortunate."

Loading continued on the afternoon of the eighteenth, once the three batteries and Headquarters Section arrived. Corporal William O'Brien in the 23rd Battery wrote: "After disembarking we unloaded guns and wagons and same were derricked on to big transport." The dockworkers did their jobs well. "The arrangements were so perfect," Bert recorded, "that one marvelled at the speed and apparent lack of fuss with which the embarkation was completed."

On each vessel men were detailed to remain below decks with the horses; standing instructions required that, "In ships carrying horses,

---

Maidan and *Novian* had transported the 1st Canadian Division artillery from Avonmouth to St. Nazaire in February 1915.

as many men as can be spared will be sent to stand at the horses' heads to keep them quiet."

The late arrivals found little space aboard *Maidan*. "Our quarters," O'Brien wrote, "are not very favorable, though with a little maneuvering, I can find a place on deck to sleep. Nearly froze trying to get asleep and finished up down below."

True to his word and learning of their destination, Bert arranged to send a cable from Southampton: ARRIVED SAFELY. STOP.

The 100-mile crossing was an easy one, without incident and with no injuries to horses or men. In the early morning hours the three ships dropped anchor at Le Havre and waited for first light. "Arrived in [Le] Havre harbor about 5 AM, perfect weather prevailing," William O'Brien recorded. "After the usual delay, we threaded our way through a host of craft and docked about 9 AM. Off came the horses and guns to the square behind the docks and we lay about here until 4 PM."

Then, hooking in the guns and wagons, the brigade marched in column of route to Rest Camp No. 1, four miles away on the outskirts of the city. It was a large camp, with rows of tents, huts, and field kitchens to support a transient population. The men unhooked, checked

SS *Maidan*, which brought Bert and Walter, with the 6th Howitzer Brigade, to Le Havre, January 18–19, 1916. *Author's photo.*

equipment, and drew gas helmets and other equipment from stores. "We picketed our horses and slept 10 men to a small bell-tent. But it was our first decent sleep for three days and we *slept.*" O'Brien's diary continued: "The bugle didn't sound reveille this morning because they don't use them in France. We were called this morning and proceeded to give the ponies their usual massage. We took an exercise ride through the city about 9 o'clock and had dinner at 12:30."

Finally, the Howitzer Brigade received its orders: the three batteries and Headquarters Section were ordered to the rail station; the column would follow a day later. O'Brien's 23rd Battery "hooked in at 4 o'clock, grabbed some hard tack and a little tea, and down we went through the town again for the station, with the enthusiastic *mesdames* wishing us *bonne chance* from every door and window."

Having a quiet evening, Bert purchased a postcard of Le Havre, another of many such purchases over the next three years, and found a few minutes in which to bring the family up to date.

Le Havre, 20/1/16

Arrived here safely yesterday AM with beautiful weather and everyone is in great shape. Le Havre is a very pretty place and as we had to march through the principal part of the town to reach the camp we are now in, we were able to see most of the town, although it was after dark. Today the weather is still fine and tent life once more is very comfortable. We expect to start up the line tomorrow but, even if I did know where we were bound for, I couldn't tell you.

I hope you received my cable OK. I had to commission someone to send it for me as we left in somewhat of a hurry.

We have just received [an] order to pull out of here at 5:30 AM, which means reveille at 2:30, but as it promises to be a moonlit night, it will be a simple matter to get away without much trouble.

Walter has been sick ever since we came back from London and has had a miserable journey of it so far, but I hope he will be better in the morning, for he will probably have a hard trip ahead of him tomorrow, as we may be aboard a couple of days.

On the twenty-first (described as "fair and warm" in the War Diary), the column returned to Le Havre, where it boarded a special train for the front. Wagons were secured to flatcars and horses pushed into boxcars that would accommodate eight animals, plus two drivers, harness, and saddles. In terms of distance, the trip was rather short, but troop trains followed no set schedule and often took roundabout routes to conceal their ultimate destination. The train carrying the column wound its way through Rouen, Abbeville, and Cassel. The men, each having been given two days' rations, were packed into the diminitive French boxcars marked HOMMES: 40 CHEVAUX: 8, many of which "bore ample evidence of having lately been tenanted by horses," as William O'Brien deftly phrased it. The "side-door Pullmans" had no windows, but the sliding doors could be left ajar to admit air.

France, 25/1/16

The railway journey on this side was very tiresome. We had the whole Column on one train of about 40 cars. There were 21 vehicles, 152 horses, and 115 officers and men and, although the engines over here are very powerful, we made rather slow time.

Then our little Major [Ernest McColl] insisted on his No. 1 being out at every stop to see that the men were OK and to issue some fresh orders, etc. so we obtained very little sleep.

The peculiar part of the whole trip was that after travelling for five days, we passed a spot the sixth day only about 25 miles from our starting point. Some route to take to disguise our movements, eh?

We had an 18-hour railway journey from Le Havre [to Cassel] and then a 2 1/2-hour route march to where we are billeted on a large farm not far from the Belgian border. We arrived here Sat. AM [the 22nd] about 9:00 o'clock, having been on the move constantly from the Monday previous when we left St. Martin's [Plain]. Most of our moves were made either at night or in the early mornings, so we had very little rest during the week.

We are now within sound of the guns and close enough so that at night from my window I can see the flares and flashes of the star shells and guns on the firing line.

As part of General Hubert Plumer's Second Army, the Canadian Corps held a six-mile front between Ploegsteert and Kemmel, 12 miles south of Ypres and the British-held Salient. It was a position of some importance, for Ploegsteert, at the base of the southwestern flank of Messines Ridge, formed the southern hinge of the Salient.

The 6th Howitzer Brigade was assigned a section of trenches near the French town of Caestre, five miles from the Belgian border. It was a quiet, stable sector, an ideal place for the newly arrived gunners to learn the basics of trench warfare. Though the area was in France and had been since the time of Louis XIV, the everyday language of the inhabitants was Flemish, for this low-lying land had once been part of Flanders. APM Arthur Jarvis called Caestre "a small, rambling town of poorly built houses and the inevitable cobbled streets, which are positively dangerous for horses." He claimed, probably without exaggeration, "In Caestre there is on average an estaminet to every five houses. These estaminets are entirely under our control. The drink sold by them — light beer and claret — is quite innocuous and there is absolutely no drunkenness among the troops here." Military Police (MPs) patrolled the streets, ensuring estaminets closed at the appointed time and no hard spirits were sold. They were favourite gathering places for Canadian gunners in off-duty hours. "Who will ever forget," asked the 4th Brigade's historian, "these places of merriment of France and Flanders with their low ceiling and scrubbed, tiled floors? Some boasted pianos but all had tables supporting the game of 'Crown and Anchor.' These places were usually thick with the smoke of Three Witches, Trumpeters and Red Hussars, or issue tobacco. At the back, dark speckled mirrors hung above side-boards lined with bottles. Over all presided a plump matron, assisted by two fair 'mam'zelles' who hustled huge jugs of dark, flat beer about the joyous tables."

The Howitzer gunners were delighted to find beer cost one cent a glass, and wine 1.74 francs per bottle. Food prices varied. "At one place, our men get a heaping dish of fried potatoes for 1/2d, eggs for 1 1/2d and 1/2d for coffee," noted Hal Fetherstonhaugh. Hungry gunners were not too fastidious. The 23rd's William O'Brien related: "In the evening went with Chet Smith on a hunt for eggs and chips and fared fairly well at a Belgian farmhouse. The squalor of these homes doesn't encourage one's appetite, but doesn't entirely discourage same."

Water in this part of the front was a problem, as the APM discovered the previous autumn. "There are no streams or lakes within a reasonable area and the water in mud holes is of very doubtful origin and dangerous for the horses." Most farm wells were polluted and, as a result, Red Cross officers had been inoculating local farmers against typhoid and paratyphoid. All drinking water for British and Canadian soldiers was brought in from great distances and had to be purified with four grams of chloride of lime* per water cart. John Teahan noted the chemical imparted a "horrible medicinal taste," which did nothing to slake the thirst. Clean drinking water for the horses was piped in over a considerable distance.

With the scarcity of clean water, baths were a rarity and were usually commented on. On January 29, William O'Brien was able to write: "Had my first bath in France this PM and it was a peach. It involved a nine-mile march but it was worth it." Bath Parade also featured a welcome change of clothing, with the men handing in their old clothes and getting new, or washed, items in return, along with clean socks and a clean grey shirt.

The quarters for our men here consist of a large barn with a good layer of straw in it. They are quite comfortable.

We eight Sergeants have secured an attic over a little estaminet and, although the thatch is low, the slanting walls [are] lined with bags of hops and grain, and the rats scurry across the floor at night. We are comfortable and the old man, his wife and two daughters all do their best to make us so. We bring our rations over here and the old lady cooks them for us. They make wonderful coffee here, the pot is always on the stove, and we can get good English beer between twelve and one and between six and eight at night, and the best of champagne at 5 francs** a quart, so we do not fare so poorly.

A ration of rum, served once daily from a one-and-a-half-gallon earthenware jug, helped the men keep warm. "The regulations are

---

*Also known as calcium hypochlorite, used today to disinfect drinking water and swimming pools.
**About 90 cents at the prevailing rate of exchange.

very strict," explained Hal. "The officer has to check each man and see the rum is drunk on the spot. The men lined up and each got his portion. You should have heard the smacking of lips. They claim great sleeping properties for it."

On arriving behind the lines, the column's first task was to learn the roads and tracks between the supply dumps, where the howitzer shells were picked up, and the gun pits. This was critical, for much of the work was done at night without lights, and it was easy to get lost in the maze of roads.

"The Front" was a place of near-constant din, with the whoosh and bass rumble of heavy guns and the thud of distant explosions, the flat crack and whine of a bullet, and the staccato tap-tap-tap of machine guns. "A man's first impulse," wrote MO Harry Pavey,* "is to duck when he hears the zing of a bullet, but after a while he pays no attention, for he gets to know that the ones which he hears are already past. The one that hits him he does not hear." When the wind shifted, the stench from the front lines could be smelled miles away. It was a nauseating mixture of excrement, urine, cordite, smoke, chloride of lime, and the stink of unburied bodies that littered No Man's Land.

Lieutenant-Colonel King, along with several officers from the batteries, went forward on the twenty-fourth to inspect the positions of the 118th Howitzer Brigade RFA, which the 6th would shortly relieve and whose gun positions it would take over. The gun pits the Canadians would occupy were about 2,000 yards behind the lines. Typically, they were enclosed on three sides by sandbag walls, with the back left open. The timber roof was topped with sandbags and earth for camouflage and protection. Inside were racks for shells, sorted by type, either high explosive or shrapnel. The guns themselves rested on platforms of timber or brick — whatever the ruined buildings of the area could supply.

King inspected the brigade's horses on the twenty-seventh. Concerned with what he'd seen, he ordered brick horse standings

---

*Pavey, who had examined many of the men of the former 21st Battery in Montreal, went overseas with the 60th Battalion.

to be constructed. As the OC 2nd Divisional Ammunition Column, Lieutenant-Colonel William Harrison (whom we shall meet again later) explained, "Mud is the special feature of this country which will always be remembered by our boys. If it was not for our brick standings, our horses would sink out of sight."

We will be here until sometime the middle of next week to give the officers and some of the NCOs of the batteries an opportunity to go up to the firing line and become acquainted with the positions of the units we are to relieve. Then we will go up and get into the game in earnest.

Saw a very interesting air fight today although we were not close enough to make it out very clearly. We could plainly see the burst of the [anti-aircraft] shells all about the spot where the aircraft was and, as the atmosphere was clear and no wind blowing, these large puffs of smoke stayed in position for some time, until at one time there must have been at least a hundred of these large balls of smoke along the route the craft was taking. Evidently the aircraft was dodging up and down so that the range could not be found, as some bursts were high, some low. There are aeroplanes flying over us constantly here, but as there were always a number of them at Shorncliffe, we don't take much notice.

And now just a few requisitions before I turn in. Cigarettes! You hear a great deal about how many cigarettes are given out to the men here. I believe there is an issue once a week although we have not seen any yet, but they are all "Virginia" and not my brand, and so far I have found it impossible to buy Turkish or, in fact, any kind, so I will be deeply indebted to anyone who will send me some Melachrinos, Benson & Hedges, Murads, Fatimas or anything else. I laid in what I considered a stock (150) before leaving England but they are about gone now.

A few other things I could make good use of, or will shortly, are: toothbrush, toothpaste and razor strop. There is nothing else I want and I will let you know if there is later. Of course, chocolates and chewing gum and candy are always welcome.

We have been having wonderful weather since we have been here, beautiful clear nights and crisp, sunny days, different to what we expected, however it may not last long, but here's hoping!

The mud around here is not bad yet, although our Horse Lines have to be changed every second day, but it will be a good deal worse than that up farther.

As an example of how good the mail system is here:— although we only settled here Sat. morning, a letter mailed in Folkestone at 11 PM Sat. night reached me by the first mail Monday AM, and was only addressed: Amm. Col., 6th Bde CFA, CEF, and letters addressed to me at Otterpool Camp came through just the same.

Must close now. Hope you are all as well and happy as I am.

While Bert acknowledged numerous letters from the family in Canada, he carefully neglected to mention a growing correspondence with Rosalie James, of whom he had so far said nothing to the family. His only previous references were a cryptic note indicating that while on leave in London he "Stayed with my friends the James'," and a request that his suit be mailed from Canada to "R.B. James."

The 6th Brigade had already brought into its new positions some of the equipment it would need on taking over the guns of the 118th Brigade. This included aiming posts (two per gun), siege lamps (two per gun), and sufficient telephones and spare cable to take over the communications network, which linked battery commanders to brigade headquarters.

Lieutenant-Colonel King's Operation Order No. 4 of January 31 provided concise instructions to the batteries and column on the upcoming relief of the 118th. As always, such orders were designed to minimize confusion, and gave details of timing, starting point, order of march, and the 10-mile route from the church at Fletre to their destination off the Neuve-Eglise road.

Just a week since I last wrote and during that time I have had a trip up to our front line and have had my first experience of

Shells trace a fiery parabola in the skies. *Author's photo.*

being actually on the firing line. I rode up there last Saturday [January 29] morning with Major McColl to look over the positions which our Brigade is to occupy and to get a line on the work of the Column. It was, as you can imagine, a most interesting trip and an experience which I have been looking forward to for a long time.

Although I was only there two days, I covered a lot of ground. I went over the positions occupied by the three batteries of the brigade we are to relieve, as well as those of a couple of our 18-pounder batteries. There I met a bunch of boys I knew, in fact, boys who had been in my sub-section in the old 21st Battery and had come over in drafts to these batteries. It sure was great to run across these boys way up there, and we had a big reunion and celebration in one of the dugouts Sunday night.

Pete Cornell, I think, is the only one who was present that you all know. He is looking fine and enjoying the life up there. I met him on the road the first day I was up there; you can imagine with what surprise, as I did not know his battery was near that place. I met a great number of our old drivers too, scattered through the Horse Lines on the various batteries. It is a shame the way the old 21st Battery men have been broken up and scattered through the whole 1st Division Artillery.

The two days I was up there were fairly quiet ones as it was quite foggy and impossible to observe the firing properly. Early Monday AM, however, there was a very heavy artillery action on our left in support of an advance by the infantry. It started at 3:00 and lasted for just an hour, but they sure did let the Germans have it hot while they were at it. Incidentally we captured two trenches and several prisoners, and the trenches were said to be filled with Germans; it is significant that only a few were made prisoners.

The position we are going into is really a very quiet one and there is very little doing right now, but as we expect to be there a month,* we may have a little work to do before we are through.

I will write again when I am up there with the Column at the end of the week. I will have to stop now as my candle just burned down.

Walter is better, but troubled with rheumatism yet.

---

*Under normal conditions of static warfare, Bert's Howitzer Brigade could expect to spend prolonged periods in the line, often a month or more. Compare this to a typical infantry rotation, usually consisting of four to five days in the frontline trenches, a similar period in support, followed by a week or more in reserve before returning to the front.

15

A Present to the Kaiser

At 5:00 a.m. on February 4, one section from each of the Howitzer Brigade's three batteries began moving to the new Wagon Lines (WL). The ammunition column quit its position at 8:00, arriving around noon, and the changeover was completed the following day when the remaining sections moved into position. The Wagon Lines to which the brigade marched were a mile and a half behind the gun positions. Under the command of a captain, it was here a battery's horses and limbers were kept, so as not to betray the locations of the guns. Here, too, were the battery's supplies, along with any men not needed at the guns, including drivers, farriers, and administrative personnel. Often, half or more of a battery's personnel were at the WL at any given time.

Bert and the column were still on French soil, north of the Bailleul-Armentières road, a short distance from the gun positions just across the Belgian frontier. The column transported two main types of shells for the 4.5-inch howitzers: high explosive (HE), used against "hard" targets, and shrapnel, employed mainly for anti-personnel work. Shrapnel shells, containing 480 lead alloy balls, were designed to burst above the intended target, mowing down troops in the open with a deadly shower of metal. The 4.5-inch howitzers could also fire gas, smoke, and star shells, and the column brought these to the guns, as well, though in smaller quantities. Shell consumption was modest compared to actions later in the war. A 15-minute bombardment on February 12, for example, involving the brigade's three batteries, called for 46 rounds of HE by each of the 21st and 22nd Batteries, and 56 rounds of shrapnel by the 23rd.

Gunners of the 23rd Battery marked an important milestone on February 4. "Our gun," recorded William O'Brien proudly, "gave its first present to the Kaiser this morning in the shape of six rounds of high explosive."

On the sixth, with the weather being fair and mild, the howitzers began the process of "registering" (or "ranging") their guns on a variety of enemy targets, usually frontline trenches, crossroads, or other facilities in the forward zone assigned to the brigade. Guided by a Forward Operation Officer (FOO) at the Observation Post (OP, or "O-Pip" in the war's phonetic language), the fall of each shot was relayed back to the battery by telephone, so the gunners could make appropriate corrections. Junior officers from each battery took turns at the OP, often located in the front lines; it was a dangerous job, for suspected British OPs were a favourite target for German gunners. OPs were manned around the clock by one officer (the FOO), two signallers, and two linemen, whose job it was to ensure constant telephone communication between the OP, brigade headquarters, and the individual batteries. These men were relieved, usually at night, after 24 hours on duty.

Once a particular howitzer had hit its target, details of elevation, azimuth, and charge were entered into a battery target table, a booklet that got thicker over time as new targets were added. In this way, in fog or at night, gunners could hit — or come close enough to — a particular target when ordered by setting the appropriate range and azimuth. So accurate were the 4.5-inch howitzers and so reproducible the shots, usually a gunner could count on dropping his shells within a few yards of the target.* When a gun was moved to another location, it had to be re-registered. When batteries relieved each other in the field, taking over howitzers already in established gun pits, the target

---

*By the end of the war, "technical" gunnery had come into its own. Gunners made adjustments based on air temperature, barometric pressure, wind direction, and velocity, as well as the muzzle velocity of each gun.

tables were handed over to the relieving battery. It was a reflection on how static conditions had become on the Western Front.

Weather was all-important to an artillery brigade. Sometimes, in poor visibility, shooting was nearly impossible, not because the gunners couldn't see their targets (most of the time they couldn't, anyway) but because the FOO couldn't observe the fall of the shell. Thus, entries like the following appeared in the War Diary:

February 11: "Observation nearly impossible on account of mist."
February 13: "Very little was done in registering on account of weather condition[s]."

At the front, almost all activity on both sides took place at night. Working parties repaired damaged trenches, strung new barbed wire, and moved up ammunition, supplies, and replacement troops. As a result, Canadian and German gunners were active by day and night. Catching the enemy during a relief was a worthy objective for the Canadian gunners, for twice as many soldiers crowded the trenches and offered an opportunity to inflict greater casualties. Naturally, German gunners tried to do the same when they suspected Canadian infantry battalions were being relieved.

Night raiding of German trenches was a Canadian innovation, dating back to the previous autumn. Raids were supported by artillery, and thus on February 7 the Howitzer Brigade received Operation Order No. 5 in connection with "an enterprise" to be carried out that night. The 2nd Canadian Divisional Artillery was tasked with providing "a Barrage to prevent any enemy reinforcements from coming up." Targets consisted of support and communications trenches, along with roads in a precisely defined rectangle.

8/2/16

As I write this letter I am sitting at a table covered with a red-checked oil cloth with a stove burning close by, four bunks in one corner and a brand-new keg of Belgian beer in another.

I have just put on water for porridge and as soon as it gets warm I will proceed to mix in a package of perfectly good

Quaker oats. The only trouble is the oats are so expensive over here, we have to pay 1 franc 30 centimes* for a package which does us one meal but, as there are nine of us in the mess, we are not worrying very much.

I should have mentioned we are now up on the line and in our position. We have been here five days and have had a fairly quiet time of it, altho' we have had a few hundred rounds to take up to the batteries. The day we left our billets down the line it was raining and blowing like the d— so our trip here was not as pleasant as it might have been, but the next day it made up for it by being so pleasant you could imagine it was midsummer. It was really beautiful and hard to realize there was a war going on.

From the top of our horse lines we can see a little village** that is mentioned every day, I think, in the papers, particularly in connection with the Canadian artillery work over here. It is less than a mile away and with the sun shining on the red roofs and what is left of the church steeple, it was a beautiful sight.

Tonight the Germans put over about 8 "coal boxes"† just over the village while we were at Stables. They sure did make a row coming over. You could imagine it was a railway train coming along, ending in a couple of heavy explosions. We couldn't see what damage they did but I suppose we will be able to go up there again one of these nights and get a few more loads of bricks for our horse standings, from the houses they demolished.

Ern Hutchison is now attached to the Column which makes it very nice, as I lost a filling the other day and it will be nice to have it replaced by my own dentist. I see a good deal of Ern these days but very little of Rus [Hutchison], as he is with Headquarters and billeted about a mile away.

Grover's 500 Fatimas reached me from New York. I was glad to get them as the [service] issue are Virginia and I do not care for them.

---

*About 23 cents.
**Ploegsteert, Belgium, known to the Tommies as "Plug Street."
†A shell that exploded with a cloud of black smoke.

It is a peculiar thing, but the dry canteen or grocery bar up here is far better and much cheaper even than any I have struck yet — even those in England — and we are able to obtain a great many things we require and will be very comfortable.

Walter is around again and attending parades regularly.

Will climb into my blankets now, so will say good-night.

Having a dentist in the brigade meant the men did not need to receive treatment in a dental clinic to the rear. Ernest Hutchison was well regarded; in a confidential report, Lieutenant-Colonel King wrote: "Capt. E.C. Hutchison has been attached to this Brigade since October 1915. I have always found him to be a very thorough and efficient dentist. He is painstaking, energetic and willing, and has been a great boon to the Brigade." The gunners were fortunate to have a man of Hutchison's diligence, for many in the Dental Corps could not be bothered with basic work. "I went to the dentist this morning to have some fillings replaced," reported Private Noel Chipman, a friend of Hal's. "He fixed it permanently by the simple process of pulling it and three others out. There aren't any frills like gas* in the army. A good husky orderly (not even a dentist) just pulled like the deuce until they came out."

Death from artillery fire was random and could come at any time, without warning. Contrary to expectations, rear areas could be more dangerous than frontline trenches; shelling of a Canadian trench invited immediate retaliation by Canadian gunners on German trenches. More often, in what was called the "Morning Hate," German gunners "swept" selected areas behind the lines. Firing blind, or aided by aircraft and balloon spotters, enemy batteries sought to demolish British billets, communication trenches, supply dumps, and road junctions.

February 15 was cold and rainy and that afternoon Bert's sub-section came under long-range shellfire. Eight horses were killed and three men were wounded; killed was Albert Bates, whose mother in Folkestone had poured tea for many Canadians. The first member of the 6th Howitzer Brigade to be killed in the line of duty, Bates was

---

*Laughing gas (nitrous oxide) was used as an anesthetic.

buried two days later at Maple Leaf Cemetery, outside Ploegsteert. As a mark of respect, the funeral was attended by senior officers, including Lieutenant-Colonel King and the divisional artillery commander, Brigadier-General Edward Morrison. The brigade chaplain read the brief service. "Forasmuch as it hath pleased Almighty God of his great mercy to take unto himself the soul of our dear brother here departed, Albert Henry Bates: we therefore commit his body to the ground...." A small white cross marked his final resting place. The graves were well tended; Montrealer Royal Ewing of the 42nd Battalion was surprised to find local farmers placing flowers on British graves.

17/2/16

Just a line as I begin to realize that it is some time since I last wrote, but it is hardly my fault as we have had a little excitement the last few days and this is positively the first opportunity I have had since Sunday.

The excitement I mention above was the result of our being under shellfire for the first time and, believe me, the Zepps at Otterpool have nothing on the German 5.9s. They found our comfortable billet at 12:45 PM on Tuesday just as we were all lined up at noon Stables, and they did give us an uncomfortable

Burial service behind the front. *Author's photo.*

time for about an hour and a half. Their third shell landed right in my sub-section amongst my horses, and certainly did play h—! I lost two men, my corporal, and eight horses. My corporal was killed outright, one man had both legs badly fractured, and the other only a flesh wound. That was all the actual damage they did, but we had to get out and leave our happy home.

To make things more interesting, it began to rain as we moved off. As it was just getting dark, you can perhaps imagine (but I doubt it) the fun we had picking out a new bivouac and gathering our men, horses and equipment together and finding cover for our men.

As luck would have it, I have been acting Sergt.-Major for about a week and consequently I had my hands *more* than full. It was about 9:30 PM before I succeeded in finding a barn for the men to sleep in and had our horse lines straightened out and the horses fed. The men had nothing to eat since breakfast and had nothing to go to bed on except what coffee and biscuits they could buy, and most of them had wet feet at least, so they were quite ready to crawl into the straw.

Personally I was so busy getting things away from the old place I didn't bother about my own coat and stuff as, of course, we left all kit, etc. to get the next day and contented ourselves with taking all our horses, ammunition, and wagons to a safer place. So, after, travelling around for about six hours in the rain and wind, I didn't have many dry spots left. I found that by burying yourself in the straw and keeping as close as possible to the next man, you can dry your clothes quite well, for by 6:20 the next morning I was practically dry except for my feet.

We are straightening things out now and by tomorrow I think will be quite normal again. We have managed to carry on our supply of ammunition to the batteries without interruption and altogether it has been a splendid experience for us all. (Except perhaps those who were unfortunate enough to get hit.)

Please don't be alarmed at anything I have told you. I have found from this experience that I am well able to take care of myself and have no fear whatsoever for the next time, when-ever it may come.

It is rather funny that the [118th's Brigade Ammunition] Column that occupied that billet were there for seven months and never saw a shell, but we got it in less than two weeks, so it is not likely we will be near it again for some time.

I hope you are all as well as I am. If you will not worry any more than I do, everyone will be happy. I had thought at first I would not mention anything about what has occurred but I decided to tell you everything that I am able to, as I feel that you want to know it all and will not worry.

Despite Bert's glib assurances, his casual description of the fall of German shells would have alarmed, rather than placated, family members reading the transcribed letter. If death was as random as he portrayed, even behind the lines, then surely he was *always* in some sort of danger.

As Bert predicted, things settled down in the next days. The weather was seasonably cold, and the War Diary for the eighteenth recorded: "Usual routine: front quiet & normal." And, a day later, "Famous old landmark, Ploegsteert church steeple, was brought down by the enemy." On clear days German aircraft roamed behind the British lines, their presence noted in the War Diary: "Aeroplane activity: 8 came across our lines at 7 AM."

The Royal Flying Corps was in the air, as well, assisting Canadian gunners. On the twenty-first, Andrew McNaughton's 21st Battery registered its howitzers by aircraft, a relatively new development. An observer in the aircraft reported the fall of the shell by wireless back to the battery, which was then able to correct the fire. Billy Bishop, the young Canadian who would score 72 aerial victories, was at that time an artillery observer in the RFC. In his 1918 memoir, *Winged Warfare*, he described his role:

You fly on until you pick up the four mounds that indicate the German battery position. You fly rather low to get a good look at it. The Huns generally know what your coming means and

A well-camouflaged British field gun. *Author's photo.*

A British field piece in a semi-permanent emplacement. Gunners will take their rounds from the limber on the left. *Author's photo.*

they prepare to take cover. You return a little way toward your own lines and signal to your battery to fire. In a moment you see the flash of a big gun. Then nothing seems to happen for an eternity. As a matter of fact twenty to thirty seconds elapse and then fifty yards beyond the German battery you see a spurt of grey-black earth spring from the ground. You signal a correction of the range. The next shot goes fifty yards short. In artillery parlance you have "bracketed" your target. You again signal a correction, giving a range just in between the first two shots. The next shell that goes over explodes in a gunpit.

"Good shooting," you signal to the battery, "carry on."

Bert's next letter demonstrated a willingness to bend rules.

25/2/16

Am taking the opportunity of sending a few snaps I took while in England but did not send before coming over here. QMS [Harold] Rolph, who has been with us for some time now, has just received his commission and goes back to England tomorrow and will mail this for me. As there is very little chance of this letter being censored, I might as well tell you a few things which I otherwise would not be able to.

In the first place, we have returned to our old billet where we were shelled and have made ourselves comfortable and incidentally have heard nothing further from our friends the Huns. We were away from there just about five days, and some rough days they were too.

We are just a few miles inside the Belgian border between Plug Street and Neuve Eglise. Armentières is further to our right and Ypres to our left. We expect to move next week in the direction of Ypres and will probably take up our position with the Second Division somewhere near Locre or Mont Kemmel. This we expect will be a permanent position for us.

We have had a change of officers this week, and Capt. George Riley has replaced Major McColl. The change is very much for the better and, if permanent, will make the work of the Column much smoother and much more pleasant.

Doc Hutch (Capt. Ernest Hutchison) is attached to us permanently now, has been with us (the Column) for about 4 weeks and he and I have some great old chats at times over home news, etc. Am also having Harold Rolph mail you a piece of one of the shells that came over here the other day; thought you might like to have it as a souvenir. We have found out they were 5.9s and they were fired from a naval gun mounted on RR trucks, back of Messines with a range of about 12,000 yards. They sure did have our range down cold, and pumped them over in good shape.

The day we came here, an aeroplane went over about five o'clock at night and dropped four bombs; fortunately they were a bit off the line, the closest one landed about 150 yards from our hut. It is a great sensation to hear these bombs come whistling down and not know just where they are going to land. I think they are even more terrifying than the big shells. You can hear these whistle almost as soon as they leave the gun, getting louder and louder as they come, until just before they land, sound like an express train and, if you are wise and can do so, you get just as close to the ground as you can (mud or no mud). If you are no closer than 10 yards to the burst of one of these shells (high explosive) and lie flat on the ground, I believe you are quite safe. The burst is upwards and in the direction in which the shell is travelling. But anyway, at best they are very unpleasant customers to run up against.

Our batteries have been making a big reputation for themselves and have done some exceptionally good work; they have been rather highly complimented by the General on several occasions.

We have had a great number of aeroplanes over us the last few days, as the weather has been clear and some very interesting air fights have taken place. All these planes carry machine guns and when you hear this rattling away up there, almost out of sight, you know there is something doing. The anti-aircraft guns on either side don't seem to be able to do anything and, although they fire hundreds of rounds, it is only a chance shot that ever hits them. You see, the planes can change their elevation and position so rapidly the gunners have absolutely nothing to range on. The new German type of machine* that has just appeared here lately has practically no body to it at all, and everything painted aluminum, it is very hard to detect when any distance up. It certainly is a pretty sight, though, when they come over in any numbers and it is nothing to see 10 or 15 machines all up at the same time.

We have had a very cold spell the last three days, with snow. The ground is frozen quite hard and covered with snow, quite a homely appearance.

Had a nice letter from Lena today. Anything sent from Harrods will certainly be gratefully appreciated by the members of the Sergeants' Mess, as a few extras are always more than welcome. Rec'd Flo's letter with the silk handkerchief inclosed; the silk is hardly serviceable here but I will send it back to London with my other things and hope to have an opportunity of using it when I go over on leave sometime in the near future.

During our travels around the country last week most of us were unfortunate, or fortunate enough, perhaps, to lose most of our kit, so I have decided to carry only the absolute necessities from now on and only what will go in a haversack. Khaki handkerchiefs would come in very handy and a couple sent with a letter every two or three weeks would be fine.

Will close now and climb into my blankets. It is snowing hard out. Hope everyone is well.

The weeks flashed past, differing little from the brigade's experience in its first month at the front. Though the weather slowly improved, there were still many days of fog when direct observation was not possible. German observers were similarly blinded. On March 7, with the temperature around freezing, Lieutenant-Colonel King noted, "Observation very difficult on account of snow. Front was very quiet & normal. Only six hostile shells reported as falling on our front."

---

*Likely Fokker E.IIIs, one-seater monoplanes with a machine gun synchronized to fire through the propeller.

At an OP in the spring of 1916, an artillery officer directs the fire of his guns by telephone. Neither the officer nor the signaller is wearing a steel helmet. The Graphic, *April 22, 1916.*

Sergeant Bert in front of a tin-roofed shack, somewhere in Flanders. Undated, but probably March/April 1916, before Canadian troops were issued steel helmets. *Courtesy of Madeleine Claudi.*

The work of the three howitzer batteries consisted mainly of trench destruction and counter-battery fire. This latter was important; silencing the enemy's artillery was one of the best ways to assist the infantry. On March 3 the War Diary recorded: "At the request of 2nd & 3rd Infantry Bde we retaliated on enemy's trenches & supposed batteries. Results satisfactory. Three trench mortars were silenced." Batteries were allowed other targets on occasion: "flash targets," or targets of opportunity, could be called in on the telephone by the FOO for destruction.

3/3/16

It is a miserable, cold, windy and rainy night but we are quite comfortable in our little hut. We have had nothing to disturb us since our experience of almost two weeks ago, although things have been stirring on our front and our guns are at it most of the time these days, keeping the Column busy nearly every night.

We don't expect to be here much longer as we move into our new position in a couple of days. We have an open field to move into this time, so if we are unlucky enough to have bad weather, we will have a rather uncomfortable time of it the first week or so, until we can put up some kind of shelter.

Pokette sent me 500 Fatimas so I am "jake" for some time. I ran short the last week and took a pipe to fill in, but cigarettes are much handier.

I have a nice hot rum waiting for me as I have a bit of a cold in my ear tonight. I am going to turn in and will write again soon.

To infantrymen, gunners appeared to enjoy an easy life. Yet, despite appearances, gunners faced their own special dangers, apart from being favoured targets for German artillery. Defective fuses and bad shell cases were a problem faced by all gunners and were by no means rare. On February 27 a premature shell exploded in the barrel of the No. 4 gun of the 23rd Battery, wounding three men with metal splinters. Lieutenant-Colonel King convened a Court of Inquiry that afternoon to "inquire into and report upon the causes." Calling Jim McKeown as a witness, the Inquiry determined the premature shell had been caused by faulty ammunition.*

At 10:30 a.m. on March 11, the brigade was relieved by the 118th Howitzer Brigade, the same unit it had taken over from five weeks earlier. As before, one section from each battery was relieved at dusk that same day, and the remaining sections the following evening. For the 6th Brigade gunners, there was no rest. Their skills and howitzers were required a few miles northeast, near the Belgian village of St. Eloi and immediately south of the Ypres Salient. As always on coming into a sector, battery commanders consulted their detailed trench maps and determined their respective zones of fire, after which the gunners began registering their howitzers on selected targets.

Muddy fields dried in the spring sunshine, and the thoughts of young men turned to activities other than artillery matters. "The sun was warm today," wrote William O'Brien on March 13. "Real baseball weather."

As in every active service unit, gifts of all sorts flooded into the 6th Howitzer Brigade, donations from individuals, Canadian companies, and charitable organizations. In one short period that spring, the brigade received books, cakes of soap, and dried fruit. As well, Lieutenant-Colonel King received 149 pairs of socks, 17 flannel shirts, and 150 handkerchiefs from the IODE, and the Canadian Field Comforts Commission at Shorncliffe sent 190 cakes of soap. The Canadian War Contingent Association in London sent 24 Tommy cookers, 25 pounds of Players navy cut tobacco, 12 sets of checkers, 12 packs of cards, and two footballs. Every donation was acknowledged in writing.

Captain Philip Cook,** the brigade ammunition column's OC, accepted 115 pipes from an anonymous donor, sent from Hyman's Tobacco in Montreal. A day later he received the following:

---

*At one point in 1915, defective shells were so prevalent that one 18-pounder shell in 5,000 could be expected to destroy the gun it was fired from. Fortunately, the situation was soon rectified.

**Cook had commanded the 6th Brigade's ammunition column in Montreal and sailed aboard *Megantic*.

Dear Sir:

We herewith hand you a package containing forty pouches to be delivered to the men of your unit.

An acknowledgment of same to us will oblige.

H.B. Hyman

To this, Lieutenant-Colonel King replied:

Will you kindly convey to the Montreal citizen who so kindly donated this to us, our heartfelt thanks for same. This tobacco was duly distributed as requested, and was much appreciated by all ranks.

To no one's surprise, Andrew McNaughton was recalled to England on March 18 from the 21st Battery. Promoted lieutenant-colonel, McNaughton, just 29, assumed command of the Third Division's 11th Howitzer Brigade, the first step in a meteoric career that saw him finish the war as a brigadier-general. The same night there was a party in the column. "Rode over to our Ammunition Column tonight and enjoyed the party given by Capt. [George] Riley to the men. It was," claimed William O'Brien, "for an impromptu concert, the best ever."

The following, extracted from Operation Order No. 14 of March 19, 1916, indicates how the firing was designed to keep the Germans off guard:

The 23rd Battery, 6th (How) Brigade, will fire as follows:—

Enemy's trenches about N.18.c.9.1., and N.24.a.7.6

1.37–1.40 a.m.	—	12 rounds Lyddite [HE]
1.40–1.44 a.m.	—	Silence
1.44–1.46 a.m.	—	8 rounds
1.46–1.58 a.m.	—	Silence
1.58–2.01 a.m.	—	12 rounds Lyddite
2.01 a.m.	—	Stop firing.

The sector in which the Canadians found themselves was an active one. German artillery often retaliated for shells sent their way by the Canadians, as the War Diary (March 21) recorded: "They retaliated at about 5.07 & lasted till 5.18, firing 5.9s and about 20 whizz-bangs,* but very little damage was done."

It was at this time that all Canadian troops on the Western Front were issued a new piece of gear — a wide-brimmed helmet of hardened manganese-steel intended to reduce head injuries. The "battle bowler" or "tin hat," designed by John Brodie in 1915, had a distinctive, bowl-shaped profile that defined a generation of soldiers. Though it offered less protection to the lower head and neck than the German M.1916 "coal scuttle" *stahlhelm*, the incidence of head wounds among British Tommies from shrapnel and shell fragments fell dramatically. As Harry Pavey wrote to his wife, "One man had a piece of shrapnel pierce his steel helmet and only scratch his scalp. The helmet saved his life." For obvious reasons, most men welcomed it. "The helmets seemed very heavy at first," wrote Hal, "but now I am quite accustomed to the weight and hardly notice it."

At 4:15 a.m. on March 27, six huge mines were simultaneously detonated under the German lines at St. Eloi. The massive explosions, heard more than 70 miles away in Folkestone, were the signal for a two-hour bombardment of enemy positions. As the guns roared, the 6th Brigade ammunition column had the satisfaction of knowing the shells it had laboriously brought to the gun pits were being used to support the advance by the British 3rd Division.

Surprise was complete. One German officer quoted in the Howitzer Brigade's War Diary claimed that of his company of 260 about 200 had been blown up when the mines were exploded.

---

*The term was first used to describe the noise made by shells fired from the German 77 mm quick-firing field gun. As these shells reached supersonic velocities, British infantrymen first heard the *whizz* of the incoming shell before the *bang* from the gun itself. Since it gave little warning of its arrival, unlike enemy howitzers, the whizz-bang was a fearsome weapon.

Captain Robert Smyth, who served briefly with Bert's Howitzer Brigade in the autumn of 1915, wrote: "On the way home last night they started to *strafe* the road I was on with whizz-bangs, but you can bet that when I heard the *whizz* I was in the ditch before the *bang*."

Tasked to provide counter-battery fire, the 21st Battery placed three observers atop Kemmel Hill. Equipped with telephones, they could call down artillery fire on any suspected German battery position. William O'Brien noted: "Our first big scrap began this morning, our battery putting over about 600 HE shells."

Despite initial surprise, the British advance soon bogged down; the immense craters made it difficult to move up supplies and reinforcements to consolidate the ground gained. So transformed was the landscape by the explosions that attacking British troops scarcely knew where they were. Unknown to the British high command, the Germans still occupied Craters 4 and 5, and three days elapsed before the British realized their mistake. In the next days, in what they called the "Crater Show," Canadian gunners continued to support renewed British attacks, though not without incident. ("I don't know why the boys call an engagement a *show*," confessed Major Harry Pavey, "unless it is because so much takes place, and one is able to see so little of it.") On March 30, Gun No. 542 of the 22nd Battery had a premature at the muzzle, which blew 16 inches off the barrel. Though the gun pit was badly damaged, there were no casualties. The gun was returned to ordnance workshops at Abeele for repair and a Court of Inquiry convened at 8:45 p.m. Again, the Court blamed defective ammunition.

As the British pressed their attack, enemy gunners exacted a heavy toll. "Hostile artillery very active" was the opening entry in the 6th Brigade War Diary for each of the first three days of April. German observers atop the Messines-Wytschaete Ridge did a remarkable job of directing fire: on April 3, 40 six-inch shells fell in the vicinity of the 6th Brigade Headquarters between 5:00 p.m. and 7:00 p.m. In the daily artillery exchanges, the Canadians gave better than they got. "Fritz caught hell," Bob Hale wrote after the battle, "as one of them told us. He was taken prisoner and, as he was wounded, he was sent down with us. Our boys were talking about the German bombardment and he said to me, 'You boys don't know what a bombardment is. They should be in *our* trenches when *your* artillery opens up.'"

Amid all this, the 6th's gunners still found time for sports. On April 2, a Sunday, William O'Brien recorded: "Had first baseball workout last evening."

By the night of April 3/4, the exhausted British troops withdrew, replaced by Major-General Richard Turner's 2nd Canadian Division, untested in combat. Though minor in overall strategic terms, the Battle of the St. Eloi Craters was a milestone for Canada, as it marked the 2nd Division's first set-piece battle on the Western Front. On April 4, the 27th Battalion attacked and, within hours, half of the Canadian assault force was dead. Throughout, the 6th BAC toiled day and night to keep the guns supplied with ammunition. "Today has been one of the busiest since being in France" the War Diary noted on April 6.

Confusion reigned in the next two weeks. Bad weather kept the RFC on the ground and, amid intense German artillery barrages and with no aerial photographs, senior commanders were uncertain what portions of the field were held by the Canadians. In the end the Germans reoccupied almost all the ground that had been wrested from them in the early hours of March 27.

For Bert, Walter, and the rest of the BAC, there was a much-deserved rest on April 7. Even as the fighting raged on, the column — joined by sections from the 21st and 22nd Batteries — marched to rest billets a few miles behind the lines, out of range of all but the longest German guns.

On the twelfth, after just four days of rest, the column and battery half-sections returned to St. Eloi, this time to take over positions previously occupied by the 30th Brigade RFA. The Canadians were not impressed with what they found. "Billet and Horse Lines in very dirty condition," the War Diary sniffed. Little had changed in five days, and the sector was still unsettled. On the thirteenth, the 6th Brigade was firing at German positions inside Craters 2 and 3 and, a day later, destroyed a machine-gun emplacement. As German infantry units attempted to retake Craters 4 and 5 at 2:45 a.m. on the fifteenth, all three batteries switched to barrage and fired for 15 minutes. "Enemy were repulsed," the War Diary noted laconically.

By the first week of May, as the exhausted infantry caught their breath and rebuilt their strength, the Canadian howitzers spent much of their time on tasks that by now were routine: counter-battery fire, silencing *Minenwerfers* (trench mortars of various calibres), and general destruction of German trenches. In this, they were highly successful.

A downed British Vickers FB-2, probably taken May 16, 1916. *Courtesy of Madeleine Claudi.*

William O'Brien exulted on May 5 that the 23rd Battery "did some rare old shooting this afternoon, getting a trench mortar battery and eliciting the approval of the infantry." In a typical entry, the War Diary for May 12 recorded: "Trench mortars were again active but 21st Battery took them in hand & stopped them." It was not all one-sided by any means. German gunners were skilled and succeeded on May 5 in putting one gun of the 22nd Battery out of operation.

On May 7, Driver Ernest Victor Grout, a distant relative of the author, was posted to the 6th Brigade ammunition column. English-born, the 28-year-old rancher from Alberta had enlisted — rather unusually — at Shorncliffe and was taken into the Reserve Artillery Brigade. His training complete, he was part of a draft for France and ended up in the howitzer brigade.

Though dogfights in the skies were now commonplace, they were mentioned on occasion in the 6th Brigade's War Diary. "One of our planes fell in our lines; pilot was killed," the War Diary recorded on May 16. Bert, among others, got a close look at the downed machine, a pusher-type Vickers Gunbus FB-5.*

---

*The plane, from No. 11 Squadron, was piloted by 2nd Lieutenant Morden Mowat, the only RFC pilot killed that day on the Western Front.

Summarizing this difficult time, Bert wrote, "The Crater Show continued for practically a month, during which time there were incessant raiding or bombing attacks by one side or the other. The craters themselves were continually changing hands and the chief difficulty from an artillery point of view was in determining from one hour to the next just who was in possession of certain ones.

"Activities on this front were now gradually diminished so that by the middle of May normal conditions prevailed once more and both sides settled down to Trench Warfare."

16

The Second Division Ammunition Column

In the third week of May, a major reorganization of British (and, by extension, Canadian) artillery units took place. Having separate howitzer brigades with their own ammunition columns was deemed inefficient; henceforth, field artillery brigades would consist of three batteries of 18-pounders and one battery of 4.5-inch howitzers. Brigade ammunition columns were disbanded and absorbed into their respective division ammunition columns. Surplus personnel, some 92 officers and men, along with 117 horses, were transferred to Calais for redeployment. Driver Ernest Grout found himself temporarily without a unit until, on May 25, he joined the 1st Division ammunition column.

"Last day of existence of 6th How Bde CFA," Lieutenant-Colonel King wrote in the War Diary on May 21. His command was broken up effective 6:00 a.m. the following day. Bert and Walter, both respected sergeants with spotless records, were two of just 13 men from the old 6th BAC taken on strength by the 2nd Division ammunition column and not sent to Calais. King's three howitzer batteries were distributed among the artillery brigades of the 2nd Canadian Division. Jim McKeown and the 23rd Battery went to the 5th Brigade CFA, the 22nd Battery to the 6th Brigade, and the 21st to the 7th Brigade.*

After reorganization, the 2DAC consisted of a Headquarters Section and four sections, numbered one through four, each commanded by a captain. Records are unclear, but Bert Sargent probably found himself in No. 1 Section, headed by Captain George Gamblin, and based in the hamlet of Reninghelst, two miles inside the Belgian border. It was the task of No. 1 Section to bring 18-pounder and 4.5-inch howitzer ammunition to the 6th Brigade, essentially the same work Bert had done since coming to France.

Commanding the 2DAC was Lieutenant-Colonel William Harrison, a 34-year-old native of New Brunswick and former barrister. He had brought the ammunition column to France in September 1915 in company with the Second Division's infantry units. "We are," he explained, "holding down the job of supplying ammunition to the whole 2nd Canadian Division, rifle, machine gun, 18-pdr, Howitzer, to say nothing of bombs, grenades, signals, trench mortar bombs, etc. which suffices to keep our unit busy." After the reorganization, the 2DAC's paper strength was 825 men and 1,010 horses, making it the largest artillery formation in the 2nd Canadian Division.

In mid-May the 2nd DAC's headquarters were in Boeschepe, a small but relatively prosperous French crossroads village close to the Belgian frontier. Here the Canadian YMCA opened a recreation hut and canteen for the column, where they could buy tinned fruit, chocolate bars, and cigarettes, and in the evenings, free hot drinks were offered. It didn't stop there: the "Y" also supplied free paper, envelopes, and books, along with baseball, soccer, and other sports items.

At the end of May, Lieutenant-Colonel Harrison's headquarters moved to Ouderdom, five miles northeast, inside Belgium and closer to Ypres. Here it remained until mid-July, while the Wagon Lines of the column's four sections were based in surrounding hamlets.

A great deal of work was necessary around Ouderdom. "In most cases accommodation in the new area was about nil, and this meant considerable rustling on everybody's part to build shacks, cook-houses and horse standings, etc." Fortunately, as the unit's history noted, the

---

*After reorganization, the Second Divisional Artillery consisted of the following Field Artillery Brigades:

4th Bde CFA: Hqrs Section, 13th Bty, 14th Bty, 19th Bty

5th Bde CFA: Hqrs Section, 17th Bty, 18th Bty, 20th Bty, 23rd (How) Bty

6th Bde CFA: Hqrs Section, 15th Bty, 16th Bty, 28th Bty, 22nd (How) Bty

7th Bde CFA: Hqrs Section, 25th Bty, 26th Bty, 27th Bty, 21st (How) Bty

average Canadian soldier was an adept "borrower," and "in about a week's time the Unit was quite comfortable."

"The DAC boasted of a fine baseball team," recorded the unit's historian, "and during the whole season did not lose a game, playing twenty-two games, tying two and winning twenty." Good teams, though, were hard to maintain in an active service unit due to constant turnover of personnel. The high point came in late July, when the DAC defeated the Engineers to capture the divisional championship.

In early June, British forces began concentrating near the city of Albert on a front astride the River Ancre, a tributary of the Somme, part of a major Anglo-French assault intended to relieve pressure on the French armies, which had been locked since February in a bloody battle of attrition at Verdun.

When the Germans got wind of the impending attack, they determined to launch a counteroffensive to gain the initiative and ruin any chance of success at the Somme. "To this end," Bert wrote, "on the morning of June 2nd, [the Germans] launched a heavy and unexpected attack on the 3rd Canadian Division at Mount Sorrel, immediately to the north of the 2nd Canadian Division zone. The attack, coming as a complete surprise and projected under a heavy artillery bombardment, was successful in its early stages, the enemy capturing the front line system and penetrating to some of the advanced gun positions in Sanctuary Wood."

In the next days, Canadian gunners were busy, along with the ammunition column. One howitzer bombardment, for example, called for three rounds of 4.5-inch howitzer ammunition per yard of German trench. It meant each howitzer would fire about 500 rounds during the bombardment, or 2,000 rounds per battery.

After 10 days of fighting in mostly rainy weather, an infantry attack by the 1st and 3rd Canadian Divisions at 1:30 a.m. on June 13 regained all the ground lost on June 2. By June 15 William O'Brien was able to report in his diary: "Rain again today. We have all our trenches back now."

It was in the Mount Sorrel "show" that Biff Notman was killed. Receiving a commission in January 1916, he joined the 3rd Division

Trench Mortar Group at the end of April, in charge of 25 men. Out of the line at the time, Biff came up to where a good friend, Lieutenant Gerry Davidson, had his dugout. "Purely voluntary on his part," Davidson later explained to the Notman family:

> He really had no right to come up in the target zone — but he was very keen on his work. The enemy must have seen him coming across some open space for, just as he got to the row of dugouts, they burst two 4.1s right above his head. A small piece went into his left kidney and a few more across his neck. It was the one in his back which told. He was only a few yards from the dressing station and was being attended five minutes after he was hit. Biff never regained his senses. I sat down by him and held his hand until just before he died.

The young lieutenant was buried in the Salient. Among those attending the brief pre-dawn funeral was Harry Pavey, who had examined Biff at his enlistment in Montreal. "We laid [him] to rest in a little cemetery beside the mill," Pavey recorded in his diary.* In Montreal a few days later, Alice Notman received the telegram all mothers dreaded:

> DEEPLY REGRET INFORM YOU LIEUT WILFRED NOTMAN THIRD DIVISIONAL ARTILLERY OFICIALLY KILLED IN ACTION JUNE 6 1916. ADJUNTANT GENERAL

For Bert and Walter, June was a quiet month. The 2nd Divisional Artillery was temporarily being supplied by other ammunition columns, and the War Diary refers only to officers going on training courses, leave assignments for officers and men, and personnel transfers.

On June 25, the men of the column began constructing an elaborate ammunition dump near Vlamertinghe, about a mile east of Ypres. Designed to store up to 60,000 18-pounder and 4.5-inch howitzer rounds, it was a reflection of the war's static nature. Rock and

---

*Biff Notman is buried in Menin Road South Military Cemetery.

A typical British shell dump on the Western Front. *Author's photo.*

Limbering up at a shell dump. *Author's photo.*

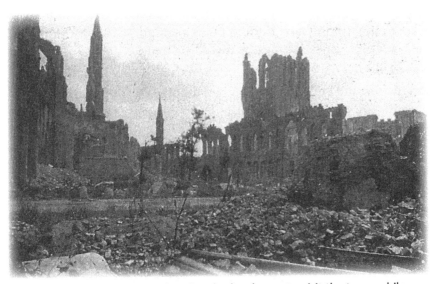

Ypres, probably June 1916, when Bert had a chance to visit the town while constructing an ammunition dump at nearby Vlamertinghe. By the time he returned in October 1917, the town had been reduced to rubble. The square tower is part of the famous medieval Cloth Hall; to the left are the ruins of St. Martin's Cathedral. *Courtesy of Madeleine Claudi.*

crushed stone were laid over the site for proper ballasting, and the whole was then covered with fine shingle and rolled. Proper drainage ditches were dug, with culverts at each end. The dump was divided into sections, separated by sandbag traverses, six feet at the base and eight feet high, so the effects of an explosion would be reduced somewhat. Ammunition was stored on wooden stands, constructed from boxes that had once contained 4.5-inch howitzer shells. This part of the British rear area was under German observation from Wytchaete Ridge, and enemy aircraft flew over frequently. Throughout its construction and thereafter, the dump was carefully camouflaged by screens of chicken wire covered with stained canvas.

Lieutenant-Colonel Harrison's headquarters moved next to the new ammunition dump on July 13. Though work on the dump continued until early August, the first deliveries to the guns were made on July 25: 680 rounds of 18-pounder shrapnel and 1980 rounds of 18-pounder HE. Overall the front was quiet enough that the "Y" organized a horse show for the Canadian Corps on July 19. The 2DAC did well: No. 3 Section won third prize for the best wagon turnout, and Driver Gus Peters — a cowboy before he'd enlisted — took third place in the trotting race, riding a horse belonging to the MO, Captain Francis Gow. So successful was the event that a further competition was organized on July 25 in the Column's No. 1 Section. Prizes were awarded to the best sub-section, best six-horsed team, and best two-horsed team, with three Veterinary Corps officers acting as judges.

By mid-July, the 2DAC was hauling 2,000-odd shells a day to the guns of the 2nd Division, mostly for routine shooting. It was not a large number and reflected the quiet state of the Canadian front. Still, the Canadians kept constant pressure on the Germans to tie down troops who would otherwise be sent to the Somme. Operation Order No. 55 from Brigadier-General Edward Morrison on July 10, referring to a minor infantry operation against German lines, noted: "The enemy will be gassed, smoked out, shot up, and raided."

At night, with artillery support, the Canadian infantry continued their trench raids. On July 1, for example, the 7th Brigade War Diary recorded:

At 1:44 AM the infantry visited frontline trench opposite and, thanks to effectiveness of barrage, got away with it with few casualties. As soon as they came out we covered their retreat by closing up the gap in our barrage. Infantry reported that our fire was very effective, hostile trenches being very noticeably damaged. Raid was in every way very successful.

On the first of July, 13 British divisions, supported by 1,537 guns, attacked along a 14-mile front in what General Douglas Haig termed the "Big Push" and history would later call the Battle of the Somme. Newspapers, under strict censorship, made it seem as though the initial attack had succeeded brilliantly, but the reality was vastly different. In the single bloodiest day in the history of the British army, wave after wave of infantry, loaded like pack animals with equipment, clambered out of their trenches and, following orders, calmly walked shoulder to shoulder toward the German lines. Assured by their commanders that the week-long barrage, some 1.5 million artillery rounds, had cut the German wire and wiped out the machine-gun nests, the New Army — the flower of a generation — advanced across the open downland to their deaths. Of the 120,000 attackers, 57,470 were casualties, including some 21,000 dead, most killed in the first hour of the attack. Only one in four officers who had gone over the top was unhurt at the end of the day — a casualty rate of 75 percent.

Despite the unprecedented barrage that began the Battle of the Somme, German machine gunners *had* survived in their deep dugouts, and much of the barbed wire in front of their positions had not been cut. High explosive was in short supply, and wire cutting with shrapnel was haphazard at best; it would become reliable only with the introduction of Fuse 106,* which exploded on impact, in combination with HE rounds. Worse, something like 30 percent of the British shells fired in the opening bombardment were duds.

Undeterred, British commanders ordered the attack to be renewed the following day, though on a smaller scale — and the day after. Only

---

*The correct nomenclature is Fuse, direct action, No. 106. Introduced early in 1917, Fuse 106 would be used to advantage in April at Vimy Ridge by Canadian gunners.

on the fourteenth did the British come tantalizingly close to achieving a breakthrough, and this came to naught when German reserves rushed to plug the hole. Thereafter, the Somme degenerated into another bloody meat grinder, an appalling battle of attrition in which the British, usually attacking uphill, were at an enormous disadvantage. Each yard of the strategically useless, shell-pocked moonscape cost far more in lives than it was worth. Anticipating they could do to the British what they were already doing to the French at Verdun, the Germans fought relentlessly. Each British attack met with a furious counterattack, often successful. In some sectors the British line pushed forward, but there were other places where it hardly budged. The hamlet of Thiepval, heavily fortified by the Germans and originally expected to fall on the first day of the battle, was finally taken on September 28. Some objectives, even when the battle ended on November 18, remained uncaptured, and the British were still four miles from Bapaume, which the cavalry expected to seize on July 1.

Sixty miles north of the Somme battlefields, things were quiet in the Ypres sector held by the Canadian Corps. In accordance with a Special Order, all batteries in the Corps area fired three salvos on the German front lines at noon sharp to celebrate Dominion Day. Recognizing this did not signify an attack, and preoccupied with developments to the south, German batteries hunkered down and remained silent. In the afternoon, all personnel who could be spared made their way to Ouderdom to enjoy various sporting events held under the auspices of the "Y."

In the 23rd Battery things were quiet, there being little real work for the howitzers. "The chief excitement," Jim McKeown noted, "was shooting up objectionable German trench mortars."

On July 14, Brigadier-General Morrison conducted a thorough inspection of the artillery brigades under his command. The following day he issued a memorandum to all brigade commanders, to be read out to a full parade of all personnel at the battery wagon lines and the ammunition column. Expressing his satisfaction with the general condition of the Wagon Lines, Morrison wrote: "In the majority of cases, the horses were in very good shape, the harness well attended to, the men as comfortable as circumstances would permit, and the general supervision showed care and intelligence." Morrison went on to stress the importance of proper care of personnel, horses, and equipment. "When the time comes to move, it may easily be found that the best shooting battery in the Division is least mobile."

The memorandum concluded with a paragraph that would have caused Bert to flush with pride. "Special commendation is due to the officers and men of the Divisional Ammunition Column for the good standard maintained in the Sections of that command. Under the new system of organization, the fighting efficiency of the Division depends to a large extent on the Divisional Ammunition Column, not only in the vital area of ammunition supply, but also in furnishing reinforcements in personnel and material for the firing line."

As July gave way to August, the British attacks at the Somme continued. South of Ypres, the Canadians spent the summer watching ... and waiting.

Hijinks at the Canadian Corps Horse Show, July 19, 1916. Drivers W. Scott and S. Werley amuse the crowd. *Courtesy of Library and Archives Canada, PA-000252.*

In the summer of 1916 the men of the Canadian Corps sported new cloth insignia at the top of both sleeves. All Second Division personnel, including the 2DAC, could be distinguished by a navy blue rectangle, measuring two inches by three inches; 1st Division men wore a red rectangle, Third Division, French grey.

On August 17, five valued artificers were removed from the 2DAC's ranks and sent to England for discharge. They were specialized tradesmen who had been recruited with the promise of working pay. When the government decided this additional pay was now not warranted, the conditions of their enlistment had been breached. Hundreds of men in the Corps who had received working pay as of December 31, 1914, then availed themselves of the opportunity to be discharged. Their skills would be sorely missed. "This seriously affected the smooth working of the Unit for some time," affirmed the 2DAC's historian, "as the class of artificers replacing them were noticeably inferior, especially in the case of shoeing-smiths." Two weeks later Brigadier-General Morrison described the division's replacement farriers and shoeing-smiths as "quite incompetent."

In the afternoon of August 25 the relief of the 2CDAC by the 4th Australian DAC began, and the Canadians handed over the new ammunition dump at Vlamertinghe. Cleanliness was always a concern for the Canadians. "All [wagon and horse] lines will be carefully cleaned and rubbish buried or placed in incinerators which will be left burning", the Relief Order directed.

Next day, in accordance with the detailed marching instructions and accompanying route map, the DAC (along with Jim McKeown and the 5th Brigade CFA) moved out of the lines and proceeded westward, back into French territory. Steady rains accompanied the column when it set out at 8:30 a.m., and the men marched with their helmets tilted low but by afternoon the sun came out and the men were dry on reaching Arneke. It was a long march, some 18 miles, and did not end until 5:30 p.m. Not surprisingly, the men were extremely tired, as this was "practically the first long march since arrival in France. Barns with lots of straw provided good accommodation." There was another reason for the slow march: the column brought with it a full echelon of ammunition, consisting of 6,311 artillery rounds, 1.8 million .303 rifle rounds, 10,840 pistol rounds, and 5,520 Mills bombs.*

A half-day's march — about 12 miles westward — the following day brought the DAC at 1:30 p.m. to its assigned area around the village of Ruminghem. Lying halfway between St. Omer and the English Channel, this sector had been allocated to Second Army for training purposes. Lieutenant-Colonel Harrison and the Headquarters Section were billeted in the château at Muncq Nieurlet, while the four sections secured billets near Ruminghem. It was pretty countryside, "slightly wooded with few hills and the people were very hospitable." All found it a welcome change from the Ypres Salient. As always, Bert purchased postcards along the route.

The column settled into a regimen of training, consisting of "harnessing and hooking in, route marching, map reading and signalling instruction." These were skills more suited to open warfare, for senior commanders never gave up hope of a breakthrough that would end the trench stalemate. It was also a time for kit reduction. As Bert explained, "Several General Service wagonloads of 'spare' blankets, gramophones and other accessories were returned to Ordnance, and most of the inhabitants of the village had been entrusted with some precious souvenir which would be called for at some future date." Not far from the 2nd DAC, the 5th Artillery Brigade was testing new techniques to camouflage gun positions. Netting, supported by poles, proved to be very successful: at 800 yards the position was undetectable.

Anticipating what was to come, Lieutenant-Colonel Harrison and 17 other 2nd and 3rd Division field artillery brigade commanders travelled on August 29 by motor bus to the town of Albert to inspect gun positions on the Somme battlefield.

Two events of note occurred on the last day of August.

In Montreal, Bert's nephew, George Kenneth Darling, the son of George and Flora —whom everyone called "Ken" to avoid confusion — enlisted as a gunner in the 66th Battery, then being formed. A mechanical engineer like his uncle, Ken was a few days past his

---

*The Mills bomb was a type of hand grenade.

twenty-third birthday. Learning later of the enlistment, Bert promised Flora and George to keep an eye out for him, once he arrived in France.

And, of greater importance, the commissions that Bert and Walter had sought for so long finally came through — both on the same day.

Extract from Divisional Ammunition Column Orders, August 31, 1916:

74. OFFICERS — STRENGTH — INCREASE

Lieut. Albert Elbridge Sargent, having been granted a temporary commission in the CFA Auth. AG's D/1900/551, MS to C-in-C No. 510/8399 and 2nd Army A/2079/49 dated 23.8.16, is taken on strength 31.8.16 (1st posting) and posted to No. 3 Sec. Auth. CRA 2nd Cdn. Div. No. C/1-95 dated 29.8.16.

A similar entry recorded the posting of Lieutenant Walter Gordon.

The two removed the three chevrons from their upper sleeves, trading them for the four stars (or "pips") of a lieutenant, worn on the shoulder straps. The Sam Browne belt and a decent uniform would have to wait. With their commissions came a pay increase — lieutenants made $2.00 a day and received a daily field allowance of 60 cents, along with a daily mess allowance of $1.00.

That evening, Lieutenant-Colonel Harrison recorded in the 2DAC's War Diary: "Lieut. A.E. Sargent and Lieut. W.H. Gordon, having been granted commissions, are taken on strength." It was the first time either had been mentioned by name in the War Diary of any unit.

It would not be the last.

17

"Hell to the Nth Power"

The first of September brought with it a Move Order to all units of the 2nd Canadian Division, in company with the 1st and 3rd Canadian Divisions. Though three entraining stations were given, for security reasons the 2nd Division's ultimate destination was not indicated. In the absence of hard facts, rumours were rife. In Jim McKeown's 23rd Battery, bets ranged from the Somme, to England, Egypt, and the south of France.

Detailed Operation Orders were drawn up and circulated to the artillery units. These specified entraining and detraining stations, departure times from billets, and departure times for 42 separate trains — all carefully planned to avoid congestion and confusion, and ensure that various units arrived at the right place and on time. In case anyone had ideas about deserting, Paragraph 12 of the Move Order specified: "Pickets must be provided at all stops for each end of the train to prevent troops leaving." Over the next days artillery units worked feverishly to repair their gear and prepare for a trip to … somewhere.

In accordance with Operation Order No. 12, the 2nd Division ammunition column began moving from its training areas at 5:39 a.m. on September 5. This time the column would move by rail — not always a pleasant prospect, for by now the men knew well the discomforts of a French boxcar, and the difficulty of loading horses and transport wagons. Broken down into small groups, the 2DAC was scattered among 18 trains. Bert's No. 3 Section made its way to St. Omer, one of three departure stations.

British field artillery pieces moving to the front by train. *Author's photo.*

Despite the complexity of the move, things went smoothly and all units of the column entrained in good order. As always, the trains followed indirect routes, and there were frequent halts. Seven hours after departure, the sub-sections of the 2DAC began detraining at three sites

A field artillery brigade on the move, early in the war. Note the gun and limber pulled by a six-horse team. *Author's photo.*

on separate rail lines. On arrival, the sub-sections had just an hour — working under the glare of arc lamps — to unload their horses and wagons and clear the railyard before the next train. Teams hooked in without delay and drivers fed and watered their horses, not knowing what lay ahead. Cooks handed the men a dixie of tea for nourishment.

Such moves highlight one of the ironies of the Great War. Although the immense armies of the day commanded unprecedented firepower and new weapons had virtually mechanized the process of killing, they relied on muscle power (either human or animal), much as the legions of Julius Caesar had done in the same part of France 20 centuries earlier. For most men, the only way from a railhead to the front lines was on foot.

Without maps, gunners of the 23rd Battery who detrained at Auxi-le-Château had no idea where they were. "As far as anyone could tell from the seemingly aimless wanderings of the train, [they] might be anywhere in Europe," observed McKeown. Arthur Jarvis of the Provost Corps accompanied the Second Division. "The country lies in a series of slopes with plateau-like tops and the farms seem badly cared-for and neglected. The roads, however, are excellent. As we proceeded the country became flat and monotonous. The several villages passed

British field artillery moving through a French town. *Author's photo.*

through indicate that we are in a very impoverished part of France. The houses are one-storey affairs of lath and much in need of repair, while the people stared at us in a listless, apathetic way, attempting no reply to the greetings called out to them by our men."

In the early morning of what developed into a fine autumn day, the sections of the 2DAC began marching toward their designated rendezvous, the small manufacturing town of St. Ouen, nine to twelve miles away, depending on each group's detraining station. Those dropped at Candas (including Bert's No. 3 Section) had the shortest march. By 8:00 p.m., most of the column had arrived at St. Ouen, where Headquarters and the four sections were billeted in a field south of town. Bert and Walter, as lieutenants, were given officers' billets in town, already crammed with Canadian troops.

The march resumed at 7:00 a.m. on the tenth, another in a string of gorgeous, sunny days. Their destination was the hamlet of Vadencourt, 16 miles to the southeast, which the head of the ammunition column

Canadians at the Brickfields, outside Albert, October 1916. The place was in poor condition when Bert and Walter arrived. *Courtesy of Library and Archives Canada, PA-000858.*

reached at 2:00 p.m. after passing through a succession of forgettable crossroads villages and hamlets. Though billeting parties had gone out in advance, Vadencourt was just too small to accommodate several thousand men. That night, recorded the 2DAC's history, "the whole of the Unit encamped in a field. No shelter was provided and the night was cold and overcast. This was somewhat evened up by a big Canadian mail arriving."

As they drew closer to the town of Albert, "it gradually dawned on the [23rd] Battery that the sustained roar in the distance was possibly caused by the noise of many guns being fired" and not thunderstorms, as some had imagined. As the 23rd marched through one village where the inhabitants were pleasantly surprised to find the Canadians spoke French, one gunner purchased a map and the men finally discovered where they were.

By late morning on the eleventh, after an eight-mile march, the column reached its destination, the so-called "Brickfields," south of the Aveluy-Bouzincourt road, outside of Albert. This was a barren section of chalky downland, prone to flooding when it rained. Here the column took over the space vacated by the Lahore Divisional Ammunition Column. The camp, which the 2DAC shared with the 4th, 5th, 6th, and 7th Brigades, was "in very dirty and unsanitary condition, manure and faeces not properly disposed of." This was a serious matter, for such conditions bred diseases that could cripple the effectiveness of the column and the field artillery brigades. The units soon set to making their surroundings habitable. Taking over dirty Wagon Lines or billets seemed to be the lot of the Canadians. In midsummer, a disgruntled William O'Brien had complained in his diary, "We are made to leave our places clean but we always step into dirty holes."

A hundred and fifty yards from the camp was the ammunition dump, which the 2DAC took over. It, too, had been neglected and required a great deal of work to get it into shape. The DAC history later recorded, "About the middle of September the Hun paid quite a lot of attention to the Bouzincourt-Albert road, also dropping a number of shells in our wagon line area and around the dump. One evening he obtained two direct hits on the ammunition dump — fortunately in the empty box pile." Lieutenant-Colonel Harrison ordered an ammunition inventory in the dump, along with what the column had brought in. The first issue of ammunition was made the same day to 2nd Division batteries, which had already assumed forward positions. As the Canadian infantry moved into place, gunners behind them feverishly prepared gun pits and dugouts.

Even as the column settled into "Brickfields," the wheels of British military justice were turning. On the twelfth, a Field General Court-Martial convened to try Gunner William Morrison, accused of contravening General Routine Order No. 1348.* His camera having been found on August 24, while the column was near Reninghelst, the 28-year-old gunner from rural Quebec had little option but to plead guilty. Morrison, described during the trial as "a splendid soldier and a most efficient man," claimed to have taken only photographs of his comrades and scenery. But that mattered little; the court-martial was more about maintaining discipline than anything else. A verdict was published the same day: four months imprisonment with hard labour. Undeterred by Morrison's sentence and knowing it could cost him his commission, Bert continued snapping pictures at the front for another year; by the summer of 1917 he was even taking shots of his superiors — who turned a blind eye.

Having secured their commissions, Bert and Walter promptly applied for transfer to a field artillery battery. Both men were well liked and respected and, from their activities with the Column, knew all the 2nd Division battery commanders.

In this late stage of the Somme campaign, the British brought two innovations to the battlefield.

Long past was the shell shortage of 1915, so that the first innovation (on August 16) was the "creeping" (or "rolling") barrage, in which attacking infantry followed about 100 yards behind a massed continuous shrapnel barrage directed at targets just ahead of the advancing troops. This concentrated fire created a pall of smoke and dirt,

---

*"No officer or soldier (or other person subject to military law) is permitted to be in possession of a camera, to take photographs, or to send photographs or film through the post."

obscuring the attack, and pinned down the defenders of a trench or strongpoint until the infantry were almost upon them. At set intervals, say, three minutes, the artillery would "lift" to a further objective, allowing the infantry to overcome the stunned defenders, and push on, following the moving curtain of fire. Though it required careful planning and synchronization between artillery and infantry, the rolling barrage became a standard fixture of almost all subsequent battles. Done well, it enabled the infantry to capture objectives with minimal losses. However, if the "lifts" were too slow, the falling shells could hit the attackers or hold up the advance. Done too fast, a gap could be opened between the barrage and the attacking troops, allowing the enemy to emerge from their positions after the barrage had passed by.

The second innovation was the tank, conceived as a way to cross trenches and crush barbed wire defences. Though slow and prone to breakdowns, the first tanks on the battlefield caused consternation and panic among the Germans. Tank tactics were in their infancy and, in the first attacks, the British used their tanks in small numbers and failed to concentrate them to create a decisive breakthrough.

The Canadian Corps — attached to General Hubert Gough's Reserve Army* — realized it was in for a tough fight. Recounted the historian of the 4th CFA Brigade, "Line after line of [German] trenches were constructed with long belts of barbed wire, innumerable communication trenches, redoubts, concealed machine-gun emplacements, and strong, deep dugouts. The nature of the country admirably adapted it for defensive warfare. The Hun made use of the chalk-pits, quarries and sunken roads, and turned ruined villages into veritable fortresses."

Infantry of the 2nd and 3rd Divisions, in conjunction with British units, moved up to their jumping-off positions. In preparation for the attack on the village of Courcelette, six miles northwest of Albert, the 2DAC hauled large quantities of ammunition forward to the guns, already registering targets and destroying key German positions.

Yellow mud, a mixture of chalky subsoil and thin brown topsoil, made ammunition delivery an arduous and dangerous task for men and animals. So churned up was the terrain and so thick the mud

---

*Later, the Fifth Army.

that horse carts could no longer be used to deliver shells. Instead, canvas carriers, each holding eight 18-pounder shells, were strapped to the horses' or mules' backs. "When loaded up," the 2DAC's history related, "the animals were led to the guns by paths or shell-plowed fields where no wagon could proceed. Several casualties to men and horses occurred, and at times the route was a veritable hell on earth."

After a three-day bombardment of enemy front lines and various strongpoints, the infantry attacked. The 2nd Division, assaulting at 6:20 a.m. on September 15, captured its first objectives in 30 minutes. The history of the 4th Brigade provides a vivid picture of what Canadian gunners experienced at Courcelette:

> A crescendo of sound rose and grew to a deafening, rushing roar as the whole front awakened to the sustained tumult of

A Canadian Mark 1 4.5-inch howitzer firing from a shell hole, September 9, 1916, at Sunken Wood, Battle of Flers-Courcelette. At this point the battlefield was still passable. Two months later it would degenerate into what one Canadian officer called "Hell to the *n*th power." Illustrated London News, *November 4, 1916.*

Gunners setting fuses at the Somme front. The Graphic, *August 5, 1916.*

"drum-fire." For miles to north and south, the front was aflame with gun flashes, the ground trembled at the concussions and plunging explosions of the newly devised rolling barrage.

Great geysers of earth continually spouted up, as the shells from the heavy guns and howitzers plunged in....

The gunners in their gun pits had become temporarily stone deaf, while blood oozed from their ears and noses. Orders were passed in writing, the noise was too terrific for words. Field gun batteries were firing four rounds per minute, ceasing fire for a few seconds to lift the range as the barrage crept forward in front of our Infantry.

"Unanimous praise is given to our artillery," enthused APM Arthur Jarvis. "Barrages timed and ranged to perfection and the success of the attack is greatly due to their wonderful work."

For the attacking infantry, conditions were atrocious. Colonel Thomas Tremblay, commanding the 22nd (French-Canadian)

Battalion wrote in his diary: "*Si l'enfer est aussi abominable que ce que j'ai vu, je ne souhaiterais pas à mon pire ennemi d'y aller.*"*

Seven tanks were allotted to the Canadians. Of these, five rolled into action, with four being knocked out by German shellfire. APM Jarvis observed: "A new and unique weapon of offense was introduced into the fighting for the first time on this memorable occasion — caterpillar forts armed with 6-pounders and MGs. These weird and uncanny machines, which can move through the deepest shell holes and trenches with astonishing ease, followed right on the heels of our advancing troops, and dealt effectively with isolated and dangerous enemy bombing posts and MG redoubts, which have proved such a costly menace to our men in all former engagements."

As always, the artillery plan was carefully scripted in advance. For the attack on the fifteenth, for example, while the 18-pounder batteries participated in the rolling barrage, Jim McKeown in the 23rd Battery received the following orders:

At Zero, the 21st, 22nd, and 23rd Howitzer Batteries will open on MOUQUET FARM for five minutes; rate of fire, one round per gun per minute, for five minutes, after which they will lift and walk up and down on the following trenches....

"We took a lot of prisoners," Royal Ewing of the 42nd Battalion recorded in a letter. "They were glad enough to give up. Never saw so many dead Huns before — the ground was strewn with them." Canadians had a high respect for the fighting qualities of their opponents. Walter Hyde, now a captain, wrote, "The old Hun is marvelously stubborn...." And it was Hyde who best described the fighting on the Somme in a memorable phrase: "It's Hell to the *n*th power all the time."

On September 16, Walter Gordon received orders to report the next day to the 5th Brigade for attachment to the 23rd Howitzer Battery. Two days later, after pulling some strings, Bert was attached to the 5th

---

*"If Hell is as bad as what I have seen, I would not wish my worst enemy to go there."

Brigade — also to the 23rd. It was a very good billet: members of the 23rd fervently believed theirs was "the best battery in the Corps."* It was a good fit for both men. They were familiar with the 4.5-inch howitzer from their days with the 6th Brigade's ammunition column, and they already knew many of the battery's officers. The 23rd's OC was British-born Captain Hamilton Geary, 31, who had served in the pre-war artillery. Joining the CEF in September 1914, and posted to the Howitzer Brigade a year later, he had brought the 23rd to France.

Commanding the 5th Brigade was Lieutenant-Colonel Russell Britton, 35, a native of Gananoque, who had been posted to the brigade on September 11 — his birthday — just four days prior to the attack on Courcelette. A manufacturer in civilian life, he had served eight years with the pre-war militia before enlisting. An avid sportsman, contemporaries held him in high esteem: "As a soldier he was keen, energetic and efficient, absolutely fearless and unswerving in his duty." Britton's command consisted of a Headquarters Section, three 18-pounder batteries (the 17th, 18th, and 20th) of four guns each, and one 4.5-inch howitzer battery, the 23rd, also equipped with four guns — in all, 729 horses and 845 men — on paper.**

For the first time, Bert and Walter were in an artillery unit that directly supported the infantry. The work was far different than bringing up supplies of ammunition to feed the hungry guns, and offered a particular sense of gratification when a hostile target was blasted to pieces by a well-aimed shell.

The Somme battles did not end with the capture of Courcelette, now a village in name only, having been reduced to heaps of ruins. Beyond were more formidable German defences, including the Zollern Trench, Hessian Trench, and Regina Trench, the latter being the longest constructed by the Germans on the Western Front.

---

*The 23rd Battery was attached to the 5th Brigade CFA in the May 1916 reorganization. Prior to that it had been part of the 6th Howitzer Brigade, where Bert and Walter had served in the ammunition column.
**Included in this total were the following attached personnel: Medical Officer (1); Veterinary Officer (1); Medical Corps men (5); Veterinary Corps sergeants (4); armament artificer (1); and batmen for VO (2).

When Bert reported to the 23rd Battery on September 19, all batteries of the brigade were firing in support of infantry advances against the Zollern Trench. While the infantry had by far the worst job, their advance could not have been achieved without the supporting artillery. "On three successive days the [23rd] Battery fired 1000 rounds per day into Zollern Trench, with direct observation from the [Pozières] Ridge, after which the infantry experienced no difficulty in taking the trench," McKeown noted with satisfaction.

The exchange of shells was not all one-sided. German gunners were experts in their craft and usually gave as good as they got. "Wagon Line vicinity shelled all night & early morning," recorded the 5th Brigade War Diary for the twentieth. And on the following day: "Hostile fire heavy in back country." When the Germans sent over lachrymatory shells in addition to the normal HE, Canadian gunners scrambled for their gas masks.

Elated that he and Walter were serving together, Bert's joy was short-lived. On September 22 the following from 2CDA arrived at 5th Brigade headquarters: PLEASE INSTRUCT LT W H GORDON TO REPORT TO THE 7TH BDE CFA FOR DUTY.

The same day, with Walter now gone, the 5th Brigade moved from the "Brickfields" to positions three miles northeast, near the ruined village of Contalmaison — a move made necessary because the advancing infantry were getting close to the maximum range of the guns that supported them. Once in their new positions, the gunners registered their weapons on prearranged targets, the results being checked by FOOs and aircraft spotters.

The 23rd Battery was tasked with "the obliteration of about three hundred yards of Zollern trench, for which task it was allotted 1000 rounds per day." The howitzers, with Bert in charge of one gun, got down to business. From one day to the next, the overall work of the brigade was repetitive. The War Diary reported "23rd firing on special targets" on September 25; "Barrage on Zollern Graben Trench & vicinity" (September 26); "Batteries busy wire cutting" (September 27). German batteries were equally active: "Vicinity of Battery positions shelled during day" (September 25); and, "Hostile fire fairly active all day" (September 26).

By the twenty-sixth, the Canadians, attacking to the right of other British divisions, secured Zollern, Hessian, and Kenora Trenches. In the next three days the line advanced another 800 yards. Determined to retake the ground yielded to the Canadians, the Germans counterattacked on September 29. With artillery support, it was successfully repulsed.

As September ebbed, the weather began to change. The fine, warm days of autumn in northwestern Europe gave way to rain and what would be the worst winter in memory. "Raining practically all day" recorded the 5th Brigade diarist for September 28, and the report for the following day was almost the same. It was a harbinger of things to come: October saw 14 days of rain, including an eight-day stretch from the twenty-third to the thirtieth. Under such conditions, the Somme battlefield, already churned up by tens of thousands of artillery shells, turned to a quagmire in which roads simply disappeared.

Supplying the batteries with ammunition became a serious problem, and moving a 3,010-pound 4.5-inch howitzer from one position

YMCA canteen in the firing zone, October 1916. *Courtesy of Library and Archives Canada, PA-000944.*

to another was nearly impossible. The mists hindered observation, with the result that German artillery could not be effectively dealt with by Canadian counter-battery units, and so became more active. With the rain, Bert wrote, "the battle changed from a clean-cut drive, in which only the resistance of the enemy had to be overcome, to a stubborn, sticky struggle against the combined forces of the elements and the enemy, of which the former provided the greater obstacles."

On October 1 at 3:15 p.m., in a heavy drizzle, the 2nd and 3rd Canadian Divisions attacked the next fortified line, Regina Trench, concealed behind a ridge and protected by thick belts of barbed wire. The 5th Brigade supported the attack by the Canadian Mounted Rifles by cutting wire and laying down barrages. Regina Trench changed hands several times during the course of the day, and the attack continued the following day in the rain. In the next days, both sides engaged in artillery duels. The Germans defended the trench with great vigour, and the first portions of Regina Trench would not be taken until October 21; its whole length would not fall until November 11, fully five weeks after the initial attacks.

11.10.16

First the usual acknowledgments. Since Oct. 2nd, letters from Alice, Mildred, and Lotta and two small (but *very* nice) boxes of fudge from Ede. Evidently this box was mailed from the office and the boy, not knowing what was in them, made a shrewd guess it was cigarettes and declared it as such. So, the box came "in bond" and took a little longer than was necessary.

I am indeed pleased to note the general satisfaction and admiration expressed on all sides for the prospective new addition [Rosalie] to our very worthy family.

Wednesday night

Was unable to go any further with this yesterday as I was alone at the old position and had too many interruptions.

In the meantime we have moved our gun further forward and tonight I am on duty. We have two guns out of action now and are in a rather crippled state but having only two guns to move simplified the operation considerably. One gun was put out of business completely the other day by a premature, the worst I have ever seen. It absolutely blew the gun to pieces and if I hadn't seen it myself, I would never have believed it possible. The shell evidently burst right in the bore, just as it left the chamber. About eighteen inches of the muzzle-end landed about forty yards in front of the pit; the breech was practically intact but the remainder of the piece was blown to atoms. Our howitzer, as you probably know, is a short, stubby piece; at the breech the steel is about three inches thick, tapering down to about an inch at the muzzle, and to see the way that steel was shattered gave me a pretty good idea of the power of our explosives.

This gun pit happened to be made of corrugated steel sections about 1/8-inch thick; the pieces went through that like paper and the roof of the pit looked like a sieve when it was all over. Luckily there was only one man in the pit at the time and the marvelous part of it was he was only wounded in about three places and none of the wounds appeared to be serious.

We are still hot on Fritz's trail and worrying him no end. He is putting up a h— of a stubborn fight here on our front. Since we have been here we have shoved him back for two big gains but he is holding his line pretty well.

It is quite a common thing to see prisoners being escorted back to the Corps "Cage" these days after a *strafe*, but saw one party the other day that sure made me laugh. We had pulled off a show at dawn that morning. About nine o'clock conditions were normal again. I had just shaved and was washing outside the dugout when three Huns came strolling down a little trench railway that ran past the Battery, hands in their pockets as though they were out for a constitutional and if their countenances expressed anything, it certainly was not sorrow. Behind them, strolling even more casually, was their escort, a little Canadian "Tommy" about four foot nothing and looked to be about eighteen years old, rifle slung, one hand in his pocket, smoking a cigarette and a broad grin on his face. We took quite

Canadian Artillery horses being watered, November 1916. *Courtesy of Library and Archives Canada, PA-000865.*

a few that day and I saw several other parties go by later. They were a scurvy-looking lot.

We have had a rather tough time of it down here. What with wet weather and frequent moves, we have got so we can put up with most anything now and be very comfortable (of course, there are a great many degrees of comfort).

Think I should call this a letter now and try to grab a little sleep. Will you ask Lena if she will please send me another statement of how my finances stand and just how much of my assigned pay she has received?

For gunners of the 5th Brigade, the days blended into a blur of mud, noise, confusion, and lack of sleep. They fired protective barrages to support local infantry advances, cut wire with shrapnel rounds,* engaged in counter-battery operations, and responded to SOS calls

---

*Wire cutting with HE rounds was usually avoided, as the resulting craters made the ground more difficult for the attacking infantry to traverse.

from the infantry to repel enemy counterattacks. As well, they poured retaliatory fire on German trenches, a sort of tit-for-tat for German shelling of Canadian trenches, and carried out special tasking orders against specific targets, most often nighttime repairs made by German working parties.

On October 17, Canadian Corps headquarters, along with the 1st, 2nd, and 3rd Divisions, marched out of the Somme and headed north, where they took over a quiet section of the line near Lens. Only the Canadian Divisional Artillery remained behind, joined a few days later by the 4th Division.

The next Canadian success came on October 21, with the capture of a portion of Regina Trench. It was a clear, cold day, and shell holes and puddles were rimmed with ice. The Canadian battalions reached their objectives in 15 minutes.

Recounted the War Diary of the 7th Brigade:

Our batteries bombarded Regina Trench at a slow rate of fire for two hours prior to the attack. At 12:06 PM all Batteries concentrated and increased their fire to two rounds per gun per minute. Barrage commenced 50 yards short of Regina Trench and lifted 100 yards a minute. 53rd Infantry Brigade followed closely behind barrage, without suffering any casualties from our fire and reached Regina Trench without the slightest trouble, where they found the enemy either very ready to surrender, or dead. Officers and men of 53rd [Infantry] Brigade said several times to our FOOs that they had gone forward under many barrages but that of the CFA was the most perfect they had yet experienced.

18

"Absolutely the Best Pal I Ever Had"

Walter Gordon, reattached to the 2DAC on October 22 from the 7th Brigade, joined the detail responsible for bringing up shells on the light railway (or "tram"), which the column had constructed some weeks before. As a result of the heavy rains, the line was in bad condition and was capable of moving only 100 shells an hour, a tiny fraction of the 5,000–8,000 shells the Divisional Artillery consumed each day. This duty lasted less than a week. On the twenty-sixth, the tramway was abandoned due to heavy mud and a lack of proper ballast. Thereafter, shells were taken to batteries by pack horse, each animal carrying eight 18-pounders in wicker baskets, or four 4.5-inch howitzer rounds in wooden boxes. It was slow, tedious work, but the shells went forward.

The next day, Walter was transferred yet again, this time to the 2nd Division's Trench Mortar Group.

At the front, conditions became more difficult as each day passsed. On the twenty-seventh, the ration of fresh meat and bread for the troops was cut to 75 percent preserved meat and biscuits, as it was nearly impossible to move hot food and supplies forward in any quantity. The 7th Brigade diarist painted a grim picture:

> The mud was frightful and guns were no sooner out of the pits when they sank into the mud up to their axles. It took all night

Hauling a field gun into position. Illustrated London News, *March 17, 1917.*

Bringing up 18-pounder shells at the Somme. Illustrated London News, *November 4, 1916.*

for batteries to get two guns per battery forward, but they did it.

> Batteries are now under very trying conditions; the guns are in the open with nothing over them, not more than 800 yards from the front lines, the men are living in the open without proper shelter and they are wet through. It is impossible to get any quantity of material through on account of the lack of roads. However we are moving forward, and on that account the men are happy and making the best of it.

By October 30, conditions at the front had gone from bad to very bad. Mules, better able to deal with the battlefield conditions, began replacing horses, so that by the end of the winter of 1916–17, nearly half of the artillery animals were mules. As a pack animal, the "moke" was unexcelled. "Ignorant and fearless of danger, he went through the thickest of shellfire, mud and water. If his master became lost, he could always be counted upon to find the way home."

Dugouts, swamped with water, began to cave in, threatening to bury the men inside. To make matters worse, in the zone allotted to the 5th Brigade, enemy artillery kept up a steady shelling all day on October 30, and into the night. Elsewhere, though, it was tranquil. "Hostile artillery was inactive," recorded the War Diary of the 7th Brigade. "Front was quieter than it ever has been since we came to the Somme."

Walter Gordon was behind the lines that same evening, some 12 miles northwest of where Bert was acting as FOO. Walking with Walter on that night full of rain, in the hamlet of Courcelles-au-Bois, were two fellow officers from the Trench Mortar Group.

Somewhere in the darkness across No Man's Land, a wet, mud-caked German gunner in *feldgrau* wiped the rain from his eyes. He'd probably never seen a Canadian soldier and, like most soldiers at the front, bore his opponents no ill will. The men across from him shared the same dangers and privations, and their courage and tenacity had earned his grudging respect. The team's loader rammed a shell into the breech, and the gunner snapped back to the present.

"Los!"

He yanked the firing lanyard. A dozen seconds later, a single, random shell burst in the main street of Courcelles in front of the three men, scattering a blizzard of jagged steel fragments. Perhaps, in the driving rain, Walter and his companions did not hear the scream of the incoming projectile until it was too late; perhaps there was nowhere to take cover. Perhaps it was just their time. The three Canadians were killed outright.

Walter was buried the next day at Courcelles-au-Bois Communal Cemetery Extension.

After several weeks in action, Bert finally managed to write home on November 18.

> Probably before you receive this letter you will have seen by the papers of Walter's death and will know what it has meant to me. He was absolutely the best pal I ever had and since leaving Montreal he has been a brother to me. He was killed about fifteen miles from where I am, was with the Trench Mortars at the time and had been with them only three days.
>
> I had some difficulty getting news of the affair so rode over there the day after and arrived just too late for the funeral.
>
> Walter was very popular over here and left a host of friends and I don't know anyone whose loss has been more generally regretted. It was indeed very tough as Walter had just made a start as an officer and was bound to make a name for himself. I have written his brother in Montreal but so far have not been able to write his mother and father. Will try to do so tomorrow.

As Bert anticipated, Walter's death was duly reported in Montreal's *Gazette*. Because of his past association with the newspaper, there was a half-column obituary on November 6, headed LIEUT. W.H. GORDON KILLED IN ACTION. "Word that Lieut. Walter H. Gordon had been killed in action will be learned with regret by a large circle of friends...."

Three days later, Bert's sister wrote to Dr. Alvah Gordon in Montreal:

CFA Christmas card, 1916. In the aftermath of the Somme, "Remembrance" was a common theme. Members of the artillery could even have personalized cards with their names preprinted inside. *Author's photo.*

So deep is the grief in my heart over your brother's death that I trust you will not deem a word from a stranger an intrusion at a time of national sorrow and sacrifice.

My dear brother, Albert Sargent, loved Walter as cleanly as one could love another. I know what this will mean to him, for in almost every letter to us he has mentioned Walter, and deplored the fact that after their commissions were conferred they were really separated for the first time since leaving home.

I should like Walter Gordon's mother to know how very deeply the sisters and brothers of Bert Sargent feel for her in the great sorrow which has come to you all.

Flora Darling

Bert also wrote to Alvah Gordon and, weeks later, received the following reply. It is the only surviving letter of the hundreds Bert received while overseas.

January 1, 1917

Dear Bert,

It is some time since your letter came telling all about poor Walter. I sent it on to our father and mother and then to another of Walter's friends, and now that I have a little time, I must try to answer it.

Needless to say that it is impossible for any of us to thank you enough for all you did and what you told us of the details which, so far, are the only ones we have received.

I had been half-expecting some word from his OC or perhaps some other information from Ottawa to amplify what the first telegram contained but so far none has come.

Ever since he had crossed to France we had always looked with some anxiety to the casualty lists but, as weeks and months passed on, and nothing happened, I am afraid that we got rather to feel that everything was going to be all right and he was going to return safe and sound.

I got the telegram on the 5th of Nov. on a Sunday morning before I was up and it struck me like something that was meant for someone else and, even yet, it is very hard to get over the feeling that there has been a mistake and he is all right still.

I can imagine that you, who will have seen so many whom you knew taken off, will have a greater notion of the reality of their deaths than we who do not see these things close at hand.

I have simply been inundated with letters from those who were his friends and I wonder how any man could have had so many real friends — but knowing him from a baby as I did, it isn't any mystery.

He was 11 years younger, and it was my business to look after him when he was a little kid. I took him to school and home, and looked after him generally, and later when our people moved up here, he fell into my hands again as he was growing up and I never knew any boy in or out of the family who was all-round as straight and decent and likable as he. In a way I fathered him till he went across and to have him picked off, and not to return — well, it's tough. Every letter we had from him mentioned you in some way or other and it seems you were one of the family.

We were fortunate enough to get through his newspaper affiliations the name of the town and cemetery where he was buried and, if this war ever ends or perhaps sooner if I am elected to be sent over myself, that will be my first pilgrimage.

My mother and father have borne up wonderfully, though as you can imagine, it was a greater blow to them than to any of us. They are now with me for a time, at least.

I am sure it would be a great source of happiness to receive any little personal belongings which would serve them as reminders, though I don't imagine that they will ever need such reminder. I have not yet made any enquiries at Ottawa as I know these things always take a long time.

Several enlargements of Walter's pictures have been made and when you return there will be one ready for you — I have one in front of me as I write, and it is a most excellent likeness.

This is New Year's night and though it is rather an irony, I wish you a Happy New Year. I do wish it shall be as happy as possible, and that sometime in this year the war may end and you may come back safe and sound to get the credit you deserve for doing what you have done.

Again, accept my and our most sincere thanks and remember that what I can express is only a small part of what I feel.

Most sincerely yours,

A.H. Gordon

19

"We Made the Usual Success of It"

The campaign sputtered into November, losing momentum with each day. Rain continued to fall, and the weather turned increasingly colder. Sleepless days blended into sleepless nights, for the artillery was always on call. By day, the fall of shells could be observed by the FOOs; at night, gunners fired on previously registered targets. Bert's 23rd Battery continued its usual work as the Canadians prepared for yet another assault on Regina Trench. On November 1 it engaged in an artillery duel with hostile batteries near Miraumont, following a wireless call from a British spotter aircraft. The next days were given to wire cutting and registering barrages. FOOs and signallers in the OPs were "sitting practically on top of their targets. The guns were located in positions varying from 600 yards to 200 yards behind, and the FOO was often 100 yards, or less, from the wire at which he was shooting."

As always, German gunners were active, their fire directed by observers in captive balloons and aircraft. On November 3, they scored a direct hit on an 18-pounder in the 18th Battery, putting it out of action and killing four men. The same night they began dropping shells into the 5th Brigade Headquarters at Pozières, necessitating a hasty withdrawal.

At midnight on November 10/11, Canadian infantry stormed Regina Trench and, as dawn broke with thick fog, they controlled its whole length. Ten days of wire cutting had reduced the once-forbidding obstacle to "a shallow ditch, twenty feet wide, littered with debris and corpses." In its assigned sector the 23rd had contributed to the Canadian success, bombarding a section of the German lines for 10 minutes at midnight.

Not content with Regina Trench, General Gough wanted to push on. There was no let-up for the tired gunners of the 5th Brigade, who spent the next days cutting wire and bombarding enemy trenches. The final assault took place at 6:10 a.m. on November 18, when the 4th Canadian Division stormed the next German position, Desire Trench, 500 yards ahead. In blowing snow on a frontage of 2,200 yards, four attacking battalions, supported by the 1st, 2nd, and 3rd Canadian Divisional Artilleries, reached their objectives with ease. One battalion, the 87th, broke completely through the German lines and surged forward — until it ran into its own barrage and was forced to withdraw.

NOTHING is to be written on this side except the date and signature of the sender. Sentences not required may be erased. If anything else is added the post card will be destroyed.

I am quite well.

I have been admitted into hospital.

{ sick } and am going on well.
{ wounded } and hope to be discharged soon.

I am being sent down to the base.

I have received your { letter dated_____
{ telegram „ _____
{ parcel „

Letter follows at first opportunity.

I have received no letter from you

{ lately.
{ for a long time.

Signature }
only.   }

Date_____

[Postage must be prepaid on any letter or post card addressed to the sender of this card.]

(M2658) Wt. W3197-293 2,000m. 9/16 J. J. K. & Co., Ltd.

Field Service Postcard or "Whizz-Bang," sent by the millions by soldiers from the front. *Author's photo.*

Bert found a few moments in the OP to scribble a letter on sheets of squared paper, torn from a service notebook.

18-11-16

Am writing this while on duty up front and I haven't my diary with me. I am unable to tell off-hand just how many letters I have to acknowledge. Will leave that until the end and attend to it when I get back to the Battery in the morning.

I know it has been a very long time since I last wrote, probably longer than any time since I have been in France. However I have sent several "Whizz-Bangs"* so you will know I have been OK.

There has been a reason for my not writing; haven't written anyone, in fact, as I just haven't been able to.

That box of candy reached me in splendid condition some days ago. It certainly was by far the best yet and will stand a repeat at any time. Don't know when I have enjoyed a box more than that one and the other boys seemed to enjoy it just as much as I did.

I am as far from getting any leave as I ever was and I have absolutely no idea when I will be over there. By tomorrow I will have been in France just ten months and am ready for a few days off any time now.

Although we are still on the same part of the front, I don't think we will be here much longer as it has been a hard spell and we are all badly in need of a change. Winter has set in now and we can look for a lot of dirty weather from now until May.

Received two more batches of NY papers from Lotta. Very glad to get them indeed. The pictorial part is most amusing. The pictures supposed to be taken here at the front are so ridiculous and unreliable, but suppose they are fully credited and accepted by anyone who has [not] been out here.

Will close now and do a little work.

---

*Field Service Postcards, bearing various standard short messages that could be crossed off by the sender.

Nov. 19

We put on another very successful little show here yesterday morning, the account of which you will no doubt have read before this reaches you. It was mostly a Canadian show and we made the usual success of it.

While the infantry rested, the 5th Brigade continued its daily exchange of fire with German batteries. Finally, on November 25, the brigade began handing over its sector to British units, a process completed the following day. "Never," Bert recorded, "was there a relief so absolute in every sense of the word." Under normal circumstances, the Canadians would take their guns with them. So badly torn up was the ground that the guns of the 20th and 23rd Batteries were left in position, and these two batteries took over the weapons of the incoming units.

Fittingly, on the twenty-seventh, the heavy morning mist burned off to a fine day as all units of the brigade assembled at the Wagon Lines in preparation for a move. Even at the Wagon Lines the liquid mud varied from four to 14 inches in depth; cleaning horses, harness, and vehicles was largely a waste of time. At the Wagon Lines, Lieutenant-Colonel Britton went around to each of his four batteries to satisfy himself things were in good order for the upcoming march, and to congratulate his men on a job well done. And, at each battery, he read the following message from Brigadier-General Morrison, written the previous day:

At noon today the 2nd Canadian Divisional Artillery handed over its sector of the front to the 51st Divisional Artillery, after being in action exactly 11 weeks on the Somme battlefield.

During that time, in addition to the routine night and day bombardments which have characterized this great battle, the Division has participated in seven special operations of the first class, any one of which in ordinary times would have ranked as a battle of considerable magnitude.

Throughout this arduous period of service every Unit of the Division has done its duty admirably, and the Division as a whole has earned the special commendation of the General Officer Commanding Fifth Army. On no occasion within my knowledge did an officer, non-commissioned officer or man fail in his duty, the result being uniformly satisfactory service during the participation of the Division in one of the greatest battles in history.

I am proud to have commanded such an Artillery Division, and have been especially pleased to note the cheerfulness and buoyant spirits with which all ranks have faced the ordinary dangers of the battlefield, and the even more trying hardships imposed by weather conditions.

There was no hiding the fact the Somme had been a bloodbath for Britain. Since July 1, the country had lost more than 419,000 men, the cream of the New Army, all to advance the front line no more than six miles. For the British, as John Keegan claimed, "it was and would remain their greatest military tragedy of the twentieth century, indeed of their national military history." It was little better for the Germans; determined to yield as little ground as possible, the Somme cost them more than 465,000 men. In 12 weeks of fighting, the Canadians suffered over 24,000 casualties, roughly 31 percent of those engaged. In the Canadian infantry, one soldier in two became a casualty — a staggering rate of loss for such minor achievements.

In London, David Lloyd George, who became prime minister on December 8, recognized the quality of the men from the Dominion. "The Canadians," he recalled in *War Memoirs*, "played a part of such distinction that thenceforward they were marked out as storm troops, and for the remainder of the War they were brought along to head the assault in one great battle after another. Whenever the Germans found the Canadian Corps coming into the line, they prepared for the worst."

Summing up the experiences of the 23rd Battery, Jim McKeown observed, "The difficulties and hardships met with and overcome in the Somme battle went a long way towards preparing the Battery for anything and everything that might be met with in the future."

The next day, beginning at 6:20 a.m., the 5th Brigade began the long trek to winter quarters in the First Army area. Wading through

Guerre 1914-1916

80 — ALBERT (Somme) - Basilique de N.-D. de Brebières (côté Est)
Après plusieurs bombardements par les Allemands.
The Basilica after several bombardments.

The famous "Leaning Virgin," atop the tower of the Basilica at Albert, familiar to every Canadian soldier who came to the Somme. Dislodged by a bombardment in January 1915, the statue was secured in place by British and French engineers. German guns finally toppled her on April 16, 1918. *Courtesy of Madeleine Claudi.*

thick mud, the 23rd finally reached the Albert-Bapaume road, where the going was slightly easier. Passing through Albert, the main British staging point for the Somme battlefields and empty of civilians, the men stared for the last time at the shell-battered spire of the Basilica of Notre-Dame-de-Brebières, whose famous golden statue of the Virgin hung head down, held in place by ropes. No one regretted leaving. "If horses have sufficient brain power, even they must have hoped to never see again this section of the world," Bert wrote. Behind them lay one of the most devastated regions on the planet. "Many small towns," noted Hal, "are merely sites, with a few odd bits of brick wall, or a few tattered roofs showing where the town used to be. Sometimes a few black holes at the roadside showed where the cellars were, but more complete destruction would be hard to imagine."

Gradually, the sound of gunfire became fainter and finally disappeared. Once past the range of enemy guns, the settlements were undamaged and fields were unscarred by trenches and shell craters. Owing to a bulge in the German line south of Arras, the gunners could not march directly back to their winter quarters but were obliged to follow a roundabout route. The first bivouac was at Amplier, little more than a few farmhouses at a crossroads. The brigade covered just over 14 miles "without mishap and in good order," even though the roads were wet and full of holes. Resuming the next morning at 10:30, it passed through the industrial town of Doullens, then swung northward. When the morning mist burned off, the day turned into a fine one for marching. Passing through Bouquemaison, the brigade swung northeast to Frévent and thence to Ligny-sur-Canche, where they arrived at 5:00 p.m. Weeks of activity at the Somme had hardened men and horses; again, the march of 12 miles was accomplished without problems.

In the next two days, the brigade covered another 20 miles, finding "good billets and horse lines" at Ruitz, in the coal-mining district of Bruay, where conical slag heaps and pithead winding towers dominated the landscape. Brigade headquarters was at Aix-Noulette, four miles west of German-held Lens, while the Wagon Lines were located at Hersin. Relief of the Lahore Divisional Artillery began the following day. As usual, this was accomplished over two days, with one section of each battery being relieved each day. "'Luxurious' is the only word which accurately describes the position into which the Battery came into action after its march from the Somme," McKeown wrote in amazement, "with a peace-time front, model gun pits in which to work and comfortable living quarters." It was as close to paradise as one could come at the front. The winter of 1916–17 was the coldest in Europe since 1880–81; the comfortable billets were much appreciated by the brigade in the next months.

Off in the distance was the rising bulk of Vimy Ridge, an escarpment more than four miles long, running from northwest to southeast. With its highest point some 475 feet above sea level, it dominated the Douai Plain. Held by the Germans since the first week of October 1914, the ridge had since been heavily fortified, becoming the strongest point in the entire German defensive system on the Western Front. The French attempted to recapture it on three separate occasions, December

1914, May 1915, and September 1915 — all without success. To the Canadians, at least for the moment, it was just another feature of the local landscape.

The gunners settled into a familiar pattern, learning the local landmarks and registering their weapons on selected points of tactical importance. FOOs soon got to know every foot of the terrain in front of them. Any changes — a new belt of German wire or an overnight trench extension, for example — were noted at once and added to the day's list of designated targets.

The Germans opposite the 5th Brigade were not in a bellicose mood. "Hostile shelling practically nil," the War Diary noted on December 6; similar entries followed on subsequent days. The 18th Battery history commented, "As far as we were concerned the war might have terminated." This tranquil state did not long prevail, as Bert explained. "As usual in quiet sectors taken over by the Canadians it was not allowed to remain so for long. Raids and destructive shoots were organized and successfully carried out, and harassing fire employed to the best advantage."

All batteries in the brigade began a general cleanup and refurbishing of equipment. "Vehicles were repainted, guns overhauled and harness and equipment restored to their usual good condition." Leave also started to open up, an important consideration for men who, for the most part, had been on active duty at the front for almost a year with scarcely a respite. A message came through from the 2CDA staff on December 4 that ten days' leave would be granted to qualifying officers and ORs. Twenty ORs and two officers per week were granted leave.

On December 15, Bert celebrated his twenty-ninth birthday, his first in France. Then, in the week before Christmas, his leave papers came through. Making hasty arrangements, on December 20 he got himself on the daily leave bus from the town major's office in Hersin at 4:00 p.m. The bus dropped him at the station, where he caught the Calais train and took a steamer to England.

Each leave train pulling into Victoria Station was greeted by female volunteers dispensing hospitality to the soldiers. "Right beside the train were large booths with tea, piles of sandwiches and cake," related

Noel Chipman. "We helped ourselves and passed into London." From the station's telegraph office, Bert sent a cable to Canada, letting the family know he was safe, then rode the Underground to the east end, where Rosalie and her parents were expecting him.

Bert had been writing steadily to Rosalie, even if only "Whizz-Bangs" to indicate he was still alive. Their growing respect and feelings for each other had stood up well to a separation of almost 12 months. For Rosalie, Bert's safe return was the answer to a daily prayer; what happened to Walter could as easily happen to her Bert.

Like any officer arriving in London after a period of frontline service, Bert took advantage of the opportunity to purchase various items of kit, which would be useful on his return to France. And, with his promotion and the rigours of the Somme, he obtained a new tailored uniform.

Sometime during this period of leave, he took in a performance of *Theodore & Co.*, a two-act musical at the Gaiety Theatre. It had

Returning to France: a typical scene at London's Victoria Station. *Author's photo.*

The cast at the finale of *Theodore & Co.*, which Bert saw in London while on leave, December 1916. *Author's photo.*

opened three months earlier to decent reviews and would run for 503 performances, in part due to a score composed by Ivor Novello and American-born Jerome Kern. The play was typical theatrical fare for the period and offered the laughs a wartime audience desperately needed.

While Bert enjoyed Christmas dinner with the Jameses' at Browning Road, the work of the 5th Brigade went on. "Flares and machine guns normal during night," the War Diary noted, "18th & 19th Batteries cut a gap in wire assisted by 23rd How Battery. Considerable damage done to trench as well."

On learning that his nephew, Ken Darling, had arrived in England and was then in training camp, Bert spent an evening of his leave at Witley Camp in Surrey, an hour from Waterloo Station. The camp was singularly unattractive, a sprawl of wooden huts on Witley Common, erected in great haste after the outbreak of war.

All too soon it was time for Bert to return to France. We can only imagine the sweet sadness of parting as Bert boarded the train at Victoria on New Year's Day, the first leg of the tedious trip back to France to rejoin the battery.

20

Prelude to Vimy

In northern France, the weather was normal, which is to say it was often misty and rainy, and made life generally miserable for frontline infantry. When Bert returned on January 2, a heavy mist had prevailed all day so that German artillery remained quiet. The New Year, though, had been welcomed in style, with all guns of the 5th Brigade firing three rounds rapid fire at midnight.

In Bert's absence the front had not changed. Over the next days he slipped easily into the accustomed routine, as the 23rd Battery continued to silence enemy trench mortars and 77 mm* field guns. A heavy snow, the second of the year, fell on January 17, while the 23rd engaged in counter-battery work, its guns thudding away for most of the day. Finding a quiet moment, Bert tore seven sheets of squared paper from his service notebook and began to write.

> Again the same old story! The time has gone before I realized it. We have been very busy, it's true, and I have had a lot of 24-hour duty to perform which rather interferes with one's "home" life, but I have managed to do a lot of letter writing — only it has been unfortunately directed elsewhere. That is, unfortunately for you people, as I hope the others appreciated it.

---

*The 77 mm was the standard German field gun during the war. The Model 1896 had a range of 9,186 yards; the Model 1916, at 11,700 yards, outranged the British 18-pounder by almost 2,000 yards.

This front which was once so quiet and peaceful has developed into a regular "bear" and there is now a real war on most of the time. Funny thing, but it has absolutely borne out my prophecy when we came here first. We heard then how quiet it was and what an easy time the others had in artillery activity, and the infantry held an inquest over every man that was killed or wounded, etc.! I said "Just wait until the Canadians have been in there two or three weeks and see how quiet it will be!"

The [howitzer] battery we relieved expended six loads of ammunition during the five weeks they were here. We are now using an average of four loads a day and some days eight! You can draw your own conclusions. We have made Fritz just about double the strength of his artillery opposite us and we have him in that nervous state where he doesn't know just where he is at.

There are about eight inches of snow on the ground today, nice dry snow too, so we feel very much at home, although I must admit OP duties are not quite the most pleasant under these conditions.

Was so pleased to hear from Lena's letters of Dec. 27 that my cable from London reached you on Xmas Eve. I knew there was quite a break between my letters before that and am very sorry you should have had that anxiety for nothing. I am afraid I haven't yet realized just how much my letters do mean to you all over there, but I will try to write more regularly, even if I do have to make some of them very short.

When we are busy, though the days are so much alike and pass so quickly, the time does slip by before one is aware of it. I positively find it hard to realize now that I actually have been to England. I haven't had a chance to think much of it since the few days I had there went so quickly it was all over before I knew it.

Expect to see Ken [Darling] out here very shortly now, probably the end of the month. Was sorry to see so little of him in England but I knew then he would be over soon, so will get around to see him as soon as I hear he is in the country. I don't expect he will be more than ten miles from us.

Lena's letter was one of the best! It was so good to get all the Xmas news of the family and if I hadn't been fortunate enough to have been in London for Xmas it might have made me quite homesick.

I will take Lena at her word and offer suggestions on the last parcel. Candy, cake, Meadow Sweet cheese, raisins, dates, etc. are a *real* treat. Condensed milk, coffee, etc. we can get here. I have a good stock of cigarettes now but a small box of cigars would be about the one best bet. Have taken to smoking cigars now, in fact, whenever the opportunity offers, so some real Canadians would sure be a treat!

Have had two or three bundles of NY papers, which I enjoy very much. *The Outing* and *Story Teller* from Auntie Stevens, *Beth Norwell* from Charles; *Literary Digest* from Grover and *Everybody* from Lena. I am really *very* glad to get these for, although I have not had much time to read the last week or so, the other boys have and I hope to have [in] the next few days.

Will say good night now and leave the remainder for another time.

Loading up with snow-covered shells at a dump. Illustrated London News, *February 3, 1917.*

Things did not slacken off in Bert's sector. On January 20, Lieutenant-Colonel Britton organized a "shoot" for all batteries to keep the Germans on their toes. Fifteen hundred shells slammed into enemy front lines, support trenches, and other targets; the War Diary claimed "much damage was observed." A day later, tasked with hitting a house thought to be a German OP, the 23rd scored six direct hits. Three days later, British observation aircraft called in a number of artillery targets. These were soon dealt with and the 23rd, its FOO having spotted movement, shelled a cookhouse and a crossroads behind German lines.

That evening, half of the 5th Brigade was relieved by the 3rd Brigade CFA — from the 1st Canadian Division — and the relief was completed on the twenty-fifth. As usual, the guns were not exchanged. The 5th Brigade hauled its 18-pounders and 4.5-inch howitzers from their pits, limbered up, and moved out with a full echelon of ammunition. All maps, photos, defensive schemes, and codebooks were handed over to the incoming batteries.

Lieutenant-Colonel Britton led his brigade to a training and rest area on the twenty-sixth. Leaving Hersin at 9:45 a.m. on a clear, bright day, the batteries passed through Barlin, a fair-sized coal-mining town. Heading northwest, the brigade passed through Haillicourt and Divion, ending the 11-mile trek shortly before noon at Camblain-Châtelain ("more familiarly known," Bert noted, "even by the inhabitants, as 'Charlie Chaplin'"). Four more souvenir postcards from villages along the way found their way into Bert's pack. The afternoon was spent searching for billets for the brigade.

The next day, Saturday, was clear and bright, and the morning was devoted to foot drill for gunners and an exercise ride for drivers. Only in the afternoon did the men get a half-holiday. A Church Parade was held next morning at 10:45, with the men again having the afternoon off. Monday, another cold, clear day, was given over to training. In the evening, new orders arrived, calling for a further move, this time to rest billets in the village of Amettes, five miles northwest. A two-hour march the following morning over icy, slippery roads brought the brigade to its destination.

Over the next days the batteries engaged in various training activities, most related to mobile warfare, accompanied by lectures by officers on a variety of topics. The drills and lecture topics were familiar subjects after nearly a year in the field, but they ensured that skills did not become rusty and new men learned the basics as rapidly as possible. And, should the stalemate of the trenches be broken, the brigade would be ready to play its part in a war of movement.

2-2-17

I don't seem to be improving any, do I? Fifteen days between letters isn't good enough. I have had two letters from Flo, one from Lena and one from Charles. Also a grand box of cigars from the firm. "Scotty" (Capt. Duguid, our OC)* and I are the only ones who use cigars, but we sure did make up for the others. The box of 50 was gone in eight days. Of course, we did have a few visitors during that time, but I must admit I wasn't very liberal to outsiders. These were real cigars and I was afraid they wouldn't appreciate them. The parcels are also very much appreciated and I hope will continue at intervals. Wonder if there is a book of sorts on its way over here, for I have read all we have here and am looking for something new.

Had my first game of bridge in almost two years the night before last and was very much surprised to find I hadn't forgotten the game. Scotty and I won out, cleaning up the fabulous sum of six francs. Play quite a lot of cribbage these days with [Lieut. George] Havers, an English chap from Vancouver. He plays a fair game but I find that I am usually declared the winner.

We are having a long spell of very cold weather (for this country). The ground has been covered with snow for almost three weeks now and the thermometer has varied from about 7° to 28° during that time. Just now the days are clear and crisp and bright moonlight nights.

As we are in a part of the country where we can appreciate these things, we don't care how long it lasts, except it is very hard on the horses. The roads are covered with ice and

---

*Born in Aberdeen in 1887, Archer Duguid was a 1912 McGill science graduate (engineering). Another of the original 8th Howitzer Brigade members, posted as a lieutenant to the 23rd Battery, he took over the 23rd Battery in December 1916 after Major Geary was invalided to England.

snow and they are not sharp-shod; you can imagine the fun they have. We moved the Battery about 2 miles the other day under these conditions. Had a d— of a time doing it, but came through without any serious trouble.

We have a very comfortable billet now in a little village, very quiet and peaceful. It is in a school, or at least there is a school attached. We are living in the "home" or whatever they call it. There are about ten or fifteen Sisters here and it does seem funny to run across them at odd times in the hall or upstairs. They certainly are doing their best for us. They have given us a large room downstairs for our mess (it has a piano and an open fire) and three bedrooms upstairs. Also our servants sleep in the school and have the use of their kitchen to do our cooking. We certainly are making the most of it and expect a comfortable time of it here for a couple of weeks.

We are very busy from 7 AM to 5 PM but have our evenings to ourselves and hope to rest up quite a bit.

Had a splendid letter from Dr. Gordon some days ago. I have often intended writing him again since I first wrote but never got around to it. Will try to do so, now that I have a little more time.

Brigade boxing championships took place February 5, once the day's lectures were completed, and a gunner from Bert's 23rd Battery, Frederick Lansdowne, qualified for the divisional finals. In parallel, the 17th Battery defeated the eighteenth to capture the brigade soccer championship on the tenth. Of the two weeks at Amettes, McKeown remembered the time "was spent in playing football and burnishing steel and head-chains."

Orders for a return to the line having come through on February 12, the brigade prepared to move on the fifteenth and sixteenth, with half-sections from each battery moving on each day. This time they'd be marching light; ammunition was left at the Wagon Lines and handed over to the incoming units. On the fifteenth, beginning at 6:30 a.m., the designated half-sections began the 16-mile trek to wagon lines at Camblain l'Abbé, where they relieved the 9th Brigade CFA. Brigade headquarters were at Mont St. Eloi, where, atop the summit of the hill, stood two ruined towers of an abbey whose roots went back to the tenth century.

The new positions taken up by the 5th Brigade were in front of Vimy Ridge, and rumours soon began to circulate among the Canadians who were gradually assembling in the area. In time, as light railways were built and access tunnels dug, the rumours became a certainty. The Canadian Corps, then holding a nine-mile segment of the front from Ecurie to Bully-Grenay, would attack along the whole length of the ridge, in conjunction with a larger operation by Third Army, to the south. Tactically important because of its elevation, capturing the ridge would give the British a commanding position over the Douai Plain and the mining town of Lens.

On the British (west) side of the escarpment, the land sloped gently upward to the ridge's highest point, designated Hill 145 from its elevation. Wide belts of barbed wire protected line after line of deep German trenches and well-constructed dugouts. Behind the German front lines, on the ridge's east side, there was an abrupt drop to the surrounding Douai Plain. German field guns were emplaced just beyond the crest of the ridge and amid the ruins of shattered villages.

The 5th Brigade headquarters at Mont St. Eloi proved to be in bad shape. Worse, the 9th Brigade handed over virtually no maps of the sector and provided no information of practical use. Despite this, the batteries, on assuming their positions, began at once to register their guns. And, as the gun pits were in a poor state, all ranks worked steadily over the next few days to improve them. New tasks for the brigade soon came down from above: it was to construct 54 gun pits for batteries, which would come up at the last minute in the forthcoming attack. Each pit was to be furnished with 1,000 rounds of ammunition. In all, it was a considerable task, requiring the brigade to haul 850 tons of ammunition in addition to material to construct the new pits. Ruined buildings in the area provided an abundance of construction material. For its part, the 23rd was to select, build, and ammunition three pits. Working steadily, the brigade completed the new pits on March 5.

Naturally, the normal tasks of the brigade went on — normal firing, supporting minor raids and retaliatory shelling on German positions. As one would expect, German batteries in the Vimy sector were also very active. "Our OPs shelled by enemy," the War Diary reported on March 2. With snow falling at intervals on March 8, an alert 5th Brigade FOO observed six men going into a haystack behind the German lines and assumed it was an enemy OP. The coordinates were then relayed to the 23rd Battery, which promptly destroyed it.

When the new gun pits and dumped ammunition were turned over to the First Division artillery on March 12, the batteries of the 5th Brigade moved to their battle positions and began to strengthen their gun pits. The 23rd's howitzers were dug into exposed positions around La Targette on the Béthune-Arras road, about 4,200 yards from the German lines. Soon the battery was pumping more than 1,000 rounds a day at selected targets.

German shelling of the backcountry and enemy aircraft were common in the weeks leading up to the Canadian attack. "Hostile aeroplanes on three occasions during afternoon flew over Battle Positions at altitude of less than 500 feet. Boche temporarily has mastery of air on this front owing to slowness and difficulty of handling our machines," the 5th Brigade War Diary groused on March 24. It was a short-lived complaint. In what the RFC later termed "Bloody April" (from the number of its pilots shot down by Albatros fighters), British planes managed to keep German aircraft away from the front lines, where evidence of a pending attack grew more obvious each day.

At this time (March 17) the Canadian artillery underwent a final reorganization, with batteries being increased from four guns to six, a number of units being broken up to accomplish this.* Lieutenant-Colonel Britton's 5th Brigade was left intact, and sections from other batteries were added to bring it up to the new strength. The 5th then consisted of three six-gun 18-pounder batteries (the 17th, 18th, and 20th) and one six-gun 4.5-inch howitzer battery, the 23rd.

---

*The Canadian Field Artillery then consisted of nine brigades of six-gun batteries, in all, 216 guns. The Lahore Divisional Artillery, supporting the 4th Division, contributed another 52 guns.
1st CDA — 1st, 2nd, and 3rd Brigades
2nd CDA — 4th, 5th, and 6th Brigades
3rd CDA — 8th, 9th, and 10th Brigades.

Added to the 23rd was one section from the 83rd Battery, just out from England. Still commanding the 23rd was Captain Scotty Duguid, Bert's bridge partner. Five days later, Duguid was posted to the 2nd CDA headquarters as brigade major. His place as OC 23rd Battery was taken by Captain Roy Muirhead, a Montrealer from the 21st Battery. Jim McKeown was the senior of six lieutenants, each in charge of a gun; Bert was second in seniority.

The artillery plan for the Vimy attack was divided into four phases. Phase I (Z minus 20 [March 20] to Z minus 7 [April 2]) and Phase II (Z minus 6 to Zero Day) comprised the preliminary bombardment, with a gradual buildup to destroy trenches, strongpoints, barbed wire, and enemy batteries. Phase III dealt with the bombardment on the morning of the attack itself, with batteries providing either rolling or standing barrages. Phase IV called for the field guns to move forward across the ridge to take up positions to support further infantry advances and defend against expected German counterattacks.

Officers designated as FOOs or liaison officers were ordered to "spend as much time forward as possible so they may become thoroughly familiar with [the] entire Group Zone while [the] Front is quiet." Taking his shifts in the OP over the next days, Bert gained a detailed perspective of the sector allocated to the 23rd Battery. Later, he provided reports on German wire, pinpointing machine-gun nests and suspected OPs.

In the last week of March, wire cutting by 18-pounders continued, while the howitzers were tasked to destroy selected German trenches. For this, two rounds per yard of trench were allocated. The War Diary recorded: "23rd How Battery continued in destruction of Balloon Trench, 395 BX* fired." Next day, the 23rd dropped 200 rounds of BX on the Grenadier Graben and Fritter Trench with "good effect." There was a purpose to all of this. At a conference at Corps headquarters on March 30, it was noted, "By harassing the enemy now in every possible way, he will be half-beaten before the infantry attack." The gunners also sought to locate and silence German batteries that might, when

---

*A shorthand notation for 4.5-inch HE shells; B denoted 4.5-inch shrapnel, while A and AX denoted 18-pounder shrapnel and HE respectively.

Pack horses of the 2DAC carrying 18-pounders to the 20th Battery, Neuville St. Vaast, April 1917. *Courtesy of Library and Archives Canada, PA-001231.*

the assault began, halt the infantry in their tracks. "Our planes located active batteries and duel kept up by our batteries all afternoon," noted the March 31 War Diary.

As the last days before the attack ticked away, the pace quickened. While 18-pounders chopped lanes through the German wire, the 23rd's howitzers continued to destroy communication trenches. On April 1 alone it dropped 250 rounds of BX on Dump Avenue, 150 on Fritter Trench, 75 on Balloon Avenue, and 85 on Grenadier Graben. These received more of the same the following day, 625 rounds in all. Observed from the Canadian front lines, the German trenches soon showed the effects of heavy shelling. "Hun trenches on 5th Brigade Zone badly knocked about," reported the War Diary on April 6.

Ammunition stores at each gun continued to increase in anticipation of the attack. Lieutenant-General Julian Byng, commanding the Canadian Corps,* had determined that victory would be purchased

---

*Byng had taken command of the Corps on May 28, 1916.

with shells and not with the lives of men. Orders for 5th Brigade specified that howitzers were to use *not less* than 150 rounds per gun per day: 120 for trench destruction, 10 to prevent repairs, and 20 for

OFFICIAL PHOTOGRAPH SHOWING BRITISH ADVANCE IN THE WEST. Taken by permission of the C.-in-C. of the B.E.F.

Supplied by The Sport & General Press Agency, Ltd.   **CAPTURED GERMAN TRENCHES.**   Crown copyright reserved
45, Essex Street, Strand, London.   Barbed wire destroyed by shell fire.

The scattered remnants of once-formidable German barbed wire defences destroyed by field artillery prior to a British attack. *Author's photo.*

Canadian gunners with 18-pounder shells, presents for Fritz. *Author's photo.*

harassing fire. It was a welcome change from the 1915 shell shortage, when Canadian gunners were rationed to no more than three rounds per day. In practical terms, it meant more than 70 tons of ammunition were being hauled each day to the 5th Brigade alone. As Bert wrote, "By the time Zero Day arrived, horses and men alike were thoroughly played out."

On April 3, Zero minus 6, Phase II began. Artillery fire would gradually increase from Z-6 to Z-3. Thereafter, there would be "no marked increase of intensity in order that no indication be given to the enemy as to the moment when the assault will be launched." All batteries of the 5th Brigade were firing day and night. The 23rd sent 950 rounds of BX onto a variety of targets: Grenadier Graben (*again!*), and Frog, Fusty, and Fudge Trenches. Roads and approaches were kept under fire all night to prevent reliefs and working parties from coming up. Later, the same targets would receive fire both day and night. With evident pride, the War Diary noted on April 4, "Group never ceases fire during 24 hours." Sleep, for gunners and infantry units taking up their assault positions, was a scarce commodity.

Across the Atlantic on April 6, the United States declared war on Imperial Germany. Though it was an important psychological boost for the Allies, a year would pass before significant numbers of Americans were at the front.

At Vimy, the Germans were catching hell, as the following entries from the 5th Brigade War Diary make clear:

April 7, 1917. Brigade again concentrated on making an absolutely safe job of wire in German Front Line Trench. Further 1800 A, 1600 AX, 175 BX were expended. Excellent results observed by our FOOs who now report that small remains of wire would offer no obstacle to infantry.

Feint Barrage by all Artillery of Cdn. Corps Front.

During afternoon, Contact Plane flew over German Trenches at altitude of 200 feet, covered by barrage of 2nd CDA on Thélus Trench to keep down MG fire. Our planes again have mastery of the air, though a good many being brought down.

Night firing continues during hours of darkness, covering wire and approaches.

April 8, 1917. Zero minus 1 day. Steady harassing fire kept up day and night. All wire kept open by 18 pdrs. Finishing touches put on trench demolition by 23rd How Battery, concentrating on Furze Trench during afternoon. Concentrated bombardment of Thélus by all artillery Cdn. Corps.

Ninety-plus years later, the heavily shelled landscape has not recovered. Overlapping shell craters bear witness to the intense bombardment and the thoroughness of the Canadian gunners in this section. The piles of rusted dud shells, stacked like cordwood by French farmers at the margins of their fields (the so-called "iron harvest"), illustrate the high percentage of shells that failed to explode — between one-third and one-quarter of all shells fired. They are still lethal, and almost every year civilians in France and Belgium are killed or maimed by shells of the Great War.*

On April 8, the 5th Brigade War Diary summarized the activities of the previous two weeks:

From Zero minus 13 to Zero Day the Group fired 45,320 rounds 18-pr. and 11,003 rounds 4.5 How, a further 18,000 rounds being expended to cover the assault on Zero Day, and reserve of some 12,000 kept in hand for counterattacks. This was all hauled by our own horses from Dumps in vicinity of Grand Servins and Camblain l'Abbé. At the same time teams were bringing up material to make pits strong enough to keep guns in action. This long haul of 9 miles each way was very hard on horseflesh and, despite greatest attention, all horses lost condition and many died.

---

*Some experts reckon that as many as 30 million unexploded British shells and gas cylinders are still buried near the former front lines. In April 2001, Vimy and several surrounding villages were evacuated when mustard gas began leaking from shells that had been gathered for destruction.

A few hours before the attack, Bert was appointed liaison officer to the 26th (New Brunswick) Infantry Battalion. Attacking in the middle of the Canadian line, the 26th was to seize a section of the Zwischen Stellung, the first objective. In all, just four officers of the 5th Brigade were appointed as LOs to the attacking infantry. In his operational order, Lieutenant-Colonel Britton stressed the importance of the liaison officers. "The whole success of the entire operation may depend," he wrote, "on the efficiency with which the duties of these several officers are discharged." Accompanied by two telephonists who would pay out separate cables as they advanced behind the infantry, Bert was to post himself in the best position to get information back to the brigade. If the 26th's attack were held up, he would call down artillery on points of German resistance. Should the phone wires be cut, LOs were to use "runners and all and any means of communication to get messages back." Thus the telephonists also carried flags and an electric Lucas signalling lamp to relay messages. LOs were permitted to carry only their identity discs. "Badges, letters, etc. must be removed," Britton ordered. "If taken prisoner, it is only necessary that you give your name and number. No other information is to be given."

As fighter pilot Billy Bishop went to bed that night, "the British guns were roaring all along the far-reaching battle line. The whole horizon was lighted with their flashes, like the play of heat lightning on a sultry summer evening."

21

The Battle of Vimy Ridge

No Canadian battle of the Great War has been more written about than the storming of Vimy Ridge on Easter Monday, April 9 — and for good reason. Attacking for the first time with four divisions simultaneously, the Canadian Corps captured the ridge in four days, a feat of arms justly hailed at the time as an important victory and one that added to the laurels of the Corps. Here was born Canada's sense of nationhood, for this was an all-Canadian victory. But the price of nationhood came high; of the 40,000 Canadians who participated in the four-day attack, 3,598 were killed and 7,004 wounded. By the distorted calculus of the Great War, and in comparison to the Somme (and its paltry gains), Vimy was a significant achievement.

The attack was characterized by meticulous planning and attention to detail, along with greatly improved wire cutting (compared to the Somme), increased numbers of tanks, massive logistical support, and careful coordination between all branches of service. Common sense also prevailed: no longer were attacking soldiers so burdened with equipment they could hardly stand upright.

In many respects Vimy Ridge was a near-perfect set-piece artillery battle. Brigadier-General Andrew McNaughton's counter-battery work was especially effective. Using a variety of techniques — flash-spotting, aerial observation, and sound ranging — more than 80 percent of the 212 enemy guns facing the Canadians were identified and silenced. Days of bombardment successfully cut the German wire on the frontage of 7,000 yards and collapsed the trenches prior to the actual infantry advance.*

When they left the front lines, the infantry followed behind a faultlessly executed barrage, moving at 100 yards every three minutes. In many cases the attackers encountered only feeble opposition so that all the first objectives were captured in a few hours, thus supporting General Henri Pétain's assertion that "Artillery now conquers a position and infantry occupies it." The gunners had deceived the Germans as to the timing of the attack. Normally, an intensified bombardment heralded the final hours before an attack. This time the Canadian gunners kept up a steady fire, giving no clue as to when the attack would be launched.

Crown Prince Rupprecht of Bavaria, commanding the Germans in the Vimy sector, committed an additional error by keeping his reserves too far to the rear. With the Canadians shelling the roads, these men could not be brought up in time to help repel the attack.

Communications techniques had improved significantly compared to the Somme. Wireless sets were employed extensively for the first time, supplementing conventional methods like buzzers, homing pigeons, visual signalling, and contact aircraft.

Even the weather helped. With blowing snow and sleet in their faces, many Germans could not see the attacking Canadians until it was too late.

Vimy Ridge was merely one part of a major British offensive, with 18 divisions attacking along a front of 12 miles on both sides of the River Scarpe, in what would later be called the Battle of Arras. In the north, General Henry Horne's First Army (which included the Canadian Corps on the left of the line) had the shorter front, but this included Vimy Ridge. To the south, 14 divisions of Third Army under General Edmund Allenby attacked on a wider front centred on Arras. All along the line, except in the south, the British attacks met with initial success, though it ended, as did most offensives, in a renewed stalemate.

---

*More than half a million rounds of all calibres were fired by Canadian gunners in the eight days prior to the Vimy attack, and a further 212,000 on April 9.

Against the broad canvas of Vimy Ridge in the early hours of April 9, we return to Bert Sargent, attached to the 26th Battalion. In the hours before the attack, Bert and two signallers reported to the battalion's OC, Lieutenant-Colonel Archibald McKenzie, who at 4:00 a.m. was with his men in the jumping-off trench. His battalion would attack on a front just 350 yards wide. Its objective, the German forward defences (Zwischen Stellung), designated by Canadian planners as the Black Line, lay about a half-mile ahead and were held by the 263rd Reserve Infantry Regiment. As the men hunkered down to wait for Zero Hour, the weather worsened. Rain, changing to snow, lashed the men. Underfoot, chalky mud turned to glue.

Huddled in the same trenches were Nova Scotians of the 25th Battalion and their liaison officer, also from the 5th Brigade, Lieutenant Claude Purchas. The 25th would follow in the footsteps of the 26th and, once the New Brunswick battalion had secured its objective on the Black Line, would leapfrog through and continue the attack.

"Four seconds before Zero, all the guns except the trench mortars ceased abruptly. The silence was deafening." Then, at exactly 5:30 a.m., "the artillery seemed to open at precisely the same moment and fell like a curtain in front of us. The whole battalion moved forward...."

Overhead in a single-seat Nieuport-17, Billy Bishop had a unique view of the attack:

The waves of attacking infantry as they came out of their trenches and trudged forward behind the curtain of shells laid down by the artillery, were an amazing sight. These troops had been drilled to move forward at a given pace. They had been timed over and over again in marching a certain distance, and from this timing the "creeping," or rolling barrage which moved in front of them had been mathematically worked out.

The First Division's Canon Frederick Scott also had a front-row seat:

With crisp, sharp reports the iron throats of a battery nearby crashed forth their message of death to the Germans, and from three thousand guns at that moment the tempest of death swept through the air. It was a wonderful sound. The swish of shells through the air was continuous, and far over on the German trenches I saw bursts of flame and smoke in a long continuous line, and, above the smoke, the white, red and green lights, which were the SOS signals from the terrified enemy.

The three-minute barrage lifted from the German front line, and the New Brunswickers overran it a minute later. Shifting to the Support Line, the artillery hammered this for eight minutes, after which it, too, was seized. Then, following a series of artillery lifts of 100 yards every three minutes, the 26th advanced across the Ridge behind the rolling barrage. Of the German resistance, Purchas observed, "All that can be said is that he had no fight left in him, even with machine guns. Only on the Zwischen Stellung (where 2 MGs were encountered and held out for a short time) was there any attempt at defence. As to their artillery, they were either too busy moving or had no observers, for their attempt to check our advance was nothing but a farce." Douglas Murdoch, a lieutenant in the 26th Battalion, described the attack to his sister: "The previous bombardment had been so heavy that our men did not know their objective when they got to it and went a little further than was expected. However, they got there and are going to continue in the same direction which, I am glad to say, points towards Berlin."

Troops advancing on Vimy Ridge. *Courtesy of Library and Archives Canada, PA-001087.*

At Zero+33 minutes, precisely on schedule, three white Very Lights arced into the air, indicating the 26th had reached and occupied its objective. The numerous Germans on the Black Line, demoralized by the artillery, surrendered readily. Mopping-up parties then dealt with any Germans in the intermediate trenches, which had been

Artist's impression of a liaison officer going over the top with the attacking troops. Note the boxed field telephone carried by the officer; the two signallers with him carry reels of telephone cable, which they pay out as the advance goes forward, and a spare boxed telephone. The officer's walking stick is a fanciful touch; Bert certainly did not carry one at Vimy Ridge. Illustrated London News, *January 13, 1917.*

overlooked in the headlong rush. While the above paragraphs make it all seem easy, the 26th paid a steep price for its advance: 26 officers and men killed, 102 wounded, and 41 missing.

To Bert's left and right, all along the Canadian line, other battalions enjoyed similar success. Not all LOs from the 5th Brigade were as lucky as Bert and Claude Purchas. Lieutenant Albert Bright of the 18th Battery was killed by a sniper early in the attack.

As the 26th dug in on the Zwischen Stellung against a German counterattack (which never materialized), Bert remained with them, calling down artillery fire as necessary while Purchas and the Nova Scotians pressed onward.

All across the Ridge the wave of khaki-clad Canadians swept on, brushing aside pockets of German resistance, occupying the third objective, the Blue Line. By nightfall all the eastern heights — the Brown Line — had been seized and the Canadians were dug in over the crest. Infantry officers, as Purchas noted, "were delighted with the artillery work and amazed at the thoroughness of the trench destruction." APM Arthur Jarvis claimed that the bombardment "surpassed in intensity anything the Hun had ever previously experienced."

Bert's bridge partner, Scotty Duguid, described one memorable incident:

In the midst of the assault, a chance phenomenon astonished the combatants. At half past ten a sudden blaze of sunlight split the dark curtain of snow clouds and disclosed endless waves of Canadians, some advancing steadily over the Ridge north and south of Thélus, while others worked methodically on the construction of positions and prepared to meet a counterattack in force. Thus for a fleeting moment was revealed the final issue of the day: the Germans saw that the Ridge was lost, the Canadians knew that it was won.

For the 5th Brigade, much remained to be done. As Bert explained, "Many targets of opportunity, disclosed by forward observing officers, were taken on and effectively dealt with. Attempts by the enemy to pull guns out of action were frustrated, transport disorganized, reinforcements dispersed, and counterattacks were broken up."

Later, American staff officers were given tours of the British and Canadian lines as part of their introduction to trench warfare. Royal Ewing, a friend of Hal's, told of an American officer being shown around Vimy Ridge. "Didn't say a word all day and his conductor was rather fed up with his silence. However, just as they were finishing up, he said, 'Well, I guess if our fellows had seen this they wouldn't have come in.'"

On April 12 the last pockets of resistance atop Vimy Ridge were over-run by the Canadians. Even before this, beginning on April 9, men and guns had moved forward all along the Ridge, taking up positions to the east and below the heights they had just conquered. Moving forward was no easy task. The weather continued unseasonably cold, with snow and rain. Then the snow melted and the churned-up battle-field became practically impassable. Horses of the 18th Battery, after many hard efforts to wade through with the 18-pounders, "quietly laid down and died." "Broken limbers, guns, dead horses and mules, barbed wire and ammunition were piled up in an endless tangle," wrote Hal Fetherstonhaugh's brother, one of the engineers busily

Canadian Field Artillery bringing up the guns, Vimy Ridge. *Courtesy of Library and Archives Canada, PA-001073.*

constructing plank roads and light rail lines by which guns and ammunition could be moved forward. In the *Official Record*, Bert observed, "The impossibility of hauling artillery and supplies across that long strip of enemy front line area which had been thoroughly torn up by a month's incessant bombardment had not been foreseen and no provision had been made to bridge or repair this gap."

Somehow it was done.

The 5th Brigade established OPs on the forward slope of Vimy Ridge, and by the fifteenth, as the War Diary reported, "much useful information [was] sent in," including the location of hostile batteries. Though these targets were beyond the range of the Brigade's howitzers and 18-pounders, the coordinates were relayed to the long-range guns for destruction.

During the battle, the 5th Brigade captured several German guns amid the ruins of the village of Farbus, along with cached ammunition. Under Jim McKeown's leadership, the 23rd Battery soon put a pair of 5.9-inch howitzers to good use, turning them around and then

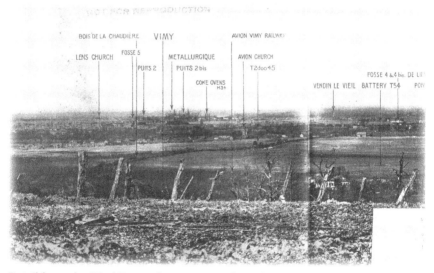

Detail from the 23rd Battery's panorama photo (No. P-109) overlooking Lens and the Douai Plain, taken April 10, 1917, immediately following the capture of Vimy Ridge. Key reference points are indicated for the gunners. Against instructions to hand the panorama over to relieving troops, Bert kept it as a souvenir. *Courtesy of Madeleine Claudi.*

Men of the 17th Battery firing a captured German 4.2-inch howitzer at Vimy Ridge. *Courtesy of Royal Montreal Regiment Museum.*

"proceeded to give the Hun a hot time in Méricourt and Acheville." Inexcusably, the Germans had failed to disable their weapons before abandoning them. McKeown's sub-section continued to man the 5.9s, firing with good effect. Ammunition was plentiful and, in three days, the two guns returned more than 400 rounds to their former owners. "The crowning achievement of the crew was the bringing down of the Méricourt church spire by a direct hit," McKeown related. This was an important target, for the Germans used the steeple as an OP, calling fire onto the Canadians spreading out on the plain below the Ridge. Having abandoned the two 5.9s, the Germans knew their precise locations and, on April 17, succeeded in knocking both of them out of action, wounding two men.

Apart from McKeown's group, the guns of the 5th Brigade were doing practically no firing. The Germans had established a new defensive line east of Vimy Ridge, stretching from Méricourt in the north to Oppy in the south.* This line was just beyond the range of Canadian

---

*Later termed the Drocourt-Quéant Line, the Germans would hold this position until October 1918.

18-pounders near Thélus and, even as late as the seventeenth, the artillery was still held up by impassable roads. In the meantime, Canadian gunners began to reconnoitre new positions on the plain east of the Lens-Arras railway line, and a few days later work began on new gun pits for the howitzers and 18-pounders.

By May 1, all guns were in their new positions and Lieutenant-Colonel Britton shifted his Brigade headquarters from Thélus to a dugout in the embankment of the Arras-Lens railway, near Vimy station. The embankment, the only obvious shelter in the area, soon became a target for enemy gunners. The Germans were determined to pay back the Canadians for the loss of Vimy Ridge, and the artillery batteries, in their new and highly exposed positions, bore the brunt of enemy anger. Batteries were heavily shelled for three days in a row. On May 2, a direct hit by a 5.9-inch shell on the headquarters dugout instantly killed Lieutenant-Colonel Britton, along with Major Alvin Ripley, the 20th Battery's OC. Britton's death was a heavy blow to the

Empty shell casings line the road near Vimy Ridge, May 1917, awaiting salvage. *Courtesy of Library and Archives Canada, PA-001349.*

brigade; fellow officers regarded him as "a born leader, beloved and respected by all who knew him."

The following day, 33-year-old Lieutenant-Colonel Charles Constantine assumed command of the brigade. A former gunnery instructor at the Royal School of Artillery at Kingston, Constantine had gone overseas as brigade major for the First Contingent. Later given command of the 7th Battery, he was subsequently appointed brigade major to the newly constituted 2nd Divisional Artillery. In December 1915, when Constantine (then a major) served as brigade major for 2nd CDA, Brigadier-General Drake had praised Constantine for the valuable assistance rendered at Larkhill and stated he had "an exceptionally good knowledge of artillery work." Junior officers found in their new OC "a soldier whose qualities of leadership, soundness and good judgment they strove to develop in themselves." And, though known as a strict disciplinarian, "his knowledge of men, his appreciation of their work and understanding of their difficulties, won from all ranks of those under him their sincere respect and regard." Lieutenant-Colonel Constantine was a commander who led by example. "In battle no one worked harder or longer. He shared with his men all their dangers and work and was always with them." Constantine was also a keen athlete, once regarded as one of the best rugby and hockey players in Canada.

The 5th Brigade was fortunate: their new commander's knowledge of artillery and leadership qualities would turn it into one of the finest artillery units in the Canadian Corps.

Enemy gunners gave Lieuteant-Colonel Constantine a hot welcome. The 5th Brigade's gun pits provided little cover from aerial and ground observation, and "Battery positions heavily shelled" was a recurring comment in the War Diary for the first two weeks of May. As McKeown acknowledged, "No one will forget the heavy shelling sustained in this position, especially with gas shell." Resupplying the exposed batteries could be done only at night. "Ammunition and other supplies," Bert wrote, "which had to be brought up by pack animals, became extremely difficult and costly to maintain, and night after night the area was drenched in gas and rendered almost uninhabitable." German gunners proved unusually adept at locating and

destroying the Canadian field guns, which made their lives miserable. In one four-week period the 1st CFA Brigade, operating in the
same zone as the 5th, had 13 howitzers and 18-pounders destroyed
by counter-battery fire. That Lieutenant-Colonel Constantine's 5th
Brigade did not suffer similar losses was more luck than anything else.

In the third week of May, as lilacs blossomed, the 23rd Battery
advanced half a mile past the railway into the hamlet of Willerval.
This, too, was an exposed position and the howitzers came under frequent heavy shelling. Relieved on May 29 by the 6th CFA Brigade,
the 23rd turned over its howitzers in their positions and took up new
positions two and a half miles to the rear on the Ridge itself, near the
ruined village of Thélus. "Front quiet" reported the War Diary on May
31 as all batteries settled into their new gun pits. The war, it seemed,
had moved elsewhere. As, indeed, it had. Field Marshal Haig's attention was now focused on a new campaign to the north, intended to
break out of the Ypres Salient.

"Quiet" was a relative term on the Western Front. In the 5th
Brigade's sector both sides continued their shelling, with the Germans
even using a 28 cm naval gun, directed by aircraft or balloon observers. Mounted on a railway flatcar, its high velocity and long-range
capability meant it could shell the British lines with impunity.

First Army Commander General Henry Horne, a former artillery officer, knew that improved training for officers and NCOs meant better
gunnery. Thus in mid-1916 he established an Artillery School at Rue
des Tanneurs in the historic town of Aire-sur-la-Lys, 10 miles southeast of St. Omer. According to its printed syllabus, the program was
intended for young officers and NCOs of and above the rank of corporal in the Field, Heavy, and Siege Artillery branches. There were
three objectives:

- train the above in the duties of their respective ranks;
- remedy faults brought about by prolonged trench warfare; and
- revive smartness and smart discipline.

Courses lasted 21 days; class size was limited to 60 officers and

60 NCOs. The syllabus for each course varied slightly, reflecting the latest tactical thinking and conditions then prevailing at the front.

With relative calm on the Vimy front, Lieutenant-Colonel Constantine arranged to send Bert to the Fifth Course at Aire. His departure was noted in the 5th Brigade Routine Orders for Sunday, June 3:

Lieut. A.E. Sargent D/23d Batty 5th Brigade proceeded to First Army Artillery School 3-6-17.

Bert's selection was an honour. For the Fifth Course, just two officers and two NCOs were selected from the whole 2nd Canadian Divisional Artillery. It was also overdue recognition for his work in the 10 months since he'd been commissioned. Only three officers from the 5th Brigade had been selected previously (of whom two were engineers), and only one further officer from the 5th Brigade would attend in the future.

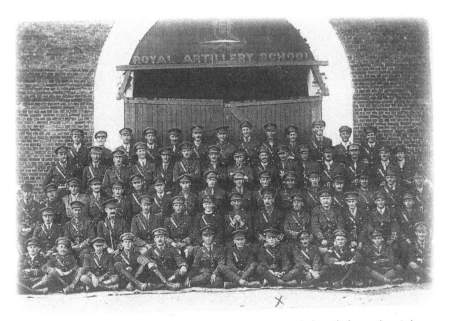

Royal Artillery School, Aire-sur-la-Lys, June 1917. Bert is fourth from the right, top row. *Courtesy of Madeleine Claudi.*

Lieutenant Sargent, astride one of his favourite horses. Undated, but likely summer 1917; the horse is probably "Flirt." *Courtesy of Madeleine Claudi.*

10-6-17

These last two weeks have gone by very quickly and if it hadn't been for letters reaching me tonight from Charles and Alice, I don't think I would have realized it was time for me to write again.

I am away from the Battery just now; left a week ago today to take a course at the First Army Artillery School. It is the first course I have ever had since I have been in the game, and I can tell you I appreciate it. Ever since I received my commission I have tried to get one of these courses, but I am rather glad now I didn't get it before, as this is absolutely the ideal time to get back here in the country. I really think the course is designed as much for a rest and refresher as for the instruction. The colonel told me before I left that he was sending me down here for a rest and now I believe him.

I will give you one of our daily schedules and let you judge for yourselves:

7:45 to 8:30 AM	Physical "jerks"
9:00 AM	Breakfast
9:30	CO's Parade
9:30 to 12:00	Gun Drill, Laying, Director Work, Equipment, Harness Fitting, Ranging, Riding, etc.

Of course, we never get more than three of these during a morning. By mixing them up, we get quite a bit of variety.

1:00 PM	Lunch
2:00 to 3:00	Map Reading, Driving Drill, or Lectures in Gunnery, Ammunition, etc. (one subject each day).
3:00 to 3:30	Buzzer work (Morse)
4:15	Afternoon tea
5:00 to 6:00	Lecture
7:30	Dinner

There is a large open-air swimming pool in the town, as well as three nice tea rooms, and a couple [of] good restaurants, so we are always able to fill in our spare hours to advantage. The mess is also a very good one and, as there are about 60 officers here on the course, one from nearly every Artillery unit in the First Army, we manage to have quite a gay time.

The country around here is simply beautiful — rolling country, fairly well wooded, generously sprinkled with villages, and canals and waterways cutting through it in all directions. The canals are invariably lined on both sides by tall trees and always a beautifully kept road running along one side.

As soon as I arrived here and had a look over the country, I wrote right back to the Battery for my horses, and Nick* just

---

*Though Bert never mentions his full name, this is Gunner 89165 Ronald Nicholson. Born in Scotland in 1885, Nicholson resided in Ottawa and was a steamfitter by trade. He first served with Bert in the 8th Howitzer Brigade at Shorncliffe in September 1915 and was posted to the 5th Brigade in June 1916.

arrived tonight at 5:30 with them. He had over 40 miles to travel, made the trip in 10 hours and neither of them turned a hair.

I have two mares now. My big one, "Flirt," is a beautiful beast; she was supposed to be "crazy" when I first took her over. She has plenty of life and [is] an interesting horse to ride. The other one I have only had about three months; she has all kinds of speed and is some jumper. I haven't tried her over the high ones yet but I'll bet she will clear six feet before I am through with her.

I expect to be here until the end of the month and will try to write again before long.

During his absence, Bert did not miss much at the front, though there was one new development of note. In a foretaste of things to come, German aircraft dropped eleven bombs near the railway embankment on June 5.

Driver Frank Hazlewood, 19, newly posted to the 23rd Battery's B-Subsection from the 2DAC, found June a dull month. "Nothing exciting has been happening to us lately," he wrote, "just the usual

Captain Robert Pearson of the YMCA umpiring a softball match behind the lines, September 1917. *Courtesy of Library and Archives Canada, PA-001921.*

daily routine: clean harnesses, graze, groom and water horses." As the weather warmed, he was pleased to find "a tank of lime juice at our disposal every day and, believe me, it is refreshing." Entertainment troupes provided welcome distraction for the 23rd Battery. As Hazlewood noted, "The YMCA have a big tent not far from our Horse Lines. There was a minstrel show a couple of nights ago and it was good."

The 23rd Battery received a new commander during Bert's stay at Aire. This was Captain Alex Paterson, a former Montreal banker, taking over from Major Muirhead. Paterson, a lieutenant in the pre-war militia, joined the 2nd Brigade on the outbreak of war. By June 1917, he was one of the few remaining "originals" of that brigade when he assumed command of the 23rd on June 8. Muirhead remained in the brigade and took over the 17th Battery, equipped with 18-pounders.

While Bert was at Aire, the baseball season got underway. "Our battery baseball team has been cleaning things up in the [2nd] Division," Hazlewood related. Bert returned to the battery on June 30 in a spell of bad weather. "It has been doing nothing but rain for the past week and it is rather disagreeable," Hazlewood noted. "The night before last it just came down in torrents and we were nearly flooded out. A little bit of thunder and lightning mingled with a bombardment which was in progress made things quite exciting."

22

July and August 1917

On July 1, to mark Dominion Day and remind the Germans who they faced, all field guns of the Canadian Corps fired a special shoot of three salvos. Eighteen-pounders hit enemy frontline trenches; 4.5-inch howitzers targeted support and communication trenches. Timing was crucial; the Operation Order noted: "it is chiefly important that each salvo should be as nearly as possible fired simultaneously by all units." Although watches were carefully synchronized, the first signal at precisely noon was given by a flare fired from a balloon tethered above Vimy Ridge. Two minutes later, another flare signalled the second salvo; a third was fired at 12:04 p.m. In response — perhaps expecting another attack and forgetting it was Canada's fiftieth birthday — German gunners responded in kind, plastering the 5th Brigade zone with more than a thousand rounds of 4.1s and 5.9s. As it was Sunday, special church services were held throughout the Corps. With July 2 being the actual day of celebration, the Corps held a sports competition at Camblain l'Abbé, five miles behind Vimy Ridge.

Following an inspection of the 23rd Battery by Brigadier-General Panet in early July, Frank Hazlewood wrote, "Everything went off fine. Our harness was in good shape as were the horses and wagons. The General seemed well pleased and I believe we had the best turnout in the Brigade."

Bath Parades were eagerly anticipated. On July 4, Hazlewood commented, "I had a long-wished-for bath today. Three minutes under the shower is all we are allowed and you have to make it snappy. We leave our dirty clothes and are supplied with clean." Sometimes it hardly seemed worth the effort, as he noted some weeks later. "We walked about three miles to the baths this morning and had about three minutes under the hot shower. I myself, in weather like this, prefer a shell-hole bathtub."

In the next weeks, as fine weather persisted, both sides continued regular artillery activity. Night after night between 10:00 p.m. and 4:00 a.m., the 5th Brigade expended anywhere from 50 to 200 rounds on a variety of targets in and around the fortified city of Lens, just to keep the Germans off guard. Enemy observation aircraft and balloons sought out the Canadian artillery positions and, ignoring the front-line trenches, pounded the batteries with a variety of calibres.

British planners, originally intending to secure the flank near Vimy Ridge and divert German attention from the impending British attack at Ypres, proposed a frontal assault at Lens. Lieutenant-General Arthur Currie, who took over the Corps from Byng on June 9, balked at the idea. Currie, a practical man with an eye for detail, recognized that an attack of this nature would entail disproportionate losses. Sensitive

Cité des Bureaux from Bois de Riaumont, August 1917. "Holes were cut in the fronts of the row of houses marked 'X' and the howitzers dropped into the cellars." *Courtesy of Madeleine Claudi.*

to the capability of artillery, he proposed instead to seize two strategic hills dominating Lens. The first, a rounded dome of chalk north of the city, was known as Hill 70, from its elevation in metres. The second, to the southeast, was Sallaumines Hill. If Hill 70 were taken, the Canadians could shell enemy positions in the city. The Germans would then have two options: evacuate Lens, or retake Hill 70 by making costly counterattacks over an open killing field where the Canadians held an advantage. Currie got his way and planning began at once. As at Vimy, the meticulous Canadians left nothing to chance.

On the nights of July 8 and 9, the 23rd Battery completed a move to new gun positions in Cité des Bureaux, one of several mining villages ringing Lens, whose *corons* — miners' diminutive row houses — had been reduced to piles of brick. "It was," McKeown wrote, "a strong and comfortable position, where the guns were placed in cellars and fired through holes knocked in the walls." Bert agreed, calling it an

A Canadian shell bursting in the outskirts of Lens, prior to the Hill 70 show. By the time of the attack, much of the city had been reduced to rubble. Illustrated London News, *September 1, 1917.*

"ideal position. Although we were only 2200 yards from the front line, we lived there for almost three months, firing steadily all the time and were not discovered." Brigade Wagon Lines were set up at Aix Noulette, a mile to the west.

The following days were a blur, not unlike the prelude to Vimy. Night brought the usual shoots on targets in and around Lens; in daylight, gunners registered their weapons on various points in the intended battle zone and responded to the infantry's SOS calls. Often, the 23rd's howitzers engaged enemy guns: "These hostile batteries have been shelling the 17th Battery for two days, and it is required to neutralize them, to take guns out tonight."

Over the next days, as Bert wrote, "The enemy was harassed on every possible occasion by enormous gas projections and repeated raids. His trenches and wire defences were incessantly pounded and reduced to impotency, and the morale of his troops tried to the utmost." And it worked. From captured German letters, enthused Hal Fetherstonhaugh, "it is quite evident they dread what they now have to take in the way of artillery fire, and the sight of the sun fills them with foreboding as to what the planes will spot." With good weather, air activity was intense; numerous observation balloons were up on most days and planes of both sides took note of activity behind the lines. FOOs watched over their assigned section of the front and, when necessary, called for artillery strikes on any German movement. "Working party dispersed 6:45 AM by our 4.5 Hows." was a typical War Diary entry.

As preparations for the attack progressed, the 23rd Battery was assigned another task: destroy portions of the enemy front line.

In the midst of all this activity, Bert went on leave on July 29. After Vimy, leave for officers and other ranks in the Canadian Corps became available again. Since April, 174 leaves were granted each day. Officers were granted 10 days' leave four times a year; other ranks, once a year. This inequality, as historian Desmond Morton noted, was "bitterly resented by men in the ranks." Bert had almost no advance notice of the pending leave. Scrambling to pack a few things, he made his way to the divisional railhead, where he took a train to Boulogne. From the crowded docks he cabled Rosalie, telling her to expect him the next day at Manor Park.

It was a leave to remember. Bert purchased an engagement ring and proposed to Rosalie. The couple also made a day trip to Folkestone to meet friends and Rosalie's cousins. As Bert had brought his camera from France, he took several photos of the young women who would be in the bridal party. Bert also sat for a portrait in the studio of Lambert Weston & Son, one of the foremost photographers in southern England. Pleased with the result, he ordered multiple copies for the extended family.

My ten days in London went like a dream and I was back here again looking forward to my next leave before I knew it!

I thought several times of writing when I was at Browning Road and Cud tried to get me down to it, but there was nothing doing! Time was too short and far too precious to waste on such

Studio portrait
of Bert Sargent
by Lambert
Weston & Son,
Folkestone,
August 1917.
*Courtesy of
Laura Norris.*

prosaic matters as writing letters. I did send a cable one day, though, and hope it reached you in due course.

I can tell you one thing I would appreciate above anything else and that is if Lena, Alice, or Edythe would write to Cud. So far, Flo and Mildred are the only ones who have written to her and I can't tell you how much she appreciated those letters!

I can't tell you much about my 10 days in London as it is just like a very happy dream to me now. We had intended going to the country for about a week, just Mum, Cud and I, but it rained almost every day I was there, so we naturally stayed at home. We weren't up town a great deal, except to do what shopping I had to do. We only went to one show, *Theodore & Co.*, at the Gaiety. It was the second time I had seen it but I enjoyed it more than the previous time.

Sat. night, Aug. 4th, I gave a little dinner party at Oddenino's.* The only guests were Per McRae and Ted Pullen. Ted is an old friend of Cud's and lives quite near. He is as fine a boy as you could meet and I feel so sorry for him; he has been turned down as unfit for service, and in England these days a man has to be in pretty poor health to be turned down. He has a rather good tenor voice and he and Cud sing together a great deal.

Rather a coincidence; this dinner not only celebrated the first day Cud wore her ring, but also the third year of the declaration of war.

While Bert was on leave, two events occurred that would ultimately affect him directly. On July 30, the following Operational Order went out to all 1st and 2nd Division units: "On a day and at a time to be notified later, the Canadian Corps will make an assault for the capture of the high ground North of Lens...."

And, on July 31, the British attacked at Ypres in the early-morning hours in bad weather. This was the opening of Haig's new offensive, whose objective was to break out of the Salient, drive up the Channel coast, and free the Belgian ports. As Bert read in *The Times*, initial

---

*This was Auguste Oddenino's Imperial Restaurant, 60–62 Regent Street, one of the capital's better eating places.

gains were impressive. On the first day, enemy lines were pushed back two miles; the following day, after fierce fighting, St. Julien, Pilkem, Sanctuary Wood, and Hooge fell to the British. "It is too early yet to talk of victory," the paper's special correspondent wrote, "because this one day's fighting may be no more than a beginning of operations, but the beginning is splendid." Similar claims had been made for the opening attacks on the Somme in July 1916, and Bert knew from first-hand experience how the Canadians had been called in near the end to close the campaign.

What he couldn't know was that history was about to repeat itself.

Bert returned to the 5th Brigade's Wagon Lines on August 10 and, in heavy rain the following day, moved up to the positions occupied by the 23rd. Little had changed during his absence, and the battery was still engaged in its normal work of trench destruction and wire cut-ting in front of Lens, along with night firing and counter-battery fire. The belts of barbed wire protecting the German trenches at Lens were four to six feet high and 20 feet wide, and Canadian gunners spent considerable effort cutting lanes for the attacking infantry. Suspecting something was afoot, the Germans retaliated by shelling Canadian

Bert looking out over the Vimy Plain from the Bois de l'Hirondelle, August 1917. *Courtesy of Madeleine Claudi.*

trenches and gun positions and, when the weather allowed, sent over observation aircraft.

Frank Hazlewood was enjoying life in the 23rd Battery. On August 12, he wrote, "Yesterday afternoon we had a half-holiday. The Battery has a box gramophone and a good stock of records. We had it in our gun pit all afternoon. With *Carry Me Back to Old Virginny* on the machine I felt right at home." The battery's windup gramophone rotated through each of the six gun pits every few days. The record collection included "the latest hits from the musical comedies in London," brought back by men returning from leave. "It is a good machine and is fairly played to death."

German gunners could sometimes get lucky — very lucky. The 23rd Battery's No. 1 gun pit at Cité des Bureaux took a direct hit, and the ammunition began to cook off. As Bert related, "Although the pit was very strongly built of corrugated iron and heavy steel rails, with double roof, only a few small pieces of the iron were found in the vicinity afterward, and only three of sixteen rails. The howitzer itself landed in a trench about 75 yards away."

The attack on Hill 70 and Lens was scheduled for August 15. Even though it was a "sideshow" designed to divert German resources from

Officers' Mess (23rd Battery), Cité des Bureaux, August 1917. Bert's "X" indicates the Mess; sleeping quarters were in the cellar, beneath the window. *Courtesy of Madeleine Claudi.*

"Interior of Fosse 3 de Liévin which I used as an OP for some time. You can see my telescope under the 'X.' I had a ladder up one of the rear walls about 75 feet above this level. This OP overlooked all of Lens and Hill 70 sectors." *Courtesy of Madeleine Claudi.*

Ypres, Canadian preparations for the assault were as painstaking as those for Vimy. From an artillery standpoint, Hill 70 was another set-piece battle with elaborate barrage plans drawn up in advance in support of the infantry advance. The artillery plan was more sophisticated than ever: gunners would fire box, rolling, and jumping barrages. On the night of August 14/15, regular night firing by the batteries continued up to the last possible minute before the barrage, to avoid alerting the Germans. Watches were synchronized at 2:30 a.m. at brigade headquarters, with runners from each battery receiving two reliable watches to take back to their gun pits. All gunners, from 4:00 a.m. onward, wore their box respirators* in the alert position.

At 4:25 a.m. the battle for Hill 70 opened with a rolling barrage, to which the Germans promptly replied with a weak and scattered counter-barrage. As the 4th Division staged a feint attack toward Lens

---

*The Small Box Respirator, a great improvement over the earlier gas helmet, was first introduced in August 1916 and was issued to Second Division troops in late 1916. Driver Frank Hazlewood of the 23rd Battery called it "a wonderful rig, but a little uncomfortable if worn for a long time."

"Light tramway which we laid and operated in Cité des Bureaux, by which we hauled our ammunition. The train is made up of mine cars and we kept a couple of mules at the position to supply the motive power." August 1917. *Courtesy of Madeleine Claudi.*

itself, 10 battalions of the 1st and 2nd Canadian Divisions attacked on a front of 4,000 yards. They pushed the Germans off Hill 70 in the first 20 minutes and stormed into the northern outskirts of Lens, bagging

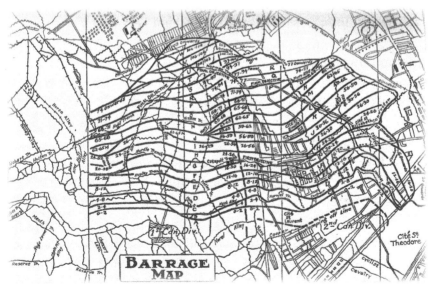

Barrage map for the Hill 70 show. *Author's photo.*

more than 1,000 prisoners. Fifty minutes after Zero, the Canadians reached their final objectives, two miles from their jumping-off point.

Canon Frederick Scott, who shared many of the frontline dangers with the men, viewed the attack from an OP. "A great silence, stirred only by the morning breeze, brooded over the wide expanse of darkness. Then, the guns burst forth in all their fury. At once, the Germans sent up rockets of various colours, signalling for aid from their guns, and the artillery duel of the two great armies waxed loud and furious."

Signaller Arthur Lapointe in the 2nd Division's 22nd Battalion described it thus: "Zero hour! A roll as of heavy thunder sounds and the sky is split by great sheets of flame. Our guns have given the signal. The noise of the barrage fills our ears; the air pulsates and the earth rocks under our feet." The Canadian gunners did their job well, for Lapointe continued, "We reach the enemy's front line, which has been blown to pieces. Dead bodies lie half-buried under the fallen parapet."

While the 18-pounders of the 5th Brigade contributed to the opening barrages, the 23rd "walked" its shells up various trenches before concentrating on the final barrage line. With a variety of ammunition types at each gun and barrages calling for specific rounds at given times, it was essential that no mix-ups occur in the darkness amid the confusion of battle. Battery commanders were thus instructed to "satisfy themselves that all ammunition is properly sorted for the different barrages, rounds bearing the same lot number being kept together and fired together, so as to avoid any possibility of short rounds. Ammunition sorted for the different barrages should be labelled in the gun pits so that no mistake can occur."

After completing the planned barrage, 5th Brigade batteries fired throughout the day in support. When the Germans counterattacked, seeking to retake their captured trenches, FOOs called down a murderous fire on the assembling enemy soldiers. "Many casualties were caused during this work," the War Diary noted dryly. Senior officers were pleased with what their men had done. Brigadier-General Morrison, for example, observed with some satisfaction, "By midnight, when the fighting died down, not a German soldier had reached our line alive." In his diary, with waves of Germans being mowed down by the Canadians, Lieutenant-General Currie recorded, "Our gunners, machine gunners and infantry never had such targets." Facing no fewer than 21 determined enemy counterattacks in the next days, often backed up with the new mustard gas* and flame-throwers (which were largely ineffective), the Canadians clung to their gains. Hill 70 would remain in British hands for the balance of the war.

21/8/17

I honestly never realize it has been quite so long since I last wrote to you but I must say in my own defence I was very busy the last two weeks before I went to London, and certainly have been on the hop since I came back.

Of course I am quite sure there is not one of you who half-realizes just how fortunate I have been and you will have to just take my word for it, for a time at least. But I must say I am *rather* pleased with my lot these days and when this little show of ours is over I wouldn't change my prospects with anyone on this earth, not even old Kaiser Bill himself!

Wednesday 22nd

Wasn't able to finish this yesterday. What I did write was done during the intervals between laying out lines to our new targets and getting the Battery in action. We are doing a lot of counter-battery work now, and yesterday they did keep us busy. We fired enough stuff to keep our shop busy just five days. So you can tell George [Darling] if he hopes to keep us supplied, he had better enlarge the plant slightly. Darling Bros. have been supplying a little more than half our daily expenditure for the last month.

---

*Dichloroethylsulphide, or mustard gas, was the most feared of all chemical weapons in the Great War, acting on any exposed moist skin and producing large, burn-like blisters. Colourless and odourless, the gas was difficult to detect. It dispersed slowly and could remain active for weeks. From the autumn of 1917 to the Armistice, mustard produced 90 percent of the gas casualties and 14 percent of all battle casualties.

George is certainly a sport to send those cigars and there is really nothing he could send that I would appreciate more. They are general favorites in the mess now and that is saying a good deal too, for both Capt. [Roy] Muirhead and the Major (Alex Paterson) have some pretty fine cigars sent them at times, but they both like my "Mercedes" better than any of them. These cigars have done one thing if nothing else: they have cured me of the cigarette habit. I began to realize about two months ago I was smoking too many of them, so began to cut down. The cigars began to arrive regularly just about that time and made the elimination process much easier. I don't suppose I smoke more than three cigarettes a day now but my pipe is going most of the time, with an odd cigar after lunch or dinner.

I can't stop for more right now. I am writing this at the OP and the light is clearing now, so I must get busy and see what I can pick up.

Shell inspection, Darling Bros. Ltd., Montreal. By midsummer 1917, the company was supplying a little more than half of the 23rd Battery's daily shell expenditure. *Courtesy of Library and Archives Canada, PA-024536.*

August 21, when Bert began his letter, was a day of particularly fierce fighting, and the 5th Brigade's gunners were especially busy. "The enemy," Bert recounted, "advancing in mass formation presented the gunners with ideal targets, of which they availed themselves to the greatest possible extent. The [23rd] Howitzer Battery alone fired 2800 rounds, which meant the handling of over 67 tons weight by the gun crews."

There were limits to what the Canadian Corps could accomplish in front of Lens and, by the end of August, the lines solidified once more. The diversionary attack at Hill 70 had cost the Corps almost 9,200 casualties, about one-third of them fatal. Writing to the Canadian Corps' artillery commander, Major-General Edward Morrison, Arthur Currie expressed his appreciation of the gunners' work during the Hill 70 operation. "The assaulting Infantry maintain that the [artillery] preparation has never been more complete, the support has never been better and the liaison has never been more perfect."

23

"Not Glad to Be Back"

With September, the Corps paused to collect its breath. Artillery activities were confined mostly to night firing on roads and trenches, designed to make life unpleasant for the Germans, while enemy gunners, in turn, did much the same to the Canadians.

Canadian infantry battalions had developed a reputation for trench raids and, when these "shows" were staged, the 5th Brigade was called on to play its part, usually providing a box barrage* around the section of trench to be raided. One typical barrage, lasting 50 minutes, specified various targets and the following rates of fire for the howitzers of the 23rd Battery:

From	To	Rate
0:00	0:10	Rapid [1 1/2 rounds/min.]
0:10	0:15	Normal [1 round/min.]
0:15	0:35	Slow [1/5 round/min.]
0:35	0:40	Normal
0:40	0:48	Slow
0:48	0:50	Very Slow [1/4 round/min.], and Stop

---

*In a box barrage, the artillery constructed a "box" of high explosive and shrapnel around the portion of the German trench being raided, thus preventing enemy reinforcements from coming up.

8/9/17

[Two days ago] I ran across [Major Osborne] Cluny MacPherson up at the guns. He had just come over with a new outfit. I knew they had been in the country for about ten days but never expected to find Ken [Darling] with them. However, I soon found Ken was still with the 66th Battery, driving lead on B Sub. Gun Team, and had just come into the line the night before.* Their wagon lines [near Liévin] are about five miles from ours and, as I expect to be down Monday or Tuesday, you can bet that mare of mine will cover that distance faster than she has ever done it.

Talking about my mare, just by way of a change, reminds me of a rather comical incident that occurred the other day. My groom had been away on leave for a couple [of] weeks and the old girl hadn't had much exercise, as the man who took Nick's job didn't take much of a fancy to her. I did not know this until afterwards. Anyway, I must admit I was a bit careless and wasn't thinking much of what I was doing for, when I went to mount and just as I was throwing my leg over, she bucked, and instead of landing in the seat, I caught on the back of the saddle and landed on her haunches. Well, I mean to say — the next moment I was over her head and — yes, go on and have a good laugh; I swear the mare did, so why shouldn't you?

By the time Nick had collected my cap and crop, I had cooled off a bit and was also wide awake, or at least sufficiently so that she didn't catch me napping a second time. Then it was my turn to laugh and her turn to sweat. She didn't buck any more that day. It is the first time she has put me off and, I hope, the last, for she is built rather high off the ground and my neck was stiff for a couple of days after.

As it is just midnight and I have to be up at daybreak, I won't write much more.

I also had another box of cigars from George on the 24th. He is a Prince to send them so regularly and I do enjoy them

---

*The 66th Battery was part of the 14th Brigade CFA and embarked from Southampton on August 21.

so. I don't think there is anything further to tell you about my London trip; my next one may be of a little greater interest to you all, but I can't say just yet. I just naturally had the most pleasant time ever but details are best left to the imagination.

Goodnight all.

I am enclosing two postcard photos; one is of the members of the Fifth Course 1st Army Artillery School. I don't think any of you know any of the others with the possible exception of Archie Gordon in the 3rd row above the X. The other is of Mr. and Mrs. James.

Everything is going along as well as can be expected. At times it seems very slow but I suppose we will have to be satisfied. We have certainly had some tough fighting lately and practically all summer we have been at it all the time. We are having beautiful weather now and if it will only last, it will mean a great deal to us.

On the night of September 9, two sections of each battery in the 5th Brigade were relieved. These sections withdrew to the Wagon Lines at Aix Noulette; the following night the remaining sections were relieved, along with brigade headquarters. In anticipation of an order to capture Sallaumines Hill, the brigade then scouted new battery positions around La Culotte, half a mile west of Avion, a Lens suburb. Working parties were soon preparing the selected sites and constructing dugouts. This time the Canadian Engineers had drawn up plans for two types of gun pits. Quantities of precut material were on hand, with the aim of reducing the time required to prepare proper gun positions. Earlier, Lieutenant-Colonel Constantine had requested, "a liberal supply of camouflage, and building material be available, as, without these, positions will be easily spotted, and the consequent losses of material and personnel, must be heavy." Adjacent to the pits would be new dugouts for the gunners, 20 feet deep, offering protection against almost anything the enemy might send over. Camouflage techniques by this stage of the war were quite sophisticated, as Hal's brother related. "Large quantities of camouflage material were made up in such a way as to represent either brown earth, grass, chalky soil, or the rubbish of ruined villages, so that the gunners could select their gun positions and then obtain suitable camouflage covers for their guns with poles and wire frames all ready to erect without unnecessary delay."

At 3:30 a.m. on September 16, the brigade moved from its wagon lines at Aix Noulette. Suspecting the Canadans were up to something, the Germans dropped a few shells in the road at Souchez, just ahead of the lead battery. Fortunately, there were no casualties and the march proceeded without further incident, with all units arriving at the new wagon lines by 6:00 a.m. After that, the day was spent in constructing improvised shelters and straightening out the positions before Brigadier-General Panet showed up in the afternoon for an inspection.

Aerial duels were by now an everyday occurrence and rarely warranted mention in the 5th Brigade War Diary. Some though, involving exceptional airmanship, were avidly followed by thousands on the ground. "On the afternoon of the 19th," reported the War Diary, "a Hun plane attacked one of our balloons but failed to damage it; it then chased one of our machines practically to the ground and, in spite of

Nissen huts, similar to those constructed for the 5th Brigade batteries in September 1917. Illustrated London News, *February 3, 1917.*

rifle and AA gunfire, rose and made his way back to his own lines. A daring piece of work."

The next day, Nissen huts began arriving at the brigade's wagon lines. Invented by a Canadian, these prefabricated structures had a semicircular arched roof of corrugated iron and were designed to fit over a poured concrete base. Each hut, 14 feet wide and eight feet high, could hold 25 men. The huts had two square windows at each end; three small heaters provided warmth. The Engineers worked hard and, several days later, after the concrete had cured, all four batteries moved into huts on the north side of the La Targette-St. Eloi road. The gunners were happy.

Over a series of autumn days described as "perfect" — clear, cool days and moonlit nights — the work of constructing new wagon lines and forward gun positions continued, albeit slowly, owing to a lack of material. Brick standings were laid in the chalky soil for the horses. Where possible, former German gun positions were taken over and improved, and Lieutenant-Colonel Constantine set up brigade head-quarters in a cellar in La Coulotte. The 23rd Battery occupied two positions, one at La Coulotte and a second in nearby Chaudière Wood. They were well camouflaged, and the new deep dugouts offered adequate protection to the gunners. Light railway tracks were laid in the area, allowing large quantities of ammunition — 4,000 to 5,000 rounds per battery per night — to be brought forward with minimum difficulty.

To the north, the Ypres offensive had run into serious trouble. Initially successful, the attack was renewed on several occasions after July 31, and the noose around Ypres had been somewhat relieved. By the beginning of October, the attack stalled for two main reasons.

First, the natural drainage system of this part of Flanders had been wrecked in the first few days. The initial assault was preceded on July 22 by the largest artillery bombardment of the war to date, with 3,091 British guns hammering the whole sector with more than 4.25 million shells.* The summer was unusually wet and, under constant

---

*Basil Liddell Hart claims the cost of this bombardment was £22 million. With 3,091 guns, the British had one gun per six yards of front.

shelling, the low-lying British areas became a sea of slime and yellow mud in which men and horses drowned. Trenches as such no longer existed. There was no real front line, and large portions of the front consisted of flooded shell holes loosely linked by duckboards. On drier ground atop Passchendaele Ridge, just 50 feet higher than the surrounding plain, the Germans could call down artillery fire on every British position in the Salient.

The second reason was that German defensive tactics had evolved over the past months. Colonel Friedrich von Lossberg had developed the concept of flexible defence in depth, rather than a linear defence. Under von Lossberg's scheme, the front line was lightly held with a series of machine-gun or trench-mortar posts, and troops were instructed to retire to a line of resistance based farther back. Anchoring the German defences were circular pillboxes of reinforced concrete containing machine guns. They were immune to almost all British shellfire, and only a direct hit from a 15-inch shell could inflict serious damage. The pillboxes represented a difficult objective for infantry, for they had been carefully sited to provide interlocking (mutually supporting) fields of fire for machine guns.

His offensive going nowhere, Field Marshal Haig called on Lieutenant-General Arthur Currie at Canadian Corps headquarters in Hersin-Coupigny on October 3. Haig's message was simple: the Canadians were needed in the Salient. It was the Somme all over again; even after three months of fighting, objectives scheduled to be taken on the first day still remained in German hands. The Canadians were being called in to retrieve an already bad situation.

Despite Currie's protests and the likelihood of great losses for little strategic gain, the four Canadian divisions made ready to head north to what was by far the worst battlefield of the war. If the Somme has since become synonymous with needless death, Passchendaele (one of eight battles collectively known as the Third Battle of Ypres) epitomizes the fearful squalor and misery of the Western Front.

While Currie voiced his misgivings to Haig, gunners of the 5th Brigade put the finishing touches on dugouts and gun pits for the attack at Sallaumines Hill. A plasticine model of the objective had been constructed behind the lines (as was done for Vimy), and the brigade's officers inspected it in detail. Next day, there was a cryptic entry in the War Diary: "Proposed operations by Canadian Corps against — postponed." In the absence of any further instructions, the men continued work, feeling the gun pits would doubtless be required at some future point.

By October 8 it was generally understood that offensive operations around Lens would be postponed. Preparations began the next day for a possible trip north; units were ordered to get rid of all surplus ordnance stores and men had to bring their personal kit down to the regulation weight of 35 pounds. Excess kit items would be stored at Villers-au-Bois until the gunners returned. All four of Lieutenant-Colonel Constantine's battery commanders took the opportunity to go on leave as reinforcements streamed in, bringing the batteries up to strength. The brigade's horses, on which so much depended, were in generally good condition despite the wet and cold weather. The new brick standings had kept the animals out of the mud and quite comfortable.

October 20 was a day of spit and polish, with all batteries at the wagon lines getting ready for the trip to the Ypres sector. In the midst of all this, new uniform regulations for Canadian gunners came into effect. The brass cap badge would henceforth be the standard Royal Field Artillery badge with a smooth-bore cannon, CANADA being substituted on the scroll for the Latin UBIQUE. The brass collar badge was standardized as the flaming artillery grenade; on their shoulder straps, all Canadian Field Artillery personnel would wear CFA in place of CANADA.

At 7:00 a.m. on October 23, the 5th Brigade began its march northward from the starting point at La Targette. "Brigade well turned out," the War Diary commented, "23rd Battery being specially noticeable." The route took them up the Arras-Béthune road, which, when the brigade had first arrived in the Vimy area in February, had been impassable due to its proximity to the German trenches. It was a long day's march, 17 miles over flat country, and took them through a series of dreary villages to Béthune, an important British staging area. From here it was a short distance to Annezin, where billets were secured for the night.

There was no rest. Haig wanted the Canadians in a hurry, and the march continued the following morning, with the 5th Brigade leading the 2nd Division. It was a fine day but cold — good marching weather. This time the planners laid out a seven-mile route, taking the gunners northwest, along the main road toward Hazebrouck, to Morbecque, where the men were billeted in farmhouses. Horse lines, for want of anything better, were set up along the road. The roads were good and well drained, but the cobblestones made for bruised feet among those who had to walk. Lieutenant-Colonel Constantine authorized passes that night for up to 10 percent of the brigade, for the town of Hazebrouck, two miles from their billets. Judging from his seven postcards, Bert was among the lucky ones who got to explore the once-quiet market town, now teeming with soldiers.

After a rainy night, the trek resumed at 7:00 a.m. It was another short march, 11 miles, and brought the brigade to billets around Godewaersvelde, a farming village a mile from the Belgian border. After three days on the road, the brigade's horses were still in fine shape, a fact noted in the War Diary. A final day of marching on October 26 — 11 miles in a cold, hard rain — brought the Divisional Artillery to its destination. Wagon lines were set up about half a mile east of Vlamertinghe, on a site recently vacated by the 3rd Australia New Zealand Army Corps (ANZAC) Division. It was a poor location, torn up by shellfire, with no standings or cover for the horses. Bert painted a bleak picture: "The area was absolutely desolate and so overcrowded that what little cover there was available was already utilized to capacity. However with characteristic resource, as soon as the horses had been attended to, 'bivvies'* were made and some degree of comfort obtained."

As the gunners of the 5th Brigade approached Vlamertinghe, they were serenaded by the steady duelling of distant artillery. With darkness came the latest German scourge, Gotha bombers. These were formidable aircraft, long-range twin-engine heavy bombers with a crew of three, carrying a 2,000-pound payload. Beginning in May 1917,

---

*A "bivvy" was a shelter constructed from a large canvas tarpaulin held up by a frame structure.

Gothas were used with great success to bomb England from Belgian bases. "As evening wore on and the trumpeters sounded 'Lights Out,' the faint drone of enemy Gothas could be heard, followed soon after by the crashing of bombs in the villages and camps around us." In the 23rd's lines, Frank Hazlewood complained, "We can't keep a light going very long at night, on account of the slogan 'Fritzie's over, lights out!' It gets dark so early these days."

Lieutenant Dick Bennett, writing in the 5th Brigade's War Diary, recorded: "Passed into Belgium at Abeele. Mud fields for wagon lines. No billets or shelters. Enemy shelling with H[igh] V[elocity] gun & dropping bombs. *Not* glad to be back."

24

"Like the Crack of Doom": The Battle of Passchendaele

Orders were soon forthcoming: the 2CDA would relieve the 66th Divisional Artillery on October 27, with the relief to be completed by 7:00 p.m. The Canadians would hand over their 18-pounders and howitzers, along with dial sights and aiming posts, in exchange for those they would take over in the line.

As dawn broke over the shattered city of Ypres, Lieutenant-Colonel Constantine, Adjutant Dick Bennett, and the brigade's four battery commanders met at the Menin Gate* with guides to take them forward. After three years of shelling, Ypres, with a pre-war population of 16,000, had been reduced to what Basil Liddell Hart called "a vast ant-heap of tumbled ruins," abandoned by its inhabitants. Streets, buildings, and shops could no longer be traced, and "the streets were piled with broken brick and twisted wreckage. Hardly a day passed without heavy casualties to troops marching through. Dead horses, broken limbers, lorries, and Red Cross trucks lay by the wayside, battered and torn by enemy shellfire."

In growing disbelief, the group made its way toward brigade head-quarters, Mill Cottage, in the pulverized hamlet of Potijze, a mile to

---

*In reality, there was no gate. The walls and ramparts constructed by Marshal Sebastien Vauban in the late 1600s were pulled down in the 1850s by the Belgian government. In 1917, a pair of stone lions guarded the spot, gateway to the Ypres Salient.

the northeast. Batteries would take positions further up the road, near the flattened ruins of Zonnebeke village. There was, however, a slight problem. When the batteries of the 5th Brigade arrived to take over the 66th's positions, the area was under such heavy fire that no one from the unit could be found to take over from. Eventually, the gunners were located and a hasty transfer took place.

Two miles ahead, scarcely visible through the mist and rain, was the low grey smudge of Passchendaele Ridge, held by the Germans since 1914. Looking down from the Ridge, enemy gunners had pre-registered their guns on all important points in the Salient, and searched up and down with shells at intervals, both day and night.

Mud was the dominant feature of the battlefield, a liquid, swamp-like ooze that filled the overlapping shell craters, very different than the thick mixture of chalk and water at the Somme, which clung to everything and made getting around so difficult. "The whole place," wrote Hal, "was full of water-filled shell holes, with some parts of the ground knee-high and more in sticky mud." Mud offered one small benefit: enemy shells bursting in it did not project shell splinters for any distance. Reflecting the nature of the battlefield, special

A German shell explodes in the mud at Passchendaele. Note the field gun at the right of the photo. *Courtesy of Library and Archives Canada, PA-002101.*

stores were issued to the men, the most important being gum rubber boots — 100 pairs per battery.

For gunners, the biggest problem was constructing a solid platform for the guns, so they would not sink into the mud. Canadian ingenuity came to the fore and two methods were found to work. Gunners constructed a "raft" of three-inch planks spiked to mud-sills and supported on piles, which were driven as deep as possible. Gun wheels rested on sandbags filled with broken brick or earth. If timber was not available (generally the case), an appropriate patch of ground was levelled. A layer of sandbags was then put down, followed by a layer of corrugated iron, atop which was placed another layer of sandbags. Some 4.5-inch howitzer batteries replaced the corrugated iron with chicken wire and reported that this was sufficient to "carry the howitzer even in very soft soil."

On arrival, the 5th Brigade found things in a disorganized state. "By dint of the most strenuous labor," Bert wrote, "guns were hauled out of the mud and set on new platforms or withdrawn for repairs to the workshops, and ammunition dumps, which were scattered in all directions, were straightened out." The 23rd, having located four

Passchendaele: "A little corner behind Zonnebeke that we used to crawl into at nights. This photo will bring back anything but fond memories to Major Alex Paterson, Major Roy Muirhead, Capt Jim McKeown, and Yours Truly." *Courtesy of Madeleine Claudi.*

howitzers deeply buried in mud and bricks, discovered that just two "looked as if they might be fired." These were dug out and set up on platforms.

Understandably, most men had difficulty relating what they endured at Passchendaele. "The Somme was no health resort," McKeown wrote, concluding somewhat lamely, "but Passchendaele — words fail to describe." More than a decade after the battle, the historian of the 4th Brigade CFA claimed Passchendaele was "a spectacle too gruesome and terrible to attempt to describe." Bert's description of the area around Zonnebeke was succinct: "this God-forsaken country," he called it, words most of those who fought there would agree with.

Battery personnel were relieved every 48 hours. At the end of that time, men were pretty well exhausted from constant work, shellfire, and lack of sleep, but not so far gone as to be unable to be quite fresh after 24 hours' rest. If serving the guns was difficult, so was the task of transporting ammunition 6,000 yards from the supply dumps. The work went on around the clock. As at the Somme, the 2DAC relied on pack animals to bring up ammunition. Each trip took the column through "a barrage that was constantly and accurately placed on the one main road, a road with deep sucking mud on either side, which formed a death trap for the animal that got into it. In most cases it was impossible to get the poor brutes out, and a bullet was the only relief for them."

Battery personnel also packed in ammunition. As Frank Hazlewood of the 23rd related, "We go up the line every other night at 2:30 AM. Each man has two horses or mules, eight rounds per horse. It takes about five or six hours return trip to the guns and back to the Horse Lines. You can bet we are ready for breakfast when we return, splashed generally from head to foot with mud." McKeown later paid tribute to the men of the 23rd who brought up howitzer rounds. "All ranks behaved in a magnificent manner, and many a driver, after having had his pack animal killed beside him, acquired a stray horse or mule — whose driver had probably been killed or wounded — and brought it through to the Battery with not one, but two or three successive loads of ammunition." By the time shells reached the guns, they were coated with mud. As a result, each round was cleaned and polished before inserting it into the breech, a process that slowed down the battery's rate of fire.

The 5th Brigade established an OP (code-named HAMBURG), manned 24 hours a day, with a rotation of FOOs from each battery who were relieved each morning at 8:00 a.m. HAMBURG was linked to the Group OP (LEVI) by telephone cable; a Lucas lamp was used when the phone line was knocked out (as it often was from enemy shell-fire), but the lamps were useless in foggy conditions. Phone lines to the batteries were cut faster than they could be repaired, so the only reliable way to send orders to the guns was by runner. The Brigade War Diary acknowledged their "marvellous" work, every order having gotten through despite heavy barrages.

The Corps bureaucracy continued to function flawlessly. Each Canadian attack was accompanied by carefully planned artillery barrages. And each day, batteries received a mass of instructions and detailed typed Operation Orders that outlined the forthcoming barrages and ammunition requirements.

The following extracts from the 5th Brigade War Diary, written by Adjutant Dick Bennett, provide a graphic impression of the battle from a gunner's perspective.

October 28: Preparation for second phase of Canadian assault on Passchendaele proceeded with, mostly firing barrage and harassing fire. Ammunition all brought up on pack animals. Road very bad. No light railway can live forward on account of heavy shellfire. Enemy [artillery] takes country by areas and plows it up. Ammunition to be brought up to 700 per gun at once, which in spite of tremendous difficulties, was accomplished.

Army Barrage & Corps Barrage fired.

October 29: Orders out for second phase of Canadian attack.

Preparations pushed on and ammunition taken forward despite continual barrage on only road. Pack mules lose one-third of strength on one trip but return and load up and proceed forward through barrage again without question. Order is to get it up at all costs.

Batteries heavily shelled, some mustard gas. Guns are just standing in mud, no protection or shelter for men, everything is rushed. Large number sick from exposure.

October 30: 5:50 AM. Barrage opens like the crack of doom. Infantry make splendid advance and capture all objectives. Our barrage goes forward in 50-yd. lifts 4 min. apart. This is much slower than we've been used to & is adapted to heavy ground and pillbox defences.*
Bursts of fire during afternoon to catch counterattacks.

October 31: Line now runs along western outskirts of Passchendaele. Corps Barrage at 5:30 AM caught enemy counterattack.
Preparations for 3rd phase of Canadian attack pushed forward. More ammunition rushed up. Enemy shelling very intense all day. Counterattacks driven off in evening. Gas very bad. Yellow Cross.**

November 1: Preparation for attack on Passchendaele by Canadian Corps on Nov. 5/17 being pushed ahead. Infantry making wonderful progress in construction of roads & duck walks. Owing to very muddy state of ground, roads have to be made of planks and more resemble bridges. No communication trenches are possible, trench mats being spread over surface of ground. A step off these in places takes you up to the neck in soft slime. These conditions make it easy for the enemy to keep roads and approaches under fire, and this he does day and night, and our casualties from this source very heavy. The Canadians are now building new road faster than the enemy can photograph it, and conditions improving.
Boche air service very aggressive, continually patrolling over our area.

---

*This was the slowest barrage on record, owing to the terrible condition of the ground over which the Canadian infantry had to advance.
**Mustard gas.

November 2: 5:55 AM. 5th & 6th Bdes fired in Army Barrage lasting 30 minutes.

During afternoon bursts of fire 4:20 PM & 5:45 PM by all batteries. Corps Barrage at 4 PM. OP maintained day & night, also Battalion & Bde Liaison.

Guns knocked out by hostile shellfire average 3 a day — record 8. Supply of guns good; teams always on road taking up and bringing out guns. Many guns left bogged by 66th DA have been salvaged.

Battery positions under almost continuous shellfire.

Lieut. J.D. McKeown recommended for immediate award for brilliant forward observation work.*

Nov. 3: 2nd Cdn. Division relieve 4th Cdn. Divn. on our front during night 2/3rd. Army Barrage fired at 3:30 AM. Bursts of fire at 4:30 & 4:45 PM.

Nov. 4: Enemy put down heavy barrage on our front at 5 AM, at same time doing heavy counter-battery work in our back area.

SOS signal up at 5:06 when our guns immediately opened. Enemy attempted counterattack all along our front. All except 1st wave were caught in our barrage. Such elements as made an entry into our trenches were immediately ejected. 4:45 PM all batteries except 17th fired in Corps Barrage.

Nov. 5: Army Barrage fired at 5:40 PM. Great rush of ammn. to guns for tomorrow's show. 34 guns [*i.e.* 18-pounders] out of 36 in Group in action. Largest number in action at once since coming to this front.

Bursts of fire at 7:40 & 8:50 PM. Night firing 200 rds. in enemy approaches.

---

*Approved on December 3, Jim McKeown received the Military Cross on January 18, 1918, for his actions on this day. The citation paid tribute to his gallantry and devotion to duty and noted: "He went twice through an extremely heavy barrage and secured valuable information."

Nov. 6: At 6 AM barrage opened for the taking of Passchendaele Ridge. Despite constant counter-battery work, every available gun was kept continuously in action and our infantry were enabled to sweep all before them under what they termed "perfect support."

After 4 1/2 hours the situation began to settle, with our infantry in all positions and the famous Passchendaele Ridge in Canadian hands. Only one immediate counterattack developed and this was promptly dealt with.

Bursts of fire during day.

Night firing kept up as usual.

As the epic battle drew to a close a few days later, the Canadians were atop Passchendaele Ridge, though the eponymous village had been reduced to a redbrick smear in a cratered sea of mud. Infantry attacks came to an end, but both sides continued to trade artillery barrages. Still, the Canadians remained vigilant. OPs on the forward crest of the Ridge were manned around the clock, although telephone communications were very difficult to maintain, due to cable breaks from shellfire and the near impossibility of laying new lines.

Infantry commanders were quick to express their gratitude to the artillery units that contributed so much to their success. Typical is this portion of a November 11 letter from Brigadier Huntley Ketchen to Constantine's 5th Brigade:

All ranks of the 6th CIB* are loud in their praise of the magnificent rolling barrage given us during the assault. We have never been better served....

Two days later, Major-General Burstall, commanding the Second Canadian Division, sent a message of appreciation to Brigadier-General Panet. "On behalf of the Infantry of the Division," Burstall wrote, "I want to express to you and to all ranks 2nd Canadian Divisional Artillery our most grateful thanks for the magnificent way in which

---

*Canadian Infantry Brigade.

your guns have supported us this year.

"Under the most difficult and trying conditions imaginable and suffering heavy casualties, the Batteries have invariably responded instantly to every call made on them by the Infantry.

"The liaison and co-operation between the two arms has been of the highest order and we feel that with such splendid Batteries behind us we can go anywhere."

Only the generals could be pleased with Third Ypres. Writing in the 1930s, former British prime minister Lloyd George (who had never supported Haig's offensive) condemned it as one of the "most gigantic, tenacious, grim, futile and bloody fights ever waged in the history of war." Writing also in the 1930s, Basil Liddell Hart termed it "the gloomiest drama in British military history." They were not alone. Winston Churchill referred to it as "a forlorn expenditure of valour and life without equal in futility," and A.J.P. Taylor in the mid-1960s called the battle "the blindest slaughter of a blind war."

British losses were something over 300,000. In three weeks, the Canadian Corps gained two square miles of waterlogged Belgian real estate at a cost of some 16,000 casualties. Though most were in the infantry, the gunners also paid their share of the "butcher's bill." The 5th Brigade had two officers and 19 ORs killed, and three officers and 158 ORs wounded. The 23rd Battery was fortunate: it lost no officers and had 10 ORs killed, with 23 ORs wounded or gassed.

25

Winter Quarters

In England, on November 19, Rosalie wrote to Bert's sister, Flora, saying she'd received a note from him. "There is a good chance of his being home in possibly less than four weeks. I am trying very hard to look serene and not excited — with indifferent success."

A day later, 378 British tanks demonstrated their true capabilities, for they had not been a great success in the mud of the Somme and at Passchendaele. Attacking over a battlefield near Cambrai, which had not been torn up by shellfire (in fact, there was not even a preliminary bombardment of German positions), the lumbering monsters rolled over enemy defences, crushing wire and opening lanes for the infantry following behind. On the first day, more ground was gained than in the three months of Third Ypres — and with far fewer casualties. The only effective defence against the tanks was provided by German field artillery. Light and mobile, the high velocity and flat trajectory of the 77 mm field gun made it a potent anti-tank weapon. The slow-moving monsters proved to be easy pickings: one battery at Flesquières, for example, destroyed every tank sent against it, firing from very close range.

Though British attacks continued for a week, each supported by diminishing numbers of tanks, the Germans staged successful counter-attacks employing new infiltration tactics, using shock troops and "bombers" carrying sacks of grenades. These tactics, developed by General Oskar von Hutier, had been proven at Riga on September 1, where von Hutier's men deliberately bypassed points of strong resistance.

In the end, the front returned essentially to its original lines, though Cambrai was a valuable learning experience for both sides. The British felt the tank offered a means to break the stalemate of the Western Front. Equally, the successful German counterattacks provided an alternative to the frontal assaults of massed infantry, which had cost the British so dearly in the past. For British gunners, Cambrai was the first use of predicted fire. When the tanks and infantry advanced, the guns — hitherto silent — opened up on their targets. With each gun previously calibrated, and by appropriate corrections for wind, temperature, and barometric pressure, lines of fire could be laid out by director or compass and gunners could reliably "shoot from the map."

A Warning Order for relief of the 5th Brigade arrived at Mill Cottage on November 18 and was promptly sent by runner to all batteries. "This will be very acceptable to all ranks," was Adjutant Bennett's understated comment in the War Diary. The first part of the relief, two sections per battery, took place early in the morning of the twenty-second, with remaining sections completing the operation by noon the next day, returning to their previous camp at Vlamertinghe.

With its howitzers left in situ, the 23rd Battery received six replacements from the relieving battery, the 174th RFA. Unusually, limbers were empty. "This is the first time we have not had to haul unnecessary weight in ammunition wagons," Bennett recorded in the War Diary. The brigade, as it prepared to march, was under-strength as a result of three weeks of combat. The number of permanent officers, 27, was the establishment strength, but ORs at 695 were 38 short. The 648 horses and mules meant it was short 81 animals.

The march to the Lens area began at 7:00 a.m. on November 24. The first day's 15-mile route took the gunners through villages already familiar from its tour of duty the previous year. Once away from the Ypres sector, the roads were in good condition and traffic was light so that the men arrived at their billets by 1:00 p.m. "All ranks pleased to be returning to 1st Army," Dick Bennett recorded.

Resuming the following morning in good weather, the brigade covered 10 miles on excellent third-class roads and arrived at Haverskerque. The march on Day Three, under 11 miles, brought the brigade to billets at Lapugnoy. "Condition of horses improving daily," noted the War Diary. And, though St. Venant was out of bounds to all ranks, passes were issued for other neighbouring towns up to 10:00 p.m, and Béthune to 11:00 p.m. Bert procured a pass for Béthune, where he purchased four postcards. A final march of eight miles brought the brigade into the Canadian Corps area, and billets at Olhain. Major-General Burstall, GOC 2nd Canadian Division, inspected the brigade on its march and was pleased with the "smartness of men and general turnout."

At Olhain, the brigade received a Warning Order for relief of the 4th Brigade CFA, near Acheville, on the plains east of Vimy. Over two nights, there was an exchange of guns, those of the 4th Brigade being taken over in situ. Horse and wagon lines moved to La Targette, the same covered standings the brigade had constructed and then vacated before the march to Ypres. Brigade headquarters was set up once more at Thélus Cave,* and batteries occupied, for the most part, the same positions and deep dugouts they had constructed in September and October.

To make up for losses, reinforcements arrived and brought the brigade almost back to strength. As the weary gunners settled into their new positions on the last day of November, they could be excused for thinking that not much had changed in their absence. "Enemy artillery and aircraft show considerable activity during day," reported the War Diary.

On December 1, Dick Bennett turned the Brigade's War Diary over to Jim McKeown, who recorded, "Enemy artillery inactive." Even so, the batteries were in action, dropping almost 400 shells on approaches to their assigned zone, and the 23rd Battery fired twice in retaliation for shelling by German trench mortars. The following day, the 23rd was directed to destroy two trench mortar emplacements, and this was speedily accomplished, "five hits being obtained." High winds on December 3 made calibration and accurate shooting nearly impossible, thus keeping the artillery of both sides fairly quiet, though the brigade fired its daily allotment of 375 rounds on various targets behind the German front line.

_____

*Also known as Mill Cave.

Making up for their silence the previous day, enemy gunners went into action in the evening of December 4, dropping gas and high-explosive (HE) shells in the vicinity of the 18th Battery and sending a number of men to hospital with gas poisoning. As usual, the 23rd's howitzers provided the retaliation fire. German heavy howitzers threw over more shells on December 6, this time around the 23rd Battery. While none of the guns was damaged, the Germans succeeded in blowing up a dugout full of ammunition, wounding one man. Overall, this portion of the front was inactive and the same general routine prevailed through the middle of the month. Enemy batteries would fire a few scattered rounds during the day, the Canadians fired on any observed movement or suspected OPs, and the 5th Brigade's allocation of shells for night firing would be sent over at irregular intervals.

In the lull after Passchendaele, Bert was granted leave to England. He left the battery on December 8, even earlier than he'd advised Rosalie. As before, he stayed at "home" on Browning Road. If he wrote anything about this time, nothing has survived. His leave coincided with

Second Canadian Divisional baths, December 1917. A welcome sight for gunners returning from Passchendaele. *Courtesy of Library and Archives Canada, PA-002236.*

his thirtieth birthday, and no doubt the event was celebrated by a small dinner party with a few close friends. Once again, Bert brought his camera from France and a few souvenir snaps were taken on December 15, his birthday.

Looking ahead and making a rough calculation as to when the next leave might come, Bert and Rosalie planned a spring wedding. In due course, Rosalie ordered some fine stationery with "April, 1918" printed in silver. Under normal circumstances it would have been a good guess, but 1918 would prove to be anything but normal.

The submarine blockade, Bert discovered, was having an effect in England. Food conditions, as Rosalie wrote to Bert's sister in Montreal, were:

> ... very serious indeed and I am afraid the coming winter has worse in store. All provision shops have a long queue of people waiting outside for butter, sugar, tea, margarine, etc. They frequently stand two by two and stretch as far as 200 yards along the road. The shops very often close several half-days in a week because they have nothing to sell. Tea is practically unobtainable now and is at least 4s per pound.
>
> We are not actually rationed yet for food (except sugar, of course — 1/2 lb. per head per week).
>
> Never mind — we must not grumble. The poor boys in France must not be stinted.

Bert returned to the battery on December 18, just as the men were beginning to think of Christmas.

On December 8, McKeown noted, "Christmas mail beginning to come in in large quantities." In anticipation of a holiday dinner, the 5th Brigade ordered 600 pounds of turkey from French and British suppliers. If the men were going to spend another Christmas away from home, they would at least do so in style. In mid-December, with the food shortages in Britain, Dick Bennett wrote to the 2nd CDA chaplain, Major James Fortier, to arrange the bulk purchase of turkey and goose in Paris on behalf of all 2CDA units. In all, for the 5th Brigade,

Bennett ordered 725 pounds of plucked turkey and 125 pounds of goose, at a cost of 2,000 francs. Of this, 100 pounds of each were destined for the 23rd Battery, at a cost of about 500 francs.

Fearing the Germans were developing their own tanks and recalling how enemy field gunners had so successfully engaged British tanks at near point-blank range, the 2nd CDA developed plans to deal with a tank attack. For the 5th Brigade, the scheme called for the 20th Battery to run two 18-pounders forward to a prepared position dug into the Vimy-Farbus railway embankment. There they would engage any advancing tanks over open sights. Two ammunition caches, each with 50 rounds of HE, were constructed nearby.

On December 19, the brigade received notice it would be relieved the following day by the 170th Brigade RFA, and this was completed by 4:00 p.m. on the twentieth without incident. Each battery left four of its guns behind and brought out two for training. The batteries then proceeded to the Wagon Lines at La Targette, where they passed the next day cleaning up. The move to Ames, planned for the twenty-second, was postponed by one day, giving the men further time to get

Canadian artillerymen attach sandbags to the feet of their horses for traction on icy roads, December 1917. *Courtesy of Library and Archives Canada, PA-002268.*

organized, though it meant Christmas dinner could not be held on the twenty-fifth. The brigade moved out at 9:15 a.m. on December 23 and, after a long but uneventful march of 20 miles to the northwest up the arrow-straight Roman road, arrived at Ames at 7:00 p.m. Despite the distance, it was a relatively easy march: limbers were empty and two trucks helped move equipment. Only on the twenty-fourth were billets provided in and around Ames, but these were only fair. The men passed much of the day getting the wagons parked and setting up horse lines on side roads leading into the village. Two miles from Ames was the bustling railroad town of Lillers, to which passes were readily granted.

All ranks attended a Christmas service in the schoolhouse at Ames. "The room was packed and service enjoyed. Orchestra provided music," McKeown reported. And, apart from a few men who remained on duty, a holiday was declared for the afternoon. A few inches of snow on the ground and frost on the trees reminded many of home. Christmas dinners for the batteries were staggered over the next few days. The 23rd, along with the Brigade Headquarters Section, held a combined dinner in the school on the twenty-ninth, with an after-dinner concert provided by local musicians. "Huge success" was McKeown's verdict.

Frank Hazlewood described the day:

We had the meal in the town schoolhouse and the remains of a lesson in French grammar on the blackboard brought back memories of school days.

It was a great success as far as the eats go and there was a good concert afterwards. Here is part of what we had:— Roast beef and turkey, mashed potatoes and turnips, bread and margarine. Plum pudding and sauce (more than we could eat), two other kinds of pie, besides the usual apples, nuts, etc.

There was lots of beer for those who had the habit.

On the thirtieth, the last Sunday of the year, another church service took place in the school, with an orchestra again providing the music.

Though the stay at Ames was supposed to be devoted to training, the brigade was nowhere near full strength, and early January saw a constant flow of men departing on specialized courses. One section of the 23rd went to Pernes to act as Depot Battery at the Canadian Corps Artillery School. Four of the 24 permanent officers and five ORs left for Hersin to attend a gas course, while other men headed to a signalling course at Houdain, and one officer and two ORs were on a veterinary course at Abbeville. Seven officers attended a one-day gas course at Lières, and one officer and eight ORs from each battery attended a course on how to fortify a gun pit with barbed wire. In addition to those absent on courses, 59 men were in hospital with a variety of ailments and 54 were on leave. In all, it meant training was often disrupted.

Lieutenant-Colonel Constantine issued a Syllabus of Training on December 26, and the following day the brigade set to work, though Wednesday and Saturday afternoons were designated as half-holidays. Battery commanders, or a captain, and all officers, were required to be present at all Stable Parades, and courses were given by captains or section commanders. The day began at 6:45 with reveille, followed by foot drill, gun drill, and — three times a day — Stables. After 4:30 p.m. the men were off duty. Though intended to prepare the brigade for open warfare, Lieutenant Bob Gillespie, one of the 23rd's junior officers, felt the training was of little value, being "as has usually been the case, cleaning steel and leather."

Constantine's syllabus was put together in haste after the 2nd CDA issued on December 14 a four-page document entitled *Notes on Training*. In it, senior artillery officers tried to distill the experience gleaned over the past year of combat. The *Notes* set out some principles for increasing accuracy of fire through the application of scientific principles, and emphasized that the skills that gunners and drivers needed to master would be quite different in a war of mobility. "A marked feature of this year's operations," the *Notes* observed, "has been the steady increase in the opportunities for the use of the rifle. Every gunner and driver must be trained with the rifle, to be ready for such happenings as occurred in the Battle of Cambrai, when wagon lines were overrun" by fast-moving German assault troops.

Old ways of doing things were not likely to work in open warfare. "In trench warfare," the *Notes* explained, "nearly all plans are settled after conferences at leisure and all positions located by aeroplane or balloon observers weeks beforehand, whereas in open warfare the opposite situation exists. Officers must have sufficient knowledge and practice in the execution of the fundamental principles of open fighting that clear, concise and intelligent orders may be given and skillful reconnaissance carried out at short notice." As a result, the *Notes* suggested, "some simple exercise in open warfare should be practised, if only to bring home to officers the necessity that arises in such circumstances for quick decision and prompt issue of orders." Some of the skills requiring attention included laying out lines of fire by night, map reading, maintaining communication, pushing out patrols, supplying ammunition, and setting up forward wagon lines.

Though all were valid observations, to the average gunner at Ames, raising a glass of beer in an estaminet as the eventful year of 1917 drew to a close, the possibility of open warfare seemed remote indeed.

Brigade officers held a dinner on New Year's Eve and was pronounced a "great success." The party was evidently a memorable one, resulting in more than a few hangovers. Bert's sole diary entry for January 1, 1918, was ambiguously short: "The morning after the night before!"

A one-day refresher in musketry began at 7:45 a.m. on January 2 at a range near Ames. Most old hands had not fired a rifle since Hythe in the summer of 1915; almost no one had aimed at a live target. Battery commanders were ordered to parade every available gunner, all possible NCOs, and two officers. Equipped with Lee-Enfields, each man fired five rounds for grouping, five rounds application, and 10 rounds rapid fire in one minute. Evidently, the men hadn't forgotten the lessons from Hythe. Summing up, McKeown recorded: "A very successful shoot."

While the brigade conducted its musketry practice, three men per battery received instruction in the Hotchkiss light machine gun, as all batteries were to be armed with this weapon for defence against aircraft under 3,000 feet. By the end of the month, though, the army had second thoughts. Instead, two .303-calibre Lewis guns were issued to each battery, along with twelve 47-round magazines per gun. Though prone to stoppages, the air-cooled Lewis was light enough to be carried by one man; strong men could fire it from the shoulder. In skilled hands it would deliver 550 rounds per minute. All NCOs and gunners, along with a small proportion of drivers, were taught to use the Lewis.

Bathing facilities at Ames were inadequate, as McKeown complained in the War Diary on January 3: "Considerable trouble being experienced getting baths for the men." This was a serious matter, and it took two days of prodding the Service Corps before he recorded, "Baths becoming available after much effort."

On January 4, a brigade concert was held in a large YMCA tent in Lières, a mile from Ames. Entertainment was provided by the "Gloom Chasers," a 2nd Divisional troupe. On Sunday, January 6, Protestants and Catholics attended a voluntary Church Parade; "Good attendance," McKeown reported. That evening there was another concert, this time in Lillers. Bert and two other lieutenants received passes. "Beautiful concert and thoroughly enjoyed," he wrote. "The Cinema was packed, all the elite of Lillers. Had tea afterwards and a very nice ride home."

The following week was one of inspections. While Lieutenant-Colonel Constantine inspected the 17th and 20th Batteries on January 7, Bert — as acting battery commander at the 23rd, filling in for Major Paterson who was on a course in England — was busy checking the battery and getting it ready for review by the OC the following day. "Held a harness inspection at 2:00 PM. and was agreeably surprised at the condition it was in," he wrote. The next day, after a heavy snowstorm in the morning, he wrote, "The OC inspected the Battery at 2:00 PM. Drill Order Mounted. Seemed quite satisfied with everything."

He did not remain in billets that evening. "Rode over to Burbure [about three miles away] at night with Dick Bennett. Cold bitter night, wind and snow. Had dinner at the estaminet. Jeanne and her sister did us very well for dinner and I found afterwards that Jeanne is about the finest little dancer in the country. If only the music would have been better it would have been the greatest treat yet. Didn't get back home until early in the AM."

Training continued through the second week of January, and the men enjoyed a half-holiday on Saturday afternoon, the twelfth. On

Sunday two services were held, the first at 8:00 a.m. for Catholics in the local church and a second, for Protestants, in the schoolhouse at 9:15. In the afternoon Bert and Dick Bennett rode once more into Lillers, where they encountered other officers, and soon a big party was in progress. Later the officers enjoyed a dinner at the Hôtel du Commerce before heading back to camp.

On Monday, January 14, the brigade received orders to relieve the 4th CDA on January 19, taking over the latter's positions in the Méricourt/Avion section of the Canadian front. "Back to our old haunts," Bert noted.

Unknown to Bert, Lieutenant-Colonel Constantine had recommended him for promotion. Ahead of him were 10 lieutenants with greater seniority; his captaincy would be slow in coming unless there were transfers or fatalities in the brigade.

Major-General Burstall, GOC 2nd Canadian Division, planned an inspection of the 5th and 6th Artillery Brigades at Ames on the sixteenth, during which he would present medal ribbons to recent winners. The men made a great effort to clean up their gear. "Inspected 'Marching Order' this AM," Bert recorded. "Rest of day spent on harness." On the fifteenth, the brigade was pelted with prolonged rain, which, with melting snow, caused temporary floods and damaged roads in nearby areas. "Impossible to do much in preparation for tomorrow's inspection," Bert wrote morosely. "It will be a sad affair if this weather holds. Haven't been out of the house all day. The joys of a Battery Commander."

With continuing rain the next morning, Burstall cancelled the inspection at the last minute. "Biggest fiasco yet in the way of inspections," observed Bert. "After turning the men out at 5:00 AM we were on the way to Parade Ground, men soaked through, harness wet and vehicles dirty, when the order came through 'Parade Cancelled.' The men's faces registered disgust!" McKeown, whose Military Cross (MC) was to have been bestowed by Burstall, received the decoration a few days later. In the afternoon Bert and other junior officers rode into Lillers, trying to forget the morning's events. "Then the fun started. Discovered a new officers' club. Dinner at the Hôtel du Commerce and some dinner!"

Anxious to get married, Bert petitioned for leave, admitting in his diary on the seventeenth, "Prospects none too encouraging, but wait and see." Not scheduled for leave again until April at the earliest, his request stood little chance of being approved. When he learned later of Lieutenant-Colonel Constantine's recommendation for promotion, Bert admitted, "Some satisfaction in having been recommended for another 'Pip' but that won't help me any next April!"

An artillery OP, January 1918. *Courtesy of Library and Archives Canada,* PA-003658.

The two-day march began the following morning, taking the brigade through familiar towns and villages. On the nineteenth, arriving at the wagon lines at La Targette at 12:30 p.m., Bert's diary noted, "Found everything in a shocking state. Most of men's 'bivvies' pulled down & all woodwork burned, even lining of Nissen huts." The War Diary echoed his dismay. The men found "an immense amount of damage had been done to billets and hutments, practically all woodwork having been removed and evidently used as firewood."

Bert did not remain at La Targette and pushed on to Petit Vimy with one section of the 23rd. There they relieved one section of the 21st Battery. Gun positions were in better condition than Bert expected, and the 21st's howitzers, spare parts, and stores were all in good order. As if to welcome the newcomers, the Germans sent over a few 4.1s.

The brigade was not prepared to let the Germans enjoy the sector's previous quiet. As Bert noted with satisfaction, "Working parties were systematically shot up, trenches raided and parties who were wont to bask in the sun behind the railway embankment were sent scurrying to their dugouts by a sniper gun...."

January 22. Showers.

Went up front this AM to look over battle positions on our charge. Found 3 of them but d— if I could find the fourth. Looks as though they gave us the wrong map location.

We get 15 DAC men tomorrow and just about time, too. To date we have 51 men on leave, 11 men in hospital, and 12 on Command, making a total of 74 — almost 40% of the Battery.

January 23. Mostly fair.

An order came in this AM to carry out night firing from our Alternative Position with one Howitzer. Very simple on the face of it, but it kind of spoiled my day and gave the boys a lot of unnecessary work. Had to call [Lieutenant Gordon] Burnett in from OP to carry it out.

Position was untenable, so had to carry on in the open. Took less than an hour to pull the Howitzer out, take up position 500 yds. away, fire 12 rds, and get her back in pit again.

Against a possible German attack, batteries began to strengthen gun positions so they could withstand a near miss from a 5.9-inch shell. Once this was done, alternative positions would be similarly strengthened. "In the area," McKeown wrote, "there is a good deal of [construction] material and as little as possible will be drawn from Engineers. There is a limited quantity of reinforced concrete blocks lying about near the water tower at La Coulotte. There is a good number of iron rails near this headquarters [at Givenchy-en-Gohelle]."

Rations and water sufficient for 24 hours were stored at each gun pit, along with 1,000 rounds of small arms ammunition, the idea being that battery positions could be used as rallying points for infantry in the event of an enemy breakthrough. Further, battery positions were to be ringed with barbed wire, though McKeown cautioned it "should not be so heavy that it will show up on photographs." Expecting the Germans to use tanks in the future, the flank guns of all 18-pounder batteries were detailed as anti-tank guns. The pits were then modified so the 18-pounders could be pulled out quickly to engage any approaching tanks. Work began at once, so that Bert could write on January 24, "Good work being done on pits." It was a fairly quiet day, though Bert recorded "Fritz tossed a few 4.1s around the position tonight. Hit the cookhouse but no damage done."

Misty weather on January 26 made for a quiet day for the artillery of both sides, as direct observation was impossible. At the end of the day's entry in the War Diary, McKeown noted, "Units being encouraged to ask for seeds and put in vegetable gardens." This referred to a plan whereby units in rear areas would grow some of their own food. It was hoped this would improve the soldiers' diet, provide an outlet for the energy of young men, and help alleviate a growing food shortage in England caused by the U-boat campaign. Batteries were expected to look after a half-acre plot, while the headquarters section was allocated a quarter-acre. It was obvious no one in British headquarters thought much for the prospects for a war of movement.

The 5th Brigade took to the idea with gusto. By mid-February the War Diary noted: "Some farm implements (plows & harrows) were salvaged by one of our batteries from Givenchy tonight to cultivate the garden allotment at the Wagon Lines." When a brigade rotated to the front, the incoming unit was expected to take over and care for the garden, though how the crop was to be divided was never specified. So successful was the scheme that by March the army even considered setting up pig farms, though this idea never went anywhere.

On January 26 two members of the 23rd Battery, Quartermaster Sergeant David Scott and Bombardier George McIntosh, were arrested for drunkenness. "Some mess," Bert wrote, "but guess there will be a cleanup this time." Three days later Lieutenant-Colonel Constantine remanded the pair for a Field General Court-Martial. "Almost a pleasure remanding the QM for the CO," Bert admitted, "but it did hurt with McIntosh, as he is one of the oldest friends I have in the Battery."

January 28. Heavy fog.

"In the midst of war we are at peace." One would think so by some of the damn fool messages "they" shoot through. For instance, working like h— getting out a report on the Battle Position, sleeves rolled up, etc. when this comes through:

To: OC GORGET

PLEASE STATE QUANTITY OF SEED POTATOES REQUIRED FOR UNIT GARDENS AAA URGENT

From: GOGGLE

Can you believe it?

Preoccupied with paperwork, Bert did not bother to respond. A few days later, 2nd CDA headquarters sent the following:

AAA CAN YOU NOW STATE REQUIREMENTS IN SEED POTATOES FOR UNIT GARDENS AAA URGENT AAA.

Gunners with farm backgrounds provided an answer: 16 bushels per acre were required, given the favourable growing conditions in northern France.

January 30. Fair.

An MG officer around today with advice about placing our Lewis guns. I think the boys will have a lot of fun when we get them, but God help the poor RFC unfortunate who flies a plane over our position which in any way resembles a Hun.

As the last entry in the January War Diary, McKeown wrote:

Very quiet day again, no doubt due to persistence of the ground mist. Outside of harassing fire, activity was practically nil.

In spite of rapid changes in weather conditions during the past month, the health of the men has been good on the whole. The Wagon Lines are again comfortable and the gun positions greatly improved since coming into action.

Wiring and defence of battery positions is being pushed forward, and new defensive positions constructed. If the enemy attack, we will not be caught unprepared, and [the] Hun is likely to have a warm reception.

26

"Looks Like One Hell of a Job!"

For Bert and the 23rd Battery, February got off to a tranquil start. His diary noted: "Quiet day. Usual harassing fire. Nothing of importance to report." One of McKeown's entries in the War Diary was not good news as far as Bert was concerned: "New leave allotment commencing this date, considerably reduced, as we have no men who have been in France over 9 months."

"Hostile artillery inactive on the whole," McKeown wrote a day later, a typical entry for the week. "Aeroplanes busy on both sides but no combats. We do the usual night firing." For the howitzers, night firing consisted of three separate targets — a headquarters, some cellars, and a crossroads. Each was to be hit with different shells (gas, incendiary, and HE respectively). To keep the Germans off guard, the bulk of the firing was done during the two hours following dusk, and two hours before daylight, with short bursts at irregular intervals during the night. If the Germans opposite didn't get much sleep, neither did Canadian gunners.

The courts-martial of Quartermaster Sergeant Scott and Bombardier McIntosh were held on February 4, with Lieutenant-Colonel William Harrison of the ammunition column presiding. Both men were charged with drunkenness while on active service; Scott entered a plea of guilty and the court ordered him reduced to the rank of sergeant. McIntosh pleaded "Not guilty." The first witness was Lieutenant Theodore

Geernaert of the 23rd Battery, who testified that on January 26 he had "found Bdr McIntosh in the [QM] Stores with an open jar of rum beside him. He was drunk." Four other witnesses corroborated Geernaert's story. Found guilty, he was reduced to the ranks. Both sentences were reviewed, as was the normal practice, by Brigadier-General Panet, who confirmed them four days later.

> *February 5.* Fair & warm.
> Left the Battery at 10 AM. Called at Brigade [Headquarters] then went on to our rear position in Cité Caumont. Work progressing very well. Walked over to 17th Battery at Cité de l'Abbatoir, arrived just in time for lunch.
> Heard of good news of Jim's & Muir[head]'s promotions. [Austin] Latchford & [Nello] Buchanon also get their other star.
> Walked more today than I have in months.

On the sixth it was decided to stage a trench raid at some future date, and McKeown got out the appropriate orders to the 23rd Battery to begin wire cutting in front of the designated German trenches. After lunch the next day, Major Alex Paterson arrived unexpectedly at brigade headquarters, his course in England for battery commanders having ended. With his return, Bert turned over responsibility for the battery. On the eighth, amid showers, Bert and Major Paterson inspected the various gun positions the battery occupied. "Quite some walk," Bert admitted.

> *February 9.* Fair.
> Had everything packed up, ready to go down and take over the Wagon Lines when a wire came in from HQ telling me to report there for a few days as McKeown had gone to hospital with pleurisy.
> Went down & looked over the position in [Cité] Caumont first & reported to the Colonel about 4:30 PM.

Lieutenant-Colonel Constantine was an astute judge of men. He appointed Bert as acting adjutant, taking over from McKeown. In effect, Bert became the OC's assistant and the brigade's chief administrative officer. As a result, he became intimately acquainted with the operations and activities of each of the four batteries, and the job brought him in contact with senior officers on a daily basis. His duties included preparing the War Diary and getting orders out to the batteries. Along with that he had to produce the day's Routine Orders, dealing with a variety of subjects. It was a position of considerable responsibility and called for an officer who could focus on details, function well under pressure, meet tight deadlines and, above all, communicate effectively. Though he did not yet know it, Bert possessed all these qualities in abundance.

In a confidential report written a year later, Lieutenant-Colonel Constantine wrote of Bert:

- good knowledge & ability
- very good disciplinarian
- good instructor
- very good leader of men
- hard working & painstaking.

To Bert, the assignment was only temporary. In his diary he wrote, "Just substituting until Bennett* gets back from leave, but anything is possible. Looks like one hell of a job!" No longer was he at the wagon lines or gun pits with his section of the 23rd. Instead he worked at brigade headquarters at Givenchy-en-Gohelle in a sandbagged dugout whose roof was reinforced with steel rails. It was sparely furnished with a battered desk, chairs, a couple of cots, and a map board. Lanterns and candles provided illumination, and the only modern feature was a small telephone switchboard with connections to the four batteries and FOOs in their scattered OPs.

Bert's first entry in the War Diary, and initialled, was for February 8:

Enemy working parties still continue to operate in spite of continued sniping by our 18-pounders. Casualties have been

---

*Dick Bennett served as adjutant until Jim McKeown took over in January.

observed. Gun in position at [Cité] St. Edouard has done effective work & is evidently causing the enemy some annoyance.

The first order bearing his signature was a short message originated by Scotty Duguid at Divisional Artillery headquarters. Duguid's message, describing the coordinates of the southern boundary of the Canadian Corps, bore a typed addition at the bottom:

To: OCs All Batteries
   The above for your information, please. Incorporate in Defence Scheme.
   (signed) A.E. Sargent Lieut.

February 10. Fair.
   Just 57 steps to get down to my new home!
   No wonder Jim went sick down here. It's the deepest dugout I have ever been in and the air is naturally none too fresh.
   I never realized what work was until I landed this job. The hours are going to be something bloody! Bed 1:30 AM last night & it will be worse tonight.

On top of his new duties, Bert was called as a defence witness in the court-martial of Farrier-Sergeant John Hamm of the 23rd Battery. Hamm was charged with two offences: stealing a mare from public property, and conduct to the prejudice of good order and military discipline while on active service, allegedly having then sold the mare to a French civilian. Compared to most courts-martial, this one was long and complicated. The prosecution called nine military and civilian witnesses, with testimony taken through an interpreter, while the defence called six witnesses. Sworn as the fifth witness, and making his first appearance in a court-martial, Bert testified, "I have known the accused since March 1915. I was at that time an NCO in the same Brigade as the accused for fourteen months. I was an officer in the same battery with the accused for seventeen months. I have always found the accused absolutely trustworthy. He has always been conscientious in his work. I have no hesitation in giving him a very good character." Scotty Duguid and Lieutenant-Colonel Harrison, each of whom had previously commanded Hamm, testified in a similar vein. The 23rd Battery was relieved when Hamm was found not guilty.

February 11. Fair.

I have certainly taken over this job under somewhat unfavorable circumstances. No one to take over from, everything seems in a mess. The Orderly Room sergeant away on leave and only the Paymaster's assistant to rely upon.

However I guess we can make the grade. Had a talk with the OC and know just where I stand, and that helps a whole lot.

Jim McKeown was recovering — slowly. Taken originally to the 5th Canadian Field Ambulance, a hospital camp five miles behind Givenchy, he was admitted on the fifteenth to the British-run No. 20 General Hospital at Camiers on the Channel coast near Boulogne. Bert and the rest of the brigade did not expect to see McKeown again for a long time, feeling their friend would soon be invalided to England.

If Bert was feeling the pressure of work, so were others in the short-handed brigade. "Our men are overworked," he wrote in the War Diary on February 17. "At present we are improving horse standings and building accommodation for personnel at the Wagon Lines, improving our present battery positions, and building six complete brigade positions in rear areas. At the same time we are in action on a, by no means, 'peace' front and engaged in important fighting operations."

At 2:00 a.m. on the night of February 18/19, parties from the 27th Battalion raided the enemy trenches. Originally planned for 11:00 p.m. on the night of the eighteenth, it was put back three hours to allow the artillery to develop a revised barrage plan. Previously, the artillery had expended considerable effort in cutting lanes in the German barbed wire; however, infantry patrols the previous night discovered the gaps were being watched by the Germans, who suspected the Canadians were up to something. Amending his previous Operation Orders, Bert got the necessary changes out to all concerned in a timely fashion. His description in the War Diary for the nineteenth is a model of clear and concise reporting. The raid, he recorded, was:

... an absolute success. Artillery barrage reported "excellent" by the Infantry in spite of its being placed only 50 yards in front of the raiding parties, and fired from varying ranges over 4000 yards. 4.5 Hows opened up 10 minutes ahead of Zero at a very slow rate on the lanes which were to be used by raiders, in order to clear them of any "knife tests" that might have been set out by the enemy. Our 18-pdrs and artillery on both flanks opened up simultaneously at Zero. Synchronization had been carefully done. Four minutes after Zero, enemy MGs opened up a desultory fire and 2 minutes later his field guns began to retaliate, and it was not until Zero+10 that his heavy artillery came into action, and then the retaliation was only light.

The demonstrations on either flank were successful in diverting his attention from the point of attack.

At Zero+14 one party returned with 2 prisoners and two minutes later the other party returned with 3 unwounded and 1 wounded prisoner.

Their return we communicated to all by a prearranged light signal. Our casualties nil.

This Bde HQ was in close touch with the infantry throughout the operation by means of telephone communication with a FOO in the front line.

On the twentieth, the brigade learned that it, along with other units, would be relieved on the twenty-second by the 3rd CFA Brigade. Guns were left in situ and the relief of all batteries was completed by noon on the designated day, though Lieutenant-Colonel Constantine, Bert, and the rest of the Headquarters Section remained behind until after nightfall. Transportation had been laid on to their new quarters at Haillicourt, eight miles northwest, near the mining town of Bruay. "At 7:00 PM the OC with HQ party moved complete by lorry, arriving there at 8:30 PM."

The men were agreeably surprised by their new home. "Billets appear to be good," Bert recorded in the War Diary. "Horse standings very good: covered stables and harness rooms." Haillicourt even had a movie theatre, a barn decorated with Allied flags, where Frank

Hazlewood took in *The Yellow Fang*, a five-reel detective drama. A few days later, the program changed to a Charlie Chaplin film he had already seen in Toronto.

The next days were spent in getting settled and organizing various details such as town picquets, water picquets, and other similar tasks. Four officers, as a result of promotion, were transferred from the brigade and three replacements arrived. A month in the line had had little adverse effect on the men. They were, Bert noted, "generally in a good state of health and the horses are in splendid condition."

With his brigade in rest, Lieutenant-Colonel Constantine developed a training syllabus that went out to battery commanders under Bert's signature. It was similar to that of seven weeks earlier, though gun drill against moving tanks was now instituted, with a horsed General Service or ammunition wagon used as a target. This special anti-tank training was given to two officers and six men per battery. Days began with reveille at 6:45, and the men were kept busy until 5:00 p.m., when dinner was served. Wednesday and Saturday afternoons were half-holidays, and Saturday morning was devoted to general grooming of the horses and cleaning of harness, guns, and equipment. With more than 55 ORs and nine officers absent on various courses, and much of the time consumed by cleaning guns and equipment, it was impossible to follow the syllabus very closely.

The 2nd Canadian Division had been in the mining district long enough for the backcountry, where infantry and artillery units took their rest, to develop an extensive infrastructure supporting more than 12,000 troops. Villagers in the area got to know the men well and regarded "their" Canadians with affection. Bob Gillespie recalled that the 23rd Battery at Haillicourt "was busy all the time — stables and steel in the daytime and the estaminets at night." Six miles southeast lay Château de la Haie, a massive building capable of accommodating two full infantry battalions (about 2,000 men). The officers of 5th Brigade were welcomed at the Officers' Club in the château, and ORs had access to a wet canteen. Also at the château was a theatre where the "See Twos," the highly regarded 2nd Divisional troupe, put on nightly revues of a professional calibre. The YMCA, which did so much for Canadian troops throughout the war, operated two cinemas and two 500-seat theatres, where the "Y Emmas" played to packed audiences.

Leave was always a subject of great interest to Bert. At month's end, he recorded gloomily, "The English leave allotment has undergone a drastic cut, from an average of 5 [men] per day during January to 4 per week during this month. In spite of this cut, there are only 10 men in the Brigade who have not had leave for over 9 months." Hopes of an April wedding began to fade.

As Bert settled into the tasks of administration, he began assembling a mass of paperwork and appendices for the February War Diary, a total of 165 pages.

France 2/3/18

Haven't the faintest idea now when I last wrote. I remember sending a couple of Field Postcards sometime during the last month and a cable shortly after I came back from leave but as for a letter — it seems somewhere in the dim past. I think I could find out just when it was by looking through my old diary but I am afraid the result might prove somewhat of a shock and I will probably feel more comfortable without it. Too much has happened in the last three months for me to try to detail it.

No doubt you have heard all there is to hear of my last trip to England from Cud. I am awfully glad Cud did write, for otherwise you might have been a bit anxious at not hearing from me, but I have hoped the odd cables and Field Postcards (very odd, as a matter of fact) would help somewhat.

I have had rather varied experience the last three months, first as Acting Captain, then Acting Major, and now I am Acting Adjutant of the Brigade and, what with one or other, I have usually found quite enough to do to keep me fairly busy.

This Adjutant's job nearly had me stopped for a while though, for I took it over under rather adverse circumstances and for about a week I was never quite sure whether I was coming or going. It happened just after the Major [Alex Paterson] had got back from seven weeks in England. I had just finished turning over to him at the Battery and had my kit packed, ready to go down and take over the Wagon Lines, when a wire came in for me to report to Brigade HQ and have my kit follow along.

When I arrived, I found the Adjutant had gone to hospital in the morning, the Orderly Room Sergeant was on leave, and the Colonel was kind of up against it. We were on a fairly active front at the time and there were some rather ticklish operations pending. If you know anything of what an Adjutant's job is, you will know what I was let in for, but if you don't, you cannot possibly imagine it. I have been on the job for about a month now, the Adjutant is expected back in a few days but whether or not I will go back to the Battery again, I don't know.

I suppose Ken [Darling] has told you some time ago I managed to see him again for a few minutes one afternoon. I must have walked twelve miles to do it, but was more than worth it to see the boy again. He is bigger and huskier than ever. Was up at the guns when I found him, and quite a typical gunner. We have moved again since I saw him, but the first chance I have to get away I will ride over and try to find him.

I can't stop for more tonight. I have had letters from everyone, I think, in the last month.

At last feeling comfortable with his workload, Bert resumed his diary.

March 5. Fair.

Went to a lecture with Major [Alexander] Donald at Theatre Bruay on "Employment of Tanks with Infantry" by Lieut.-Col. [Christopher] Baker-Carr [Tank Corps]. Extremely interesting. Went down to 2nd CDA [at Chateau de la Haie] afterward for tea.

March 6. Fair & warm.

17th & 20th Batteries inspected by the General [Panet] this AM.

Rode to Bruay in evening with [Major Roy] Muirhead, took in the 4th Div. Show & had dinner at the [Hôtel du] Commerce after. Good party.

Even with the brigade at rest, military justice could not be ignored. Next on the rotation and not in the chain of command of either of the two accused, Bert was appointed prosecutor for the courts-martial of the 20th Battery's Gunner Harry Coltran and Driver Stanley Lewis. It was not a job any junior officer enjoyed, but it was an essential part of their duties. Following the *Manual of Military Law*, officers appointed to prosecute or defend had to collect witnesses and gather evidence, a time-consuming distraction from their other duties.

As these were the first cases in which Bert acted as prosecutor, they are worth reviewing. Major Roy Muirhead served as president of the court; the two officers constituting the court were Captain Ernest McColl and Lieutenant Hyndman Irwin. Coltran was charged with absenting himself without leave from 6:30 a.m. on Feb. 16 to 11:50 a.m. on the twentieth, having been apprehended that day in Paris at the Gare du Nord. After the charge was read, Coltran pleaded guilty. Declining to call any witnesses or make a statement, he was sentenced to 90 days Field Punishment No. 1,* a verdict that was confirmed a week later.

In the second court-martial, Lewis entered a plea of "Not guilty" to the charge of "Stealing a stove and stove pipe on or about February 22nd, 1918." Bert then called three witnesses, one of whom was Lieutenant Beatty. "On the morning of February 25th," Beatty testified, "I entered a small room off 'A' Subsection Harness Room and saw there a stove which I had not previously seen. I was ordered by Lieut.-Col. Constantine, who I was with at the time, to have this stove removed. I had it removed and put in charge of Sergt. Webb at Billet No. 74, where QM Stores of the 20th Battery are. The accused was accompanying me at the time." Lewis testified on his own behalf, along with another witness, Corporal James Clarke.

After the court was cleared for deliberation, the officers reached a verdict and Lewis was led back in. Then the verdict was pronounced: "Guilty." Beatty, then testified to Lewis's character: "He has always been an exceptionally good man. His harness and horses have always

---

*A humiliating form of punishment, in which the soldier was tied standing upright to a fixed object, like a post or a wheel, for up to two hours a day, in view of his fellow soldiers. As well, the soldier was assigned as many fatigues as possible during this period, his rations were reduced, and he was denied the use of rum and tobacco.

been among the best, if not the best in the unit. I have always found him during these three years to be of exemplary character." No matter. Lewis received five days Field Punishment No. 1.

Unexpectedly, Jim McKeown returned to the brigade at noon on March 8 after a month's absence. "Sure is a relief to hand over to him. Feel I had nothing to do right now," Bert wrote in his diary. In the evening, the brigade received a Warning Order: it would relieve the 14th Brigade on March 14 and 15. "A little sooner than we expected," he admitted ruefully.

A new shoulder patch, blue with a capital "C" and superimposed "II" in gold wire, became available for all officers of the Second Division in early March and was to be worn on both shoulders. Routine Orders of March 10 called for "Batteries to indent immediately for necessary supplies."

Though McKeown was back at brigade headquarters, the workload was such that Bert was retained as assistant adjutant, having gained Lieutenant-Colonel Constantine's confidence. Throughout the month, Bert continued to prepare the War Diary, though he had other tasks as well, as his diary attests.

> *March 9.* Fair & warm.
>
> Started off with the OC at 9:30 AM in a "Tin Lizzie." Ran through Barlin, Hersin, Grand & Petit Servins, Carency, Souchez, Angres & Liévin to 14th Bde HQ. Looked over our future HQ. Came back to Chateau de la Haie & had lunch at the [Officers'] Club.
>
> Came around through Braquement to 1st CDA, saw [Lieutenant Dick] Bennett & tried to make a horse deal.
>
> Back home at 5 PM. The OC sure is a corker to travel with.

By chance, the brigade was returning to about the same sector it had covered in the Hill 70 show the previous September, with gun positions and brigade headquarters in Liévin, and wagon lines in Sains-en-Gohelle and Fosse 10.

Two days later, Lieutenant-Colonel Constantine sent the following to 2nd Division Artillery:

To: 2nd CDA
Lieut. A.E. Sargent
The marginally noted Officer has been selected as Orderly
Officer for this Brigade.
May this appointment be approved, please, from this date.
(signed) C.F. Constantine Lieut.-Col.

The OC's request was granted and Bert's appointment became effective the same day.

March 13 was Bert's last day at Haillicourt; still hoping to get leave in April, he rode in the morning to Béthune, where he purchased some items of clothing for the wedding, along with other odds and ends. "Very warm ride," he wrote, "just like summer."

March 14. Showers in AM. Back in Action.

Left Haillicourt at 1:15 PM with Signal outfit. Went through Barlin & Hersin to Sains-en-Gohelle. Stopped there long enough to see Ken [Darling]. Found him on kitchen fatigue & enjoying it! Left Signals to come on after dusk & rode up through Petit Sains, Bully-Grenay, Maroc, to Fosse 11. Walked from there to Liévin, arriving about 5:30 PM.

March 15. Fair & warm.

Went around the OPs in AM. This front has changed wonderfully since we left it last September. A great many landmarks have disappeared.

Got back late for lunch and found the OC and Jim had arrived. We took over about 2:30 but the other crowd [the 14th Brigade] didn't get away until about six-thirty.

All ranks were relieved to find "the gun positions in good repair," and Bob Gillespie observed that the 23rd Battery "took over the best Wagon Lines of our history." Once more, the brigade settled into its accustomed activities. Guns were registered on various targets, orders came down for the usual harassing fire at night, and plans were drawn up for nighttime raids, supported by artillery.

March 16. Fair & warm.

McKeown arranged my leave for 10th inst. That means April 11th will be The Day, providing nothing turns up in the meantime.

27

Operation Michael

At 4:40 a.m. on March 21, the German Army launched a massive offensive along a 40-mile front held by the British Fifth Army and part of Third Army. Code-named "Operation Michael," it was only the third major German offensive on the Western Front since the outbreak of war in 1914.*

Planning for the attack began the previous December, when the High Command realized time was running out for the Imperial Army. The German economy was in dire straits, manpower reserves were nearly depleted, and by the summer of 1918, a large, well-equipped American army would be in the field. The collapse of Russia and the Bolshevik peace meant Germany could redeploy more than 60 divisions from the Eastern to the Western Front, and this was done over the months of January and February. By the end of March, Germany had 192 divisions in the west, giving it a temporary numerical superiority over the Allies. Even with American divisions arriving in France in growing numbers, Germany could expect to enjoy a manpower advantage until midsummer. Quartermaster-General Erich Ludendorff's strategy aimed to achieve a war-winning decision in the west before the advantages in men and *matériel* shifted irrevocably in favour of the Allies.

Operation Michael, the first of five separate large-scale attacks between March and July, was intended to punch a hole through the

---

*The first two were the invasion of Belgium and France in August 1914 and the attack at Verdun in February 1916.

Allied army on the Somme. Following this, the Germans would wheel to the northwest and pin the BEF against the Channel, thus ending the war.

The attack employed von Hutier's tactics, which had proved so effective in reversing the British gains at Cambrai the previous November. Elite storm troops (*Stosstruppen*) — specially trained, highly mobile assault forces — were taught to bypass and not be held up by British strongpoints, leaving these to be overcome by following waves of infantry, while the storm troops pressed the attack against command, control, and communications targets. Such tactics required intelligent and well-trained men who could make on-the-spot decisions, and placed great emphasis on personal initiative, speed, and surprise.

As well, von Hutier brought to the Western Front his artillery specialist, Lieutenant-Colonel Georg Bruchmüller, whose innovative tactics at Riga the previous year were so successful he had been nicknamed *Durchbruchmüller* — Breakthrough Müller. For Operation Michael, Bruchmüller's five-hour bombardment consisted of three phases: a short attack on British command and communications centres, followed by counter-battery fire to destroy any possibility of British retaliation, and concluded with a hurricane bombardment of British frontline defences with gas and high-explosive shells.

The offensive was a stunning tactical success, smashing through the southern end of General Gough's Fifth Army. By the end of the first day, advance elements of the German Army were into open country, having taken more ground in one day than the British captured in four months at the Somme. On that first day, 7,500 British soldiers were killed and 21,000 were taken prisoner. In the following days, Fifth Army was pushed relentlessly back over the old Somme battlefield. To the north, General Julian Byng's Third Army mostly held its front, its defensive positions having been largely constructed before the attack.

Ludendorff's offensive finally came to a halt on April 5, when his exhausted army outran its artillery and logistical support. By the standards of the Great War, it was a brilliant success, driving the Allies back 40 miles, capturing vast quantities of supplies, and taking more than 80,000 prisoners. Nonetheless, it was a hollow victory, for it achieved no strategic goal. The territory gained was of little value and cost Germany almost 240,000 men, most of them specialized assault troops. Worse, the Allies continued to hold the important rail centre of Amiens, the capital of Picardy, from which future attacks could be launched against the German-held salient.

In the Canadian lines around Lens, there was no inkling of the disaster about to befall Fifth Army, 35 miles to the southeast.

March 21. Fair & warm.

Day commenced very noisy. Huns put on a very heavy area *strafe* from the north portion of our front. An SOS went up on our front and we opened up. The shoot started at 5:30 & lasted until 6:15.

Rest of day quiet. The Col. goes on leave this PM.

Made a trip around the OPs in the afternoon.

The next day, Bert noticed strange orders coming through. Relief of an infantry brigade was cancelled, and then a trench raid, planned for March 24, was scrubbed. Rumours of a major enemy offensive swirled through the Canadian lines, preparing the gunners for a Warning Order that arrived at 1:00 p.m. It called for the brigade to withdraw to the Wagon Lines, complete with 18-pounders and howitzers, at 7:30 that night. "This was eventually carried out," Bert's diary recorded. "The last battery reported 'All Clear' at 8:50 PM." On arriving at the Wagon Lines at 10:30, the gunners found new orders. They would march at 9:00 the next morning toward Arras. As Fifth Army crumbled, no one knew whether the Germans could be stopped, or what they might do next. "Three days of uncertainty followed," Bert wrote, "during which orders received and issued were no sooner issued than they were cancelled." All leave was stopped and those on leave were recalled. Lieutenant-Colonel Constantine, who got as far as Boulogne, returned in the early hours of March 24.

The men took the opportunity to pare down their kits, and Bert sent a package of boots, jacket, and breeches to Browning Road for safekeeping. In all, the brigade divested itself of seven wagonloads of excess gear, depositing them with the town major at Acq.

March 24. Fair & warm.

Army Reserve and under orders to move at 1 hour's notice.

Rode over to Aubigny with Major Paterson and came back to 23rd for dinner. Seemed very much like old times again. [Lieut. Julius] Waterous, just back from Nice, had some interesting yarns. Got into a game of poker with somewhat disastrous results.

March 25. Fair & warm.

Evidently things are not going any too well down south and the powers don't know just what to do with us.

The next day orders arrived at 4:40 p.m. from Scotty Duguid at 2CDA for all batteries to harness up and prepare to march. The gunners moved fast. The last battery, Bert noted, reported ready at 5:20 p.m. The men stood to until a Warning Order arrived at 7:00 p.m.: they would march at 2:00 a.m. on the twenty-seventh. Horses were unhooked and fed, and the men rested. Over very congested roads, the brigade arrived at Basseux shortly after 7:00 a.m. "We secured a rather nice billet in an estaminet which had just been evacuated!"

Though Bert and brigade headquarters were well housed, most of the men were not. "Horse lines in the open, little shelter for the men," he wrote in the War Diary. Bob Gillespie described the uncertainty in the 23rd Battery. "We all watched our maps with anxious eyes as report after report of Hun successes to the south came in. Finally the line settled down and we were kept on our toes for some weeks by a repetition of such messages as 'Hun is expected to attack on this front tomorrow morning. Take all necessary precautions.'"

Third Army released a series of orders that McKeown circulated to battery commanders on behalf of Lieutenant-Colonel Constantine. "The situation demands," the instructions read, "that the line of Third Army be maintained at all costs. There must be NO withdrawal; if breaks occur, the line must be linked up again on the general line of our present position with the aid of such troops as can be made available....

"It must be borne in mind by all Commanders that conditions approximating open warfare exist at times, and no precautions will be neglected to guard against surprise."

In light of this, Duguid issued orders that all units were to main-tain an inlying picquet, armed with rifles and Lewis guns, under the command of an officer. They will be, he wrote, "particularly alert and should be visited at frequent intervals by an officer." A day later, he cir-culated further details of the "no withdrawal" order. "All officers and ranks are to be made to understand this. Most stringent orders must be issued by all Commanders to this effect, and officers who fail to observe the spirit of this order are to be relieved of their commands."

28/3/18

My correspondence has completely got out of hand now, and I don't know when I last wrote to anyone or when I last received letters from anyone. I am sorry to say I have had to let my diary drop away too, I hope not beyond hope of catching up, but it will require a lot of work. Ever since I left the Battery, or as a matter of fact before that, when I took over from the Major at the Battery, I have had very little time to do anything outside of the work for which I was responsible.

I think the last time I wrote I was doing Adjutant, while McKeown was in hospital. We never expected to see him back again, but he turned up apparently none the worse for his expe-rience. In fact, he seemed to have enjoyed it. And, if it had been anyone else but him, I am sure we would not have seen him for at least a month longer, as they evidently have pretty good times at the base when they have sufficiently recovered to be able to get out of hospital.

By the time McKeown got back I was just in a position where I could handle the Adj. job in about half the time it took me at first, so I was really sorry to have to turn it over, apart from the fact that it meant 50 cents a day extra to me, which is very much worth considering these days.

However I am still at Brigade Hqrs. doing Reconnaissance Officer and Assistant Adjutant. It is an interesting job and has possibilities of leading to something better.

Since the new Corps Seniority came into effect, it is the only chance I have of getting any promotion for, as a regimental officer, I have dropped about a hundred places at least, in the Corps. You see, ever since the Canadians first came to France, seniority out here dated from when you came to France as an officer and under that ruling, I would now be Senior Subaltern in the Brigade, if not a Captain. But in January, the new lists were issued and seniority dated from leaving Canada or date of receiving Commission, whether in England or France. I dropped 9 places in the Brigade alone, and have the pleasure of seeing officers who have only been in the country three to six months senior to me. It has been rather a sore point with me for the last month or so, and somewhat discouraging, just at this time when I was counting on it, but it is one of the things you get used to in this game. I have the satisfaction, however, of knowing I was recommended twice for my captaincy before the new lists came out.

While on the subject of disappointments, I might as well continue and give you my latest and greatest. You have heard from Cud that we had planned to be married in April. I had everything arranged, including a special leave to be dated from April 10th to May 1st, and we were to be married on the 11th of April. However, all leave was cancelled the other day when the Boche let loose a little hell over here, and now the chances don't look very good for weddings and such-like affairs. Another thing one gets used to in this pleasant little game.

I won't stop to write any more tonight as I am rather tired. We have had irregular hours for the last week or so and I find it pays to get to bed early, as we never know how long we are going to be there.

I was in the saddle about five hours today and covered almost 50 miles.

Good night all, and don't worry about me. You will read a lot of startling stuff in the papers no doubt, but don't let your imagination run away. I am absolutely fit and quite happy under some of the circumstances I have related.

If Bert's letters to the family had flagged, the two-way flow of correspondence between France and Browning Road had not. Bert's diary reveals that in the first three months of 1918 he sent 49 letters and cards to Rosalie, along with two cables, receiving in return 36 letters and cards, and one cable. Despite his administrative workload, he would maintain this rate of correspondence for the balance of the year.

In this period of uncertainty, Currie issued a Special Order to the Canadian Corps. While the first part was overly sentimental, raising hoots of derision in dugouts and billets, it concluded on a positive note:

> Canadians, in this fateful hour, I command you and I trust you to fight as you have ever fought, with all your strength, with all your determination, with all your tranquil courage. On many a hard-fought field of battle you have overcome this enemy. With God's help you shall achieve victory once more.

The 2nd CDA took up positions around Neuville-Vitasse to protect the southern approach to Arras. It came into the line on March 29–30, holding a front of 6,000 yards. The main feature of the Division's new area was a series of narrow ridges running from southwest to northeast. "The whole of my area within 3000 yards of the front line was under direct [German] observation," Major-General Burstall, the Division commander, later wrote. "There were very few suitable locations for my artillery to come into action, and such positions as were available quickly became known to the enemy."

March 30. Fair in AM. Rain in PM.

Left Basseux at 7:00 AM with Hqrs party and reached our new Hqrs [at Agny, 2 1/2 miles south of Arras] about 8:30. Not quite so *bon* as yesterday, as he [Fritz] scattered the odd whizz-bang over the lot. Had to leave the mess cart behind & go in on foot, but brought it up later when the shelling stopped.

On the thirty-first, Bert visited the various gun positions in the morning and then walked to the village of Beaurains with Harry Jardine to look for a suitable OP. On their way back, the two lieutenants came under fire from German 4.1s. Bert was disconcerted to find batteries of heavy howitzers had taken up positions behind the 5th

Brigade. "Does not look *bon* to me," he wrote, knowing they would soon be targeted by enemy gunners. Any German "shorts" would land in the 5th Brigade positions.

Bert's narrative section of the March War Diary ended on an upbeat note. "The men," he wrote on Easter Sunday, "are in good physical condition and horses are in excellent shape." The War Diary he assembled for the month was the largest to date for the brigade, amounting to 209 pages, of which just seven were handwritten narrative; the remainder consisted of orders, maps, artillery overlays, and other similar documents.

To close the month, Second Division staff circulated a five-paragraph situation report and instructions. "For the time being," the paper began, "the enemy has been checked all along the line. He will probably renew the offensive at an early date as soon as he has had time to bring up fresh divisions, guns and ammunition."

For once the staff got it right.

As the reserve positions of both the 5th and 6th Field Artillery Brigades required additional work, six officers and a hundred Other Ranks arrived from the Trench Mortar Group to lend a hand. They reported on April 1 and, for the next weeks, traded their mortar tubes for picks

Shell holes near Telegraph Hill, southeast of Arras. *Author's photo.*

and shovels. In their support line, 5th Brigade gunners stumbled across a large cache of ammunition in former battery positions, which had been evacuated in recent operations. Bert went to inspect the dump on April 1 and counted about 1,000 18-pounder shells, 500 4.5-inch howitzer rounds, and 1,000 for the 9.2s. Though the dump was just 600 yards from the front line, in full view of the enemy and within machine-gun range, the gunners decided to salvage the ammunition. Working at night to avoid detection, they recovered more than 1,500 shells by April 6.

On the whole, the brigade front was quiet, for many German field guns had been removed to support Ludendorff's next offensive. In the War Diary for April 2, Bert wrote: "the total absence of heavy calibre is very noticeable." The brigade still needed to find suitable OPs, and Bert went out again with the signals officer to Beaurains, then to Telegraph Hill, a prominent landmark two miles southeast of Arras, rising to 325 feet above sea level. "Most wonderful view of Hunland from there," he recorded, "but it is not a place one would choose for a home, as he has it covered with a whizz-bang battery all the time, shooting from very close up."

By now the 5th Brigade had established phone links to two six-inch howitzer batteries, one eight-inch howitzer battery, and one 60-pounder battery, enabling targets beyond the range of its 18-pounders and 4.5-inch howitzers to be attacked. Over at 2CDA headquarters, Scotty Duguid drafted the following: "Every opportunity is to be taken to fire on all targets of opportunity. Movement during the day will be fired upon, or if beyond the range of field guns, reported to Heavies and to this office, so that action can be taken at once." Duguid meant to harass and confuse the Germans. Night fire, he wrote, would be "intermittent throughout the hours of darkness — roads and trenches will be swept with bursts of fire, and creeping barrages of short duration put down, commencing as close to our line as possible and creeping by 100 yard lifts to +500 yards, to prevent the enemy digging any trenches in front of our line." Should any battery have any unused ammunition from its daily allowance of 60 rounds per 18-pounder and 50 per 4.5-inch howitzer, the unused portion would be expended on harassing fire.

April 3. Rain.

[Major]-General Burstall, [Major-]General Morrison and [Brigadier-]Gen. Panet all in here at the same time this AM. All seem quite confident of future events.

All kinds of movement shown by the enemy on our front today, and our guns had a regular field day. Had the Heavies working overtime.

Expecting the Canadian sector to be the target of the next advance, new orders went out to infantry and artillery units. If the Germans raided or penetrated a narrow section of the Canadian front line, "an immediate counterattack will be launched by commanders on the spot." In case of an attack on a large front, troops were expected to offer all possible resistance to the enemy advance. "There will be NO VOLUNTARY RETIREMENT," the order stressed. "If our troops are driven out of the front line they will fight their way back to the intermediate line where a firm stand must be made to delay the enemy as long as possible."

April 8. Rain & mist.

Duty from 4:00 AM.

The Boche started in at 9:45 AM to shell the country at large with gas and HE. Our people living in Beaurains got the worst of it. They got into the 23rd Bty's advanced WL with 5 HE [shells], wounding 1 man, killing 7 horses, and wounding 15 others. One of our shelters [at Headquarters in Agny] occupied by two signallers was hit by [an] 8" gas shell & 1 man buried. Seven men assisted to dig him out and he was apparently unhurt & felt no ill effects. It was not until about 5 PM that he was taken violently ill and removed to hospital. A little later all the others who had come in contact with it, including the 2 Gas Sergeants, became affected & went to hospital.

It was merely a diversion; the Germans had no intention of launching a full-scale attack against the Canadians, whose tenacity and fighting qualities they had come to respect. Thus, 30-odd miles north of Bert's position, Ludendorff's second offensive (code-named "Georgette") opened on the Lys sector at Armentières and Neuve Chapelle on April 9. Again employing the tactics of von Hutier and Bruchmüller, the attack on a front of 12 miles met with great initial success, capturing places that were familiar to the Canadian Corps and threatening to envelop Vimy Ridge from the north. The British were driven back more than 10 miles and the Channel ports were threatened. By April 11 the situation was so serious that Haig issued a now-famous Special Order of the Day, addressed to all ranks of the British Army in France and Flanders:

> There is no other course open to us but to fight it out. Every position must be held to the last man: there must be no retirement. With our backs to the wall and believing in the justice of our cause each one of us must fight on to the end.

During Georgette, the British abandoned — without a shot — Passchendaele Ridge, won at so great a cost the previous autumn, and once again the German Army knocked at the door of Ypres. The British finally rallied in front of Hazebrouck, an important railway centre; though the offensive was abandoned on April 29, Ludendorff had achieved another great tactical success. A strategic result proved as elusive as ever.

Brigadier Panet, feeling his 2nd CDA was stretched too thinly, had earlier requested additional artillery resources to cover his front. He was given three British brigades, just returned from Italy. Of these, two were assigned to Lieutenant-Colonel John Mackay's 6th Brigade and one to Lieutenant-Colonel Constantine's 5th Brigade. When Major Sir Henry Imbert-Terry of the Royal Field Artillery's 175th Battery appeared at brigade headquarters on April 9, Bert gave him a tour of the front. "After we had been out fifteen minutes," Bert noted, "he said he had heard more shell[fire] than all the time he was in Italy."

The next days were tranquil as the Germans pressed the attack at Armentières. On April 15, Bert noted "Another exceptionally quiet day. In spite of all our bursts of fire and harassing shoots, he has no come-back. He is either lying very low to fool us, or has withdrawn most of his artillery, and I am inclined to think it is the latter."

As a result of the severe fighting, all schools of instruction were temporarily discontinued and, worse — from Bert's point of view — all leave was stopped until further notice.

April 17. Fair but dull.

Duty 4:00 AM to 6:00 AM.

One requires a wonderful stock of optimism these days to keep afloat.

April 18. Dull & showery. Cold NW wind.

Duty to 2:00 AM.

Situation up north slightly improved. Looks as though we have him stopped now!

Tired of living like a mole, on April 22 Bert arranged to have new sleeping quarters built above ground. "This dugout life is getting me," he noted. That day he took Lieutenant-Colonel Constantine on a tour of the battery positions, the OP for the 18-pounder "sniper" gun, and the headquarters of the two infantry battalions immediately in front of the 5th Brigade. "Made quite a decent hike." The two men went out again the next afternoon inspecting the OP for the 17th and 18th Batteries. "Had some sport with 17th Sniper Gun shooting up a Boche plane which was brought down by one of our Camels NW of Neuville-Vitasse."

April 25. Dull & sultry. Thunderstorm 5:30 PM.

Duty from 3:30 AM.

Had lunch at 23rd and enjoyed a little music on the new gramophone.

April 26. Dull & misty.

No excitement at all these days. Wonder what they are keeping the Canadians for. Guess we are likely to find out sooner or later.

April 28. Dull & cloudy. Heavy ground mist.

[In the afternoon a] Hun plane made three successive trips over our rear and Battery areas at a low altitude of 2000 ft. Every

MG & AA gun in the country opened on him & still he got away each time.

Bert's War Diary consisted of 10 pages of handwritten narrative, followed by 74 appendices, amounting to an additional 130 pages. He summed up the month by observing, "There has been a noticeable improvement in the general health of the men during the month, compared to when the Brigade was out of the line, probably due to better accommodation and being away from congested civilian areas."

28

Holding the Line:
May and June 1918

By May, life in the still-quiet 2nd Divisional Artillery sector assumed a familiar pattern. The brigade continued its nightly harassing fire, targeting roads and approaches, often using information from prisoners. In addition, gunners provided support for Canadian trench raids and responded to SOS signals from the infantry when the Germans sent over raiding parties. In turn, the brigade came in for its share of enemy shelling, taking casualties almost every day. Despite this, the gunners realized they were lucky. As Bert frankly admitted, "There are probably lots of worse places than this we might be in."

Duty as orderly officer took Bert all over the rear areas, checking battery positions scattered over several square miles.

May 2. Fair & warm.

Duty 3:15 to 6:00 AM.

Increased activity on the part of the Boche artillery, particularly in rear areas.

General Panet up this AM and General Sir Julian Byng* and [Major-] General Burstall were around just after lunch.

---

*Byng commanded the Canadian Corps at Vimy as lieutenant-general; he took command of Third Army in June 1917. In 1921 he was appointed Canada's twelfth governor-general.

Up front all afternoon making a further reconnaissance of two anti-tank positions, determining arcs of fire and dead ground, etc.

May 3. Fair & warm. Sultry.

Duty to 3:15 AM.

20th Battery forward section got in the way of a burst of fire tonight: one gun out of action, one man killed and one wounded.

Took Jim & [Lieutenant] Mat Scott over to OP on Telegraph Hill in PM. Sniped at so hard [we] had to take to trenches.

Bert's reconnaissance of May 2 led the brigade to create two positions from which gunners could fire directly at any German tank that might come crawling across the open spaces of No Man's Land. The positions, each for one 18-pounder, were stockpiled with 200 rounds of HE and manned by picked detachments during daylight. Great care had been taken to conceal the positions from enemy observation. During construction, the gun pits were screened with camouflage netting. Thereafter they were covered with turf to blend in with the surroundings. The assigned crews lived about 50 yards from their gun, and all foot and wheel tracks were carefully covered up. Within a few days this arrangement changed. Not content to rely on fixed anti-tank positions, the entire 26th Battery of the 6th CFA Brigade was withdrawn from the line and formed into a mobile anti-tank unit. Three weeks later, having obtained an old 15-pounder, the gunners set it up in a forward gun pit and Bert went over to watch the trials. Some questioned its reliability, and the gunners fired the first test shell with some anxiety. "She worked steady as a rock but a little slow," Bert wrote. It went into action that night as an anti-tanker, replacing an 18-pounder that could be better used elsewhere.

May 5. Warm & sultry.

Duty to 5:15 AM.

Made a rather busy day of it. Didn't get to bed until 5:30 AM, up again at 9:30. Rushed my [Summary of] Intelligence through and met Maj. Bennett of 186th Battery at 11:45. Took him up front & showed him his anti-tank proposition. Fritz must have heard us coming, as he gave us a warm welcome.

May 6. Overcast and sultry.

The 18th Battery were rather badly shelled this afternoon with 5.9 How. No damage or casualties but will have to move tonight. The old Hun is becoming somewhat more active around these parts.

On May 7, Bert's diary noted: "A great deal of sickness around here these days, everyone seems to be having a tour at it. The OC is down today." The sickness was identified the following day in the War Diary. "A mild epidemic of botulism amongst all ranks in the forward area. Symptoms: headache, soreness in back and limbs, temperature at night, lasting for two to three days."*

May 8. Fair & warm.

Quiet day.

The 18th Battery has moved main position about 300 yards NW, as old position still shelled at intervals.

Went up with [Lieutenant John] Trewhitt in afternoon to OP NE of Mercatel. It is only 20 yards behind our front line and has a splendid view.

We are the only Div. of the Cdn. Corps in the line at present.

May 11. Dull. Perfect "dud."

Staff captain up from [Third] Army says leave will re-open the 1st of June. Here's fervently hoping!

May 12. Some showers in AM. Beautiful afternoon.

Duty from 2:30 to 6:30 AM.

Telephone message at 4:15 this AM that [Lieutenant Theodore] Geernaert has been killed at "Shrap" OP [on Telegraph Hill].

He is the first officer to be killed in the 23rd Battery.

May 13. Cold wind with rain.

_____

*In reality, this was a mild form of influenza that swept through the armies on the Western Front in the next six weeks.

An absolutely "dud" day.

Kept a fire in the "Mansion" all day & made ourselves as comfortable as possible.

Geernaert's funeral from Wagon Lines at 10:00 AM. The OC attended so Jim & I had to stay at home. There was a large attendance of officers and men.

Scientists had now developed techniques to locate German batteries by sound ranging and triangulation from listening posts. Over the next few nights, periods of complete silence were arranged for the Canadian guns (except, naturally, in the case of an SOS from the infantry), so specialists from the Engineers could pinpoint enemy guns for destruction.

May 16. Fair & warm.

Nothing doing, so got [Lieutenant] John Trewhitt and buggered off up through Mercatel. Travelled light, without serges, & just as well, as it *was* hot. Left at 4:00 PM & didn't get back until 9:00 PM.

Found a "pukka" OP in the front line from which the rear slopes of Neuville-Vitasse and also the Heninel Valley can be seen. Wonderful view. Never thought it existed on our front.

Located a [German] 5.9 How battery and saw one of the best air fights yet. Of course, the Boche crashed.

Wonderful day!

On May 18, Bert took the afternoon off and rode to Berneville to watch the 23rd Battery play an American team. "A mighty good and exciting game for the first of the season," he wrote. "The 'Sammies' led all the way but our boys tied the score in the 1st, 5th, 9th and 11th innings and won out in the 12th. Score 6–5. Good crowd present and the rooting in the 9th inning was [the] best part of the game."

Senior commanders were concerned that units had neglected other means of communications during three years of trench warfare, during which telephones became practically the sole means of relaying information. VI Corps (to which the brigade was temporarily attached) thus decreed that communications on designated days would be by alternate means. While phones could still be used to report an enemy attack or deal with an urgent tactical situation, for training purposes all other communications would be by visual signalling, runners, or mounted orderlies — the only means of passing information should there be a return to mobile warfare. Only one exception was allowed: officers at OPs, whose concealment might be endangered by the use of visual signals, could continue using telephones.

> *May 19*. Fair & warm.
> Had a wonderful trip this afternoon with [John] Trewhitt & Capt. [Ernest] McColl up through Mercatel to the front lines (25th Battalion) & from there through the 29th, 31st and Middlesex Bn to Telegraph Hill, & back through Telegraph Hill Switch to Beaurains & cross-country [to] home. Over 10 miles in a straight line & over 7000 yards through trenches, walking steadily from 2:45 to 8:15 PM. Don't think I ever enjoyed a bottle of beer quite as much as the one I had when I got back. We stopped at all the company Hqrs on the way & did some good "liaison."

The same day, amid a rumour of spies, a signal arrived from Division:

> THREE AMERICAN OFFICERS REPORTED IN THE FORWARD AREA WITHOUT ESCORT AAA ONE GIVES NAME OF "HARRY" AAA IF FOUND, HOLD IN CUSTODY AND WIRE THIS OFFICE

Not until the following morning did Bert realize what excitement they had created the previous day. "Guess the Infantry are so unused to seeing Artillery officers in the front line that they thought something was phony," he wrote. "The wires were kept hot all over the country last night looking for us." Later, an Imperial infantry officer showed up at brigade headquarters and was sure he'd captured two of the presumed spies when he stopped Bert and Jim McKeown. Such zeal was not surprising: anyone capturing a German spy received a £20 reward and 14 days' leave.

May 21. Fair & very warm.

All gas helmets were worn from 10:00–11:00 AM. Bloody business it was too, but good practice.

The 17th & 186th Batteries were shot up for a couple of hours this AM [by 10.5 and 15 cm howitzers]. Four gun pits blown up & about 400 rounds destroyed. One man killed and two wounded, but not one gun out of action.

The howitzers, which shelled the 17th and 186th Batteries, were dealt with later in the day: "Sound bearings were obtained from the OP to these batteries and they were eventually neutralized by the heavies."

May 25. Fair & cool.

Went down to Wagon Lines this afternoon. Hqrs were playing the 18th Battery at baseball and, as they were a man short, I played second base. Great to get into the game again but I certainly didn't do very much toward winning the game — score 6–5.

Went around with the OC after the game & inspected the 17th & 23rd Wagon Lines. Got back home at 7:15, just in time to get some of the last rounds of 5.9 How which he had been tossing around all afternoon. Had to cut dinner short as he was coming uncomfortably close. Four windows broken. More gas at night.

May 26. Fair & cool.

Boche artillery very active all day, both forward and rear. Heavy shelling of front line trenches between Neuville-Vitasse and Mercatel, and very scattered blind shooting through the back areas. He has taken quite a fancy to our sunken road and vicinity for 5.9" and 8" Hows. Has made it rather unpleasant but not exactly uninhabitable yet. This has been the most activity on our front since we have been in here.

On May 27, Ludendorff's third offensive, code-named "Blücher," opened on the Aisne between Soissons and Reims, 65 miles southeast of the Canadian positions. The attack was a near-total surprise and met with great initial success, with the Germans punching a pocket

Canadian gunners filling their limbers with 18-pounder shells from a roadside dump, May 1918. *Courtesy of Library and Archives Canada, PA-002587.*

15 miles deep on a front of 40 miles. Reaching the Marne on May 30, they were in a position to threaten Paris as they had done in September 1914. Checked by the Americans at Belleau Wood, the offensive continued until June 13. Again, a strategic result proved elusive.

To keep the Canadians pinned down, the Germans went into action around Arras.

May 27. Fair & cool.

We thought the big day had come when the Boche opened up at 2:00 AM very heavily on the front line and, at the same time, all the battery areas, HQs and OPs were bombarded with gas.*

Signals and I had to make a very hurried exit and descent to the lower regions. We broke all records dressing and donning gas masks. Bombardment lasted for over two hours and extended over three Corps fronts. Altogether over 7000 gas

---

*The War Diary clarifies that the gas used was mainly Green Cross (phosgene, or carbonyl chloride, an asphyxiant), with some Yellow Cross (mustard gas).

shells landed in our area. At no time were we out of communications with at least one OP and 3 out of 5 of our batteries.

Only one gas casualty in the Brigade, out of about 500 men exposed.

He attempted a big raid at 6:00 AM on the 24th Battalion east of Mercatel with two parties of 45 [men] each. Not a man reached our trench. Many casualties caused.

Despite the extensive use of gas, the low casualty rate among the Canadians was due in part to good training. For the past six days the men spent more than an hour a day wearing their gas masks. Though this was cumbersome, the War Diary noted: "The men have become accustomed to carrying out their duties under gas conditions."

The next day was much quieter in comparison, but the 20th Battery came in for some scattered shelling. "The unlucky 20th," Bert called it.

May 29.

The Boche is doing a lot of counter-battery work these days but not getting very many guns. Leave is open again but the allotment is so small it does not give one much encouragement.

A battery of six-inch howitzers located in a sunken road behind Bert's headquarters moved out on May 30. "They have fired thousands of rounds from that position during the past two months and the Boche is beginning to get wise," he noted. The following morning the position was hammered by enemy guns. "They just moved in time. The pieces were flying around our shack."

Infantry units in front of the 5th Brigade had complained for weeks of "short" 18-pounder shells, a matter of great concern. When samples were recovered, they were all found to be shrapnel rounds. On some the fuse had detached during the shell's flight, leaving behind a complete shell minus the fuse, along with a number of fuses on the ground in the line of fire. Other whole shells were found with the copper driving bands stripped off. "These samples," the War Diary acknowledged, "have all been sent back for examination by experts." No written explanation for the "shorts" ever came back to the brigade.

The War Diary that Bert assembled for May was another thick volume: eight handwritten pages of narrative and 200-plus pages of appendices.

June 2. Fair & warm.

The dirty old Boche put on another good gas show at 2:00 AM. I had just turned in and got nicely off to sleep when it started. Signals & I had to go downstairs, as it got a little too close to be pleasant or safe. He used Yellow Cross and phosgene, about 3000 rounds, and the 186th [Battery] were in the center of it all. They had a h— of a time. Shelters crumpled in, men buried, etc. Altogether they sent 33 men to hospital. The 20th sent 2 and we [brigade headquarters] sent 2 [signallers].

Altogether a bad show. Lasted 2 hours.

German shelling continued over the next days, and Bert was in the thick of it. On June 3 the former positions of the 186th Battery and the 17th were again hit by eight-inch howitzers and, with what Bert called "a h— of a concentration" of 5.9s, succeeded in putting two guns of the 18th Battery out of action near the Beaurains road. On June 6, returning from a baseball game, Bert arrived at brigade headquarters "in time to miss a little excitement. A 4.1 landed at top of dugout, wounded [Driver John] Miller and [Driver Frank] Cooke, the latter very badly. Made quite a mess generally." For the night of June 6-7, he wrote, "Was just going to bed at 2:00 a.m. when he started pumping them over, 4.1s on "Datchet" [OP] in rear of us. This was uncomfortable but, when he switched on a 77-mm battery on the road and track beside us, it began to get serious. Another battery shooting gas just put the can on it, and Signals & I made our getaway in some haste. He kept this up until 4:00 AM and by that time the gas was pretty thick in the road but I had to go through it and spent a very uncomfortable half-hour."

News of the King's Birthday Honour List reached the 5th Brigade on June 4, and Bert recorded with evident satisfaction, "Major Paterson and Scotty Duguid both get DSOs and no two men deserve them more." He noted as well that Regimental Sergeant-Major Tom Double* was awarded the MC.

---

*Double joined the old 21st Battery on November 30, 1914, and sailed aboard *Megantic*.

June 6. Fair & warmer.

The OC offered to recommend me for a job in England and, after some consideration, I accepted for only one reason. Now I am pulling for the job!

The fourth German offensive of 1918 began June 8 between Montdidier and Compiègne, 50 miles southeast of the Canadians defending the approach to Arras. After four days, Ludendorff called off the attack. Again, a German diversion pinned down the Canadians.

June 8. Fair & cool.

The 20th [Battery] Forward Section was shot up by 4.1" [10.5 cm] Hows. Direct hit on No. 2 [gun] set the ammunition off and blew everything to h—. Gun badly damaged but no casualties.

At 9:45 p.m., while Bert enjoyed dinner and a bridge game at the 20th Battery, the Germans raided the trenches of the 22nd (French-Canadian) Battalion. The gunners responded at once, dropping shells just in front of the Canadian line. "Then," as Bert's diary related, "[we] added 500 and gave him hell. From infantry accounts our fire was very effective." The next day, Major Arthur Dubuc, commander of the 22nd, sent a note to Lieutenant-Colonel Constantine:

Sir,

Allow me to express to you personally the sincere thanks of all ranks of my battalion for the superb support we got all through [the] tour just completing from the artillery under your command. Last night particularly, during [the] enemy raid, although no SOS went up, your prompt and quite adequate answer to [the] enemy's vicious bombardment went a long way to spoiling whatever chances he had of achieving his object.

The constant moanings heard all night in distant No Man's Land further proved that your retaliation had dropped well and true.

The enemy outside Neuville-Vitasse had little respite from Canadian guns. As Bert wrote in the War Diary: "In addition to the normal harassing fire on roads, tracks, trenches, HQs and centres of activity during the hours of darkness, special shoots have been arranged which have caught the enemy transport on roads immediately east of Neuville-Vitasse. Casualties and much confusion have been caused, as the shouts of men and noise of galloping horses have been heard by our infantry."

June 11. Fair & cool.

Spent most of the day writing up my War Diary and felt very virtuous when it was done.

There is a devil of a lot of sickness going around these days. They call it "pink" fever and is very contagious. A good many of the officers have it and any number of men. Some batteries have as many as 25 to 30 on their daily sick parade. Luckily it only lasts three or four days.*

June 12. Fair & cool.

Very busy this morning finishing up the barrage maps for the raid night of 13/14th.

Rode down to Wagon Lines in PM and played [baseball] for HQ against the 23rd. Played a rotten game — we lost 8–13!

Rode down to Div. Arty after with the Major [Alex Paterson] and had tea and went to the ball game [at Basseux] — Machine Gunners *vs* Engineers — to decide who would represent the Div. troops in semifinals. Wonderful game! MGs pulled it out in 9th inning by 6–5. Good band, large crowd, lots of red tabs [staff officers] from Lieut.-Gens. down, and good seats.

June 13. Fair & cool.

First strawberries of the season.

Very quiet day. The Hun isn't showing much "pep" these days. We put over 200 gas projectors on him at 2:00 AM and

---

*Bert is describing the classic symptoms of the early and less virulent form of influenza, not the so-called "Spanish Flu" pandemic that claimed at least 20 million lives around the globe in 1918–19 — more lives than the war took.

accompanied it with a short burst of fire [from all batteries of the Group]. I don't imagine he is having such a good time of it these days, on this front at least.

At 1:00 a.m. on June 14, the 25th Battalion raided "The Maze," a portion of the enemy's front line at Neuville-Vitasse. The Germans were caught during a relief and (in Bert's words) "a good many were killed." Canadian losses were one officer and four ORs killed, 13 wounded and three missing. To support the infantry, the 5th Brigade had several tasks. While 18-pounders placed a box barrage around the objective, the howitzers blanketed machine-gun and trench-mortar sites, blocked approaches, and laid a smokescreen across the northern portion of Neuville-Vitasse. "The enemy retaliation was very light and scattered, showing the effect of our counter-battery work."

"According to reports," Bert's diary recorded, "the Artillery was magnificent."

June 20. Mostly fair. Showers in evening.

Field Day at Basseux.

Decided at the last minute to go down to the Divisional Sports and arrived just in time for the baseball game. The 26th Bn beat the Engineers 6–0, and thereby hangs the tale of 75 francs. The 26th have a wonderful team and played the snappiest ball I have seen out here yet. Saw part of the soccer game between 29th Bn and DAC, and some of the wrestling, but it started to rain and I beat it for home.

June 21. Generally fair. Rain at night.

Got busy on my War Diary again today and cleaned it up to date.

The Tunnelers started a new dugout for us today. The shaft goes down by the door of our hut and it will eventually join up with our present dugout.

June 22. Cloudy & cool.

Busy day getting out barrage maps for the raid by 27th & 31st Bns night of 24/25th. This will be the biggest raid yet and will include the whole of Neuville-Vitasse.

There was great excitement at 5th Brigade headquarters on June 24 when word arrived of the routing of Austrian troops on the Piave. Bert exulted in his diary:"180,000 prisoners taken and the army in full and disorderly retreat." Next came even better news — the brigade would be relieved before the end of the month, confirmed shortly with the arrival of senior officers from 10th Brigade.

June 26. Fair & warm.

Inter-battery competition for VI Corps Horse and Transport Show.

Went down to Wagon Lines in the AM and completed arrangements for the Inspection. By the time the OC arrived, sections from each battery were on the field. The 23rd, as expected, had the best turn-out but the 17th [Battery] surprised everyone and ran a close second.

In the driving competition the 20th was very well handled by [Lieutenant] Bill Little and took first, but were too far behind in equipment to beat out the 23rd, who took first by a good margin.

Got into a game of [base]ball after lunch. The officers played the 20th Battery and very nearly beat them. Dinner & bridge with the 20th. Back home at 11 o'clock.

June 27. Fair & warm.

OC sails for "Blighty" on leave.

My opposite number from the 10th Bde is here to look over the job, one [Lieut.] Bruce Chown* by name, an Arts '15 McGill man. Took him up to "Sniper," "Super," the front line and Right Bn Hqrs this afternoon for a starter, and a good four-hours' walk it made too.

Bert spent the morning of the twenty-eighth completing the Orders and Administrative Instructions relating to their relief by the 10th Brigade and ensured they were sent to each battery. In mid-afternoon

---

*Bruce Chown (1893–1986) received his medical degree in 1922. Later specializing in pediatrics, he is remembered today for his pioneeering work in Rh disease (erythroblastosis fetalis).

he and Chown went to inspect the rest of the brigade's positions. The pair visited the 18th and 23rd Batteries, the anti-tank guns of the 17th and 18th Batteries, the 17th's sniper gun, and three more OPs — "Safety," "Stable," and "Shrap." "Made the trip in 3 hrs. 30 minutes," Bert noted. The next day, with Bert feeling under the weather, they toured the brigade's reserve positions, 16 in all, completing the trip on horseback in about two and a half hours. "Felt somewhat better by the time I got back."

29

A Much-Needed Rest

While 2nd Canadian Division infantry battalions rejoined the Corps and went into reserve, the division's artillery units remained detached from the division.

On July 1 the 5th Brigade began a march of 15 miles to its assigned rest area around the village of Berlencourt, following a route that took it first southward, toward Basseux, where it was inspected by Brigadier Panet, and then in a short arc to the northwest. "Very hot, dusty march," Bert recorded. On arrival at Berlencourt at 4:35 p.m., Bert discovered he'd gotten lucky. With a majority of the brigade under canvas, he had drawn "a very nice little room off the Mess in the Curé's house next the church. Real bed with sheets! This place does look good — even boasts of a swimming pool." For hot, tired soldiers, the River Canche flowing through the town provided "fair swimming accommodation, which was immediately taken advantage of by all ranks."

There was no getting away from the war, as Frank Hazlewood acknowledged: "We just hear an occasional faint rumble of the distant guns." Apart from normal details like Stables, this was a period of relaxation for all ranks. After three months in the line, the men (and horses) deserved a break, and no training activities were scheduled for the first week. It was the first time since the brigade arrived in France that it would be out of the line for almost a month in summer. "We shall remember Berlencourt," Bob Gillespie reminisced, "more by the good old swimming hole than by the training we did there. That was a real treat and we all appreciated it." A sports committee convened the next afternoon and agreed on a program of baseball, football, swimming, and field sports. Bert, a member of the committee, spent the rest of the afternoon trying without success to find a ball field. The area was under intensive cultivation, leaving little acreage untilled and suitable for baseball.

With the officers pooling their money for something special, Bert sent the mess cart into Avesnes-le Comte on July 3 and followed later on horseback with two other junior officers. "Spent most of the morning in the market — great sport!" he wrote. "Good run home across country for lunch." Looking again for a field, Bert finally located one, though he admitted it was "not as good as it might be."

July 4. Fair but cooler.

Held the first swimming meet this afternoon. [Bombardier Ronald] Johnson of the 23rd [Battery] won the 25-yd. Championship, with [Driver James] Sugden of Bde Hqrs second.

Only had time for one heat in the 75-yard.

July 5.

Finals of the 75-yd. Swim won by [   ]* of the 18th Battery with [Dvr Milne] George of the 23rd Battery second.

Over at 17th Battery for dinner and the usual game of bridge, in which it was my turn to pay for the dinner, to the tune of 5 francs.

July 6. Fair & warm.

Started a new game — volleyball, Hqrs Forward *vs* Hqrs Rear.

We then went down for a swim and got back in time for a feed of strawberries and cream.

As officers and men of the 5th Brigade unwound at Berlencourt, their 18-pounders and howitzers were trucked to the Corps range behind Amiens. Here each field gun was calibrated and its muzzle velocity determined using methods devised by Andy McNaughton. This was important work. It meant the fall of shells from a particular gun could be calculated with greater precision, thus avoiding the

---

*Bert left this space blank, evidently hoping to learn the winner's name later.

need to register the weapon on a target in advance. The problem arose because, as the gun barrel wore from use, the velocity of a shell as it left the muzzle began to drop. An 18-pounder, for example, firing at a range of 8,000 yards, could expect a loss of 300 yards in range over its life. A correction table for each gun could thus be prepared, enabling gunners to engage targets without any preliminary (and warning) ranging shots.

Sunday, July 7, saw a mandatory brigade-wide Church Parade at 9:15, the first for the unit as a whole in four months. After the service, Panet arrived to present medals. Of the 18 medals presented to the brigade, 10 were won at Passchendaele. The lone MC went to RSM Tom Double for heroism at Passchendaele. "Quite a good ceremony," Bert commented. After a pickup ball game in the afternoon, Bert and the other officers trooped off for a swim.

Training began on Monday, though Wednesday, Saturday, and Sunday were half-holidays. Following orders from 2CDA, every effort was to be made by all officers, NCOs, and men to "bring their respective units up to the highest degree of efficiency in offensive and defensive tactics." Of the first day's training in battery manoeuvres, Frank Hazlewood wrote: "Those howitzers are not exactly a light load and my pair of blacks did sweat and there was also *beaucoup* dust and horse flies galore." The program placed great importance on the training of NCOs. "In conditions of open warfare, NCOs may often be called

Church Parade in the field. *Author's photo.*

upon to act on their own initiative. This quality should be encouraged and developed in them." And, since good driving skills were critical to future success in open warfare, drivers practised turning wagons and teams in narrow ditched roads in a given time and replacing horse casualties and damaged wheels.

Anti-gas training, in which the men wore box respirators for not less than a half-hour per day, would pay handsome dividends in the future. Gunners had to be able to work their guns under *all* conditions, providing critical support for attacking infantry. In combat the men were expected to have their respirators on within eight seconds.

The 5th Brigade's MO, Captain John Stewart, took advantage of the rest period to inoculate all ranks that had not been vaccinated since December 1917. Next day, more than half of the brigade nursed sore arms and were excused from duties. Estaminets in town provided a convenient gathering place, though the Town Picquet (one sergeant and six ORs) had instructions to ensure they closed at 9:00 p.m. and that men were in billets by 9:45, with lights out at 10:15.

July 8. Mostly fair & cool. Thunderstorms at night.

The first ball game of the new series was played today. 17th Battery beat Hqrs 15–2 in a *rather* loose and poorly played game. The 17th rooters had a lot to do with winning the game.

July 9. Showers.

Rode into Avesnes-le Comte in the PM and ran across Major [William] Scully for the first time since Dickebusch in 1916. He has the 11th Siege Battery (6″ Hows.). Had tea with him and invited him over to dinner tomorrow night.

Good bridge at night. MO & I played Major [William] Hendrie and [Lieutenant] Ernie Jordan. Very close fight all the way; we finished 1 franc up.

July 10. Showers.

Field sports held in afternoon.

[a/Bombardier Albert] White of 23rd [Battery] won the 100 yards & broadjump; the 17th won the horseback wrestling; the 20th the obstacle race and baseball throw. [Gunner William] Nightingale beat me out by 3 feet in the latter.

Had a little workout at ball after the sports.

Major Paterson and Major Scully in to dinner, and a "pukka" dinner it was too. The best fruit salad I have ever tasted and some very good benedictine.

Bert's hospitality was reciprocated the next day when he rode into Avesnes and lunched with Bill Scully. In the 11th Siege Battery's Mess, he ran into old friends from Montreal and passed a lazy afternoon catching up on news.

July 12. Mostly fair.

Had dinner at the 20th Battery and some good bridge after, in which I won 6 francs.

The OC arrives back from leave full of "pep" as usual and had such a good time that it is the first time I have heard him say he could have stood more of it.

[Lieutenant Arnott] Minnes goes on leave and [Lieutenant Gordon] Burnett decides to drop, making me *fourth* on the [leave] list.

Sports and games continued. "Managed to sprain my wrist again," Bert noted on July 13, after a baseball match. There was also a soccer game, with headquarters beating the 23rd Battery 4–1. "Played bridge at the 23rd, [Lieutenant] Harry Beatty and I *vs* the Major [Alex Paterson] & [Captain] Cecil [Gordon]. We were only 500 points down."

July 14. Showers.

Good church service in the big tent with the piano and violin to accompany the singing.

Played some *Vingt-et-un* and Red Dog* at 23rd and lost a few more francs.

Ludendorff's fifth offensive began on July 15 in the Champagne sector on both sides of the historic city of Reims, 90 miles southeast of the

---

*A card game for three to eight, in which a player bets whether any of the five cards in his hand will be the same suit as, and higher, than a card dealt from the deck.

Canadians. With Germany nearing the end of its manpower reserves, the attack met with limited initial success. French and American counterattacks two days later caused the Germans to retreat from the huge salient created by the Blücher offensive in May, and Ludendorff shelved plans for an attack ("Hagen") on the British in Flanders.

The 5th Brigade received orders to return to its previous area around Neuville-Vitasse, southeast of Arras. While the brigade marched in the heat eight miles to Gouves, an advance party (including Bert) arrived in Arras. The move to Arras was cancelled on July 18, and the brigade marched six miles from Gouves to Berles, where it went into General Headquarters Reserve.

July 16. Fair & very warm.
[Lieutenant Norman] Rattray's Leave Warrant comes through for the 19th. I am now 3rd on the list.
July 18. Warm, some showers.

Château at Berles, where the 5th Brigade rested from July 19–24, 1918. Each officer had a separate room and there was a good Mess. *Courtesy of Madeleine Claudi.*

Championship ball game between 17th [Battery] & 23rd won by 17th, 9–6. Rather exciting but not very good ball. A lot of money on the game.

July 19. Very warm.

We have managed to "cop" the chateau and ought to be able to live in some style. A beautiful spot — extensive grounds with beautiful trees, walks and driveways, a baseball and football field. We all have separate rooms with beds & a good Mess.

Horses all in stables & men comfortably billeted.

Went over to 23rd at night. Disastrous game of Red Dog.

As First Army was planning a Rifle Meet in August, Bert spent part of the afternoon of the twenty-first inspecting a range at Hermaville, and spent most of the following day with a work detail, getting it into shape. Shortly after, he drew up a schedule of practice and elimination rounds, hoping to form a team of one officer, one NCO, and 10 ORs. "Busy on the rifle ranges all day. Put 60 men from each of the batteries through 5 rounds application, and 5 rounds rapid," he noted.

On July 22, newly transferred Lieutenant Donald Macpherson reported to the 23rd Battery. "At last I am back with a fighting unit again," he wrote in his diary. "I am sleeping tonight in one of the luxurious bedrooms of the chateau here, the windows of which overlook a beautiful stretch of green grass and lovely shade trees." That afternoon, the whole divisional artillery staff, including General Panet, arrived for a baseball game against the 5th Brigade. Bert, playing shortstop for the brigade, was surprised when they were defeated 14–6. Panet, at six feet two inches, had a long reach, and Bert acknowledged "the general played a wonderful game at first base and the game attracted a big crowd." Among the fans was Lieutenant Macpherson, who described it as "a good game" and also paid tribute to Panet's skill.

In London on the twenty-second, Rosalie wrote to Flora Darling, her future sister-in-law. "I just can't sit still long enough to write a decent letter," she confided. "I wonder if you can guess the reason?" She went on to explain, "Bert wrote on Saturday and he said he may be home BEFORE THE MIDDLE OF AUGUST. Of course, I am trying hard to look calm and collected and dignified, with distinctly indifferent success. It seems too good to think of." Alluding to the upcoming wedding, Rosalie added, "I do wish you and all Bert's sisters could come over. It does seem a shame the poor old boy should have none of his family with him on that day."

With new orders, the brigade returned to Berlencourt on July 24. "Arrived at our old home at 11:45 AM. Everyone glad to see us back again and by the time it took everyone to settle down it looked as though they were glad to be back." It would be a short stay, for another batch of orders soon arrived. On July 25, Bert and Lieutenant-Colonel Constantine rode through light showers into Frévent in the morning to inspect entraining facilities. The brigade, it seemed, would travel by rail — to an as yet unspecified destination. Riding back through divisional artillery headquarters, the two officers learned Brigadier Panet was away at a meeting of Second Army artillery commanders. "Looks like a bad business to me," Bert wrote ominously.

July 27. Rain.
    Our movements still very much in the air, but it looks as though we will go north to St. Jans Capel to relieve the X Corps of Second Army & retake Mt. Kemmel.
July 29. Fair & warm.
    Had verbal orders to move early in the AM but this was postponed later to "late in the day." Don't know yet whether we are going north or south & whether we will entrain or not.

Secret Orders finally arrived. On the twenty-ninth, Currie informed his divisional commanders that the Corps was being detached temporarily from Byng's Third Army to participate in an offensive with General Henry Rawlinson's Fourth Army. Next day, the Corps began to move, with only a handful of men knowing their ultimate destination. In the 2nd Canadian Division, infantry brigades prepared to move by train and bus. Only the Divisional Artillery and other mounted units would move by road — at night, to hide their movement from German aircraft.

July 30. Fair & warm.

Pulled out for the south.

Last day in Berlencourt a busy one. While the others were sleeping in preparation for a night march, I got my War Diary written up to date and typed. Had a good swim before dinner & wrote a letter [to Rosalie] after.

We pulled off the [Wagon] Lines at 10:15 PM. My big mare is still lame, so I had to ride the little one. Beautiful night to march, starlit and cool.

As I was responsible for finding the road, I had my job all the way, particularly going through Doullens.

Arrived Orville at 4:30 AM, having covered about 18 miles.

In the War Diary, Bert added, "As this is the first night march we have made since that of Frévin-Capelle to Basseux in March, careful attention was paid to march discipline and special care was taken to maintain communication between batteries." McKeown's Operation Order stressed that "Section Commanders will be particularly alert to see that Drivers do not fall asleep on their horses." In the early morning, the 5th and 6th Brigades and the 2DAC camped in fields around Orville, sleeping in the open or under wagons.

"Slept all morning," Bert wrote, "and went into Doullens in the afternoon with Major Paterson [and Lieutenant Donald Macpherson]. Did the odd shopping, etc. and got back by lorry at 6:30 PM, to find we were moving earlier than expected."

The brigade pulled out of Orville at 9:15 p.m., July 31. Bert had no difficulty finding the way, except through Bertangles. It was a cool, moonlit night, which made for easy marching, but the distance — 22 miles — meant men and horses were tired by the time they arrived in Argoeuves at 4:30 a.m., with the first hint of dawn. "Very nice little village, but crowded with troops. People a different class altogether from those up north. The old lady at our mess was awfully decent to us and made us coffee and bread and butter while we were waiting for our breakfast."

August 2. Showers.

Finished up my War Diary and squared away a few odd jobs.

No one knows yet just where we are going and it wasn't until late in the evening we knew we would not move until tomorrow night.

Over at the 23rd at night, and got back 150 francs.

Amiens, four miles away, was declared out of bounds. The German spring offensive brought the city within range of enemy guns, and the population of 80,000 was evacuated, creating a ghost town. Having ridden into Amiens on August 3 to scout the brigade's route, Bert wrote, "Things are certainly somewhat different to what they were two years ago. It is the City of the Dead now, and a good many of the big buildings are in ruins."

The next day, commanders received their first notice of the pending assault. "On a date and at a time to be communicated later," began Artillery Instructions No. 1, "the Canadian Corps is carrying out an attack, in conjunction with the French on our Right and the Australian Corps on our left." "Surprise," it cautioned, "will be the essence of the attack. There will be no previous bombardment." After describing the general artillery plan, it warned, "The success of the operation will depend on our ability to conceal our intentions up to the moment of attack."

One last night of marching brought the brigade through Amiens to Château Longeau, where the officers took over most of the ground floor for the night. "There weren't many vacant spaces on the floor," Bert admitted. The extensive grounds were well wooded, sufficient in Bert's view to provide cover for the whole Divisional Artillery and more. Over in the 23rd Battery, Frank Hazlewood wrote:

We are in a pretty woods, all "camouflaged" so to speak. We landed in here at 2:30 in the morning and, after getting the horses unharnessed and tied up, had a nap ourselves. The ground was our bed and the sky our roof. We are really taking the fresh-air cure and it is a treat after those stuffy barns accompanied by the barnyard smells.

Also in the 23rd, Lieutenant Macpherson confided, "Great things are pending in the next few days!"

At the château, the elaborate deception continued. As Bert explained in the War Diary, "All horses and vehicles are placed under cover of the trees in the Chateau grounds, and all ranks have strict orders that no movement will take place during daylight that is not absolutely necessary." The orders passing through Bert's hands were very specific. "Every Officer, NCO and man must be made to realize that concealment of our intentions is the primary stage of the attack itself. He should understand that by neglecting to observe the necessary precautions, by careless conversation, neglect of care as regards tracks and cover of gun emplacements and ammunition dumps, he is directly endangering the success of the operation and the lives of his comrades."

Exceptional steps were taken to hide the growing concentration of troops. In the woods, undergrowth was removed so horses, guns, wagons, and bivouacs could all be placed under trees. At night, every light was shaded. "No candles or other illumination will be lit in tents after dusk unless tents are so situated that observation of the light is impossible. Cooking fires if visible from the air must be extinguished after the hours of darkness."

For once, the men appreciated bad weather. Rain and mist made for poor aerial observation, though officers and ORs, on duty or not, took cover on the approach of an airplane. When British reconnaissance aircraft overflew the area, they reported some horse and transport sections had failed to make adequate use of natural cover, and that "this is most conspicuous." Commanders took immediate steps to correct this and ensure "that movement by day is reduced to a minimum."

30

Amiens: "Black Day of the German Army"

August 4, the fourth anniversary of the declaration of war, dawned fair and warm. "Not a vehicle or a horse showing anywhere," Bert noted with evident satisfaction. Early in the morning he accompanied Lieutenant-Colonel Constantine and the four battery commanders to the front. "Good country and prospects look better all the time." Starting positions for 5th Brigade batteries were a short distance southeast of Villers-Bretonneux, "only 1000 yards from the present frontline trenches and will be occupied the night before the show."

By this time most of the Canadian guns were in place, and Bert was pleased to see 60-pounders within 1,500 yards of the front line, and two 12-inch howitzers just 4,000 yards behind the line. To achieve complete surprise, not a single gun fired in the next three days. As at Cambrai the previous autumn, targets for the opening salvos would be attacked without previous registration — unthinkable earlier in the war.

Men from each battery went forward to inspect the terrain over which they would later move. "Spent a busy day with Capt. [Frank] Tingley reconnoitering forward areas," wrote Don Macpherson on the sixth, "and now am at our present gun positions assisting in preparations for the strenuous work ahead." The terrain over which the Canadian divisions would attack was ideal: an open, rolling plateau, hard and dry, unmarked by shell craters, with scattered villages and wooded areas. Much of the area was under cultivation and covered by crops of standing grain. Given the opportunity, horse-drawn artillery could move rapidly, as could tanks and cavalry.

On August 5, the brigade's orders changed; that night it began to relieve an Australian field artillery brigade, holding these positions only until the attack began. "At Zero Hour the day of the show we become mobile reserve and go forward in support of the infantry. Looks like a rather good job!"

August 6. Showers.

"X" Day.

Battery Commanders meeting at 6:00 AM. Laid out plans for assembly areas, routes of advance, etc. This mobile reserve stuff takes a little figuring out.

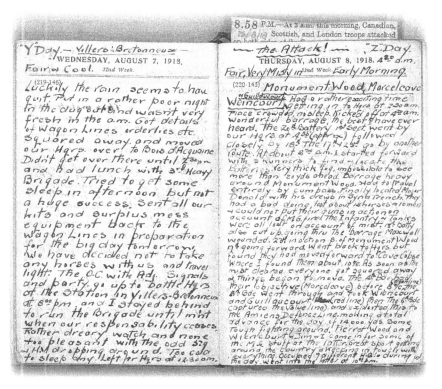

Bert's diary pages for August 7 and 8, 1918, describing the Battle of Amiens. *Courtesy of Madeleine Claudi.*

Rode up with the OC at 9:30 AM then went on into Villers-Bretonneux and located our Battle Hqrs. Had a narrow call with a whizz-bang.

Final Operational Order in tonight, and we have a busy night getting it out to batteries. Assembly Area for batteries, & routes forward have been changed slightly, which necessitates a further reconnaissance.

Only on August 7 were final details of the assault confirmed. The 2nd Division would attack on a front of just over 2,000 yards. "Zero hour and day will be 4:20 AM August 8th 1918" read the VERY SECRET message from Brigade Major John Ball. Meanwhile, ammunition columns struggled to get 600 rounds and 500 rounds respectively forward to each 18-pounder and 4.5-inch howitzer to ensure the 900-odd guns would not run short of ammunition.

August 7. Fair & cool.

"Y" Day.

Luckily the rain seems to have quit. Put in a rather poor night in the dugout [at Blangy Wood] and wasn't very fresh in the AM. Got details of Wagon Lines, orderlies, etc. squared away and moved our Hqrs over to Bois d'Aquenne.

Tried to get some sleep in afternoon but not a huge success. Sent all our kits and surplus mess equipment back to the Wagon Lines in preparation for the big day tomorrow.

The OC with Adj. [Jim McKeown], Signals and party go up to Battle Hqrs at the [railway] station in Villers-Bretonneux at 8:00 PM and I stayed behind to run the Brigade until midnight, when our responsibility ceases.

Rather dreary watch and none too pleasant with the odd 5.9 and heavy mortar dropping around.

That night, runners from each battery in the 5th Brigade brought two watches to headquarters for synchronization. Over in the 23rd Battery, Lieutenant Bob Gillespie (whose section would lead the battery) described the last hours before the attack:

It was cold and miserable as it always is on such occasions, and the nervous tension increased as the minutes grew fewer and fewer between then and Zero. Somebody always kept us posted, as we could hear: "Two minutes to go"; "One minute to go"; "Thirty seconds to go"; then two 18-pdrs barked and, a second later, hell broke loose.

Immediately "Get mounted the Center Section — Walk march!" and our part was begun at last.

An hour later we had guns in action far beyond what had been the German front line.

At 4:55, Lieutenant Don Macpherson led his section forward, following the infantry as soon as the Engineers had filled in enemy trenches to make lanes for the 23rd's howitzers. Shortly after, he was badly wounded and evacuated to England. The weather continued to co-operate. On that moonless night, banks of dense ground fog drifted across the front, making it difficult for those leading the batteries into action, but masking them from observation.

August 8.

"Z" Day. The Attack!

Had a rather exciting time getting in to Hqrs at 2:30 AM. Place crowded, no sleep.

Kicked off at 4:20 AM. Wonderful barrage, the best I have ever heard.

The 20th Battery (1st Section) went by our Hqrs at 4:35 followed closely by 18th; the 17th & 23rd go by another route [via Cachy, passing south of Monument Wood].

At about 5:30 AM I started forward with three runners to find and locate the batteries. Very thick fog, impossible to see more than 20 yards ahead. Had to travel entirely by compass.

Lost in the mist were tanks and various infantry units. Bert finally located Major Alexander Donald of the 20th Battery and his crews in the former British front line. They'd come under heavy fire from machine guns, losing 10 men and more than a dozen horses. At brigade headquarters, McKeown was concerned about the 20th and sent a note by runner: "Get into action. Get parties forward and see what infantry want." It wasn't quite *that* simple, and McKeown had no way of knowing what was happening farther forward. At 7:00 a.m. Bert scribbled a message for Lieutenant-Colonel Constantine and handed it to a runner. "Have seen Major Donald. Mist very heavy & machine guns still active. He has not yet fired. On account of very heavy fog Infantry having difficulty locating themselves. Have not yet seen any other batteries...."

Other batteries in the brigade also came under fire as they crossed the old German front line with the infantry. Bert wrote: "18th Bty also cut up going through the barrage, 23rd in action south of Monument Wood, 17th going forward." He returned to brigade headquarters, only to find it had moved to Cave Copse, near the village of Marcelcave, a mile and a half inside the former German lines. When the mist cleared about 7:30, he related, "everyone got squared away and things began to move." This was mobile warfare at last, though gunners' recollections

A Canadian six-inch howitzer in action at the Battle of Amiens, August 8, 1918.
Courtesy of Royal Montreal Regiment Museum.

are somewhat jumbled. "It all happened so quickly," confessed the 18th Battery historian, "that one did not get the opportunity to get a fair idea of what was actually happening."

The Canadians were unstoppable that morning. The 4th Infantry Brigade seized its objective, Marcelcave (Green Line), before 8:00 a.m., whereupon the 5th Infantry Brigade leapfrogged at 8:20 and took Wiencourt and Guillaucourt on the Red Line. In the early afternoon the 6th Brigade captured the Blue Line and exploited this to the former Amiens Defence Line, making a total advance for the day of 14,000 yards. The headlong advance left isolated pockets of resistance to be mopped up later. "Jim and I came in for some of the machine gun stuff at Wiencourt," Bert recounted, almost lightheartedly. "Great sport getting around the country and keeping in touch with everything. Occupied seven different HQs during the day." By the time he caught up with the brigade, it was 10:00 p.m. He was exhausted.

His narrative in the War Diary adds: "During the day all batteries took up at least five different positions and were at all times in close support of our advancing infantry. Fairly heavy casualties occurred in the 18th & 20th Batteries when going through the enemy's initial barrage, but from then on the going was good and no further casualties occurred."

Recalling McKeown's success in putting to use German howitzers at Vimy, Lieutenant Gerry Aldous headed a detail of four NCOs and eight men. Their instructions were simple: put into action any enemy guns that might be captured. Fifty minutes after Zero, Aldous and his detail went forward. Around 8:00 a.m., three 77 mm field guns were discovered in an orchard just south of Marcelcave and these were soon turned around. In the next couple of hours, Aldous's team dropped about 250 shells into German positions. By the end of the first day, seven guns were in action against their former owners, firing some 400 rounds on a variety of targets. In all, in five days, the 5th Brigade put 10 enemy guns into action, firing almost 1,000 rounds in support of the infantry. So stunned were German gunners by the speed of the advance that some field guns were captured with muzzle covers still in place.

Mobile warfare demanded special arrangements to keep the guns supplied with ammunition. When the field gunners moved from their initial positions, ammunition columns at once began picking up any remaining shells. These were then dumped at selected points along the roads, collected by trucks, and moved forward.

Hal Fetherstonhaugh was also on the battlefield. "The German prisoners coming down in streams do improve the morale, and there is the wonderful hope we are getting on with the war. The ground captured is not the usual trench area of mud-holes, strung together with strands of barbed wire and brown weeds. The country here is lovely and green."

Against all odds, the Canadians had managed to deceive the Germans. Surprise was complete and captured officers were dumbfounded to find themselves taken prisoner by Canadians, whom their intelligence had reported as being farther north, supposedly planning an attack near Arras or Ypres. The attack on the first day — on a front of more than 20 miles — exceeded all expectations of the British High Command. The Canadians alone bagged 5,000 prisoners and 61 field guns, and in nine hours the Allies advanced seven miles into open countryside, which offered scope for movement to tanks, cavalry, and motor machine guns. It was the largest one-day advance of the war thus far. Canadian losses on the first day amounted to 1,036 killed and 2,832 wounded — tolerable numbers considering the gains.

The real victory of August 8 lay not in the territory seized but in the way it had been won, and the panic that spread through the German Army, with even the Kaiser voicing his opinion that the war must be ended. Amiens marked the beginning of the so-called "Hundred Days," in which the Canadian Corps served as the spearhead to Allied victory. Such a role, though, cost the Corps dearly. From August 8 to the Armistice, the Corps sustained 45,835 casualties — one-fifth of Canada's total wartime dead and wounded.

Tributes flowed in from all sides. Haig congratulated Henry Rawlinson, Fourth Army commander, on the "magnificent success," and praised "the brilliant manner in which the operation was prepared and successfully carried out, with comparatively small losses." In turn, Rawlinson wrote to Currie, congratulating the Corps on a fine performance. One of the keys to success, he noted, was "the energy and drive in pushing forward mobile artillery immediately the enemy front line had been broken."

Historian Basil Liddell Hart called the success of August 8 "the most brilliant ever gained by British arms in the World War, and, better still, the most economical...." Certainly the most decisive battle of the war, Amiens merits a special place in military history as one of the first examples of combined arms operations, with infantry, tanks, artillery, and aircraft in close coordination, a taste of what was to come in the rest of the twentieth century.

To the Germans, August 8 was an unmitigated disaster, their worst defeat in four years. It was, Ludendorff confessed in his postwar memoirs, "the Black Day of the German Army in the history of the war ... the worst experience I had to go through...." He was not alone in this view. Prince Maximilian of Baden, Imperial Germany's last chancellor, described August 8 as "the turning point" in the war.

The attack continued the following day. "Bad staff work," Bert grumbled. "The show was allowed to cool off & we didn't get going again [from the Blue Line] until 11:00 AM. We managed by some damn good work to give the [6th CIB] boys a barrage to go over with, but the tanks were late coming up and the clear day gave the Boche every advantage, which he took to the full with MGs. Their fire was simply hellish. He had also brought up some guns during the night, so the going was not good." The 5th Brigade gunners received only 45 minutes' notice of the advance. Despite this, and the brigade's frontage of 1,500 yards, "A creeping shrapnel barrage, remarkably good under the circumstances, was laid down in support of the attack."

At noon McKeown dashed off a quick note to the 18th and 20th Batteries: "It is reported that our troops are near the edge of Rosières [-en-Santerre]. Push forward sections at once and endeavor to avoid observation from Rosières church tower." Bert, at brigade headquarters, did not remain long. "I went up with the 3rd infantry wave and was the first Artillery officer to get into Rosières [around 1:00 PM]. Got some useful information which I got back to [Brigadier-] General [Arthur] Bell at 1:20 PM."

That afternoon the disorganized Germans mounted their first counterattack since the battle began. The buildup of troops was spotted in its early stages and all batteries in the brigade turned their guns on the massing infantry. The threat never fully developed and was easily beaten off by Lewis gun and rifle fire. In the meantime, the brigade's other batteries pressed forward. The 23rd, bombed by an aircraft, had six horses killed and seven men wounded. Among them was Frank Hazlewood, who suffered a neck wound, a "Blighty" that ended his active service.

When the brigade set up its headquarters in Rosières that night, Bert climbed to the top of the church tower. "Wonderful OP."

After two days of combat, the 1st, 2nd, and 3rd Canadian Divisions went into reserve, but their respective artilleries remained in action. Designated as a reserve, the 5th Brigade enjoyed two welcome days of rest on August 10 and 11.

The church at Rosières-en-Santerre. The village was taken by the Second Canadian Division on August 9, the second day of the Battle of Amiens. Bert was the first artillery officer into the village. "Wonderful OP," he recorded after climbing the tower, which had been used previously by the Germans for artillery spotting. *Author's photo.*

August 11. Fair & warm.

Chance to get a bit of a rest today but my War Diary takes up most of my time.

General [Panet] in this AM and the OC fixes my leave up so that I will get away next.

Battery Commanders' meeting at 5:00 PM.

Instead of going into positions west of Méharicourt for a show tomorrow, we remain where we are [Rosières].

August 12. Fair & warm.

There was no attack launched today; looks as though we will let this bit of front quiet down a bit now.

Went up front with the OC in the afternoon to reconnoitre new positions but did not take much interest, as all leave has been cancelled again by Gen. Burstall and I am once more out of luck.

Some bombs tonight.

August 14. Fair & warm.

Went down to see General Panet tonight about my leave. He has promised to see Burstall in the AM & the chances are I *may* get away on the 19th!

A day later Bert recorded sourly, "Nothing doing in the leave line! General Burstall refused to make any exception in my case, so there is nothing for it but to carry on!"

In the morning of August 16, the 5th Brigade received notice of its relief over the next two nights by Australian units. That afternoon, Bert and officers from each battery went into Cayeux-en-Santerre to arrange billets. "Not very successfully," he noted, "as the 10th Brigade is in our area and don't like the idea of getting out, but when Divisional Artillery get my report, things start to happen." He returned to head-quarters in Rosières. "The piano in my room was a big attraction and with [Frank] Tingley & Jim [McKeown] to play it, we had a real party in spite of Fritz and his bombs. As our responsibility had ceased, we did make a night of it," he mused.

When McKeown and the OC rode back from Divisional Artillery on August 18, they brought the welcome news that leave, inexplicably, was open again and Bert's name headed the list. Bert worked feverishly to get the War Diary up to date, but commented, "I won't believe I'm going until I'm on the way with my [Leave] Warrant in my pocket." As Bert prepared to depart for England, the mood of the Canadian Corps was positive. Hal's brother, Edward, summed it up neatly: "Everyone feels very much bucked up here at being on the offensive once more. It is wonderful what a difference it makes."

31

Wedding Bells in "Blighty"

Tidying up the last of his administrative paperwork, Bert turned the War Diary over to Lieutenant Gerry Aldous. No longer would the narrative pages bear the intricate "AES" with which Bert had initialled each entry over the past six months. While the brigade continued its rest at the château, refitting and preparing for future operations, Bert was on his way back to England on August 19. It hadn't been easy, though. "In spite of all the arranging I have done," he wrote, "they did their best to ball up my leave again, and sent a Warrant through for 'Boyer' instead." Disgusted, he rode at once to 2nd Divisional Artillery to see Captain Lewis Duncan, then over to Wiencourt where Major Frank Spry amended the Leave Warrant. By the time Bert arrived back at brigade headquarters, he found they'd already received orders to move out the same night. "I made myself scarce as soon after lunch as possible."

Getting a lift to the station in Amiens, he nearly took the train to Paris but opted instead to try for the morning boat from Boulogne and thereby reach England a day earlier. Taking a civilian train from Amiens at 5:50, he arrived at Abbeville two hours later. At the Officers' Club he enjoyed a fine dinner with an officer of the 27th Battalion and an Australian surgeon. "The WAAC waitresses are a big improvement," he noted. On account of recent bombing, the club shut early and the three men returned to the Dormitory about 10:00 p.m.

About the same time as Bert finished dinner, the 2nd Canadian Divisional Artillery began marching northward to the Arras sector, and the Corps came once more under General Henry Horne's First

Army. To mask the move from the Germans, marches were conducted at night; the enemy would have no inkling of the next target of the British Army or the presence of the Canadian Corps.

At Abbeville Station, the railway transport officer informed Bert that the 4:30 a.m. to Boulogne was a civilian train, thus closed to military personnel. Undeterred, Bert and a couple of other officers persisted, with the result that "it did not pull out without us." Arriving at Boulogne at 8:30, Bert made his way to the dock but failed to wangle a passage: the one boat making the crossing was packed solid. "Went back to the hotel, had breakfast and a general clean-up," he wrote. After that he wandered back to the docks and had a talk with a regimental sergeant major, "and was put wise to the ropes." Bert's subsequent direct approach to the military loading officer paid off: he secured permission to cross by the afternoon boat.

> Left Boulogne at 2:45 PM, arrived Folkestone 4:50 and Victoria Station 7:30 PM.
> Arrived at Browning Road at 8:45 PM!
> Decided that wedding would be on Friday, 23rd.
> Cabled the Folks to that effect.

Back to "Blighty" — boarding the leave boat. *Author's photo.*

Not surprisingly, the next day was hectic. Despite a bus and tram strike, Bert headed into London on the Underground and purchased two critical items: a wedding ring and the marriage licence. Then he telephoned Shorncliffe and spoke to his best man, Major Eslie ("Tiny") Birchard, OC Canadian Troops. Birchard's nickname stemmed from his great height — six feet three and a half inches — "a frail, wee mite," Rosalie liked to joke. Birchard drove up from Kent on his Indian motorcycle and arrived at Browning Road in the evening, followed by Bo, another of Bert's close friends.

The next day, he met Tiny and Bo at Oddenino's for what Bert called a "very nice little luncheon." Tiny and Bo agreed to make

Bert and Rosalie on their wedding day, August 23, 1918. *Courtesy of Madeleine Claudi.*

reservations for the honeymoon but refused to provide details in advance. "Don't know yet where we are going for our trip but am leaving it entirely up to them," Bert admitted. They made reservations at Cromer on the Norfolk coast and purchased return rail tickets. At the last minute this fell through and someone suggested Mundesley-on-Sea, a few miles from Cromer, known for its tranquility and sea-views. A telegram was quickly sent and reservations confirmed at the Clarence Hotel. Bert and Rosalie could scarcely have cared less where they went. Reverend Kendrick Sibly, then in his tenth year at St. Barnabas Church on Browning Road, had no objections to the last-minute arrangements. This was wartime and his schedule was clear for Friday morning.

As a parody of the artillery orders and reports he typically generated in the field, Bert described his wedding day in the following tongue-in-cheek fashion:

August 23. Fair but cloudy.

The Day!

Final objective: Clarence Hotel, Mundesley

Zero Hour: 11:00 AM

Jumping-off Line: St. Barnabas Church, Little Ilford

Order of March: Major E.R. Birchard & Lieut. A.E. Sargent, Mr. R. U. James, & Miss R.J.B. James, Misses E.H.B. James, H.B. Austin & L.B. Hall.

Rolling Barrage by Curate Sibley from Zero to Zero+45 (Both flanks in the air).

First Objective (The Vestry) reached at Zero+48 (amidst some confusion).

Position consolidated by Zero+75.

Enemy barrage came down very heavy at the church door but by skillful maneuvering and the aid of a fast armoured car, the barrage was penetrated & next objective reached at Zero+90.

Rested on objective, watered & fed & prepared to move at Zero+180.

During the halt on this line, the enemy had brought up strong artillery reinforcements and another heavy barrage of all calibres was encountered but successfully penetrated by the aid of Bo's car.

A further halt was necessary at Liverpool Street Station but the advance was pushed forward at Zero+250 & Final Objective reached at Zero+595.

The following day at Mundesley, Bert wrote in his diary: "Details of this period of my life are, and always will be, too fresh in my memory to require chronolization." A day later, he added: "For those who may be curious or wish to profit by another's experiences, my advice is: — to marry the sweetest and purest and best little girl in the whole world (there may be another one left) and work out your own destiny."

As souvenirs, over the next days Bert and Rosalie purchased post-cards of Mundesley and the area. The diary was silent with respect to the couple's activities, apart from notations like "tennis," and the nearby places to which they made side trips: Trimmingham and Overstrand on the coast, and Wroxham.

Inevitably, the war intruded into the honeymoon. Each day Bert devoured *The Times* for the latest news and explained its significance to Rosalie. Tucked into the diary's pages were clippings with terse bulletins from France describing the Canadian assault at Monchy-le-Preux.

Clarence Hotel, Mundesley, where Bert and Rosalie honeymooned.
Author's photo.

There was one further clipping from *The Times*, a wedding announcement inserted by Rosalie's father on Tuesday, August 27. It served notice that, even in the midst of history's most destructive war, love would not be denied.

> SARGENT: JAMES. — On the 23rd Aug., at St. Barnabas' Church, Little Ilford, LIEUT. ALBERT ELBRIDGE, Canadian Field Artillery, to ROSALIE JULIA BURBIDGE, youngest daughter of Mr. and Mrs. R.U. James, of Browning Road, Manor Park.

As British papers were generally available in the trenches just a day or two later, it meant the officers of the 5th Brigade outside Arras could share in Bert's happiness.

Mundesley-on-Sea

4/9/18

Just a line to send along with some snaps which I have taken in France & should have sent you when I was over here last December. Please be careful with these and don't show them promiscuously to people outside of the family. As you probably know it is absolutely against orders to carry a camera over there. I don't intend to take it back with me this time as a matter of fact, as it is practically impossible to get films for it over here now.

I have quite a number which I took over there during 1916 and 1917 and if I can find them at Browning Road will send them along as I think they will be of interest to you all. I have taken some down here but the films were so poor that they are not worth much, but will send them along later after I have shown them to the folks at 237.

The news in the papers is exceptionally good these days, isn't it? I have evidently missed out on some good fighting since I have been over here; however, I think there is still plenty ahead to make things interesting.

We return to town tomorrow evening by the 5:25 which ought to get us back at Browing Road about 11 PM.

This is all I have time for just now but will try to write again soon after I get back to France.

Love to all from both of us.

Bert and Rosalie returned to the capital on September 5. The next day, Bert went to the Canadian Pay and Record Office at 7 Millbank, near the Houses of Parliament. There he produced two key pieces of paper to amend his assigned pay. First, written approval by his OC, Lieutenant-Colonel Constantine, to get married, and second, his marriage certificate. With these, he designated Rosalie as his next-of-kin and assigned $25.00 (effective September 1) from his monthly pay to her, in addition to the $10.00 still being assigned to Lena in Montreal. The pay office clerks were used to such requests: by late 1918, Canadian soldiers were being married at the rate of 300 per week.

That night there was a large party at Browning Road. Tiny Birchard's Indian broke down on the way from Shorncliffe and "he missed the fun."

September 7. Showery.

Yes, Uncle! at the Shaftsbury [Theatre].

Decided about 11:30 we would have a photo taken. Some rush getting over there and the loss of a lot of good humor. Didn't think much of the old "jonnie" that propped us up like a couple of sticks.

Rushed back to the house for lunch as we were due at the Shaftsbury at 2:00 PM. Cud is certainly a lightning change artist; never saw a girl take so little time to change.

By good connections & taxi made the theater by 2:30. Fair show.

Back to Browning Road in the early hours.

September 8. Mostly fair; some showers.

Rather nice breakfast in bed!

Joined the civies again today and nested around in slippers.

"Tiny" arrived before we were downstairs.

Got my things together in the afternoon and then I began to realize my "little bit of heaven" was about to end.

32

Back to the Front

During Bert's absence, the 5th Brigade moved into the line south of Arras, the same area it occupied from April to June. At 3:00 a.m. on August 26 the Canadian Corps attacked, in what would be called the Battle of Arras. Overcoming no less than five separate trench systems, the Canadians pushed the Germans back more than five miles. Two days later, the Second Canadian Division assaulted the heavily fortified Drocourt-Quéant Switch. Days of heavy fighting ensued, at the end of which it had successfully penetrated the Hindenburg Line,* outflanking enemy units to the south and compelling them to fall back. By September 3, the Canadian front, now 10 miles long, faced the heavily defended Canal du Nord. Here, the Corps paused for almost three weeks, refitted, and made ready for the next assault.

Relieved on September 6 and designated as Corps Reserve, the 5th Brigade profited from the brief respite. Equipment was checked, deficiencies made up and, as always, harnesses were cleaned and steel chains burnished. The 18-pounders and 4.5-inch howitzers were calibrated on the range and batteries were brought up to strength in officers, men, and horses.

---

*Known to the Germans as the Siegfried Stellung. In reality, it was not a line and had nothing to do with Hindenburg. Rather, it had been developed under von Lossberg's principle of defence in depth and consisted of barbed wire entanglements supported by entrenchments and pillboxes, in turn backed up by independent forts and strongpoints. It was the most formidable defensive system constructed by either side in the Great War.

September 9. Fair & windy.

Back to France!

Was rather hard to get up at 5:30 AM. Mum had breakfast for us at 6:30. Caught a train at 7:05 which got us to Victoria Station at 7:40. Landed a compartment with only four of us in, and able to sleep most of the way.

The toughest proposition I have had to face yet, going back, but Cud was braver even than I expected and it did help a great deal.

Made Folkestone in just two hours & my embarkation card was marked for the 4:30 boat. But, as I was particularly anxious to make the morning boat, I promptly "lost" my card, secured a fresh one from the sergeant-major at the gangway, filled it in and walked aboard.

Very rough passage — many sick, but I smoked my old pipe all the way.

Arriving at Boulogne at 12:30, Bert wandered over to the Officers' Club where he lunched with Captain George Gamblin and Lieutenant Wolfred Wurtele, old friends from the 2DAC, and Captain Frank May, an electrical engineer from Montreal. After he cabled Rosalie to let her know he'd arrived safely, the four men went to find a car. "Left at 3:30 and made one of the fastest runs ever, arriving Officers' Club Aubigny at 5:30." They had beaten the Leave Train by a half-hour, even though it had left Boulogne eight hours before their departure. Overnighting at Aubigny, he caught a lift with an army truck headed for Etrun, then transferred to another going to Arras. A last ride, of eight miles southeast, brought him to the ruined village of Hendecourt-lez-Cagnicourt. Bert "jumped the 23rd Battery mess cart through the village and walked to Hqrs, arriving at 12:30." On being told by Lieutenant-Colonel Constantine that Brigadier Panet had been asking about him, Bert reported to Divisional Artillery that he'd arrived the previous night. His return was duly noted by Harry Beatty in the War Diary: "Lieut. Sargent reported back from leave."

Success at Arras and the Drocourt-Quéant Switch had come at a price, as Bert soon discovered. Gone were many friends and familiar faces in the 5th Brigade, among them Major Alex Paterson who had been gassed and evacuated to England.

September 13. Mostly fair. Showers in AM.

Fritz shot 3 balloons down in flames on our front today.

September 14. Showers.

Fritz has been getting so many of our balloons on this front that a trap was set for him. A balloon with a good charge of ammonol in it has been up for three days now but he hasn't gone near it until this afternoon, when the charge was set off too soon and Fritz turned and went quietly home, undamaged.

September 15. Very fair and warm.

Plenty of activity in the air, mostly supplied by Fritz. He played about with our balloons all day and burnt them up by twos and threes at odd intervals when he felt so inclined. Altogether he accounted for seven on our immediate front — just cleaned up the whole row, and we only got one of his planes.

Bert saw his nephew, Ken, on September 16 for the first time since March. Over lunch in Bert's office at brigade headquarters he was surprised "how the kid did tuck away the grub." A Warning Order arrived in the afternoon, with the 5th Brigade relieving the 6th on the nights of September 17/18 and 18/19. "Got out my first Operation Order," Bert noted with satisfaction, after issuing the necessary paperwork to all battery commanders.

Gotha bombers droned over that night, dropping bombs near the 18th Battery and killing Major William Hendrie's horse. Bert watched as searchlights caught the raiders and a British fighter succeeded in bringing one down. While still in mid-air, the bombs exploded, blowing the Gotha to pieces. "Great cheers all around the country."

Two sections per battery began the relief on the night of the seventeenth, even as Gothas rained down bombs. Next afternoon, Bert and Harry Beatty rode over to 6th Brigade headquarters at Bois de Bouche. Approaching the headquarters, the two lieutenants were spotted by enemy gunners, who fired a single "Whizz-Bang." Rather close," was Bert's offhand comment. Handing over to Beatty and Bert was Lieutenant Frank Jennings, an old friend from *Megantic* and the 6th Howitzer Brigade.

At 9:00 a.m. on the twentieth, Lieutenant-Colonel Constantine convened a meeting of battery commanders to discuss the orders for a new attack by the Canadian Corps. The officers then went out and reconnoitred gun positions 1,500 yards to the west of the Canal du Nord. The positions were "absolutely open," in full view of the Germans occupying the high ground at Bourlon Wood where, amid tall oaks, artillery pieces were dug in on the forward slope. As a result, the Canadians did all the construction work and ammunition hauling at night, and the positions were not occupied until a few hours before the attack.

September 20. A few showers.

Recommendations for [Captain] Jim Ellwood, [Lieutenant Arnott] Minnes and myself for MCs turned down by [First] Army Commander [General Henry Horne]. Just as well not to expect these things.

Next morning, the brigade Signals Officer, Lieutenant Robert Christie, and Sergeant Harold Buck were at the 23rd Battery when the Germans shelled the position. Christie was killed outright and Buck, taken to a casualty clearing station, died shortly afterward. "Kind of put our signal outfit in a hole," Bert noted.

September 22. Some showers.

Two Hun planes brought down today. Pilots jumped out in parachutes. First instance I have heard of.

Hun very nervous on our front tonight. He suspects something.

New procedures went into effect concerning replacement of damaged guns. Any artillery piece damaged in combat was taken back to the IOM depot.* Unless it could be repaired in four hours or less, repair artificers issued a condemnation notice. Gunners then took the slip to

---

*Inspection, Overhaul, and Maintenance depot.

the Corps gun park at Louez, where they received a new weapon. It was a good arrangement: batteries could replace damaged guns quickly, an important consideration in mobile warfare.

> *September 23. Fair.*
> One month today.
> Went around the batteries this afternoon, took [Gunner Kenneth] Carter with me. Had a h— of a time coming back from 17th [Battery]. Got caught in front of Bois de Bouche by 5.9s and had two rather close calls. The dirty bounder mixed gas with it, and we had to run for it. Carter nearly lost his lunch but it only got to my eyes, nose & throat.
> Our assembly areas heavily shelled tonight. The old Boche is wise!

On September 25 orders arrived in the morning by dispatch rider. Bert convened a meeting of battery commanders at the 18th Battery and Lieutenant-Colonel Constantine, up from Divisional Artillery, provided a final briefing. Though the Second Division was withdrawn to Corps Reserve, its artillery brigades remained in place, coming under temporary control of the 1st Divisional Artillery. "Most complicated barrage map I have ever seen," Bert admitted. "Barrage lasts 6 1/2 hours, and on our front we have one gun per 22 yards. The First, Third, and Fourth Armies are all taking part, so it ought to be the big show of the year. First phase is capture of Bourlon Wood and high ground beyond. Second phase includes Cambrai and crossing of Canal de l'Escaut [Scheldt]."

Bert worked late into the night at brigade headquarters to prepare the orders and barrage maps, which went out to the batteries in the morning by runner. Only at 9:20 p.m. of the twenty-sixth did Bert and Major William Hendrie leave for the brigade's new headquarters on the outskirts of Inchy-en-Artois; in the rain and darkness the two men had considerable difficulty finding it. "Luckily the Hun was very quiet."

Not until after midnight did the batteries take up their battle positions. Over at the 20th Battery one 18-pounder got stuck in a shell hole, but the determined gunners wrestled it free and into position.

33

Open Warfare and the Cambrai "Show"

The third major Canadian "show" of the year, the Battle of Cambrai, began before dawn on September 27, with the Corps attacking on a front of 4,000 yards. Compared to Amiens and the Battle of Arras, Cambrai was judged to be the most arduous. Another set-piece attack, it was planned with great care and executed with near-flawless precision. By October 8, the Canadians were eight miles east of their starting point, having taken more than 7,000 prisoners and hundreds of field guns, trench mortars, and machine guns.

The most difficult aspect of the show was crossing the 100-foot-wide Canal du Nord on the offensive's opening day. Meeting stubborn resistance, the 1st and 4th Canadian Divisions pressed their attack across a short dry section of the canal, just 2,600 yards long, where work had ceased in August 1914. Two hours after the assault began, the 4th Division on the right had secured Quarry Wood, 1,000 yards past the canal, while the 1st Division on the left was rolling up the Canal du Nord line to take the Marquion Line, a mile beyond.

Thereafter, German resistance hardened, but by nightfall the Canadians had punched four miles east of the canal.

September 27. Rain in early AM. Fair before Zero Hour.
Barrage opened at 5:20 AM much the same as for the Amiens show. Hun came back rather nasty through our valley and got into the 18th Battery rather badly. [Lieutenant Alexander] Ness

The desolate and exposed landscape in front of Bourlon and Bourlon Wood, over which Bert made a solo reconnaissance, September 27, 1918, for which he was later awarded the MC. *Author's photo.*

and [Lieutenant Herbert] Simmonds both wounded, 1 OR killed and 1 died of wounds, 11 wounded. 17th had 1 OR wounded.

The barrage lasted six and a half hours, and at its end the infantry had advanced so far that only three long-range 18-pounders from the 18th and 20th Batteries could still provide support. Shortly after the barrage concluded, batteries received orders to move across the Canal du Nord to new positions north of Bourlon. Brigade headquarters moved at 2:00 p.m. but Group refused to allow anything forward of Quarry Wood, due to the uncertain situation on the left.

Bert then embarked on a hazardous solo mission, determined to get the batteries into advanced positions, an action for which he later received the Military Cross.* When he returned to headquarters in Bourlon Quarry, the batteries started moving again, though the 23rd got lost and was not found until the following morning.

---

*The citation reads: "For marked gallantry in making reconnaissances of forward battery positions in front of the main Buissy Switch on 27th September 1918. He went forward and made an exhaustive reconnaissance of battery positions, being most of the time under extremely heavy shellfire" (*Supplement to the London Gazette*, October 4, 1919, pages 12365–66).

The history of the 4th Brigade offers a vivid account of the artillery action at the Canal:

As the mist began to rise from the valley, a few hours after Zero, the leading gun teams of the Brigade trotted down the long slope towards the canal, followed by the rest of the batteries. Each unit wheeled left and right to their positions 200 yards beyond the line previously occupied by the infantry. Behind us, machine guns and field guns were firing steadily. The noise was almost deafening. Officers ran about with directors, and men with aiming posts, while linemen laid their telephone wires to batteries on the flanks. Gunners unloaded and piled the shrapnel and high-explosive shells in neat rows on the ground; the wagon teams moved off to the rear as rapidly as the rough going would permit.

Meanwhile the Forward Observation Officer and his party began to establish connection with the forward zone.

Bert's Military Cross and close-up of his diary for the attack on Bourlon Wood, September 27, 1918. *Author's photo.*

Captain Norman Guiou, the 6th Brigade's MO, wrote:

Our guns opened up [at 5:20] and in minutes the retaliatory enemy barrage came right down on them. A runner came to Headquarters for me — "there were wounded at the guns."

As I approached the flashing guns, shells seemed to be bursting everywhere. The eighteen guns of the Brigade were arranged in a slight arc. Centrally placed and back about thirty yards were the six 4.5-inch howitzers firing over the 18-pounders. The 18-pounder closest to the aid post ceased firing. I looked up — the gunners were fallen against it, apparently all dead.

Ammunition was being brought up in General Service wagons, the horses at the gallop. The wagons were hastily unloaded and the drivers immediately wheeled and started back at the gallop out of the heavy shelling.

On Day 2, the 5th Brigade was in support of the 4th Canadian Division. Zero Hour was 6:00 a.m., and it meant all batteries had to move forward 1,000 yards or more from where they were and be prepared to fire a rolling barrage in less than two and a half hours. "Required some doing, but it was done," Bert noted. Infantry attacks met with strong opposition and counterattacks. Late in the day, the brigade laid a heavy concentration of fire on the Cambrai-Douai road, enabling the infantry to regain positions they had been thrown out of earlier.

Gunners soon discovered mobile warfare was very different than what they had experienced in the years of trench warfare. Gun pits were a thing of the past. And, after the second day of the offensive, the 5th Brigade War Diary noted: "The great problem in an advance is to keep up communication with your infantry and your brigade HQ. The procedure from an artillery point of view is to run a line from Brigade HQ to a point where FOOs can signal back. Runners are also employed. This is a much surer but slower method.

"It is also essential for a part of the Brigade HQ to move forward with the batteries, so that communications can be kept up in case of an emergency."

September 29. Windy, some showers.

Zero Hour 8:00 AM.

Very little progress made today. The show was not a success and we only advanced a few hundred yards.

Out all day for the first time since I came back. Rode down to Wagon Lines in AM (Inchy). Went up front in afternoon to find a Headquarters. Called at 17th, 18th & 23rd, then went down across Arras-Cambrai road to Raillencourt and Sailly. Picked out some good Hqrs in Sailly.

Next to Dead Man's Trench in front of Pozières, the Raillencourt Trench is a close second — dead Huns piled 3 deep in some places. A beautiful sight!

Bert went to bed in the early hours of September 30 and "at exactly 2:30 AM a large-sized Operation Order [No. 3] came in over the wire, which required some doing to get out in time." It was a complicated order, calling for a 21-lift barrage at 9:22 a.m., supporting an attack scheduled to begin at 6:00 a.m.* "Our batteries were required to be in action between 1500 and 2000 yards east of their present positions." Bert drafted the orders, getting them out at 5:45. "All batteries got forward into positions — but the show did not progress as it should, and 23rd and 17th were d— lucky to get out of their positions between the Cambrai-Douai road and the railway, when our infantry had to fall back [due to heavy machine-gun and artillery fire]. This is the second time the Boche has beaten us in this show!"

With the new month, Bert took over the War Diary from Harry Beatty. When McKeown returned from leave on October 4, he corrected and signed off the daily entries.

Under a full moon, enemy pilots stepped up their night missions, doing great damage in the crowded Canadian Corps sector. "Never saw enemy planes so active with MGs and bombs. Wonder he did not get more of our men and horses," Bert wrote.

The Canadians resumed the advance at 5:00 a.m. on October 1, seeking a bridgehead over the Canal d'Escaut and a vantage point

---

*The rolling barrage was divided among three artillery groups, with the 5th and 6th CFA Brigades commencing the last part at 9:22 a.m.

over the valley of the River Sensée. Lieutenant-Colonel Constantine's group of two artillery brigades, the 5th and 6th, were supporting the 6th and 5th Infantry brigades respectively. The attack began well and German prisoners streamed back from the front, but heavy counter-attacks pushed the Canadians off their earlier gains. Digging in, the Canadians held but called off any further attack for the day.

For Bert and the 5th Brigade, it was a day of confusion. As the brigade was not taking part in the barrage, "Batteries were instructed," as the War Diary noted, "to engage any targets that presented themselves. The situation, however, was so obscure that very little could be done. Each Battery and Brigade HQ had an FOO out with communication. The infantry themselves were not sure of their disposition until 9:00 PM."

Wisely, the brass decided to pause for a few days before the next offensive.

October 2. Fair & warm.

Looks as though we will have to try some other tactics, as we have been turned back there three times.

Batteries withdraw somewhat from battle to defensive positions.

The Corps found itself in an area consisting of (as Brigadier-General Harry Burstall described it) "a succession of flat-topped ridges and small hills with broad open valleys in between." As the terrain offered little cover for advancing infantry, staff officers began putting together plans for a night attack, a rare occurrence.

Supporting the 2nd Canadian Division on a narrow front of 4,000 yards were no fewer than seven field artillery brigades, along with two brigades of six-inch and eight-inch howitzers. These units were concentrated around the village of Sailly, due to a scarcity of water elsewhere. Even at Sailly, though, the "supply was very bad, consisting of the usual village reservoir of surface rain water," which "seemed nothing more than liquid mud."

In the 5th Brigade, McKeown was not pleased. "There are a good many guns around Sailly, and there are far too many troops here. A good many horses are around the place. We will probably be shelled."

His words were prophetic. When six-inch howitzer batteries camped just behind brigade headquarters, they immediately brought down enemy fire. "Some close ones during the night," Bert wrote. "Boche continues to *strafe* us at night but doesn't put anything closer than our front yard, scattering the dirt down my ventilator and over my papers." Having so many gunners crammed together made it easy to find old friends. "Saw Harold Fetherstonhaugh," Bert noted, and he also found his nephew, "looking as tough as ever."

On October 4, the War Diary recorded: "All ranks are suffering for the want of a bath," though this was soon remedied. Baths with a capacity of 150 men per hour were located at Sains-lez-Marquoin, four miles away, and the 5th Brigade received two time slots, three hours in the morning of October 5, and a further three hours the following day.

Around this time a new type of gas shell began to fall into Canadian positions. Containing a considerable quantity of high explosive, they could not be recognized as gas shells by the sound of their flight or their burst, and the deadly gas was masked by the fumes of the explosive. As a result, all ranks were warned to be on guard for gas in any HE attack. The Canadians, too, had a new shell. On October 7, 18-pounders of the 5th Brigade fired their first lot of ABB — mustard gas in an elongated shell — sending more than a thousand rounds into enemy positions. Though prisoners left little doubt as to the effectiveness of Canadian HE and shrapnel fire, it was a different story for the mustard gas bombardments. Both sides, as the War Diary admitted, were so well trained to deal with gas that "it neutralizes the fatal effects."

October 5. Fair & cool.

The Boche doesn't intend to leave much of Cambrai, as he has started to blow it up and burn it.

That same day Lieutenant-Colonel Constantine submitted to 2CDA a short list of men recommended for decorations. Among the names were two lieutenants he put in for the Military Cross: James Wilson, and Bert Sargent ("on the basis of extreme gallantry in action"). Of Bert, Constantine noted as well that "this Officer's services while he has been under my command have been all that could be desired" and that "he had been previously recommended for decoration." Constantine's suggested wording for the citation was adopted with only minor changes.

Each day brought good news on the military front. The Germans retreated in the Verdun sector, while Bert's diary of October 7 mentioned a proposal by Austria and Germany for an armistice to discuss peace. He was probably voicing the opinions of many when he wrote, "Great stuff that, and now is the time to hit him!"

On October 7, Bert prosecuted two courts-martial down at the headquarters of the ammunition column, though he had a difficult time leaving his own headquarters. German gunners started shelling the area, and he was obliged to take cover for three-quarters of an hour. "I couldn't get shaving water or breakfast," he noted. Bert's case against 20-year-old Gunner James Graham of the 18th Battery was straightforward. The second — that of Corporal Alexander Robertson of the 20th Battery — was postponed.

While Bert was prosecuting Gunner Graham, Rosalie was writing to Flora Darling on letterhead embossed with the cannon emblem of the Royal Field Artillery. Along with it was a silver-printed envelope with "April, 1918" crossed out and "August 23rd" substituted by hand.

I am sending you a copy of each of the snaps taken on our wedding day. I had intended waiting until I had several of each to send you — but the photographer seems so slow and also Bert is very anxious for you to have them. However, as soon as I receive the fresh supply I will send you sufficient for a set for each member of the family.

Bert is ever so pleased with them but I don't think it is nearly good enough of him, for he looked just splendid! Of course you can pick out Mum and Dad in the group, also my sister [Emily], sitting at Mum's feet. She was my chief bridesmaid.

It is four weeks today since Bert went back and it seems almost like years. Somehow the wedding and honeymoon seem but a dream now, but it is one I never tire of dwelling upon. We are looking forward to February 8th — the earliest date he could possibly come!

I had a letter from Bert this morning. He is very busy and is in the thick of it and is scarcely ever able to write until after midnight. I feel I ought to tell him to go right to bed and not trouble about my letters, but I am ashamed to say I haven't the pluck! I don't mind a Field Card or even two or three lines — but I dread not getting any at all. I think I must be a bit of a coward, for Bert has always been kept safe and well and I ought to rely more upon my faith, oughtn't I? However, *c'est la guerre* and one day peace will be declared and we shall all be happy again, shan't we?

Bert received the brigade's new orders on October 8 for an attack the following day at 1:30 a.m. The orders were complex, and it took almost six hours to figure it all out and get them circulated to four brigades of artillery. This time, instead of a barrage, the 5th Brigade would lay down a series of "crashes" on roads, trenches, and known enemy strongpoints in advance of the infantry. Some last-minute changes came through from division, and Bert rushed out an addendum to his Operation Order.

With the Canadians holding the high ground north and west of Cambrai, the Germans began to evacuate the city. Jumping off at 1:30 a.m., the infantry pushed into the city. To the east, the 2nd Division rushed the bridges of the Canal d'Escaut, while the 3rd Division, fighting from house to house, thrust the Germans back. "Put up a poor scrap," Bert observed. By daybreak, much of the city had been taken. Hoping to spare the civilian population, most of whom were already fleeing, Canadian gunners refrained from shelling Cambrai in advance. As the Germans retreated, they set numerous fires and began blowing up buildings. It took almost three days to extinguish the flames, by which time the city centre and eastern suburbs had been consumed.

To keep up with the Canadian advance, the 5th Brigade moved its headquarters from Sailly — with regrets. "Probably the best Headquarters we have had in some time! I hate to leave my little brass bed behind," Bert groaned. The batteries advanced 4,500 yards to be able to support the infantry, taking new positions around the hamlet of Ramillies. It was after dark when Bert and Lieutenant-Colonel Constantine made their way from Sailly to Ramilles. "If it hadn't been for the fires in Cambrai we never could have found the place."

With Cambrai in Canadian hands, "There was not a moment's lull in the fighting," the *Official Record* declared. "The enemy was in full retreat along the whole front and constant heavy pressure was necessary at all points and at all times." Under these conditions, gunners often had little time to prepare positions in support of the advancing infantry. Headquarters for 5th Brigade moved on October 10 to Escadoeuvres, a mile away, then again the next day to Croix St. Hubert. "Communications very hard to keep up," Bert noted.

On October 11, the brigade was relieved by an RFA Brigade. "Some job turning over our own Brigade and two others as well, particularly in the midst of a battle," Bert commented.

October 12. Cold, some rain.

Sad awakening this AM! The Brigade Major [John Ball] came in at 6:30 with verbal orders for us to be back up in the line to fire a barrage in support of 5th CIB at 12:00.

With all batteries back at Wagon Lines in Ramillies and Tilloy, we sure had some job ahead of us. Warned the orderlies and wrote an order.

Operation Order No. 223 arrived in writing from Divisional Artillery at 7:00 a.m. and mounted couriers went out soon after to all batteries. The brigade staff worked hard to allocate zones and set up barrage tables. Bert then met with officers from all batteries, handing out barrage tables and getting the precise locations of the guns. Under the circumstances, the brigade performed admirably, as Bert described in the *Official Record*.

When it is considered that all Batteries were at this time more than 2000 yards as the crow flies from Brigade Headquarters and the farthest one, more than 6000 yards from the position which would have to be occupied, that the only system of communication was by mounted orderlies, and the roads congested with traffic, that an operation order had to be written and Battery Zones allotted in the barrage before Battery Commanders could either select their positions or make their calculations for the barrage, that men and horses were tired out with their exertions of the past few days and, on being relieved, had relaxed to enjoy the anticipated rest, it is a matter of no small wonder and one which reflects the greatest credit upon the Brigade Commanders, Battery Commanders, and all concerned that all Batteries were in action, firing the opening barrage, at Zero Hour, and the supply of ammunition was maintained until the barrage was shot out.

Bert's handwritten instructions stressed the importance of the barrage. "Battery Commanders must realize that this is a matter of extreme urgency and batteries must be in action as required at all costs." Major William Hendrie's 18th Battery thrilled onlooking infantry "as it galloped down the Escadoeuvres-Iwuy road and swung into position at 'Action Left!'" with thirty seconds to spare before the first round was fired."

The attacking 24th Battalion met with little opposition and took the village of Hordain shortly after 1:00 p.m. Thereafter, progress was slow, largely due to the wide and deep drainage ditches around villages like Thun-St. Martin. Once more, 5th Brigade batteries moved forward, through the village of Iwuy, but the 51st Division on the right was checked and the batteries halted. Acting on erroneous reports that the Germans were withdrawing, the 17th and 23rd Batteries pushed to within 1,000 yards of the enemy artillery. This was too close for comfort and they later withdrew to a safer distance.

The area was a welcome change from the villages around Arras, shattered by years of shellfire. Here, the countryside was fresh and green, the hamlets often untouched by the storm of war. The Germans, pushed back too rapidly by the Canadians, had no time to lay waste the villages they were abandoning.

On October 13 the brigade established a report centre at Château Richon in Iwuy. This became a collecting point for telephone lines between infantry, artillery, and other units operating in the forward zone. Lieutenant-Colonel Constantine and Bert elected to remain at brigade headquarters in Thun-St. Martin, a lucky decision as it turned out, for the Germans dropped just three shells near the château, killing one man and chasing everyone downstairs. The following afternoon Bert arrived at Château Richon to set up brigade headquarters. "Beautiful spot. Most elegant furniture. Makes a great layout. Mess, bedrooms, etc." The officers settled into their new home and tried to get comfortable. "Got a load of coal," Bert wrote. "A good grate fire in the Mess makes things very much more home-like but not conducive to much work." A day later he admitted, "This is the best piece of country we have ever fought through. All kinds of fresh vegetables, good billets, and not much harassing fire." The men, too, were well looked after at Iwuy. The War Diary observed, "Troops are being splendidly fed, as there are many gardens in this area. Coal is also quite plentiful, and sufficient to keep forward troops comfortable. All ranks are under cover in houses not too badly damaged. Horses for the most part are splendidly housed."

Because the places through which the Corps was advancing were still inhabited, gunners received special instructions on October 14: "Destructive artillery fire on ... towns and villages of importance will, as far as the situation permits, be confined to gun positions, railways, approaches and points of tactical importance." As each town was liberated, the Canadians were greeted as heroes. "The people could not do enough for us," the 4th Brigade history recorded. "Every time the column halted, cups of steaming hot coffee and biscuits were handed to the men, and our horses were garlanded with flowers."

October 16. Fair & cool. Misty.

Our front remains quiet. 1st and 4th [Canadian] Divisions working east from Douai put us in a peculiar position, as we are firing due north, and eventually they will work across our front and do us out of a job.

Moving 18th and 20th Batteries west of the Canal [de l'Escaut].

Infantry crossed the Canal de l'Escaut on October 17 and the gunners made ready to follow. The brigade received an Operation Order on October 19 for a 2:00 a.m. barrage the next morning, only to have it cancelled, "as the Boche was moving too fast." The brigade then went into Corps Reserve and batteries remained in position until October 22, when they finally crossed the canal. Headquarters and the report centre moved again on the twentieth, this time to the château in Hordain. Bert described it as "the most comfortable Hqrs we have occupied for some time," while the War Diary noted "All ranks [were] very grateful for a few days rest in such splendid surroundings."

Civilian refugees, hollow-eyed and undernourished, were a wrenching sight as they trudged along the roadsides. Bob Gillespie of the 23rd later wrote, "Most of us will never forget that long procession of men, women and children, carrying or wheeling what little personal belongings they could, back to what had once been home. We all know what a disappointment they invariably met." The 4th Brigade historian added, "Many had no shoes. The clothing they wore was of all sorts and shades. Some carried huge bundles, others pushed along little dog carts and baby carriages to carry their meagre belongings, while still others dragged wagons in which had been placed their bedding and other necessaries."

October 21. Dull, some rain.

Steady stream of civilians coming down from Denain all day yesterday and today. Very pitiful sight in many cases. The old Boche sure is foxy. He strips them of everything except their clothes, knowing we will have to feed and look after them. The 220,000 he let loose on us at Lille just delayed our advance three days.

Just as the brigade was getting ready for a week or so of rest, orders arrived for the 22nd to move to the village of Wavrechain. The brigade got underway at 9:45 a.m., crossing the Canal de l'Escaut, one vehicle at a time, by a pontoon bridge at Bouchain. "Not a pleasant trip," Bert recorded, "as it rained most of the way." Though Wavrechain had been badly damaged by the Germans, headquarters were set up in Château Lahure. "With a lot of work, [it] will be very comfortable," Bert wrote. The officers got the place fixed up quickly enough, so that when it came time to move on, Bert recorded, "Will be sorry to leave." Wavrechain held enough barns to provide cover for all the brigade's horses. Given a respite from action, the men engaged in "general fatigues," which included clipping the horses, cleaning equipment, securing baths, overhauling kits, and replenishing stores.

October 23. Dull and cold.
Today is the 2nd Monthly Anniversary of the greatest day of my life.

Lieutenant-Colonel Constantine put together a training schedule, sent out under Bert's signature. Implemented on the twenty-fifth, it was a typical syllabus, and gave no hint the war would end in less than three weeks.

October 26. Fair & warmer.
Went out with the OC at 08:45, mounted. Spent the morning on the training ground galloping from one battery to the other, watching the drill and giving them schemes to carry out. Very interesting, as well as good sport. The OC sure does know his Battery Tactics and Driving Drill. Managed to get some of the new subalterns considerably fussed.

The training was short-lived. On October 28, the brigade moved again, with new headquarters at La Pyramide-de-Denain. As in Wavrechain, Bert "grabbed a very nice billet with the usual piano. Mademoiselle came in and played for us. Quite a respectable evening." Extract from Routine Orders October 27, 1918:

2104. Prevention of Venereal Disease
The presence of Venereal Disease amongst the prostitutes inhabiting the recently captured area makes it necessary that immediate preventative measures be taken.
It is known that a number of diseased prostitutes have been deliberately released by the Germans from their venereal hospitals.

This fact will be communicated to all ranks on three successive parades and every precaution taken.

October 29. Fair & warm.

A little long-gun stuff around this morning. Got a couple of horses in the 23rd. It didn't take the civilians long to cut up the one that was killed. They haven't had fresh meat for years.

That afternoon, Bert and Lieutenant-Colonel Constantine rode ahead to the village of Maing, looking over prospective positions. At 3:45 the Germans laid down a heavy barrage of gas shells. "By the time we came through," Bert related, "the village was full of gas and we both got quite a dose."

October 30. Fair & warm.

Rode into Denain in afternoon. Surprising number of civilians in the town. Conditions practically normal again. Shops open and business as usual.

The Boche still playing about with his long-gun stuff; came *very* close to getting my two mares.

Château de Pres, at Maing, occupied by the 5th Brigade, October 29–31, 1918. *Author's photo.*

As expected, the brigade's next move was to Maing, four and a half miles away, on October 31. Batteries had to be in place by 11:59 p.m., in time for the next offensive. Barrage maps and reams of paperwork soon arrived by dispatch rider. Bert's headquarters was just 500 yards from the battery positions. "Looks good for communications," he observed. It wasn't a quiet night; the Germans strafed Maing and killed one man in each of the 20th and 23rd Batteries.

October 31. Dull in AM. Rain in PM.

Great news this morning. Armistice was signed at 12:00 hours with Turkey under very favorable terms. Looks more than ever like the beginning of the end! More good news: Austria has cashed in and *begs* for an armistice.

This is the stuff to give 'em.

34

Valenciennes and
the Pursuit to Mons

At 5:15 a.m. on Friday, November 1, the 4th Canadian Division, push-ing from the south, attacked the wooded heights of Mont Houy on a front of just 2,500 yards, aiming toward Valenciennes, an industrial city of 30,000 that had been held by the Germans since August 1914. Supporting what would be the last Canadian battle of the war was a highly sophisticated barrage in which Canadian gunners, in just over three hours, fired 2,149 tons of ammunition, about three-quarters of what both sides had used in the entire Boer War. It was the most intense barrage ever fired in support of the Canadian Corps,* another confirmation that Canadian lives were more valuable than shells. Or, as Andy McNaughton later phrased it, the corps commander's policy was "never to employ men where shells would do the work."

The attack cost the Corps just 80 killed and 300 wounded.

Batteries of field and heavy artillery had been sited to provide over-head, oblique, enfilade, and reverse fire, this latter designed to make the Germans believe they were being shelled by their own guns, further demoralizing an already disheartened enemy. Following the barrage, one section per battery of the 5th Brigade moved forward to continue supporting the infantry, after which the remainder of the battery moved up. This was accomplished with relative ease, as the roads were good and the ground had not been torn up by enemy shelling.

---

*Eight field artillery brigades participated, along with six heavy artillery brigades, a total of 296 guns.

November 1. Fair & warm.

Show went with a good swing at first. Reports that Fritz was not fighting very hard at first. I don't blame him, considering the barrage that was let loose at him. Objectives occupied practically on schedule time.

Hun casualties very heavy. Saw more wounded Huns than in any recent shows and reports indicate great number of dead ones. Barrage lasted 3 hours 25 minutes.

That night Valenciennes was captured, almost intact, for neither side had shelled the city, though Gothas bombed the railway station and canal locks. The Germans, however, had looted much of the city's machinery, including electrical equipment.

November 2. Rain.

Jim and MO [Captain Alexander Campbell] in Valenciennes in afternoon. Had a wonderful time. MO came back with pockets filled with cocaine, morphine, etc. — over $100 worth altogether.

Earlier, RAF observers reported seeing large-scale movements of troops and guns around Estreux in front of the Canadians. These were interpreted as German transport moving westward to support a counterattack. "We may have a good scrap on our hands," Bert enthused, as orders arrived for the brigade to prepare for 30 minutes of counter-battery fire in the morning. Before the Canadians fired a shot, the mistake was discovered. "It turns out that [enemy] concentrations on roads, instead of being artillery coming in, were limbers, etc. coming up to pull his guns out! So, when the patrols get out in the AM they find the Boche gone, with only the usual fringe of MGs left [as a rearguard]. We take on a few targets for them and answer the odd Neutralizing Fire call, and our advance goes well again."

The pursuit continued unabated as the Germans withdrew to the northeast toward the Belgian city of Mons, 18 miles away. In full stride, the Canadian Corps was hot on their heels.

Given a day's respite from action, the 5th Brigade spent the time at Le Poirier cleaning up.

November 4. Fair & warm.

Armistice signed with Austria.

Advance going rapidly. The 4th Division will follow him up until they push him out of France, then our Div. will relieve. So, will probably go back into action again tomorrow night.

Valenciennes itself is the finest and richest town I have been in out here. Very gay — flags flying and a band playing in the square. The Prince of Wales, General Currie and others of lesser degree are amongst the crowds today.

November 5. Rain.

Interesting talk with some of the civilians in Estreux. They talk a very funny patois, half-French, half-German, and rather hard to understand. Told us of how scared the Huns were of our counter-battery work. They would man their guns and fire five or six rounds fast, then beat it and await results.

The betting in Paris is it will be over in 6 days! I am not quite so optimistic.

German prisoners related, on interrogation, how their troops retreated before the withering Canadian artillery fire. Bert's Operation Order No. 67 urged, "He is to be given every opportunity of so doing...."

New artillery tactics evolved to exploit the Canadian momentum. One 18-pounder battery per brigade was instructed to move forward in close support of the infantry on a moment's notice. "Section Commanders will work more or less independently and will be prepared to engage any target that presents itself or that may be holding up the advance of the infantry." Artillery officers now accompanied infantry reconnaissance patrols, so "batteries could be rushed forward as rapidly as possible." Batteries moved forward before dusk each evening so they would be properly situated for the next morning's barrage. So rapid was the advance that Bert had to caution all battery commanders there would be "... no unobserved shooting on the front of [the] 5th CIB without reference to this office, except by mobile batteries acting in conjunction with their infantry." Otherwise, Canadian gunners shooting purely by the map risked hitting their own fast-moving battalions.

Brigade headquarters moved again on November 6, this time to Onnaing, six miles away, while McKeown went forward to reconnoitre battery positions. Bert and the Headquarters Section arrived at Estreux at 11:30 a.m. in a steady rain. After lunch they pulled out, heading for Onnaing. German sappers had blown many of the roads, forcing the gunners to make long detours, but the brigade arrived at Onnaing at 3:30 p.m. Headquarters were set up in a château that had been badly shattered but was still habitable. "Usual piano, some beautiful furnishings, mostly ruined," Bert recorded. Communication would be next to impossible: "We are about 5000 yards from our nearest battery."

November 6.

Infantry going strong. They require a kick-off in AM to help them on their way.

Great news these days. The delegation has left Berlin to confer with Foche re an Armistice. The betting is it will be all over by Sunday.

Crossroads mined by the Germans, outside Mons, to impede the Canadian Corps, November 1918. *Courtesy of Library and Archives Canada, PA-003537.*

Heralding the Canadian advance on the seventh was another series of artillery "crashes" in which gunners pounded a variety of pre-determined targets — sunken roads, slag heaps, and suspected strongpoints — for varying lengths of time. Desperate to delay their dogged pursuers, the Germans mined the roads behind them, blew bridges, and tore up railway lines. It didn't help much. Engineers filled in the massive craters, some 18 feet deep, and swiftly rebuilt bridges using anything at hand. Communications, though, remained a huge problem. "Very great difficulties were encountered in getting reports," Brigadier Harry Burstall related. "The telephone lines were very lengthy and owing to the bad weather, leakage and interference were excessive. The general state of the roads and of the whole country rendered communications by cyclists or by mounted orderlies very slow, while visibility was so poor that visual signalling and general observation was almost impossible." Burstall added that Belgian civilians had become so terrified of German road mines they believed "every piece of telephone wire was some sort of fuse for blowing up roads. The result was that our telephone wires were being cut the whole day long."

November 7. Dull and cold.

Belgium!

Hqrs move to Quiévrain.*

Day mostly busy keeping track of our infantry and batteries. Boche going fast.

The OC goes forward at 15:00 hours. After 17:00 before I get away. Road lined with traffic and held up all the way by the enormous craters blown by the Boche. Night pitch-black and raining. Guns and lorries stuck in holes or turned over in craters. Never have I seen such traffic before.

Had a h— of a job to find our new Hqrs.

The people had vacated their perfectly good house and turned it over to us. Seems funny to sleep between sheets when in action. Village full of civilians.

---

*This was the only point where horse transport could cross the swollen Honnelle River.

In a curt handwritten note to the four battery commanders, Bert referred to the German delegation arriving in the Allied lines. "This should not interfere with shooting Boche until further orders." There was no let-up in the Canadian attack. Orders arrived on the night of the seventh for an advance the following morning, supported by artillery "crashes" from 7:30 to 8:10 a.m., when the 5th Canadian Infantry Brigade (CIB) started its attack.

November 8. Dull, some rain.

Hqrs move to Elouges.

Started out at 09:00 hours to locate new Hqrs. Rode up through Elouges [at 1:00 PM]. Roads blown up as usual.

By the reception I received from the civilians they might have thought I was the C-in-C. Every door and window crowded with men, women and children and every house with a flag flying.

Hqrs moved in shortly after noon and by 15:00 hours we were in communication with all batteries, who had taken up positions close by.

The infantry encountered opposition near Bois-en-Boussu, but mobile batteries soon broke this up. Fooling the Germans, the Canadians continued the advance after dark, supported by further "crashes." On the morning of the ninth, the 4th CIB passed through the 5th CIB without artillery support, for the advance was unopposed. The gunners were on the march early, making what amounted to a route march over good roads until they finally came into action near Frameries at 5:00 p.m. This, however, was a route march with a difference. In the *Official Record*, Bert described it as "a triumphal procession through villages, where every house was bedecked with flags and the inhabitants, delirious with joy at their delivery, lined the streets and expressed a welcome born of four long years of tyranny and oppression." For the 23rd Battery, it was "the wildest day of the war." Bob Gillespie described it thus: "We started forward about 10 AM and, instead of stopping a mile or two ahead, as had usually been the case, we found the Hun had beat it, so we went after him."

For Bert it was a day of wild confusion, trying to communicate to batteries on the move and keeping up with the fast-moving Lieutenant-Colonel Constantine. "Found the OC at the church in Frameries. Moved into comfortable billets and batteries take up positions of assembly as the Boche is still beating it! The people simply can't do enough for us."

At night Gothas struck the Wagon Lines of the 20th Battery at Frameries with deadly effect: 43 horses were killed or wounded.

November 10. Fair & warm.

Hqrs move to Sucerie. My two horses have a close call.

Started out at 06:30 hours with a party of mounted orderlies on a reconnaissance to keep touch with the infantry.

Civilians in all the houses insist on my stopping for coffee. Had a h— of a job to get away from them.

The historic message flimsy to the 5th Brigade CFA, announcing the end of hostilities at 11:00 a.m., November 11, 1918.
Courtesy of Madeleine Claudi.

The infantry were ordered to advance during the night to seize the high ground at Bois la Haut, southeast of Mons. The country was open and the Canadians met with little opposition, though the Germans continued their stubborn rearguard action by blowing up road junctions. These were quickly repaired or bypassed entirely. Though word of an armistice was received at infantry headquarters, the advance continued until the last minute, supported by mobile batteries of the 5th Brigade, helping to overcome light resistance from machine guns.

At brigade headquarters in Obourg, someone thrust a "C" Form message flimsy into Bert's hand. He scanned the pencil scrawl, then shoved it into a pocket.

TO: 5TH BDE CFA

FOLLOWING RECEIVED FROM 2ND CDN DIV AAA BEGINS AAA HOSTILITIES WILL CEASE AT 11 HOURS TODAY 11TH STAND FAST ON LINE REACHED WHICH WILL BE REPORTED TO BDES AT ONCE AAA DEFENSIVE PRECAUTIONS WILL BE MAINTAINED AAA THERE WILL BE NO INTERCOURSE WITH THE ENEMY FURTHER ORDERS WILL BE ISSUED LATER AAA BATTERIES WILL REMAIN IN PRESENT POSITIONS UNTIL FURTHER ORDERS AAA ACKNOWLEDGE

FROM: 2ND CDA

PLACE & TIME: 08:35*

Into his leather-bound diary that night, Bert tucked the pencilled transcript of the historic message announcing the Armistice. Eighty-six years later it was still there.

While wild celebrations took place in London and elsewhere, the 5th Brigade front was strangely quiet, with only sporadic fire as Canadians advanced into Mons, an appropriate place to end the war; here, in August 1914, British forces had first clashed with the advancing Imperial Army. A great and unaccustomed silence settled over the Western Front as the guns fell quiet and millions of men sought to make sense of what they had endured. At 5th Brigade headquarters

---

*The wording of this historic message differs slightly from that of similar wires reported in other unit histories, including the one in Bert's *Official Record*.

the mood was sombre, and "feelings of infinite relief" were mixed with slight disappointment as batteries deployed to cover the infantry on the positions they had reached at 11:00 a.m.

Writing that evening, Bert tried to summarize the most momentous day of the war:

> Well! I mean to say — but it was funny how calmly everyone took it. So hard to realize it is all over that one cannot appreciate the fact.

Bert's instructions to battery commanders — in longhand — cautioned, "Under present circumstances it is very necessary that the present high standard of discipline be maintained, and every opportunity must be taken to clean up men, horses, equipment, and reduce loads." In the afternoon of the eleventh, Bert rode through unknown territory, seeking McKeown and the OC. His diary continued: "Rendezvous at church in Hyon. Pick up an orderly on the way directing me to Obourg. Dark and raining by the time I get there. Had a h— of a time finding the place. The Boche hadn't time to blow up any of the roads around this part of the country. When we got the Infantry [telephone] line in, we find we are in No Man's Land."

Gunners of the Canadian Corps could take great pride in their achievements. Field Marshal Haig, summarizing the last six months of the war, later paid special tribute to the artillery. "The accuracy and intensity of our barrages, frequently arranged at short notice and with little opportunity being given for ranging or previous reconnoitring of the ground, have contributed largely to the success of our infantry attacks. The intimate cooperation between artillery and infantry, which is the first requisite in modern war, has been a marked feature of our operations."

The 23rd Battery's Bob Gillespie wrote: "Now our great task is done. At what price we do not yet realize. Of our bravest, many now sleep on European soil; many more will bear henceforth on their persons the marks of war; still more will remember the war as the donor of weakened health and constitution. But we all — maimed, weakened, and untouched alike, unite in a common sorrow as well as a common pride in those who sacrificed their all — but not in vain."*

Not all Canadian gunners welcomed the Armistice. "Unless [the Germans] feel in some measure what the people in captured France and Belgium have gone through, I do not think they will have learned the lesson which the war should teach them," Hal wrote in August. Some months later, he mused, "I wonder, did we stop too soon? The feeling out here is that if the war had continued a few more weeks, it would have produced an overwhelming disaster for the Germans." Lieutenant Don Macpherson of the 23rd Battery wrote, "Germany will have to be soundly whipped before we shall obtain a peace worth having."

A former McGill engineering professor saw it the same way. "Bloody fools!" railed Brigadier-General Andy McNaughton. "We have them on the run. That means we shall have to do it all over again in another twenty-five years."

---

*In the course of the war, Bert's 23rd Battery (with a nominal strength of about 140 men) mustered more than 560 officers and men, thus reconstituting itself more than four times over. In all, 50 men were killed in action or died of wounds, and 148 were wounded, a casualty rate of almost 36 percent.

35

Into the Rhineland

As the guns fell silent at last, the German Army commenced its march eastward, a disciplined return to the defeated Second Reich. In accordance with the terms of the Armistice, the leading troops of the Canadian Corps stood fast on the line reached at 11:00 a.m., and checkpoints were set up on all roads. No British troops were to advance east of this line and airmen were directed to remain not less than a mile behind it. Fraternization was not permitted with any enemy troops who remained, nor were German soldiers permitted to approach the halt line. Though it was soon apparent the Germans were retiring in an orderly fashion, the British High Command took no chances. No one was yet certain what an armistice actually meant, how long it would last, or whether hostilities might resume.* As a result, caution was the watchword of the day. "In order to maintain the highest state of efficiency throughout the Corps," Currie reported, "I ordered Commanders to pay the strictest attention to discipline and smartness." But Currie knew what his men had endured and, concerned for their well-being, ordered all troops not on duty to be given "every opportunity for rest and recreation."

A plan was soon put in place for the British Second and Fourth Armies to advance to the Rhine, where they would occupy strategic bridgeheads. The Canadian Corps would form part of the Second

---

*The Armistice was to remain in force for 36 days from November 11, with provision for extension or annulment on 48 hours' notice being given.

Army. The advance was scheduled for November 17, but the plans soon changed. On November 22 new instructions stipulated that only Second Army would advance into Germany, and just the 1st and 2nd Canadian Divisions would participate in the occupation, along with Corps headquarters and various Corps units; the 3rd and 4th Divisions would remain billeted in Belgium. The change arose because planners expected difficulty in supplying such a large number of men, and a great deal of repair work was necessary in Belgium to ensure the safety of the army and the civilian population.

At the 5th Brigade, Lieutenant-Colonel Constantine made one thing very clear: "Strict discipline and smartness [were] to be maintained to prove that the British in general and Canadians in particular can be good soldiers as well as good fighters." And because no one knew what the Germans might yet do, "every precaution [would be] taken against surprise or treachery on the part of the enemy."

On November 12, 5th Brigade headquarters moved to be closer to the batteries. McKeown found a nice château in Havré, which the officers shared with the 17th Battery. "Everything squared away shortly after noon," Bert wrote. "Located in a very nice room in west corner of Château. Madame perturbed that her house is in such disorder and can't understand how we can live in it. Very apologetic. The Boche occupied it for ten days and, as usual when they left, took everything with them. She refuses to come back to live here, so the place is ours as long as we care to stay." Orders went out in the afternoon to the batteries to get cleaned up and have the horses properly shod in anticipation of a long march, though no one knew anything definite. At a major conference the next afternoon at 2nd Divisional Artillery headquarters, brigade commanders and adjutants were briefed on the planned move into Germany. Later, Bert and Lieutenant-Colonel Constantine rode into Mons. "Very interesting old town but not to be compared with Valenciennes for beauty."

The brigade's four batteries began cleaning equipment. Surplus articles were turned into ordnance and salvage depots; the trip would be tiring enough for the horses without carrying a lot of excess baggage. Lieutenant-Colonel Constantine visited each battery position, where he addressed the men. After thanking them for their support during the last operations, he expressed the hope they would conduct themselves "in such a manner while passing through Belgium and during [the] occupation of German territory as will reflect the greatest credit on the Unit."

After weeks in the field, the men were in dire need of new clothing and underwear, but these were difficult to obtain as the Corps had outrun its supply lines. Personal hygiene could not be neglected, and the men managed to obtain good baths at the mines surrounding Havré, whose mayor and council never ceased to demonstrate their gratitude at being liberated.

> *November 14.* Fair & cool.
> The Burgomaster of Havré dined with us tonight. A very interesting old boy.
> *November 15.* Fair & cool.
> Official Entry into Mons.
> The official entry of the British Army into Mons was staged this morning [at 11:00 AM]. We supplied a composite battery [one battery each from the 2nd and 3rd CDA] which Major [William] Hendrie commanded. All the notables were to be on hand. Jim went in so I couldn't get away.

Two pending courts-martial remained on Bert's docket as prosecuting officer, and he was anxious to dispose of them before the march into Germany. These were set to begin at 10:00 a.m. on the sixteenth at 4th CIB headquarters. After getting the witnesses and "riding h— out of my horses to get there on time," he was upset to find that "the whole show was called off." Raising a fuss after riding over to 2nd Division Artillery, he succeeded in having both trials reinstated for 5:30 that evening. It was late when Bert returned to headquarters in a foul mood. "Had to turn down a perfectly good invitation to the Burgomaster's dinner, also to a big reception and dance in Mons on account of these d— FGCMs."

The journey to the Rhine commenced on Monday, November 18. More than 20,000 men of the 2nd Canadian Division began marching on roughly parallel courses, which would terminate at Bonn, the university town of 90,000 on the west bank of the Rhine, best known as the birthplace of Ludwig van Beethoven. Included in this number were three brigades of the division's artillery — the 5th, 6th, and 13th. Following other routes a dozen or so miles to the north, the 1st Division began making its way to the historic cathedral city of Cologne.

Officers were on horseback, as were drivers; gunners rode in the seats built into their weapons or rode on limbers and General Service wagons. Although Belgium had been liberated, the columns took no risks. "All precautions are to be taken as by an army marching through hostile territory," McKeown noted in the War Diary, "advance guards of all arms being thrown out." In Belgium, at least, this was soon seen as a waste of effort. As the *Official Record* marvelled, "A wonderful reception was tendered the Brigade on its way through Belgium, where the warm hospitality of the inhabitants left nothing to be desired. Every house was hung with flags and bunting and the streets of the villages festooned with garlands."

That same morning in Montreal, under the headline TRAMP! TRAMP! TRAMP! THE BOYS ARE MARCHING, *Gazette* readers learned of the move of Allied armies toward Germany, and the plan for Canadians to garrison certain parts of Germany, though no details were given.

The route to the Bonn bridgehead — 131 miles away in a straight line — would require 16 days of marching to cover 211 miles on the ground, and took the brigade on a southeasterly swing through Belgium and into the forested Ardennes region. For some units in the Corps, the trek to Bonn was farther than they'd marched during the entire war.

Field Marshal Haig, in his last published Despatch, acknowledged that the march would not be an easy one. "The country through which our troops were passing was of a most difficult character. Practicable roads were few, villages were far apart, and facilities for billeting very limited. Our way lay across a country of great hills rising to over 2000 feet, covered by wide stretches of forest, and cut by deep and narrow valleys, along the steep sides of which the roads wound in countless sudden curves. Even under conditions approximating to those of peace, severe demands were made upon the spirit and endurance of the troops."

The eighteenth was dull and cool, with rain and occasional flurries as the brigade stuck to back roads, leaving the main roads for infantry. After a march of 10 miles through pretty countryside, the column arrived at Trivières, a historic town on the River Haine.

November 18.
    Pulled out at 10:30. Inspected by General Panet en route. Pulled into Trivières at 13:30. Very comfortable billet with the Deputy-Burgomaster.
    Some of the people are sore because they haven't any of the boys billeted with them.
    The civic authorities declared a holiday in honor of our arrival and tendered us an official reception at 17:30. Gathered at the Church Square and "strolled" through the village to the Town Hall to the music of the town band and preceded by the Municipal Police.

At the eighteenth-century town hall, Lieutenant-Colonel Constantine received an illuminated scroll and a large bouquet of flowers. Burgomaster Paul Latteur led off a series of short speeches. "Gentlemen," he began in French, "it is a great honor for us to welcome the allies who have liberated us, the soldiers of Great Britain and the valiant Canadians.

"When in 1914, treacherous Prussia, despite her treaty obligations, violated Belgian neutrality, it was Great Britain that unsheathed the sword to defend and protect tiny, oppressed Belgium.

"Thanks to the tenacity of the allied armies, thanks to their unflagging bravery, the terrible enemy has been crushed forever and Belgium has regained its independence and liberty." Latteur continued in the same vein for a few moments, then concluded, "We will never be able to properly convey to you the feelings of profound gratitude which stir our hearts; but the recognition of Belgium, gentlemen, will endure forever. *Vive la Grande Bretagne! Vive l'Armée Canadienne! Bienvenue à ses héroïques soldats!*" He then led three cheers for the assembled officers.

Though few understood the mayor, no one could mistake the depth of feeling underlying his words. As quiet returned, Deputy-Burgomaster

Ernest Descamps added his own thoughts. "Gentlemen," he said, speaking in stilted English, "the municipality and people of Trivières begged me to be their interpreter near you so as to thank quite specially the Canadian Army for the large part it has taken in this awful war and thanks to which we are liberated of the dominion of the German Army." Descamps's speech was short, ending with, "Welcome to you! Hurrah for the Canadian Army! Hurrah for the Allies!"

After embraces and backslapping, Lieutenant-Colonel Constantine replied for the Canadians. Speaking in French, the OC kept his remarks brief. "On behalf of the Canadian Army, I want to express our gratitude for the very cordial welcome which you have given us. Please believe that the tokens of sympathy from the Belgian people have touched us deeply, and that we will remember them always. *Vive la Belgique! Vive son roi!*"

All the Canadian officers then signed the town's Golden Book* and the celebration was over. As the gunners drifted back to their billets, they learned they would remain in Trivières for two more days. Many purchased postcards, either as souvenirs or to be sent home with short messages assuring their families that everything was fine. A local printer rushed out a souvenir brochure of the official reception, available for purchase the next day.

The next two days saw the brigade engaged in foot drill and cleaning equipment.

November 20. Heavy fog.

Orders issued at noon for the march to be resumed tomorrow. Went for ride in the afternoon to La Louvière, a large town of about 18,000. Quite a busy place. When I got back I found the orders had been changed, which meant getting out a new bunch. Just the way when you get everything squared away early.

All over Belgium, civilians dug up family treasures and vintage wines from caches where they'd been hurriedly buried in 1914. Many

---

*Official register of important visitors.

were more than anxious to share the latter with their liberators, as Bert discovered in the evening. "Monsieur Descamps invited us all in to drink a bottle of wine with him, which we did several times, and 1881 Burgundy too! Coffee and liqueurs followed. Very nice party!" The second day's march, a total of 12 miles to Courcelles, began under bright skies. "Rather a poor march," noted the War Diary of the 2nd Divisional Artillery, "owing to the congestion of traffic." Passing through Morlanwelz early in the day, the brigade received a "wonderful" reception. "Streets beautifully decorated and crowded with people. Girls giving away flowers and biscuits," Bert noted.

In the next day's mail, Bert was surprised to find a Leave Warrant — for himself. From the telegraph office in Courcelles he sent a cable to Rosalie, telling her to expect him shortly and to arrange a large party at Browning Road. Bert went for a long ride into the countryside and didn't return until almost 6:00 p.m. Then, "Our host did the usual and opened up several bottles of the old vintage. Peculiar the ceremony these people attach to it."

The march resumed on November 24, a clear, cold day. The cobblestone roads were slippery and villages were small and widely scattered. Five and a half hours brought the gunners to Wanfercée-Baulet, where they found billets not quite what they'd had in the past, though Bert and Lieutenant-Colonel Constantine secured "wonderful rooms in the Burgomaster's house. Our host at the Mess does the usual honors with several bottles of 1906."

The fourth day began at 8:30 on November 25, with enough rain to make the trip unpleasant. "Very pretty scenery going through the deep valley south of Onoz before coming to Spy," Bert recorded. The brigade would spend two days in the village of Flawinne, whose people could not do enough for the Canadians. "Billets good," McKeown noted in the War Diary. "Majority of horses under cover."

With the twenty-sixth a day of rest, Bert rode into Namur to arrange a Leave Warrant for the colonel. When Brigadier Panet learned that both Bert and the OC were planning to be away at the same time, and both had had leave in the last five months, he cancelled both warrants. "About the coldest touch I have had yet in this game," Bert recorded glumly, "but there's no use arguing with a general, particularly this one." From Namur he got off another cable to Rosalie and, having already sent his canvas bag ahead to Calais, wondered how to get it back. "A blue night!"

On the twenty-seventh, Bert took over the War Diary from McKeown. Between them, in the last months of the war, they produced one of the most descriptive and readable War Diaries of any Canadian military unit. McKeown took over as billeting officer for the brigade, responsible for arranging each night's accommodation in conjunction with billeting parties from each battery.

The march resumed that day, making 11 miles to the village of Samson on the Meuse River. Poor roads and occasional showers made the march less than perfect, though the scenery along the Meuse was remarked on in the War Diary. There was the usual halt for one hour at 12:30 to water and feed the horses, and lunch for the men. The gunners discovered on arriving at 3:15 p.m. that accommodations in Samson were limited and, as a result, batteries were somewhat scattered. "Received the usual very cordial reception from the inhabitants." The town band performed a concert and civic officials dined with the officers.

November 28 was day six, covering 15 miles to Havelange. It was hard going after leaving the Meuse, a steady uphill climb "through six distinct valleys and over the corresponding ridges." Roads were judged "fair," but rain throughout the last part of the journey did not improve conditions. "Stopped one hour for lunch but too cold and wet to be enjoyed." Accommodations for the men were "fair," but officers got comfortably fixed in a small hotel. In the War Diary, Bert commented that drivers were becoming "somewhat discouraged with the condition of their harnesses," due to the rain and lack of time for proper upkeep. More worrying, because the brigade had to contend with an ever-lengthening supply line through difficult terrain, he wrote, "Ration and forage issue short."

With few roads in the area, the three Second Division artillery brigades were strung out along the route, with the 5th in the lead. At night, billets occupied by the following brigade were those vacated that morning by the men of the 5th Brigade. On the twenty-ninth the brigade advanced a further 11 miles to Durbuy, under cloudy skies and cold conditions, passing through picturesque, slate-roofed villages. Accommodations were "good," but the ration and forage situation did not improve. While some supplies might be purchased from the locals, there was a limit to what the countryside could offer after four years of iron-fisted German occupation. Things were no better elsewhere. In the 2DAC, for example, "The mail was irregular in arriving, and the rations poor, a large percentage of bully beef and hardtack being received."

Confusion in orders prevented the brigade from resuming its march on November 30 until 12:15 in the afternoon. In the War Diary, Bert recorded:

Hardest march so far. Roads generally in poor condition and mostly up-grade. Add to this the fact that most of the 17 miles were done in the dark and on short forage issue, credit is due to all concerned that the Brigade arrived [at Vaux Chavanne] about 20:30 hours without casualties to men, horses, or vehicles. Accommodation poor and very limited.

During this period of the advance to the frontier, all supplies such as rations, forage, fuel and ordnance bulk stores have been limited.

He went on to compliment the brigade: "The general condition of men, horses, and vehicles has been beyond expectations. The men in particular have always made the best of trying conditions and with very few exceptions have made every effort to keep themselves and their equipment in the best possible condition and carry out the object of the march with cheerfulness and good spirit."

On the thirtieth, the following order went out to all 2nd Division units:

1. As the 2nd Canadian Division is about to cross the German Frontier the Divisional Commander directs that all ranks of the Division shall strictly comply with the following instructions:-
2. There shall be no fraternizing with any of the inhabitants of Germany.

3. While the Division is entering Germany as part of the Allied Armies which have conquered that country, the men shall conduct themselves with that high discipline which has always been characteristic of the British soldier.
4. All necessary arrangements such as billeting, etc., shall be entered into through the official representatives of the village, etc. Direct arrangements with civilians are forbidden.
5. Any unusual arrangements requested by the inhabitants, or their official representatives, shall be referred to Divisional Headquarters without delay, and no action taken by the Unit concerned until approval is given.
6. Damage shall not be done to public or private property.
7. There is reason to believe that the Germans will endeavor to fraternize with the troops. It will be remembered by all that this is merely propaganda on their part for the purpose of obtaining something which they desire and do not deserve.
8. The Divisional Commander will expect the record of the 2nd Canadian Division, whilst in Germany, to be as outstanding as it has been since its mobilization.

With the new month, McKeown took over the War Diary, while Bert assumed responsibility for getting out orders and circulating them to the four battery commanders, usually by runner. For December 1, when the brigade made a further 16 miles, McKeown recorded: "With the exception of the 23rd Battery who marched with the Advance Guard, the Brigade moved to Longchamps. The march was without incident. In Longchamps billets were limited and less accommodation found by far than at any other place en route. Majority of the horses in the open. Weather cold." The brigade remained at Longchamps for two days, "owing to difficulties in getting rations up." In cool and rainy weather, the men attempted to clean up, but without cover for the horses or harness it was a discouraging task.

On December 1, a handwritten order to battery commanders, signed by Bert on behalf of Lieutenant-Colonel Constantine, directed: "Every opportunity will be taken to improve the general appearance of personnel and equipment before crossing the Frontier.

Particular attention will be paid to the shoeing of horses." In a postscript reflecting the shortage of fodder, he added: "If grazing can be obtained, horses should be turned out. The Interpreter is available for making arrangements."

The same day, he circulated a two-page pencilled order outlining precautions to be taken once the brigade entered German territory. Warned that small bands or individuals might try to harass the advance, he instructed: "Batteries will increase the vigilance of all guards and picquets and take all necessary precautions against surprise."

Food supplies continued to be a concern, as Bert's March Orders of December 2 indicated. "Battery Commanders will keep a close check on iron rations and any deficiencies will be made up at once, for it is quite possible that the brigade may be ordered to march on iron rations at some future date."

The atmosphere changed when the brigade left Belgian soil. Dismounting for the occasion, Lieutenant-Colonel Constantine, with Bert a step behind, were the first two men of the Second Canadian Division to enter Germany at 11:23 a.m. on December 4. "Flags and bunting were seen no more," the *Official Record* noted. "The inhabitants, with characteristic German servility, made the best of the circumstances, and provided, without complaint, the necessary requirements for the men's comfort." Civilians stared impassively at the marching columns of men from across the sea. Technically, their country was still at war with the Allies, for the naval blockade was still in force and the Armistice, due shortly to lapse, would be renewed on December 15, but only until mid-January. Gunners and drivers were not permitted to walk around alone and officers carried revolvers at all times. Lieutenant-General Currie later recorded: "The German people had been well schooled regarding the attitude to be adopted towards conquering troops, and our presence was marked by a quietness approaching indifference on the part of the inhabitants. Whatever apprehensions they may have entertained were quickly set at rest by the exemplary conduct of the men of the Corps."

The gunners passed through quaint villages of half-timbered houses, better-kept and more prosperous-looking than their Belgian counterparts. That evening two batteries were billeted in the bucolic village of Rodt, with brigade headquarters and one battery in Hinterhausen, nestled in rolling hills. "Billets very fair and sufficient in number to get all into fairly warm rooms," McKeown recorded. "Stables for a considerable number of horses. Inhabitants appear to be anxious to create a favorable impression and are quite prepared to do all that is required as regards billeting." Other units had similar experiences; the 2DAC history noted: "Accommodation, such as it was, was willingly given up by the inhabitants, who included a number of self-demobilized soldiers, still wearing most of their military uniform."

The brigade overnighted in the small village of Andler on December 6, where there was room for just the headquarters and 17th Battery. Roads improved as the brigade marched the next day to Kronenburg, where accommodation was equally limited. On December 7 the brigade reached Eicherscheid, after "a long march of about twenty miles over roads which were good but hilly." The horses and men were standing up well to the rigours of the journey. A march of 11 miles over good roads on December 8 brought them to

Münstereifel, where Bert and the 5th Brigade arrived on December 8, 1918, on the march to the Rhine. The intact villages of Germany, where the Canadians were politely received, contrasted sharply with looted Belgian villages. *Courtesy of Madeleine Claudi.*

Kuchenheim, a good-sized town with plenty of accommodation for all ranks. Passing through Münstereifel, Bert purchased eight postcards with various views of the town. Writing "8/12/18" on each, he packed them away.

Despite long supply lines, the Canadian Field Artillery managed to get embossed Christmas cards up to the marching units. In the next few days the men finished addressing them and mailed them to friends and family back home.

Only on December 8 did the Canadian public receive news of the men who had left Belgium almost three weeks earlier. In Montreal, Flora and George Darling would have wondered and worried about Bert's prolonged silence, and their mood of disquiet was not helped by the newspaper story. Although it listed many of the units then in Germany, it failed to mention the field artillery.

December 9, when Lieutenant-Colonel Constantine went on leave, was a wet day and the brigade remained in Kuchenheim, maintaining and cleaning equipment. Routine Orders that day brought good news to the brigade's lieutenants: the separation allowance was increased, effective September 1, from $30.00 per month to $40.00. If anyone had lingering doubts of the importance attached by senior commanders to properly maintained equipment, they were dispelled by the following from Brigadier-General Henri Panet:

Commanding Officers will see that every endeavor is made to represent to all ranks the importance of having horses, equipment, harness and personnel clean and tidy, so as to impress the German people with the efficiency of the 2nd Canadian Division and of the Canadian Corps. The only way to accomplish this is to make use of the spare time on the march. During the 10-minute halts after feeding horses and men at the noon halt the driver can clean the steel work, the gunners, etc. by means of buckets can wash the mud off the vehicles. If this is done little more time will be required to complete the cleaning up in billets.

At the bottom of Panet's order, McKeown added a handwritten comment for each of the four battery commanders: "Please note for your action, and return by Bearer."

With clearing weather on December 11, a march of 15 miles over good roads brought the brigade headquarters and two batteries to Bornheim, slightly north of and downriver from Bonn, with the remaining two batteries nearby at Roisdorf. "The Brigade [is] now within 1 mile of the Rhine," McKeown noted in the War Diary. With that, he turned the record keeping over to Bert.

Bert, who tended to record more detail than Jim, wrote from Bornheim:

December 11 & 12: Preparations made for the official crossing of the Rhine on the 13th inst. Far too little time to get harness and equipment into shape again after the severe conditions of the last few days and the men are expected to accomplish in two days what would normally require at least a week.

The people here are maintaining a very friendly attitude towards our men and have done everything possible to make them comfortable.

In a delayed story, published in the *Gazette* on December 16, the Canadian Press correspondent summarized his impressions of the trip from Belgium. "The men are tired out by the long march which has continued without intermission almost since the capture of Cambrai two months ago. They will welcome rest in permanent billets on their new front. It has been a long and arduous road, cut off practically from the outer world. The mail was often four to five days late; even rations were irregular." On the reaction of German civilians to the Canadians, the correspondent wrote, "In Bonn and Cologne ... the people are true Germans and regard us with sullenness, but all express joy that the war is ended, even on such disastrous terms to themselves." That was pure rubbish and pandered to lingering anti-German sentiment at home. By contrast, the War Diary of the 2nd Divisional Artillery noted: "The inhabitants of Bonn and vicinity seem quite friendly and

Hohenzollern Bridge, Bonn. On December 11, 1918, Bert rode down to the Rhine, where he watered his horse. *Courtesy of Madeleine Claudi.*

willing to help our men as much as they can." This was echoed by Hal's brother, Edward, in the Engineers. "There was not the slightest sign of hostility on the part of the inhabitants. In fact, they would come running over at the slightest sign and give us all the information about roads, etc. that we could want."

On the eleventh, Bert purchased a booklet of colour postcards depicting various scenes around Bonn. On a postcard of the Rhine bridge,* he pencilled "Rode down here and watered my horses in the Rhine at 11:30 this morning, then crossed the bridge. Didn't stay long as no one is supposed to cross before a certain date."

As the two-day respite at Bornheim came to an end, Bert finally found an opportunity to write a letter home.

---

*Completed in 1898, the elegant 1,417-foot Rheinbrücke linking Bonn to Beuel on the east bank of the Rhine was destroyed in March 1945 by the retreating Wehrmacht. A new bridge was built on the same site in 1948–49, and later named the Kennedy Bridge.

12/12/18

I forget now when it was I last wrote you a real letter. Have taken advantage of [field] post cards to such an extent lately that I haven't paid much attention to letters. Then, too, I have been without my diary for about three weeks and, as I used to keep track of my letters in it, I don't know just where I stand now.

The history of the temporary loss of my diary makes quite a story, so I guess I had better spill it before going any further.

When we began this march to Germany, everyone was so keen on the prospect that very few cared about going on leave, and all the officers who were ahead of me on the list decided they would rather pass up their leave than take it at that time. I didn't see it quite that way myself, for various reasons, and, as the OC was agreeable, I put in for leave about the 25th of Nov. and my Warrant was issued to me.

We were on the move at the time; however, it was impossible for me to get away for a few days but, as I had my Warrant in my pocket and there didn't appear to be the least chance of my not getting away, I wired Rosalie I would be home about the 28th. I made my arrangements accordingly and was ready to leave the Brigade at Namur on the 26th, so sent my bag on ahead to Calais by one of the men going down that morning.

The OC was expecting to go on leave also in a couple of days but was quite satisfied under present conditions to have me away at the same time. However, that noon the General came around, just happened to be in a very perturbed mood and, when he heard the OC and I were to be away at the same time, he went completely up in the air and, as the OC was going on a month's leave, mine was of course the one cancelled.

Well, you can see the hole it put me in — with Rosalie expecting me home and my bag with all my personal effects in Calais! I wired Rosalie that I couldn't get away, and sent a couple of urgent messages to Calais for my bag, which I haven't seen or heard of since, but haven't given up for lost yet.

You can imagine the disappointment these two wires caused at Browning Road!

Operation Order No. 69, dated December 13 and signed by McKeown, appointed Bert as billeting officer. The brigade was now looking for permanent accommodations, intending that "all troops be provided with beds in properly heated buildings." McKeown's order also specified the following for the historic crossing of the Rhine: "Dress: Battle Order. Steel helmets will be worn by all ranks...."

The Canadians would cross the Rhine at two locations. While the 1st Division crossed at Cologne, the 2nd crossed at Bonn, a dozen miles upstream. Here the corps commander took the salute from a column of battle-hardened men, which stretched for 18 miles and took more than four hours to pass Currie's reviewing stand. Bert recorded the event in the War Diary:

> *December 13, 1918.* The triumphal march across the Rhine was made in a steady downpour of rain. The Division marched over by groups with the 4th CIB leading, followed by the 5th CIB and the 6th CIB. A platform had been erected near the eastern extremity of the Bridge and from here the salute was taken by the Corps Commander and the Divisional Commander. The march past was made in battle order and an order issued to all ranks that no coats of any description were to be worn. Some considerable trouble was experienced in enforcing this order, owing to the very severe weather conditions and the fact the men were not at all impressed with the object of making a show at the expense of their health.
>
> Three Batteries obeyed the order on strong protest but the fourth absolutely refused to comply.
>
> There is a certain amount of unrest amongst the personnel of all the batteries, which is only natural under present circumstances. It is the issuing of such orders as this one, in which the men cannot see any good reason and compliance with which necessitates a great deal of personal and unnecessary discomfort, that produces this unrest and makes the handling of the men much more difficult.

The last typewritten paragraph was subsequently crossed out, presumably by Major Hendrie, acting OC while Lieutenant-Colonel

Constantine was on leave. Given the sensitivities of senior officers, it seems nothing short of a miracle that Bert was not relieved of duty and put on charge for insubordination.

Once over the Rhine, the 5th Brigade moved into its final area. As billeting officer, Bert had done well. For brigade headquarters, he selected Schloss Commende in the nearby village of Ramersdorf. The schloss, dating to the thirteenth century and modernized in the 1880s, belonged to Baron Simon von Oppenheim, a prominent Cologne banker. The 17th and 20th Batteries were billeted in Küdinghoven, the 23rd in Limperich, and the 18th in Ramersdorf. The men were all in large halls and school buildings fitted out with frame beds and straw mattresses, though suitable permanent accommodation still needed to be found for the 20th Battery's horses and harness.

For almost everyone it was a time to relax. The men purchased postcards and war souvenirs, many shop windows displaying genuine

CFA unit, having crossed the Rhine, heads to its billeting area. *Courtesy of Library and Archives Canada,* PA-003773.

Iron Crosses. In most units, as Currie explained, "the greatest possible freedom from duty was allowed all ranks, and everything was done to brighten what all hoped would be their last Christmas spent away from Canada." Bert used the time to catch up on administrative paperwork, which had lagged during the march. On December 18 he issued a list of personnel in the 5th Brigade regarding entitlement to service chevrons, complete with 28 pages of attachments.

As no one was sure of German intentions, and fearing a possible popular uprising, division headquarters circulated a Provisional Defence Scheme on December 14. Officers of the 5th Brigade then scouted out, but did not occupy, potential OPs and battery positions. "Locations will be recorded," McKeown directed, "but will not be marked on the ground nor will any action be taken that might cause enemy agents to suspect these positions." It was soon apparent the Germans had no hostile aims, and occupation authorities relaxed a little. Bonn, originally out of bounds to all ranks, was placed in bounds, with daily passes authorized for up to one-fifth of the brigade's strength. Canadian troops travelled free of charge on trains and streetcars in the occupied territory, and Bert found time for a hasty visit to Cologne, marked by more postcards. Soldiers found restaurant meals were of good quality and, when converted from Reichmarks into Canadian currency, inexpensive.* The Canadian YMCA set up canteens, and the men felt very much at home "to find Montreal biscuits and Canadian chocolate." Discipline on the east bank of the Rhine was more relaxed than on the west. Passes were not required and off-duty men were not subject to curfew, though canteens and German drinking establishments closed at 8:00 p.m. On December 19 British authorities issued a new order: "Cases have come to notice of troops fraternizing with the inhabitants of the occupied territory. Any man seen walking with a German woman will be arrested."

With the weather dull and raw, keeping the men of the 5th Brigade occupied was a constant concern. "An attempt is being made to organize sport and recreation for the men," Bert wrote in the War Diary, "but the chief difficulty is in securing a suitable field where games can

---

*On December 16 the exchange rate was 5RM=2s8d=3.50 francs. A Reichmark was thus about 12.5 cents Canadian.

be played." It was also a time for souvenir pictures. On December 20, photographs were taken on the Rheinbrücke of all officers who came to France as officers with the 2nd Division, and also those officers who came to France with the division other than as officers, and who crossed the Rhine on December thirteenth. It is a measure of the toll of war that Jim McKeown was the only remaining original officer in the 5th Brigade, while just five lieutenants — Bert included — had come with the division other than as officers.

Ten officers and 157 men of the 23rd Battery, along with two of their stubby howitzers, posed on a grassy hillside for posterity. McKeown also stood for another photo, this time with 22 other men — all that remained of the original members of the 23rd. Similarly, eight officers and 116 men of the 18th Battery posed at Ramersdorf with two of their 18-pounders.

On December 15, Bert's thirty-first birthday, an order crossed Lieutenant-Colonel Constantine's desk that had important consequences for the newly decorated lieutenant. "Units should take in hand at once the preparation of war histories and should notify this office when it is desired to send Officers to England to complete the same." One officer from each of the 5th and 6th Brigades would be appointed, and one from the Trench Mortar Brigade. Assigned to write the 6th Brigade history was Bert's friend from *Megantic* days, Lieutenant Frank Jennings, a newspaper reporter before the war.

It took Lieutenant-Colonel Constantine a couple of days to make up his mind.

Ramersdorf, 15/12/18

We are now supposed to be occupying our winter quarters and, provided such is the case, I think we will be able to exist until such time as they see fit to send us back home.

I have done the billeting for the Brigade ever since we reached Germany and usually managed to secure the best our allotted area had to provide. In this last case, however, I was out to secure something rather exceptional for our Headquarters, and I am quite satisfied with the results.

You have, no doubt, in childhood days and even later, read of the castles on the Rhine. I know I have, but it hardly seemed at that time within the bounds of possibility I should one day occupy one.

After fixing the batteries up with accommodations, I took the Commissioner of Police along with me to look for a place suitable for Brigade Headquarters and told him it had to be something pretty fine. He thought he knew of a place which would suit us and brought me up to this Castle which is built on the side of a hill overlooking the Rhine Valley, the Seven Mountains [*Siebengebirge*] and the city of Bonn. You go through a very imposing gateway, past the Lodgekeeper's House (which resembles some of the houses on Sherbrooke Street). The driveway winds through beautiful grounds, over a bridge between two artificial lakes and, after about a ten-minute walk, you suddenly come out in front of the Castle, a most imposing structure with turrets, towers, etc. The driveway leads through a *porte cochère* and you pull up in front of the main entrance with a great central flower bed and a beautifully laid-out garden with fountains, glass houses, etc. etc. In front of it and to one side is the courtyard with the stables, coach houses and servants' quarters, very well designed and laid out, so that they add to, rather than detract from, the general appearance of the place.

The front door admits you into a large reception hall with a massive hardwood staircase leading to the first floor.

In the Castle, the Servants' Quarters and Stables, we have accommodation for 10 officers, 14 NCOs, 50 Other Ranks, and 36 horses. The OC, Jim McKeown, and myself, each have suites consisting of bedroom, sitting room and bathroom, and all the other officers have single rooms.

We don't use the Reception Room or Music Room, as they are too large and too hard to heat, but we have moved the big Steinway grand piano into the Breakfast Room, and use it as a sitting room.

The furnishings throughout are in absolute good taste and the best that money could buy. Beautiful hardwood floors throughout the rooms on the ground floor, and the walls of the Reception, Breakfast and Music Rooms are all tapestried. All windows are hung with most gorgeous portieres and the electric lighting fixtures are most complete and elegant.

My suite is in the southwest corner of the Castle and was evidently furnished for female occupation, with heavy silk-lined portieres over the door, the bed and both the large bay windows of the bedroom, from which a beautiful view of the Rhine Valley, the Seven Mountains and the city of Bonn can be obtained. In the Sitting Room is a lady's desk, clothes closet, the odd comfortable sofa and chairs, and lots of big plate-glass mirrors.

18/12/18

I don't appear to have progressed very favorably with this epistle. I am afraid the billiard and card tables have been chiefly responsible, for usually both of them are going at nights and it is certainly a treat to be able to get into a game.

On reading part of this letter over, it seems I have gone ahead a little too fast and passed over a few details of how we came to occupy the place.

The first day I came up here to look it over, I decided of course that it was an ideal layout for headquarters but, as there was only the gardener and a couple of odd servants about, I sent one of them off to Cologne to tell the Baron we were coming in and that it would probably be better for all concerned if he would send someone down to take charge of putting the place in order and preparing it for occupation.

He sent his housekeeper and one other servant back the same night and, by the time we arrived, they had the fires going and all the beds made, so we settled right down in comfort. The housekeeper insists on making all the beds and will only allow our boys to make the fires and do the sweeping. The old gardener is very proud of his greenhouses and keeps the rooms decorated with fresh flowers and plants. He has some of the most beautiful chrysanthemums I think I have ever seen.

The Baron is evidently a good sport, for he sent a message back that he was sorry there was so little wine in the cellar but, if we would just let him know what we wanted, he would have it sent down to us from Cologne.* Needless to say, we will take advantage of his offer.

I was over in Bonn yesterday with Jim McKeown, attending to some Brigade affairs. After lunch we took a trip around some of the shops to see if there was anything exciting to be procured. All shops except the provision shops are well stocked and even they are not exactly empty. The old Hun is a great deal better off than he had led people to believe and, as compared to those in France and Belgium, particularly those in the area near the old fighting zone, he is mighty well off.

The people all have the appearance of being well-fed and well-clothed and are certainly not suffering one bit. For its size, I think Bonn is probably the wealthiest city I have been in yet. The houses in the residential district along the banks of the Rhine are magnificent and any of the ones I have been in have been most lavishly furnished.

I called to see [Brigadier-]General [William] Dodds to get some information about the early organization of this Brigade, as I have been given the job of writing up its history. The General, of course, remembered my name and asked me to give George [Darling] his kindest regards when next I write.

I don't know whether you have seen any notification of the fact that I was awarded the Military Cross some time ago.** As I was recommended for it both in the Amiens show on August 8th and the Bourlon Wood show about the 1st of October, and as I have not seen the official account of the award, I don't know yet just which I got it for. However I am very glad I won it after the new regulations came into force, by which the Cross could only be awarded for work done in the line and under fire, for up till then it had certainly been abused greatly.†

---

*Baron Simon von Oppenheim (1864–1932) was well disposed to the occupying Canadians. He had married an Englishwoman, Florence Hutchins, in London in 1890.

**Bert's MC was noted in the 5th Brigade Routine Orders of December 8, published on the march.

†Effective August 1, 1918, the DSO, MC, and DCM were to be awarded only for services in action.

Schloss Commende at Ramersdorf, into which Bert and the 5th Brigade headquarters moved on December 13, 1918. *Courtesy of Madeleine Claudi.*

I am sorry this letter is going to be so very late for Xmas and the New Year but you will know my thoughts will be with you all on this Happiest Xmas which you have been able to have for some years, and I hope that the present prospects of a very cheerful and prosperous New Year will be fulfilled.

Efforts to get the horses under cover finally succeeded. The 18th Battery obtained a large shed at the cement works outside Oberkassel, a 10-minute walk from its billets. The 20th moved to the eastern outskirts of Beuel on December 22, where a large warehouse accommodated the horses and harness, and the officers and men secured "excellent" billets nearby. The 17th and 23rd remained in Küdinghoven and Limperich respectively. In an encouraging sign of normalcy, the "See Twos" opened *We Should Worry* in Bonn's Stadttheater on December 23, playing to packed audiences of Second Division soldiers with little else to occupy their time.

As Christmas approached, the War Diary noted that "Preparations are being made on a larger scale than ever by all batteries, and efforts are being made to make this Xmas in Germany the most pleasant the

Bert (left) and Captain Jim McKeown at the elaborate gateway to Schloss Commende. *Courtesy of Madeleine Claudi.*

Officers of the 5th Brigade CFA at the billiard table, Schloss Commende, December 1918. *Courtesy of Madeleine Claudi.*

boys have spent in the army. The YMCA has obtained a good supply of apples and oranges, nuts and dates, and the ASC* has broken all previous records and managed to get the plum puddings through on time, but the EFC** has not yet delivered the supplies of turkey which had been ordered."

The brigade held a compulsory Church Parade for all batteries at 10:15 on Sunday, December 22, in Ramersdorf. Christmas Day was cold and an inch of snow lay on the ground when the men attended another — voluntary — Church Parade at the 23rd Battery's hall in Limperich.

Sadly, the brigade's turkeys failed to arrive. "To make matters worse," Bert wrote, "the meat and bread ration was very short, so all batteries except the 23rd were forced to cancel all dinner arrangements. The latter had foreseen the possibility of the turkeys not arriving and managed to secure pork *in lieu*. The men of the other batteries were, naturally, very much disappointed but, as usual, made the best of it."

As the momentous year of 1918 drew to a close, Bert put the final entries in the brigade War Diary. "Information received that the Brigade will be relieved in the early part of January and will go back to join the Fourth Army. Weather has been very inclement and only routine work has been possible."

---

*ASC — Army Service Corps.
**EFC — Expeditionary Force Canteen.

36

"Blighty" and the Official Record

If the 5th Brigade officers missed a proper celebration at Christmas, New Year's Day offered an opportunity to make up the loss. At Schloss Commende an elaborate dinner, complete with printed menu, was held at 7:30 p.m. and attended by 33 officers. The castle echoed with good cheer and laughter from men hoping for a swift return to Canada. The War Diary, now entrusted to Lieutenant Hyndman Irwin, termed the dinner "excellent."

Steady rain in the first week of January prevented much participation in sports or training. However, the brigade exercised its horses two hours per day and, to keep the men in condition, a weekly route march was instituted. A large hall in the brigade area was used for entertainment; the YMCA loaned films and nightly screenings attracted audiences of 400 or more. Drawing on the varied backgrounds of officers and men, classes began under the aegis of the Khaki University, another YMCA initiative. Subjects included French (four times a week), Motor Mechanics (daily lectures, and practical demonstrations three times a week), Bookkeeping (three times a week), and Agriculture (three classes per week). For men wanting a practical skill when they returned to Canada, battery farrier-sergeants offered instruction in horse shoeing. Other subjects were soon added: Citizenship, Money and Banking, and Commercial Law.

Regimental censorship of letters ceased and the issue of green envelopes for this purpose was discontinued. One of the first signs of demobilization arrived when married men, coming off leave, were retained at bases in England. A week later, coal miners in the Corps were recalled, and five men left the brigade on January 7 for speedy repatriation.

Just as the brigade was getting used to life in the Occupation Zone, Bert received 14 days' leave.

I left Bonn on the 5th of January; went to Cologne that night and caught what is fondly called the "Cologne-Boulogne Express" the following morning, which brought me into Boulogne early on the morning of the 8th. I took a run over to Calais the same morning to see if I could locate my grip (which, by the way, I have track of, but have not managed to get hold of yet). I fully intended to run from Calais to Paris just to have a look around for a day or so but the attraction across the water was a little too strong for me, so I beat it back to Boulogne about noon and caught the afternoon boat, which got me to Browning Road about 9:30 that night.

As you can imagine, my unexpected arrival caused quite a flutter in the household, for I hadn't mentioned a word even of prospects of coming home for, after my sad experience in November, I wasn't taking any chances on further disappointments. I had known for some time I would get over, for I had been given the job of writing the history of the brigade but, as I have found that nothing is sure in the Army, I just kept my mouth shut about it.

Once in London, Bert secured from HQOMFC* an extension for a further two weeks, for what was termed "private affairs." After senior officers realized the amount of work involved in preparing a history of the 5th Brigade, Bert received subsequent two-week extensions. The assignment evidently required him to travel around London and to various Canadian camps. On January 29, he received a travel allowance of £12 15s, followed by further allowances of £15 (February 18),

---

*Headquarters Overseas Military Forces of Canada.

£16 5s (March 17), and £18 5s (April 14). There was one final payment on May 6 of £14 10s to cover the last of his expenses.

The errant bag, containing clothing, personal papers, and diary, finally arrived in London. The diary proved to be a useful tool as Bert and a couple of clerk-typists began work. At the Canadian War Records Office, they pored over a mountain of paperwork, including service files, War Diaries, Routine and Daily Orders. As well, he drew on his own and the first-hand experiences of other Canadian officers passing through London.

Bert soon fell into a comfortable rut at Browning Road with Rosalie and his in-laws. Work at Canadian Military Headquarters at Argyll House was not overly demanding and, in off-duty hours, he and Rosalie sampled the sights and offerings of the metropolis that was his second home. He was encouraged when, in the first week of February, Canadian soldiers with dependents in England learned that arrangements would be made to enable families to return home together. There were, at that time, some 50,000 soldiers' dependents in England and France, the vast majority being war brides. Late in January, the Borden government agreed to pay the cost of transporting them from Europe to their destination in Canada, subject to two restrictions. First, the government would pay for third-class transport only, and second, it would pay only for those who sailed on or after November 11, 1918.

HQOMFC often arranged for Canadian servicemen who were entitled to a decoration to receive it directly from the King. Thus, in the third week of February, a telegram arrived at Browning Road:

YOUR ATTENDANCE IS REQUIRED AT BUCKINGHAM PALACE ON SATURDAY NEXT THE TWENTY-SECOND INSTANT AT TEN AM SERVICE DRESS REGRET THAT NO ONE EXCEPT THOSE TO BE INVESTED CAN BE ADMITTED TO THE PALACE PLEASE TELEGRAPH ACKNOWLEDGEMENT
LORD CHAMBERLAIN LONDON

With Sam Browne belt polished to a high gloss and his uniform neatly brushed, Bert presented himself at the palace well before the appointed time. In the fourth general investiture since the monarch returned to public life after a month of mourning following the death of 14-year-old Prince John, the King presented almost 200 men with a variety of decorations, including six Victoria Crosses. The largest group was 138 recipients of the Military Cross — Bert among them — from all branches of service and every country in the empire. In all, there were 20 Canadians, but just two others from the CFA. The ceremony, held in the white-and-gilt ballroom, the largest room in the palace, began at 11:00 a.m. Up in the musicians' gallery, the band of the Welsh Guards played as the monarch handed out decorations, commencing with the VCs.

Hal Fetherstonhaugh, who received his MC two years earlier in a similar ceremony, described the event:

I went at ten and, by 10:30 was in a huge room with about a hundred others standing around. Our names were all checked, then we were lined up nominally, and some people in civilian togs, looking rather like undertakers, put a small hook like a picture hook on each of us.

Shortly the head of the line moved through a doorway, and the bread-line started. It must have been about two hundred yards long, and we serpentined through huge rooms — turkey red rugs, gold furniture, and white walls with huge oil paintings of historic interest.

Finally I arrived at the threshold where the King was. As your name is called out, you walk up, bow, take a step forward, and the Cross is pinned on with an appropriate remark. You take two steps back, bow, and away you go.

After the ceremony, Bert joined Rosalie outside the palace for a photograph. On the Monday, Rosalie pointed with pride to the Court Circular in *The Times*. There was Bert's name, along with other recipients of the various decorations.

Though preparation of the brigade history consumed his working hours, Bert acknowledged the pace of work was fairly relaxed:

When I came over I thought I would be here for six weeks or possibly two months (the General thought the work could be done in a week!) but although I have been working for just over two months I am not nearly through yet. I haven't overexerted myself by any means, for it is slightly more comfortable living over here at home than it would be in Belgian billets, but I have been working steadily and keeping strictly to "union" hours, which in this country seems to average between four and six hours a day.

As Cud has remained on at her work, we have managed to lunch together nearly every day and I have called for her on the way home every day at 4:30.

I am hoping the [2nd] Division will be back from France before I have completed the work, for I am not at all anxious to have to go back over there, particularly now when there is absolutely nothing doing. The latest advice is that the Division will be back in England about the middle of April and sail for home sometime in May, but whether they will be able to keep to that schedule remains to be seen.

Bert, Rosalie (left), and Emily (right) outside the gates of Buckingham Palace, February 22, 1919, when Bert received his MC from George V. *Courtesy of Madeleine Claudi.*

I wrote over to France some time ago to see if I couldn't be struck off strength in France, so I could get back to Canada as soon as I finished my work over here but, so far, I haven't had any success and I don't expect it will go through now, but I still hope to be able to take Cud with me when I go.

If, when the time comes, I find I will not be able to do so, I will book a passage for her by the CPR so she will get over as soon as possible after I do. I am going to pack her wedding presents and other odds and ends in a couple of cases which I have here, and ship them off through the Estates Branch OMFC in a week or so.

In Ramersdorf the 5th Brigade wound down its activities, in what Lieutenant-Colonel Constantine, back from leave, termed the "trying period pending demobilization." On January 27, responsibility for the field artillery defence of the Ramersdorf area passed from the 2nd CDA to a British unit. Two days later the 23rd became the first to leave Germany and return, this time by train, to Belgium, where it was formally disbanded two months later.

13.3.19

I am at least going to make a start on a letter for I have put off writing for so long now it seems impossible to pick up the lost threads. I was so glad Ern Hutchison had told you I was here in London for, otherwise, you no doubt would have been anxious for, as far as I can remember, I haven't written since Dec. 15th or thereabouts.

25.3.19

Sorry, good people, but I have had a sad lapse. However, I will try to finish this up tonight. Have been busy all day packing wedding presents and hope to get them away the end of the week. I intend to ship them c/o Darling Brothers, as I imagine they will have an odd corner in the warehouse where they can stick them until I can make other arrangements.

We also have a piano and a couple [of] other small cases which will go over later by CPR freight, but I haven't decided yet just where to ship them to, as I don't like sending them to Darling Bros. without first finding out whether they could look after them for me until I find some other place.

I am sorry Grover and Louise [Robinson] have decided to pull off the big event so early, for I don't see much chance of our being present. We may make it by the end of May but hardly the end of April. The sad part of it is that I have had some rather "toff" clothes built after the latest London designs and I would like to break them in at such an auspicious occasion. By the way, Grover, are clothes such an exorbitant price in Montreal? The rumor over here has it that $75 and $80 are required to purchase suitable raiment for the office from the common garden-variety of tailor. On the strength of this, I laid in a stock to last me over the first few months while looking for a job. My thoughts slipped fondly back to old Joseph Duhamel and the clothes he used to build me at $10 and $12 a throw plus the cloth, but for all I know he may be dead now or working for the aristocracy, so I decided 8 and 9 guinea suits were a good investment.* I didn't indulge in overcoats, silk hats, etc., for I have hopes the moths have left me a few threads of those I left behind some years ago!

How are houses or apartments going these days in Montreal?** Anything doing for about $10 a month? Of course, it is impossible for me to form any idea of what we are going to do when we get out there, as it seems I have been away from Montreal at least 1000 years and I don't know what to expect to find on my return.

Charles' donation of cigars was thoroughly enjoyed by Dad and myself. I intend, and have intended for some time as a matter of fact, to write to George [Darling] to acknowledge the box of cigars from the firm, also his unfailing supply which is still

---

*Bert need not have worried. In February, Goodwin's department store in Montreal offered returned soldiers complete eight-piece civilian outfits ranging in price from $33.35 to $55.60.

**The cost of living in Montreal increased by 50 percent during the war. With peace, prices fell and Canada experienced a recession.

Witley Camp, where Bert began the demobilization process in April and May 1918. *Author's photo.*

Demobilization medical checks, Witley Camp, April 1919. *Courtesy of Library and Archives Canada, PA-006053.*

arriving monthly. Please tell George to stop the supply now, as I don't know how much longer I will be over here but, in case I get away sooner than I expect, I would hate to lose one of those perfectly good boxes.

Good night all. I am going to mail this tonight or I don't know when I will get it off as Cud and I hope to get down to St. Margaret's Bay on Saturday for a week or ten days. Cud and the family all send their love.

On April 2, Bert received orders to report to Witley Camp where, for administrative purposes, he was attached to the camp's headquarters wing pending his return to Canada. In practice, it meant he continued to live at Browning Road while completing the brigade history. With peace restored, Witley became one of five camps in Britain where Canadian soldiers were re-mustered into units with a regional association, prior to sending them to Canada for demobilization.* Second Division headquarters was at Witley, and the camp commandant was Bert's old nemesis, Brigadier Panet. Hal, who passed through in mid-March, wrote "Life here consists principally in passing [medical] boards, seeing that others do or don't, getting papers signed, etc."

Recalled to Witley in late April, Bert appeared before various boards as a part of the preliminary demobilization process. On April 28 he was examined by Captain Harry Harding of the Dental Corps, next day by Captain William A. Macdonald of the Eye, Ear, Nose & Throat Clinic. His myopia was noted, and Bert acknowledged his vision in both eyes had been poor since childhood and had not been aggravated by his military service — thus saving the Canadian government a disability pension. "Well muscled and healthy" was how Captain Macdonald summarized Bert's overall condition. Captain Eldon Coutts, president of the medical board, then read portions of the report to Bert. Satisfied, Bert signed the medical history. Also at Witley, Bert's discharge papers and other documents were made out, minimizing delays in Canada.

With his unit history nearly complete, Bert and Rosalie travelled into London on Saturday, May 3, to witness the victory march of

---

*The others were Kinmel Park (near Rhyl), Bramshott (Surrey), Ripon (Yorkshire), and Seaford (Sussex).

12,000 Dominion troops. A hundred thousand spectators lined the route as men from Canada, Australia, New Zealand, South Africa, and Newfoundland paraded through the city, while George V took the salute in front of Buckingham Palace. Despite an early threat of rain, the sun came out on occasion in the afternoon, highlighting "these honoured colours, gleaming guns, and beautiful horses." In what *The Times* termed "the most stirring military pageant that has been seen in this country since the outbreak of war," 5,000 men of the Canadian Corps, led by Lieutenant-General Arthur Currie and his staff, headed the parade. Units of the Second Canadian Division, including the artillery, followed the Canadian Cavalry Brigade. Among the gunners and marching infantry, in battle order with caps rather than steel helmets, Bert found many familiar faces, pointing them out to Rosalie.

On May 5, Bert submitted the final draft of the *Official Record of the 5th Canadian Field Artillery Brigade*. Consisting of some 140 pages of double-spaced text and 11 appendices, it was a significant achievement. Though it contained a few blank spaces for additional bits of information, and required some light editing, it more than met his original objective. In the preface, Bert acknowledged the officers in charge of the various sections of the War Records Office and thanked them for "the

Second Canadian Division Field Artillery passing Australia House on The Strand, Victory March, May 3, 1919. *Author's photo.*

courtesy shown the writer throughout an extended search for informa-tion." Acknowledging that the document tried to maintain the official point of view, the preface admitted to another purpose, as well. "It is hoped," he wrote, "that the work will still be of some personal interest to those at least, who contributed their share towards the splendid suc-cess attained by the brigade and the enviable reputation gained by it throughout the four and a half years of its existence."

With that, he was cleared to go to Canada.

Not surprisingly, the next days passed in a blur. Bert secured pas-sage for himself and booked a ticket for Rosalie on HMT *Northland*,* due to depart Liverpool in mid-May. A cabin together was out of the question: there were just too many people. As the government paid for third class for dependents, Bert happily contributed an addi-tional £10 for first-class passage for Rosalie.** Their departure was far from certain; dock strikes at Liverpool cut the number of sailings for Canada so that by mid-April more than 149,000 Canadian troops still remained overseas. With the available vessels capable of transporting about 30,000 soldiers and dependents per month, many would not get home for a while.

Household and other items, including Rosalie's piano, were readied for crating and shipment by freighter, consigned to Darling Brothers. The couple visited old friends and said their goodbyes, knowing they would probably never see them again. On May 12, seen off by a small group of well-wishers, Bert and Rosalie took the train from Waterloo Station for Milford, the closest railhead to Witley Camp. There they joined the group designated as Sailing No. 62 — a total of 904 men and 16 nursing sisters under the command of Major David McKechnie, a Montreal-born physician. At 5:15 a.m. on Tuesday, May 13, McKechnie's group marched out of Witley to entrain at Milford. Baggage was stowed in good time and the train, with a couple of shrieks from its whistle, departed promptly at 6:30. For the Witley group, the Liverpool docks lay nine hours away: the Canadians were shunted aside to let regular trains go by.

---

*This was the former Red Star liner *Zeeland*, renamed in 1915 because it sounded too Germanic.

**As third class was fully occupied by soldiers, the £10 ($48.67 in Canadian cur-rency) was refunded by cheque on June 21 in Montreal.

37

HMT *Northland* and Canada

On May 13, delegates of many nations assembled in Paris to sign the Treaty of Versailles, which would end one war and serve as a pretext for another. Though the Great War was over, fighting continued elsewhere. Russia was rent by civil war, while Greeks and Turks were locked in a struggle for Anatolia. In Central Asia, Afghans clashed with British and Indian troops. Near-anarchy prevailed in a score of German cities, and in Munich, an Austrian-born firebrand with a newly discovered talent for oratory was attracting followers to his cause. In Italy, a newspaper editor, having founded a new political party, the *Fasci di Combattimento*, prepared to enter the political fray.

Across the Atlantic, the U.S. Congress debated a constitutional amendment calling for female suffrage, while citizens of Winnipeg prepared for a general strike. And, reflecting the great strides in wartime aviation, two groups readied aircraft in Newfoundland, attempting to win the £10,000 prize offered by the *Daily Mail* for the first transatlantic flight.

In Liverpool at 3:30 p.m., Bert and Rosalie disembarked from their train. While soldiers formed up on the platform, Bert secured a porter for their baggage and the couple walked the short distance to the Landing Stage. A single gangway led aboard His Majesty's Troopship *Northland*, under time charter to the Admiralty. Army clerks at the gangway checked names off the typed manifest of returning soldiers, and their dependents, listed separately. Stewards directed Bert

HMT *Northland*. (May 1919). *Author's photo.*

and Rosalie to their respective accommodations. As a lieutenant, Bert shared a first-class cabin with other junior officers. Rosalie was quartered with nursing sisters, also in first class. Loading of passengers and baggage proceeded smoothly and at 5:00 p.m. *Northland* was ready to depart. The gangway was landed and, with a long blast of her horn, the lines were let go at 5:15. Amid much cheering and waving, tugs eased *Northland* into the River Mersey. Khaki-clad soldiers, uniformed nursing sisters, and civilians — men, women, and children — lined the rail, taking a last look at England.

Two and a half hours later, *Northland* discharged her pilot off the Bar Lightship. On the bridge, 48-year-old Captain William Morehouse, a Nova Scotian, ordered his vessel to full speed. Halifax lay some 2,500 nautical miles to the west and, at an average speed of 12 knots, the voyage would take nine or 10 days.

Of the 149 civilians aboard, 94 were regular passengers — a handful of tourists, some emigrants with a variety of trades, and a few women going to Canada to be married. The remaining 55 were on a separate manifest of military dependents, an equal mixture of U.K.- and Canadian-born. Twenty-three were children, the youngest a two-and-a-half-year-old boy.

The 2,539 officers, men, and nursing sisters came from a variety of units. The largest of these was the 27th (City of Winnipeg) Battalion, whose OC, Lieutenant-Colonel Harold Riley, was the senior officer aboard. Also aboard was the 6th Field Ambulance of Montreal — a number of whose members Bert knew well — commanded by Lieutenant-Colonel Richard Hardesty, junior to Riley in terms of seniority. Captain Helena Dulmage headed 61 nursing sisters of the CAMC, and there were various details from the Rhyl Camp. Junior officers were a rarity. Bert was one of just three lieutenants aboard *Northland*, one of whom, John Clout from the 2DAC, was the only other artillery officer on the ship.

Northland was crowded. Rated to carry 348 in first and second class, and 1,412 in third class, the 2,500-plus passengers strained her capacity to the limits.

As on most returning troopships, discipline was relaxed. Under the King's Regulations and Orders, the men came under the authority of the senior combatant officer aboard. Duties were light, though the men had to assist the crew in cleaning their quarters and washing dishes. Of the nursing sisters, two were detailed for duty during the voyage and they reported to Lieutenant-Colonel Hardesty on arrival. Their duties were minimal, assisting at the daily Sick Parade and, if necessary in the ship's small hospital. *Northland* already carried a ship's surgeon, Dr. H.T. Keating, responsible for the vessel's regular passengers.

Reveille was at 6:00, with breakfast at 7:00; Sick Parade was held at 9:00 and 4:00 p.m. Dinner was at noon, with tea at 5:00 p.m. The routine left most aboard ample time to relax and prepare for the return to Canada. In the ship's smoke-filled bars, battles were fought and re-fought over pints of bitter, with glasses hoisted to the memory of friends who would never return. The YMCA, which had served the CEF so admirably, was not about to let the men down as they were repatriated and demobilized. On every westbound troopship a "Y" officer performed a variety of functions. He carried a supply of literature, writing materials, games, a magic lantern, and slides, along with a gramophone and a selection of new and old records. To this officer military authorities had delegated responsibility for recreation and entertainment of the men during their voyage. As a result, he organized concerts, lectures, singsongs, and religious services, along with various sports and games. As well, he distributed booklets and helped soldiers understand how the government planned to re-establish them into civilian life.

Most returning soldiers, Bert among them, worried about finding jobs in postwar Canada. The skills Bert had perfected in the past four years — the ability to drop a shell within a few yards of its target — were no longer required by a society determined to forget the war. Still, he was a mechanical engineer, with a proven talent for organization, leading men, and for writing clear, logical prose. Surely those counted for something.

May 14 was a dull day, with thunderstorms and fog off the Irish coast. Lifeboat drill, as usual, took place at 10:00 a.m on the first morning after departing Liverpool. Just six men reported for Hardesty's first Sick Parade. Of these, four suffering from scabies were admitted to the ship's hospital. The remaining two were medicated and discharged. Meals aboard *Northland* reflected postwar realities. Ration levels for returning soldiers had been suggested by the Admiralty in October 1918 and were later approved by militia headquarters in Ottawa. The daily ration consisted of 52 1/4 ounces, of which bread (12 ounces) and fresh meat (10 ounces) composed the major part. In all, the Admiralty ration was 13 1/4 ounces less than the standard Canadian ration that the soldiers were used to.

It was warm and sunny on the fifteenth, though by afternoon it became (as Hardesty recorded in his journal) "dull and windy; rather rough in evening." Next day he noted, "Morning strong NW wind with heavy seas — many sick. Calmer towards evening."

Due to the large number of passengers, deck space was very limited. As the boat deck was not available to passengers, *Northland*'s promenade deck was divided, one-half allocated to officers and women and children, the other half to NCOs and ORs.

Like most soldiers, Bert acquired a variety of souvenirs during his service. In addition to four diaries detailing his military career, he had a thick stack of letters, photographs, and postcards. Carefully rolled was a 13-panel, high-resolution panoramic photograph showing the countryside around Vimy Ridge, the view he'd seen many times from the 23rd battery's OP. Another showed the area around Villers-Bretonneux, from the Amiens show. As well, he had aerial mosaic photographs, barrage maps, and mimeographed orders of no further military value. There was also a 9 mm Luger P.08 pistol with a 32-round snail-drum magazine.* Though theft and looting were capital offences under the *Army Act*, Bert also had a carved wooden panel depicting St. George slaying a dragon. Probably dating to the eighteenth century, it was salvaged from some ruined church.

Saturday, May 17, featured various sports competitions. Given the number of passengers, Sunday featured two Church Parades, at 10:30 and 11:30, held in the dining saloon, and the band played at various times.

As *Northland* passed her fifth day at sea, Harry Hawker and his partner lifted off from Newfoundland, the first to attempt a non-stop Atlantic crossing. When passengers learned of this from *Northland's* wireless, Captain Norman Guiou recounted that "everyone was on deck trying to get a glimpse of the daring flyers. All to no avail."

"Rough and cold during night and forenoon," Hardesty recorded, "calming down during afternoon." When the two aviators failed to make their landfall, an Admiralty signal instructed all vessels along the intended route to look for the men and their downed Sopwith Atlantic. Aboard *Northland*, Captain Morehouse ordered extra lookouts to the bridge. For the next days, until the liner was well past the plane's route, they scanned the endless swells, seeking some sign of the flyers.**

As was common on transatlantic crossings, a program of entertainment was held aboard *Northland*, using talent recruited from the passengers and crew members. Lieutenant-Colonel James Hutchison, a Montreal doctor, agreed to serve as chairman for the event. He spent the first days of the voyage seeking passengers who could sing, dance,

---

*The Luger was unknowingly loaded and would remain so until accidentally discharged by Bert's grandson, 45 years later — fortunately with no ill effects.

**By the twenty-third, by which time *Northland* had docked at Halifax, it was evident the flyers had been lost at sea and newspapers on both sides of the Atlantic printed their obituaries. Two days later, newspapers joyously reported that Hawker and Kenneth McKenzie-Grieve had been picked up in mid-Atlantic by the Danish steamer *Mary* and brought to England aboard a British destroyer.

or play an instrument. Given the numbers aboard, it wasn't hard to assemble a troupe that was known for the evening as the "Northland Artists." The ship's print shop put together a one-page souvenir program, which was sold outside the dining saloon, where the event was held. During the intermission, Hutchison briefly addressed the packed audience, after which a collection was taken up in aid of various seamen's charities in Liverpool and New York. The evening concluded with lusty renditions of "O Canada" and "God Save the King."

During the crossing, a transport officer checked the medical and pay documents of every returning soldier, thus reducing delays at the Dispersal Station. When *Northland* was 24 hours from Halifax, roughly 350 miles, the transport officer sent a wireless message to alert the port authorities of the ship's estimated arrival time, so the allotted trains would be ready and waiting. Lieutenant-Colonel Riley, OC of the *Northland* contingent, wired a list of the arriving soldiers to the Soldiers' Aid Commission in each province. In turn, the commission notified each man's relatives.

The last two days of the voyage were fine, and with smooth seas *Northland* made up a bit of time. "Officers and men returning on the *Northland* agree that all were made most comfortable throughout the voyage," reported the *Gazette*. "The food was very good, every man had a berth and the general health of the troops was excellent."

By chance, three troopships arrived at Halifax within hours of one another on Thursday, May 22. First, in the early morning, was *Caronia* with 3,826 soldiers; next came *Northland*, at 3:00 p.m., with its 2,539, followed by *Minnekarda* with 2,547. Arriving passengers gaped at the city, still showing extensive damage from the massive 1917 explosion, in which hundreds had been killed and 4,000 seriously wounded.* A doctor came aboard *Northland* and, at 3:15, began his inspection of the civilian passengers, completing the task in 45 minutes. In parallel, the civil examination of these passengers took place.

On the dock, under a red triangle, smiling female volunteers in white uniforms staffed a YMCA canteen, where disembarking

---

*The explosion on December 6, 1917, of the French munitions ship *Mont Blanc*, after colliding with the Norwegian relief ship *Imo*, was the largest man-made explosion in history until the atom bomb.

Northland military personnel enjoyed free hot coffee, tea, cold drinks, snacks, and cigarettes. Other volunteers provided information to those who needed it, and there were also facilities nearby to send telegrams home. Representatives of the Women's Reception Committee were on hand to greet British war brides and make them feel welcome.

Seventeen trains of the new Canadian Government Railways were required that day to move the arriving soldiers. Of these, four were for the *Northland* contingent, of whom 305, taking up one train, would be demobilized in Montreal. On arrival, Lieutenant-Colonel Riley sent a telegram to the Dispersal Station in Montreal, alerting them to the arrival of another batch of returned soldiers. The Montreal-bound dependents were processed quickly and led to their "military special"; already aboard were 29 officers and 276 ORs.

A YMCA officer helped enliven the monotony of the train journey. Providing entertainment and information, he also handed out cigarettes, candies, and snacks, along with reading materials and games — all free of charge. As the train steamed through the night, Hardesty made a final entry in his log:

May 23. Rainy and cold. Food good, men very comfortable.

Montreal-bound gunners entraining at Halifax, March 1919. Note MONTREAL and WE DON'T GIVE A DAMN chalked on the side of the coach. *Courtesy of John Fetherstonhaugh.*

Along Sherbrooke Street and on the slopes of Mount Royal, the trees were leafing out with the soft greens of springtime. *Northland*'s arrival at Halifax with the Montreal-bound contingent was noted in both the city's major English-language dailies on Friday. Among the long list of names of those aboard the train, Flora Darling found the name of her brother. By chance, Friday was also Empire Day and the hundredth anniversary of the birth of Queen Victoria. As a result, the city was in a joyful mood, the holiday spirit being boosted by the return of more of the city's sons.

It was a fine morning as the Halifax train pulled into Bonaventure Station at 9:30. A considerable crowd was on hand, and it is safe to assume that Grover Sargent, along with Flora and George Darling, were there to welcome Bert and meet Rosalie.

The Army Medical Corps furnished an honour guard for the 6th Field Ambulance. The 4th Canadian Garrison Regiment's brass band provided suitable music, while MPs and city police tried to keep a semblance of order. Half an hour late, the Halifax train's arrival coincided with the departure of a holiday special, and the soldiers detrained amid a great deal of confusion. It was the kind of joyous homecoming any soldier would have wished for, the kind Bob Hale and others had talked about in the far-off summer of 1915. Crowds cheered, flags waved, a band played, and speeches by military and civic authorities were mercifully short.

Kit bags were left on the platform, to be brought to the barracks by a CGR fatigue party. Guards cleared a space and the men were ordered to fall in. Then, as the *Gazette* recounted, "headed by the band of the 4th CGR, with the escort and the guard of honor, the 300 incoming soldiers marched up Windsor Street to the dispersal area at the Peel Street barracks." Flag-waving civilians lined the route, cheering as the soldiers and medical personnel marched past.

Once inside the barracks, the soldiers assembled in the immense canteen, where they would wait their turn to "go through the mill." The lines of men were drawn to attention with a barked "Ten-SHUN!" After a few instructions, names began to be called in alphabetical order, by rank. ORs lit a cigarette and found a place to sit; if nothing else, the army had taught them patience.

Over the previous two months, the process of discharging returned soldiers at the former High School had sped up, with as many as 500 being processed a day. The men had already gone through their medicals in England, thus eliminating the slowest part of the process, and additional inspections had been conducted aboard *Northland.*

After a man's name was called, he entered the ordnance office, where he returned any small arms and equipment but kept the permitted quantity of clothing — one complete uniform and his greatcoat — and, if he wished, his steel helmet. Next was the Department of Soldiers' Civil Re-Establishment. "Here," as a newspaper article by the Repatriation Committee explained, "each man is given advice and information on the many questions relating to his return to civilian life — employment, housing, vocational training, medical treatment." Officers of the Repatriation League of Montreal waited to interview him, and he could register for employment. That done, the next step was the paymaster's office, where he received a cheque for his back pay, a clothing allowance of $35.00, and the War Service Gratuity, based on an individual's length and nature of service. The maximum amount payable for overseas service of three years and over was 183 days' pay and allowances.

In the last office the Dispersal Station's commandant handed the soldier his certificate of discharge, officially making him a civilian again. At the next desk he received the Class "A" War Service Badge, a small bronze pin with a screwback. Intended to be worn in a suit lapel, it bore the legend FOR SERVICE AT THE FRONT CEF around a shield bearing an enamel Union Jack. At the last desk, the soldier received a transport voucher to any destination in the military district.

Slowly, the smoke-filled room began to empty. At length, sometime around 11:00, a voice bawled, "Sargent, Albert E."

In just over 20 minutes, Bert passed "through the mill." In haste, the discharge officer stamping Bert's papers neglected to record the serial number of the War Service Badge that he'd just handed Bert. In the paymaster's office, Bert's file was brought up to date and he was handed a cheque for $789.00. It was a considerable sum, more than adequate to set up a home with Rosalie.

Pocketing the badge without a second glance and folding his discharge papers into a neat package, ex-lieutenant Albert Elbridge Sargent strode briskly into the bright May sunshine, bringing to a close an exemplary military career that had lasted 1,649 days, of which 818 were under enemy fire.

In the crowd on Peel Street he found Rosalie, surrounded by members of the family, laughing and chatting as though they'd known her for years. There were handshakes and fond embraces before Bert was able to break free. Then, reaching for Rosalie's hand, he led her to a nearby taxi.

It was time to begin a new life.

Epilogue

Bert and Rosalie Sargent enjoyed full and happy lives together. Of their four children, the eldest, Walter Gordon Sargent, died in 1927 at the age of six. The second, Albert Elbridge Sargent, Jr., studied at McGill and joined the Royal Canadian Artillery in the Second World War. He was killed in action in Normandy in 1944.

After returning to Canada, Bert worked for Dow Breweries in an engineering capacity. He was a member of the Montreal YMCA for many years and was active on the board of directors and various committees. In 1962, when Montreal's Sir George Williams University decided to make an addition to their campus, Bert played a prominent role in the planning and construction of the Hall Building, then the largest academic building in Canada. It was essentially the same role he'd played eight years earlier when the university's Norris Building was erected. In 1973, the university's assistant vice-principal paid belated tribute to Bert's contribution: "Bert Sargent seemed to absorb our enthusiasm and transform it into appropriate action." For an engineer, there could be no higher tribute.

Throughout his life, Bert remained an avid sportsman. For many years he was an active member of the Royal Montreal Curling Club and had been out curling the night before he died on April 2, 1967.

Rosalie died on January 1, 1989, at the age of 94.

Jim McKeown sailed from England on May 19, 1919, aboard the White Star's *Cedric*, accompanied by hundreds of men from the 2nd Division artillery (including the 18th, 20th, and 23rd Batteries, and the ammunition column). Demobilized in Montreal, he soon reconnected with Bert and Rosalie.

Jim and Bert remained lifelong friends.

On extended leave in England prior to his departure, McKeown co-authored with Lieutenant Robert Gillespie a short history of the 23rd Battery entitled *From Otterpool to the Rhine*, published in 1920. He died in 1975 at the age of 83.

By great coincidence, the author stayed in McKeown's home in Knowlton, Quebec, on a number of occasions in the early 1960s. As a guest of McKeown's grandson, I spent Christmas and Easter holidays in the house, skiing while Jim and his wife were in Florida.

Once, after a day on the slopes, I settled into a comfortable chair with *All Quiet on the Western Front*, which I found in the library. As a teenager, it was all new and strange to me and I devoured the book, my first exposure to the First World War. Even then the Great War seemed so remote, and I wondered what it must have been like. On the walls of the guest room were photos of a man on horseback, and a shell-pitted landscape, along with a framed certificate attesting that James Day McKeown was a member of the Vimy Ridge Veterans Association. Appropriately, the doorstop to my room was a deactivated 4.5-inch howitzer shell, its brass nose cap highly polished.

Hal Fetherstonhaugh returned to Montreal and resumed his profession. In the 1930s he was one of the city's foremost architects and designed a number of important buildings that still stand on Sherbrooke Street. He served as president of both the Quebec Association of Architects and the Royal Architectural Institute of Canada, and died in 1971 at St. Anne's Military Hospital.

Three times wounded in action, **Robert Hale** returned to Montreal in March 1919. He married his sweetheart, Alice Heath, in June 1920 and settled in Verdun, resuming his pre-war career as an iron moulder. Bob and Alice had three sons, all of whom served in the Second World War. He died in 1980.

Charles Constantine remained in the Canadian Army after the war. He taught at Royal Military College, then attended staff college in England. He returned to RMC as commandant in 1925 and was named district officer commanding at Saint John, New Brunswick, in 1930. Four years later he became adjutant-general in Ottawa, and in 1938 became commanding officer of the Kingston Military District.

On the outbreak of war in 1939, he was sent to Halifax, and ended a 48-year military career with the rank of major-general. He died at Kingston in 1953.

William Scully, first (and only) commandant of the 6th Brigade's 21st Battery, ended the war in command of the 9th Siege Battery. He died in Montreal in 1947 after a lengthy illness, mourned by all who knew him.

William O'Brien was promoted to lieutenant in 1917 and was posted to the 1st Battery, 1st Brigade CFA. Returning to Canada in May 1919, he completed his legal studies at Toronto's Osgoode Hall. He died in Toronto in November 1943, aged 57.

Bibliography

Adell, Jacqueline. *Architecture of the Drill Hall in Canada 1863–1939*. A Report Prepared for the Historic Sites and Monuments Board of Canada, June 1989.

Barnes, Leslie W.C.S. *Canada's Guns: An Illustrated History of Artillery*. Canadian War Museum Historical Publication No. 15. Ottawa: National Museums of Canada, 1979.

Bishop, Chris, and Ian C. Drury, eds. *Battles of the 20th Century*. New York: Military Press, 1989.

Bishop, W.A. *Winged Warfare*. New York: George H. Doran & Co., 1918.

Canada in the Great World War Vols. I–VI. Toronto: United Publishers, 1920.

Clark, Lieutenant H.D. *Extracts from the War Diary and Official Records of the Second Canadian Divisional Ammunition Column*. Saint John, NB: J. & A. McMillan, 1921.

Clarke, Dale. *British Artillery 1914–19*. Oxford: Osprey Publishing, 2004.

Duguid, A. Fortescue. *Official History of the Canadian Forces in the Great War 1914–1919, Vol. 1*. Ottawa: King's Printer, 1938.

_____. *The Canadian Forces in the Great War 1914–1919: The Record of Five Years of Active Service*. Ottawa: King's Printer, 1947.

Field Artillery Brigade, Canadian Expeditionary Force. Issued with Militia Orders, 1915.

Field Artillery Training 1914. London: HMSO, 1914.

Field Service Manual; Field Artillery Brigade (Q.F. 18-pr.). London: HMSO, 1915.

Goodspeed, D.J. *The Road Past Vimy: The Canadian Corps 1914–1918*. Toronto: Macmillan of Canada, 1967.

Guiou, Norman Miles. Transfusion: *A Canadian Surgeon's Story in War and in Peace*. Yarmouth, NS: Stoneycroft Publishing, 1985.

Handbook of Artillery Instruments 1914. London: HMSO, 1914.

Handbook of the 4.5-in. Q.F. Howitzer, Land Service 1915. London: HMSO, 1915.

Hogg, I.V., and L.F. Thomas. *British Artillery Weapons and Ammunition 1914–1918*. London: Ian Allan, 1972.

James, Fred. *Canada's Triumph: Amiens — Arras — Cambrai, August, September, October 1918*. London: Canadian War Records Office, undated.

Kay, Hugh R., George Magee, and Finlay MacLennan. *Battery Action! The Story of the 43rd (Howitzer) Battery, Canadian Field Artillery, 1920*.

Keegan, John. *The First World War*. Toronto: Vintage Canada, 2000.

Lapointe, A. *Soldier of Quebec 1916–1919*. Trans. R.C. Fetherstonhaugh. Montreal: Éditions Édouard Garand, 1931.

Liddell Hart, Basil H. *History of the First World War*. London: Pan Books, 1972.

Love, David W. *A Call to Arms — The Organization and Administration of Canada's Military in World War One*. Calgary: Bunker to Bunker Books, 1999.

Lovell's Montreal Directory for 1913/14 and 1914/15. Montreal: John Lovell & Son, Ltd.

MacDonald, J.A., ed. *Gun-Fire: An Historical Narrative of the 4th Bde CFA in the Great War (1914–18)*. Toronto: Greenway Press, 1929.

Macpherson, Donald Stuart. *A Soldier's Diary*. St. Catharines, ON: Vanwell, 2001.

McGill Daily War Contingent Supplement March 1915. Montreal, 1915.

McKeown, J.D., and R.S. Gillespie. *From Otterpool to the Rhine with the 23rd Battery Canadian Field Artillery*. London: Charles and Son, 1920.

Morton, Desmond. *When Your Number's Up: The Canadian Soldier in the First World War*. Toronto: Random House of Canada, 1993.

Morton, Desmond, and J.L. Granatstein. *Marching to Armageddon: Canadians and the Great War 1914–1919*. Toronto: Lester & Orpen Dennys Ltd., 1989.

Nicholson, G.W.L. *Official History of the Canadian Expeditionary Force 1914–19 — Official History of the Canadian Army in the First World War*. Ottawa: Queen's Printer, 1964.

Nicholson, G.W.L. *The Gunners of Canada: The History of the Royal Regiment of Canadian Artillery, Vol. I, 1534–1919*. Toronto: McClelland & Stewart, 1967.

Nominal Roll of Officers, Non-Commissioned Officers and Men, 6th Canadian Overseas Service of the 18th Battery Canadian Field Artillery. Undated, probably 1919.

Prince, Grace Keenan. *Diary Kid*. Ottawa: Oberon Press, 1999.

Returned Soldiers' Handbook. London: Issued under the Authority of the

Repatriation Committee of the Government of Canada, undated.

Scott, Frederick George. *The Great War as I Saw It.* Toronto: F.D. Goodchild, 1922.

Statistics of the Military Effort of the British Empire During the Great War. London: HMSO, 1922.

Swettenham, John. *McNaughton. Vol. 1 1887–1939.* Toronto: Ryerson Press, 1968.

Toland, John. *No Man's Land: 1918, the Last Year of the Great War.* Garden City, NY: Doubleday, 1980.

Twenty-Third Battery Field Artillery: Active Service 1915, Canadian Expeditionary Force. London: Roberts & Leete, 1915.

Worthington, Larry. *Amid the Guns Below.* Toronto: McClelland & Stewart, 1965.

Unpublished Sources

Currie, A.W. Lieutenant-General *Interim Report Covering Operations of the Canadian Corps from Jan. 1st 1918 to Dec. 31st 1918.* Headquarters Canadian Corps. Mimeograph dated March 3, 1919.

Fetherstonhaugh, R.C. *War Letters & Diaries.* Nine volumes of transcripts of letters and diaries of various Canadian soldiers and nursing sisters, including those of his brothers, Captain Harold Fetherstonhaugh, and Major Edward Fetherstonhaugh. Rare Books and Special Collections Division of McGill University Libraries.

Official Record of the 5th Canadian Field Artillery Brigade. Typed manuscript dated May 5, 1919, with handwritten corrections. (Prepared by Lieutenant Albert E. Sargent, London.)

War Diaries of various units and formations of the CEF, Library and Archives Canada. Available online at *www.archives.ca.*

Archival Sources

Library and Archives Canada

Soldiers of the First World War. Library and Archives Canada holds the service records of all soldiers and nursing sisters in the CEF.

Court-Martial Records of the First World War (microfilm).

Andrew George Latta McNaughton fonds. Militia and First World War materials. Ref. no: R2689-0-6-E.

Commission to Investigate Alleged Ill-Treatment of the Men of the Canadian

Expeditionary Force While on Board the Transport *Northland* on her Voyage from Liverpool to Halifax fonds. Report submitted January 19, 1919. Ref. no: R1139-0-X-E.

William Joseph O'Brien fonds. Ref. no: R2566-0-9-E.

Frank Hazlewood fonds. Ref. no: R2036-0-9-E.

5th Brigade, Canadian Field Artillery fonds. Ref. no: R611-137-5-E.

6th Brigade, Canadian Field Artillery fonds. Ref. no: R611-138-7-E.

2nd Canadian Divisional Ammunition Column fonds, Ref. no: R611-220-3-E.

New Brunswick Museum

William H. Harrison fonds (Harrison, W.H. CB-DOC-1[a]).

Murdoch Family fonds (Murdoch F9-3[2]).

Principal Newspapers Consulted:

Montreal *Gazette*

Montreal *Daily Star*

New York Times

Halifax *Herald*

The Times (London)

Index